Volume 22

Environmental & Natural Resource Economics

Economics Reading Lists, Course Outlines, Exams, Puzzles & Problems

Compiled by Edward Tower, September 1995
Duke University & The University of Auckland

NOTE TO USERS AND POTENTIAL CONTRIBUTORS

These teaching materials are drawn from both undergraduate and graduate programs at 105 major colleges and universities. They are designed to widen the horizons of individual professors and curriculum committees. Some include suggestions for term-paper topics, and many of the reading lists are useful guides for students seeking both topics and references for term papers and theses. Thus, they should enable faculty members to advise students more effectively and efficiently. They will also be useful to prospective graduate students seeking more detailed information about various graduate programs and to librarians responsible for acquisitions in economics. Finally, they may interest researchers and administrators who wish to know more about how their own work and the work of their department is being received by the profession.

The exams, puzzles and problems include both undergraduate and graduate exams contributed by economics departments and individual professors. They should be especially useful to professors making up exams and problem sets and to students studying for Ph.D. exams. They may also serve as the focus for study groups.

From time to time, we will reprint updated and expanded versions. Therefore, we welcome new or updated teaching materials, particularly those which complement material in this collection or cover areas we missed. Potential contributors should contact Ed Tower, Economics Department, Box 90097, Duke University, Durham, North Carolina 27708-0097, U.S.A., **tower@econ.duke.edu**

While Eno River Press has copyrighted the entire collection, authors of the various parts retain the right to reproduce and assign the reproduction of their own materials as they choose. Thus, anyone wishing to reproduce particular materials should contact their author. Similarly, those wishing to make verbatim use of departmental examinations, except as teaching materials for one's own class, should contact the department chair concerned.

Associate Compilers for this series are:

Ömer Gökçekuş, Visiting Lecturer, Duke University
Chao Jing, Graduate Instructor, University of Colorado
Wells D. Tower, Senior at Wesleyan University

Dan Tower helped produce the volumes with creativity and energy. Nancy Hurtgen and Tom Hurtgen advised on many aspects of the project. Members of the Duke Economics Department have been helpful from the inception of the project, and belated thanks go to Allen C. Kelley, who suggested in 1980 the usefulness of collecting syllabi.

Eno River Press
115 Stoneridge Drive
Chapel Hill, North Carolina 27514-9737
U.S.A.
Fax & Phone: (919) 967-8246

ISBN for the volume: 0-88024-302-3
ISBN for the series: 0-88024-160-8
Library of Congress Catalog Number: 95-061333

ENVIRONMENTAL & NATURAL RESOURCE ECONOMICS

Contents

***

U = Undergraduate, G = Graduate
RE = Reading List with Exams, Problems and/ or Term Paper Topics

Rachel Cleetus
Duke University

Introduction:

The field of environmental economics has become an increasingly dynamic one in the last few years. The fundamental issues of resource scarcity and externalities, which have long been a part of the economics literature, are being examined in a new and rigorous light in this area. More than any other field of economic study, environmental economics has come to highlight the importance of interdisciplinary work; the input of natural scientists, survey researchers, and lawyers, to name a few, is invaluable.

The standard fare for most environmental economics classes is the analysis of the exploitation of renewable and non-renewable resources. In recent years, the emphasis on pollution control measures has taken this problem from being merely an engineering or biological constraint to one that has economic implications and solutions. Marketable permits, which were just a theoretical nicety a few years ago, are now being seriously considered as tools to reduce pollution efficiently. C. Kling and Hilary Sigman indicate the important references for permits and other environmental policy tools. There is also a trend toward making the field far more mathematical than before through the use of dynamic optimization theory and rigorous resource modeling.

Possibly, the subject of the most prolific research in environmental economics now is that of identifying use and nonuse values for natural resources through hypothetical valuation techniques. That people can assign value to resources that they will never see or use is a fundamental insight that has been gained through survey research. This will continue to be a hotly debated issue as contingent valuation and other non-market valuation methods come to be routinely used in deciding legal issues in natural resource damage assessment cases. Thus a new phenomena that will be noticed in this edition of the book is that there are reading lists for entire classes devoted to the study of natural resource damage assessment. V. Kerry Smith and Glenn W. Harrison both provide excellent references to specific case studies of natural resource damage as well as the relevant legislation.

Government regulations concerning the environment, both in the United States and abroad, have become far more stringent lately. Environmental impact statements and cost-benefit analyses that take into account these environmental impacts are now an integral part of any investment decision process. See Stavins for a comprehensive listing of environmental policies as they pertain to various media like air, water and soil. The EPA's superfund regulation has lead to a new growth in interest in the analysis of risk and environmental hazards. Shogren's list places risk evaluation and regulation within the context of environmental issues. Freeman has a specialized reference list for risks as they pertain to chemicals in the environment.

Increasingly, it is being realized that damage to the environment is rarely a local issue, and global problems like acid rain and the greenhouse effect have become the focus of much concern. Environmental economists have important insights about how it can be in the interests of several countries to come together in solving some of these problems. Another new area of interest is the impact of trade liberalization on the environments of developing and developed nations, and whether this conflicts with the goals of sustainable development. Tietenberg's reading lists for both his beginning and advanced undergraduate classes are useful and unique. Apart from the generic discussions of forests and fisheries, his basic list includes references for subjects like the population problem, the hunger problem, and environmental justice. The advanced topics readings cover sustainable development, global warming, and trade and the environment. Russell and Weinhold also have an interesting bibliography for trade, economic development, and environmental quality.

This volume is an important starting point for the researcher in environmental economics. The reading lists compiled here give a good basis for investigation into the issues mentioned above and many other key topics.

8

UNIVERSITY OF ILLINOIS

Agricultural Economics 210[1]   **U**

Economics of the Environment

Prof. John B. Braden   Fall 1994
Office: 278 EASB, 1101 W. Peabody Dr.   MWF 11 am
Phone: 333-0536   209 Huff Hall
Office Hours: To be announced

Course Objective

This course will introduce economic dimensions of environmental problems and provide experience with the analysis of those problems from an economic perspective. The course will cover a wide range of environmental problems, including but not limited to problems associated with agriculture.

Prerequisites

Economics 102 or Agricultural Economics 100.

Literature

The required readings are:

Field, Barry. *Introduction to Environmental Economics.* McGraw-Hill Book Co., New York, 1993.

AgEc 210 Casebook. Mimeo available from the Instructional Copying Service, Illini Union Bookstore, Wright Street

The text should be in the bookstores. At least one copy of each reference will be on reserve in the Agriculture Library, 226 Mumford Hall. In addition to the required materials, you may purchase the class lecture notes from the Instructional Copying Service in the IUB.

---

[1] Revised title and outline approved in Spring, 1994. Course approved for cross-listing as Economics 210, Environmental Studies 210, Forestry 210, and Urban and Regional Planning 210.

Organization

The class will involve lecture/discussions, small group discussions, debates, quizzes, and examinations according to the following outline:

Exercise	When	Consequence
Lecture/discussion:	Most Mondays and Fridays.	
Quizes:	Fridays when announced. Based on text, lectures.	Top 5 grades together worth 20%. No make-ups or retakes.
Small groups:	Most Wednesdays Based on *Casebook*.	Two absences excused. Each additional absence reduces final grade 0.5%. No exceptions. At end, members will evaluate each other and an outstanding rating can warrant extra credit.
Debates:	Last 2.5 weeks of course.	Scored by team; worth 15%
Term papers:	Due 8:00am, Dec. 17. Based on Debate topic.	Scored individually; worth 20% Late papers lose 3% + 1%/day.
Midterm Exam:	October 3	Worth 20%
Second Exam:	December 9	Worth 25%
Extra Credit:	Special projects or contributions prior to Thanksgiving Holiday. Also, based on ratings of small group contributions.	Up to 5% supplement, at teacher's discretion.

Debate topics and assignments will be formulated with student input. Further guidelines for both the paper and the debates are provided in the *Casebook*.

You may earn extra credit up to a 5 percentage point supplement to your grade. You may earn it through valuable contributions in class, writing short (e.g., 2 pages) papers relevant to the class, leadership in small groups, or in other ways: Make a proposal. (I reserve the right to say "no," but try not to.) The credit must be earned before Thanksgiving.

Periodically during the semester, you will have a chance to provide annonymous feedback about the content or conduct of this class. Please help me take care of your concerns before they become problems.

Course Outline and Reading List

Readings denoted *Field* are chapters from the text. Supplementary reading materials and background readings for the Wednesday small group discussions are compiled in the *AgEc 210 Casebook*.

Week	Topic/Assignment
1	**Introduction to the Economics of Environmental Quality**
	Field 1, 2
2	**Review of Microeconomic Analysis**
	Field 3, 4 *Casebook*, week 2
3	**"Optimal" and "Efficient" Environmental Quality**
	Field 5, 6 *Casebook*, week 3
4	**Benefit-Cost Analysis of Environmental Quality**
	Field 7, 8 *Casebook*, week 4
5	**Environmental Policy Analysis; MIDTERM EXAM**
	Field 9 *Casebook*, week 5
6	**Decentralized and Regulatory Policies**
	Field 10, 11 *Casebook*, week 6
7	**Incentive-based Policies**
	Field 12, 13 *Casebook*, week 7
8	**Water Pollution Control Policy, and the Case of Agriculture**

3   210-94.syl 20/02/95

Field 14
Casebook, week 8

9   **Air Pollution Control Policy, and the Case of Ozone**

Field 15
Casebook, week 9

10   **Waste Disposal Policy, and the Case of Hazardous Wastes**

Field 16, 17
Casebook, week 10

11   **International and Intercultural Environmental Issues I**

Field 18, 19
Casebook, week 11

12   **International Environmental Issues II**

Field 20, 21
Casebook, week 12

13-15 **Student Debate Presentations (1 topic/day selected by lottery)**

Second Examination: Friday, December 9

Term Papers Due: 8:00 am, Saturday, December 17

12

AgEc 210
Fall 1994

First Examination

Put your ID number on each page and your seat number on the first page. All examinations are due promptly at 11:50 am. There are 100 points on the exam divided equally among 10 questions, so each question is worth about 5 minutes of your time.

Answer in the space provided. (You may continue on the back if necessary, but try to be brief.) Write clearly -- if we cannot read your work, you won't get credit.

University rules about examination conduct are in force.

---

1. What is an externality?

2. Imagine that the aggregate demand curve shown below is for helicopter excursion tickets to view Mt. Everest in clear weather.

   a. Show how the demand curve will be affected if the Government of Nepal builds a power plant that will cause a haze around Mt. Everest.

   b. Based on your answer to (a), identify and label the graphical area that represents the total willingness-to-pay to prevent the haziness.

   Demand (Clear Weather)

   0   # of trips

3. Suppose you were hired by the homeowners located around a lake to determine the economic benefits of improving the water quality in the lake. How would you go about estimating the benefits?

4. An environmental regulation is expected to have the costs and benefits shown below. If the prevailing annual interest rate is 10 percent (0.10), what is the benefit-cost ratio of the regulation? (You may round to tenths. Show your work.)

	This Year	Next Year	THE FOLLOWING YEAR
BENEFITS	50	260	290
COSTS	300	130	100

B/C RATIO:_____

5. Suppose we are comparing two ways of reducing urban smog: (1) requiring vapor collection devices at companies using lots of hydrocarbon-based solvents; and (2) developing a new generation of water-based solvents. The two approaches are studied with benefit-cost analysis. How would a higher discount rate affect the comparison of these alternatives and why?

6. Why might the future costs of environmental protection depend on the types of policies that we enacted in the 1970s, even if those policies are changed?

13

7. Show graphically the "efficient" level of pollution and <u>explain</u> how an increase in per capita income would affect the efficient level. Be sure to label <u>all</u> important features of your diagram.

8. What is the "equi-marginal principle" and what does it have to do with pollution abatement?

9. How would you gauge whether the U.S. is doing enough to protect the environment?

10. (a) What do economists mean by "technology"?

    (b) U.S. laws set tighter pollution limits on new factories than on old ones. How do you think this affects the adoption of new production technology and why?

Answers to Homework 1

Question 1

(a)   Let "prevention" refer to measures taken by polluters and "precaution" refer to defensive (avoidance or remedial) measures available to victims. If damages can be <u>both</u> prevented and avoided, an efficient solution is likely to entail some of each. Compensation diminishes the incentives for precaution and leads to over-reliance on prevention.

(b)   If the compensation is not tied to the amount of damages actually experienced and, thus, to precautionary activities (that is, the payment is not affected by the amount of precaution), then precaution will still be considered on its own merits, as a means of reducing damages that continue to be experienced. Thus, the incentives for efficient precaution remains in force. In the long-run, both forms of compensation make victim status less repugnant. Too many people will voluntarily remain victims rather than leaving the location or occupation associated with victimhood.

(c)   Powerlessness implies no potential for precaution or exit from victim status. In this case, compensation does not affect the efficient solution, which relies entirely on prevention in any case. In the long-run, if entry is possible (even though exit is not), the compensation will reduce the deterrents to entry and result in too many entrants.

(d)   This question could be interpreted in several ways. As a result, the grading is pretty loose.

One interpretation raises the prospect of comparative negligence. This is a legal standard where compensation is permitted only if the victims did what they reasonably could do to avoid injury, yet they still suffered. The incentive for precaution includes not only the avoidance of damage, but also the eligibility for compensation that depends on precautionary effort. As long as the standard of "reasonable precaution" equals the "efficient" amount of precaution, compensation will not promote inefficiency.

Another interpretation looks at compensation in the context of Coasian bargaining. Neither party will argee to be made worse off than in the initial condition. The party who gives something up will require compensation. The payment of compensation does not lead to inefficiency as long as people cannot "come to the nuisance" in order to profit. That is, information is complete enough to rule out compensation payments in excess of both the costs of entry and the level of damage.

Question 2

(a) Min $s/(3d) - (2/3)s^2 + 6d$
   $s, d \geq 0$

   K.T.C. s^*: $1/(3d) - (4/3)s \geq 0$; $s \times (\bullet) = 0$
   d^*: $-s/(3d^2) + 6 \geq 0$; $d \times (\bullet) = 0$

   Solving: $s^* = 18d^{*2} = 1/4d^* \implies d^* = 1/2(9)^{1/3} \implies s^* = (9)^{1/3}/2$.

(b) Firm minimizes $(ts - (2/3)s^2)$, where t is the tax rate. We wish to find t^* such that the firm will choose s^*.

   F.O.C. $t - (4/3)s = 0$.

   If $s = s^*$, then $t^* = (4/3) \times (9)^{1/3}/2 = (2/3)(9)^{1/3}$.

(c) Min $s/(3d) - s/(3d) + 6d$ [Note: middle term is compensation]
   $d \geq 0$

   K.T.C. $d^\#$: $6 \geq 0$; $d \times (\bullet) = 0$

   Obviously, the only solution here is $d^\# = 0$.

(d) Min $s^*/(3d) - s^*/(3d^*) + 6d$ [Note: s^*, d^* are constants]
   $d \geq 0$

   K.T.C. $d^@$: $-s^*/3d^2 + 6 \geq 0$; $d \times (\bullet) = 0$

   Solving: $d^{@2} = s^*/18 \implies d^@ = (s/18)^{1/2} = 1/2(9)^{1/3}$ [same as d^*].

2

UNIVERSITY OF ILLINOIS

Econ/Ag Ec/Env St 464   **G**

ENVIRONMENTAL ECONOMICS: THEORY AND APPLICATION

Prof. John B. Braden
Office: Room 278 Env. & Ag Sci. Bldg.
1101 West Peabody Drive
Office Hours: To be announced

Fall 1994
Phone: 333-0536
e-mail: j-braden@uiuc.edu

Course Objective:

This course will familiarize students with the theory and application of economics to environmental problems.

Prerequisites:

Econ 400 or intermediate microeconomics (Econ 300) and strong quantitative skills are the minimum requirements. Econ 402 or an equivalent course is strongly recommended.

Requirements:

1. Term Paper (30% of grade) - The topic can be either an analytical exercise extending received theory, a critical analysis of policy instruments, or an empirical investigation of a new problem with existing methods. But, a theoretical framework must be included in any case, and the paper MUST be an original contribution, have clear relevance to the environment, and be more than a problem description. The ideal, of course, is a manuscript worthy of publication in a scholarly economics journal, but the standards will be realistic for term papers in a graduate class.

    To encourage study and reflection, you will be expected to commit to a topic early in the course and meet the following deadlines for turning in evidence of the development of your topic:

    >   Problem statement (2 p.) - October 5
    >   Extended outline or rough draft - November 16
    >   Presentation of paper (15 min. limit) - November 21 or later (by lottery)
    >   Final draft of paper - No later than Tuesday, December 15

2. First examination (20%) - Week of September 26

3. Second examination (25%) - Week of December 5

4. Homework (15%) - Occasional, to be handed in by the assigned dates.

5. Presentation of an Applied Article (10%) - Each student will lead the class in a discussion of one or more applied papers on the reading list (marked with an **). The summary should last no more than 10 minutes and promote group discussion.

In addition to the requirements, I encourage your questions and observations in class, both about technical material and about current events relevant to the class. I am prepared to award up to 5% "extra credit" to recognize especially constructive class participation.

Texts and Readings:

The following books should be available in a local bookstore and on reserve in the Agriculture Library, 226 Mumford Hall; if you don't find them on first glance, check under the labels of all listing departments-- Econ, AgEc, and EnvSt:

Baumol, W.J. and W.E. Oates. 1988. *The Theory of Environmental Policy*, 2nd Ed. Cambridge University Press, Cambridge, England. [Required] [Denoted B&O]

Oates, W.E. ed. 1994. *The Economics of the Environment.* Edward Elgar Publishing Co., Brookfield, VT. [Denoted OATES].

Freeman, A.M. III. 1993. *The Measurement of Environmental and Resource Values.* Resources for the Future, Inc., Washington, DC. [Denoted FREEMAN].

Also on reserve are the following books which contain wide-ranging discussions of topical issues. They provide a good deal of institutional background and some scientific insights that are important but not dealt with extensively in the course. They may also provide ideas for term paper topics.

Portney, P.R., ed. 1990. *Public Policies for Environmental Protection.* Resources for the Future, Inc., Washington, DC. [Hereinafter Portney].

World Resources Institute. 1993. *World Resources 1993-94.* Oxford University Press, Oxford, England.

Finally, I have arranged for the journal articles (except those in OATES) to be purchased as a set from the Instructional Copying Service, in the Illini Union Bookstore. The articles marked with * or ** in the reading list are included in the set, if they are not in OATES. You will need to place an order. One copy of the set will be placed on reserve in the Agriculture Library.

Outline and Reading List:

The following journal titles appear in the reading list:

AER -	American Economics Review	*JET* -	Journal of Economic Theory
AJAE -	American Journal of Agricultural Economics	*JLE* -	Journal of Law and Economics
		JPAM -	Journal of Policy Analysis and Management
CJE -	Canadian Journal of Economics	*JPubE* -	Journal of Public Economics
EJ -	Economic Journal	*LE* -	Land Economics
JEEM -	Journal of Environmental Economics and Management	*NRJ* -	Natural Resources Journal
		QJE -	Quarterly Journal of Economics
JEL -	Journal of Economic Literature	*REStud* -	Review of Economic Studies
JEP -	Journal of Economic Perspectives	*RJE* -	Rand Journal of Economics

I. *Economics and the Environment* (1 week)

B&O, Chap. 1
Ayres, R.V. and A.J. Kneese. 1969. Production Consumption, and Externalities. *AER* 58:282-97. [OATES 1]
Cropper, M. and W.E. Oates. 1992. Environmental Economics: A Survey. *JEL* 30: 675-740.

II. *Theory of Externalities and Public Bads* (3.5 weeks)

A. The Nature of Externalities

B&O, Chaps. 2-3
**Plott, C. 1983. Externalities and Corrective Policies in Experimental Markets. *EJ* 93:106-127.

B. Property Rights and Transactions Costs

Coase, R.H. 1960. The Problem of Social Costs. *JLE* 3:1-44. [OATES 5]
**Crocker, T.D. 1971. Externalities, Property Rights, and Transactions Costs: An Empirical Study. *JLE* 14:451-464.
**Harrison, G., E. Hoffman, E. Rutstrom, and M. Spitzer. 1987. Coasian Solutions to the Externality Problem in Experimental Markets. *EJ* 87:388-402.

C. Price Instruments to Correct Externalities

B&O, Chaps. 4, 6, 7, 14
**Braden, J.B. and Ascente, C. 1993. Consumer Taxes vs. Producer Taxes to Correct an Externality: Experimental Evidence on Equivalence. University of Illinois, Mimeo.

D. Quantity Regulation

B&O Chaps. 5, 11
*Helfand, G.E. 1991. Standards versus Standards: The Effect of Different Pollution Restrictions. *AER* 81:622-634.

* - included in article set
** - candidate for student presentation and
   included in article set or in OATES   3

E. Nonconvexities and Optimality

B&O, Chap 8
**Repetto, R. 1987. The Policy Implications of Non-convex Environmental Damages: A smog Control Case Study. *JEEM* 14:13-29.

III. *More on Environmental Policy Instruments* (4 weeks)

A. Transferable Permits/Pollution Markets

B&O, Chap. 12.
Montgomery, W.D. 1972. Markets in Licenses and Efficient Pollution Control Programs. *JET* 5:395-418. [OATES 12].
Tietenberg, T.H. 1980. Transferable Discharge Permits and the Control of Stationary Source Air Pollution: A Survey and Synthesis. *Land Econ.* 56:391=416. [OATES 13].
Hahn, R.W. 1989. Economic Prescriptions for Environmental Problems: How the Patient Followed the Doctor's Orders. *JEP* 3:93-114 [OATES 17].
**O'Neil, W., M. David, C. Moore and E. Joeres. 1983. Transferable Discharge Permits and the Economic Efficiency: The Fox River. *JEEM* 10:346-55. [OATES 14].
**Seskin, E.P., R.J. Anderson, Jr., and R.O. Reid. 1983. An Empirical Analysis of Economic Strategies for Controlling Air Pollution. *JEEM* 10:112-24. [OATES 15].
**McGartland, A. and W.E. Oates. 1985. Marketable Permits for the Prevention of Environmental Deterioration. *JEEM* 12:207-228.
**Atkinson, S. and T. Tietenberg. 1991. Market Failure in Incentive-Based Regulation: The Case of Emissions Trading. *JEEM* 21:17-31.

B. Uncertainty

B&O, Chap. 5
Weitzman, M. 1974. Prices and Quantities. *REStud* 41:477-491. [OATES 7].
Roberts, M.J. and M. Spence. 1976. Effluent Charges and Licenses under Uncertainty. *JEEM* 5:193-208. [OATES 9].

C. Long Run Effects

Spulber, D.C. 1985. Effluent Regulation and Long-Run Optimality. *JEEM* 12:103-116. [OATES 3].

D. Stochastic Emissions

B&O, Chap. 13

E. Uniform vs. Differentiated Policies

*Kolstad, C.D. 1987. Uniformity vs. Differentiation in Regulating Externalities. *JEEM* 14:386-399.

---

* - included in article set
** - candidate for student presentation and
    included in article set or in OATES   4

F. Enforcement

Harford, J.D. 1978. Firm Behavior under Imperfectly Enforceable Pollution Standards and Taxes. *JEEM* 5:26-43. [OATES 32].
*Polinsky, A.M. and S. Shavell. 1979. The Optimal Tradeoff between the Probability and Magnitude of Fines. *AER* 69:880-891.
**Harrington, W. 1988. Enforcement Leverage when Penalties are Restricted. *JPubE* 37:29-53. [OATES 32].

G. Liability and Insurance

*Shavell, S. 1984. A Model of the Optimal Use of Liability and Safety Regulation. *RJE* 15:271-280.
*Tietenberg, T. 1989. Indivisible Toxic Torts: The Economics of Joint and Several Liability. *LE* 65:305-319.
**Menell, P.S. 1991. The Limitations of Legal Institutions for Addressing Environmental Risks. *JEP* 5:93-113.

H. Political Economy of Instrument Choice

Buchanan, J.M. and G. Tullock. 1975. Polluters Profits and Political Response: Direct Controls Versus Taxes. *AER* 65:139-147.
**Hahn, R.W. 1990. The Political Economy of Environmental Regulation: Toward a Unifying Framework. *Public Choice* 65:21-47.

I. Jurisdiction and Environmental Problems

B&O, Chaps. 16, 17.
*Maler, K.-G. 1990. International Environmental Problems. *Oxford Review of Economic Policy* 6:80-108.

IV. *The Demand for Environmental Quality* (3 weeks)

A. Basic Theory

FREEMAN, Chaps. 1-4, 7, 8.
*Schulze, W., D. Brookshire, and R. d'Arge. Valuing Environmental Commodities: Some Recent Experiments. *LE* 57:151-172.
Hanemann, W.M. 1991. Willingness to Pay and Willingness to Accept: How Much Can They Differ? *AER* 81:635-647. [OATES 28].
**Hazilla, M. and R. Kopp. 1990. Social Cost of Environmental Quality Regulation: A General Equilibrium Analysis. *JPE* 98:853-73. [OATES 29].
**Shogren, J.F., S.Y. Shin, D.J. Hayes, and J.B. Kliebenstein. 1994. Resolving Differences in Willingness to Pay and Willingness to Accept. *AER* 84:255-70.

* - included in article set
** - candidate for student presentation and
included in article set or in OATES   5

B. Revealed Preference ("Indirect Methods")

1. Hedonics

FREEMAN, Chaps. 11, 12

Rosen, S. 1974. Hedonic Prices and Implicit Markets: Product Differentiation in Pure Competition. *JPE* 82:34-55 [OATES 22].

**Harrison, D., Jr. and D.L. Rubinfeld. 1978. Hedonic Housing Prices and the Demand for Clean Air. *JEEM* 5:81-102.

**Bayless, M. 1982. Measuring the Benefits of Air Quality Improvements: A Hedonic Salary Approach. *JEEM* 9:81-99.

2. Household Production

FREEMAN, Chap. 13

Bockstael, N.E. and K.E. McConnell. 1983. Welfare Measurement in the Household Production Framework. *AER* 73:806-14. [OATES 23].

**Smith, V.K. and W.H. Desvouges. 1985. The Generalized Travel Cost Model and Water Quality Benefits: A Reconsideration. *Southern Economic Journal* 52:371-381.

**Dickie, M. and S. Gerking. 1991. Willingness to Pay for Ozone Control: Inferences from the Demand for Medical Care. *JEEM* 21:1-16.

C. Constructed markets ("Direct Methods") and Nonuse Value

FREEMAN, Chaps. 5, 6

**Bishop, R.C., T.A. Heberlien, and M.J. Kealy. 1983. Contingent Valuation of Environmental Assets: Comparisons with a Simulated Market. *NRJ* 23:619-633.

**Brookshire, D.S., W.D. Schulze, M.A. Thayer, and R.C. d'Arge. Valuing Public Goods: A Comparison of Survey and Hedonic Approaches. *AER* 72:165-177. [OATES 27].

**Kahneman, D. and J.L. Knetsch. 1992. Valuing Public Goods: The Purchase of Moral Satisfaction. *JEEM* 22:57-70.

**Harrison, G.W. 1992. Valuing Public Goods with the Contingent Valuation Method: A Critique of Kahneman and Knetsch. *JEEM* 23:248-257.

**Desvouges, W.H., V.K. Smith, and A. Fisher. 1987. Option Price Estimates for Water Quality Improvements: A Contingent Valuation Study for the Monongahela River. *JEEM* 14:248-267.

Rosenthal, D.H. and R.H. Nelson. 1992. Why Existence Values Should **Not be Used in Cost-Benefit Analysis. *JPAM* 11:116-122.

Kopp, R.J. 1992. Why Existence Values **Should be Used in Cost-Benefit Analysis. *JPAM* 11:123-130.

V. Student Papers (2.5 weeks)

STUDENTS PAPERS DUE - Saturday, December 17 (or before)

* - included in article set
** - candidate for student presentation and
   included in article set or in OATES   6

Econ/AgEc/EnvSt 464
Fall 1994

Homework 2

1.   Say that pollutant S is related to production by: $S = \propto Y$. The production function is: $Y = f(x,z)$, where Y is output and x and z are inputs. If cost-effectiveness is your chief concern, and you are limited to the imposition of standards, would you restrict the output Y or limit the use of one or both inputs? Explain your answer.

2.   A smoker and a nonsmoker work together in an office. The smoker realizes daily marginal smoking benefits of (24 - x) where x is the number of cigarettes smoked each day. The nonsmoker incurs marginal damages of 2x each day from smoke inhalation.

   a.   What is the "socially optimal" level of x?

   b.   The employer wants to make the work place as comfortable as possible. She strongly favors incentives rather than regulations. What incentive should she apply to achieve the best possible amount of smoking? Explain.

   c.   A local company is advertising a new air filter machine that is guaranteed to remove 50% of cigarette smoke from a room. How would such a machine affect the "socially optimal" smoking rate and tax?

   d.   The air filter machine rents for $18 per day. If, as a result of the rental, the tax adjusts to the level determined in part c, would it be worthwhile for the smoker to rent this machine? Would it be worthwhile for the nonsmoker to rent the machine?

   e.   Now assume that the employer's only realistic policy options are:
      •   Permit smoking freely
      •   Ban all smoking
   Once the policy is set, the workers would be free to negotiate a modification. The filter machine has been taken off the market, but they can rent an additional office to separate the smoker and nonsmoker, so there would be no damages. The office rental is $30 per day. How will her policy choice affect the equilibrium smoking rate? Explain.

Econ/AgEc/EnvSt 464
Fall 1994

Examination 1

This is a take-home examination. All answers are due by 4:00 pm Tuesday, October 4, in 278 EASB. Late papers will be penalized 5 percentage points plus 2 percentage points per day.

You may consult books and your lecture notes, but you may NOT consult classmates or any other person. Receiving advice about this examination from someone else is grounds for serious disciplinary action. Your must agree to this condition in writing.

Please identify your answer pages (all of them) with your ID number only -- no names. **Start each question on a new page.** Be sure that your writing can be read and your logic followed. Do not feel compelled to fill up all the allowable pages, and do not exceed the limits. Work for quality, not quantity.

---

1. (20 points; 4 pages) Two companies, A and B, both pollute the environment within a 20 mile radius of their respective factories. Company A is located in Acrid Acres (A^2), the population of which is 90,000. Company B is located in Bilious Bay (B^2) with a population of 10,000. Both cities have a circular configurations and homogeneous densities. They are far apart.

    In the absence of any public policies, the emissions of A and B yield ambient levels of 100 mg/m^3 in the respective cities. The marginal cost of achieving ambient level x (in mg/m^3) is:

    $$MC(x_i) = 1000(100 - x_i)^2 , x_i \leq 100,$$

    where x_i, i = A,B, is abatement of ambient pollution (in mg/m^3) by company i in city i^2. Each mg/m^3 causes $10 in damage to each exposed individual (in lost work time and added health care costs).

    a. What is the efficient level of x_i in A^2? In B^2?

    b. What emission tax rates would you set to achieve the efficient outcome in A^2? In B^2? Explain why the optimal rates are similar (or different).

    c. What would be the effect of the taxation on long-run economic performance in the two cities?

d.   In lieu of a tax on emissions, what could city officials do to achieve the optimal levels of emissions, and what would be the likely efficiency properties of the alternative policies?

2.   (30 points; 4 pages) Two firms in a given region both emit the same type of pollution. The firms' respective marginal costs of abatement equal: $MC(x_1) = 3x_1$ and $MC(x_2) = 2x_2$ where x_i, $i = 1,2$, refers to units of abatement for firms 1 and 2. Initially, firm 1 emits 60 units of pollution and firm 2 emits 40 units. The marginal benefits of abatement are: $MB(X) = 100 - X$, where $X = x_1 + x_2$.

a.   Solve for the <u>regional</u> marginal cost of abatement function.

b.   What is the regionally efficient level (X^*) of pollution abatement? The regionally efficient level of abatement for each firm? The regionally efficient level of remaining pollution for each firm?

c.   Suppose the government sets a standard for each firm equal to $X^*/2$. How much would each firm abate? How much would each spend in total abatement costs? How would their expenditures compare to the case in part (b)?

d.   If we take part (c) as the starting point and allow firms to buy and sell permits to pollute, which firm(s) would buy, which would sell, and how many. What price would clear the permit market?

3.   (20 points; 3 pages) Why should we care about transactions costs as they relate to externalities?

4.   (30 points; 4 pages) Someday you may teach a graduate class in environmental economics, so why not begin now to develop exam and homework questions? Your assignment is to pose, then answer, a problem about externalities. The problem should have the following minimum features:

a.   A mathematical specification. The specification should satisfy the requirements of conventional producer and consumer theory (convex preferences and technologies) and be amenable to solution, analytical or numerical.

b.   The problem should analyze and compare social and private optimizing behavior under at least two types of policy instruments to resolve an externality.

Your question may have several parts. It will be graded for originality, cleverness, and depth of insight, as well as for satisfying the basic requirements listed above.

2

Econ/AgEc/EnvSt 464
Fall 1994

Second Examination

There are four questions worth a total of 100 points. Use a different exam book for <u>each</u> question. Write your ID number, not your name, on each book. All answers are due promptly at 4:30 pm.

1. What sort of enforcement regime would you recommend to an environmental regulatory authority faced with a limited budget and imperfect information about pollution levels? (Be sure to identify your key assumptions and indicate the consequences of relaxing them.) [20 points]

2. Give an assessment of the advantages and disadvantages of transferable discharge permits for pollution control. Include in your answer a brief review of key theoretical results and as much empirical insight as you can. [30 points]

3. Explain concisely the following concepts and their importance in nonmarket valuation: [5 points each]

    a. "Exact" welfare measurement   d. Weak complementarity

    b. Equivalent variation   e. Existence value

    c. Willingness to accept compensation f. Starting point bias

4. The U.S. Fish and Wildlife Service (USFWS) recently announced a plan to reintroduce grey wolves into Yellowstone National Park. (The indigenous wolf population was hunted to extinction several decades ago to protect cattle and sheep herds.) The USFWS estimates it will cost $6.7 million over the next eight years to achieve a sustainable reintroduction. The Service also expects losses of approximately 19 cattle and 68 sheep each year, at a cost of up to $30,000 annually. On the other hand, the USFWS estimates that the wolves will generate $28 million in spending on added visits to Yellowstone and another $8.3 million in existence benefits.

    The American Farm Bureau is contesting these projections. It has hired you as an economic expert with two assignments: a) identify possible errors in the USFWS benefit-cost analysis; and b) propose and justify a research plan to produce better estimates of the benefits of wolf reintroduction. Submit your draft report as part of this examination before sending the final version to the Farm Bureau.

UNIVERSITY OF ILLINOIS AT URBANA-CHAMPAIGN
AG ECON/ECON/ENVST/FOR 463: NATURAL RESOURCE ECONOMICS
G
Dick Brazee

Spring 1995
SYLLABUS

Instructor: Dick Brazee
Department of Forestry
Addresses: W-523 Turner Hall (Office)
W-503 Turner Hall (Mailbox)
brazee@ux1.cso.uiuc.edu (internet)
333-6271 (phone)
244-3219 (fax)
Office Hours: Tues. 11:30-12:00 & 4:30-5:15
Thurs. 11:30-12:00, 1:00-2:00 & 4:30-5:15
& by appointment

Goal: to prepare students as researchers in the field of natural resource economics.

Course Objectives for Participants:
  i) to develop an overview of the field of natural resource economics and policy,
  ii) to achieve sufficient competence with dynamic optimization techniques to understand scholarly papers in natural resource economics and to be able to generate professional quality arguments, and
  iii) to improve research and professional communication skills.

Substantive Focus. Intertemporal efficiency issues that arise in the modelling of natural resource problems.

Format. The course consists of lectures, discussions and student presentations. To achieve the course objectives it is crucial that assignments be completed by the due dates.

Preparation. Economics 300 or the equivalent is required. Completion of or enrollment in Economics 400 and/or 402 is desirable. Familiarity with static non-linear optimization methods is helpful.

REQUIREMENTS AND GRADES:
Course requirements are class participation and presentations, a final exam, 2 literature reviews, a modelling assignment, paper reports and 4 problem sets. For tentative assignment due dates and presentation dates, see the attached course schedule.

Class Participation and Presentations. Everyone is expected to participate in class discussions by both asking and answering questions throughout the semester, and by leading discussions on paper reports. All participants are also expected to present their literature reviews and modelling assignment. Presentations on the literature reviews and modelling assignment should be a maximum of 10 minutes. Attendance is expected at all literature review and modelling assignment presentations.

Final Exam. The final exam is scheduled to be distributed during class on April 27, and will be due at the end of the university scheduled exam period (4:30 pm May 10).

Literature Reviews. 2 brief (maximum of 5 double-spaced pages) literature reviews are required. Literature reviews should critically evaluate and synthesize several (4-6) scholarly papers within a narrowly defined subject area. The first literature review is expected to be on an exhaustible resource topic. For the second literature review participants are free with instructor consent to choose a topic of personal interest within the field of natural resource economics. The reading list by Hoagland and Stavins in the coursepack is a good source of topics and references. In addition participants are expected to write peer comments on another student's literature review.

Modelling Assignment. A short (maximum of 7 double-spaced pages) modelling assignment is required. In this assignment participants should verbally justify, mathematically develop and verbally interpret a dynamic optimization model on a natural resource economic or policy question of personal interest. Ideally the economic question developed will be associated with the topic of one of the literature reviews. Modelling assignments will be evaluated on the basis of thoroughness, verbal clarity and originality. Participants are also expected to write peer comments for another student's modelling assignment.

Problem Sets. 4 problem sets, each covering a major area of the course, (dynamic optimization, exhaustible resources, fisheries and forestry) are required.

REQUIREMENTS AND GRADES (continued):

Paper Reports. Understanding of many natural resource economic papers comes only through detailed written analysis. Verbal reports and mathematical reports are required to ensure adequate understanding of key papers. Verbal reports are a structured evaluation and overview of a paper. Verbal reports should be a **maximum of 1 single-spaced typed page.** A possible format for verbal reports is attached. Mathematical reports consist of verifying mathematical derivations within a paper or a portion of a paper by either detailed verbal description or direct mathematical proof. Ideally verbal reports should be written with standard word processing software, while mathematical reports should be neatly handwritten. Students are expected to complete 15 out of 20 verbal reports and all 5 mathematical reports. Report due dates are listed on the tentative course schedule. Without prior instructor approval late reports will not be accepted.

Study Groups. Discussion often promotes understanding. Participants are encouraged to form 2-4 (ideally 3) person study groups for discussions and joint work outside of class. Study groups may meet to discuss lectures and readings, and to jointly work on paper reports and problem sets. The final exam, literature reviews, modelling assignment and the peer comments on the literature review and the modelling assignment are to be done individually.

Course Grades. Approximate assignment weights for calculating course grades will be:
  20% Final Exam
  20% Literature Reviews (Including Peer Comments &
        Presentations)

15% Modelling Exercise (Including Peer Comments and
        Presentations)
30% Paper Reports
15% Problem Sets
100% Total

READING LIST

The texts for the course are:
P.H. Neher, 1990. *Natural Resource Economics.* (Cambridge
    University Press)
A.C. Chiang, 1992. *Elements of Dynamic Optimization.* (McGraw
    Hill)
M.I. Kamien and N.L. Schwartz, 1991 (Second Edition). *Dynamic
    Optimization: The Calculus of Variations and Optimal
    Control in Economics and Management.* (Elsevier/North-
    Holland)
D. Leonard and N. Van Long, 1992. *Optimal Control Theory and
    Static Optimization in Economics.* (Cambridge University
    Press).
Purchase of Neher and at least one of Chiang, Kamien and
Schwartz, and Leonard and Van Long, is encouraged. Additional
readings will be drawn from relevant scholarly journals. These
readings will be available on reserve in the Agriculture Library,
226 Mumford Hall. Photocopies of the readings are also available
for purchase at the Illini Union Bookstore.

I. **INTRODUCTION** (January 12-19)
Neher, pp. vii-ix, 4-10, 113-114, 349-350
Solow, R.M., 1974. The Economics of Resources or the Resources
    of Economics? *American Economic Review Papers and
    Proceedings* 64:1-14.
Hotelling, H., 1931. The Economics of Exhaustible Resources.
    Journal of Political Economy 39:137-175. (Assigned pp. 137-
    140.)
Devarajan, S. and A.C. Fisher, 1981. Hotelling's Economics of
    Exhaustible Resources: Fifty Years Later. *Journal of
    Economic Literature* 19:65-73.
Lofgren, K.G., 1983. The Faustmann-Ohlin Theorem: A Historical
    Note. *History of Political Economy* 15:261-4.
Scott, A., 1955 The Fishery: the Objective of Sole Ownership.
    Journal of Political Economy 63:116-124.
Young, R.A., 1986. Why Are There so Few Transactions Among Water
    Users? *American Journal of Agricultural Economics* 68:1143-
    1151.

II. **TECHNIQUES OF DYNAMIC ANALYSIS** (January 24 - February 9)
A. Economic and Mathematical Background
Neher, pp. 52-57, 126-144 and 282-283

B. Costless Production--Nonrenewable Resources
Neher, pp. 93-101
Hotelling, pp. 140-146
Neher, pp. 271-281

C. Methods
Neher, pp. 120-124, 145-150 and 162-173
Williams, B.K., 1989. Review of Dynamic Optimization
    Methods in Renewable Natural Resource Management. *Natural
    Resource Modeling* 3:137-216.
Dorfman, R., 1969. Economic Interpretation of Optimal
    Control Theory. *American Economic Review* 59:817-31.

29

Handout: Dynamic Optimization
References: Chiang, Kamien & Schwartz, Leonard & Van Long

III. **NONRENEWABLE RESOURCES** (February 14-March 9)
A. Costly Production
Neher, pp. 102-111, 287-302 and 311-313
Rowse, J. and D. Yeung, 1993. Resource Price Dynamics with
    Non-Malleable Extraction Capital. *Economic Letters* 42:425-
    431.
    Slade, M.E., 1982. Trends in Natural Resource Commodity
        Prices: An Analysis of the Time Domain. *Journal of
        Environmental Economics and Management* 9:132-137.
Hartwick, J.M., 1993. The Generalized r% Rule for Semi-
    Durable Exhaustible Resources. *Resource and Energy
    Economics* 15:387-396.

B. Market Structure
Hotelling, pp. 146-148 and 150-152
Stiglitz, J., 1976. Monopoly and the Rate of Extraction of
    Exhaustible Resources. *American Economic Review* 66:655-661.
    Fishelson, G., 1993. Backstop Technology for an Exhaustible
    Resource: A Fresh Look at an Old Problem. *Resource and
    Energy Economics* 15:387-396.

C. Taxation
Hotelling, pp. 164-171
Neher, pp. 321-326 and 238-244
Burness, H.S., 1976. On the Taxation of Nonreplenishable
    Natural Resources. *Journal of Environmental Economics and
    Management* 3:289-311.

D. Discount Rate
Farzin, Y.H., 1984. The Effect of the Discount Rate on
    Depletion of Exhaustible Resources. *Journal of Political
    Economy* 92:841-851.
Porter, R.C., 1982. The New Approach to Wilderness
    Preservation through Benefit-Cost Analysis. *Journal of
    Environmental Economics and Management* 9:59-80.

E. Uncertainty and Irreversibility
Arrow, K. and A.C. Fisher, 1974. Environmental
    Preservation, Uncertainty, and Irreversibility. *Quarterly
    Journal of Economics* 88:312-319.
Gaudet, G. and P. Howitt, 1989. A Note on Uncertainty and
    the Hotelling Rule. *Journal of Environmental Economics and
    Management* 16:81-86.
Olson, L.J., 1990. Environmental Preservation with
    Production. *Journal of Environmental Economics and
    Management* 18:88-96.

F. Safe Minimum Standards
Bishop, R.C., 1978. Endangered Species and Uncertainty: The
    Economics of a Safe Minimum Standard. *American Journal of
    Agricultural Economics* 60:10-18.
Ready, R.C. and R.C. Bishop, 1991. Endangered Species and
    the Safe Minimum Standard. *American Journal of Agricultural
    Economics* 73:309-312.

IV. **OPEN ACCESS, COMMON POOLS AND FISHERIES** (March 21-April 6)

    A. Open Access
30

4

Neher, pp. 28-30
Ciriacy-Wantrup, S.V. and R.C. Bishop, 1975. Common
    Property as a Concept in Natural Resources Policy. *Natural
    Resources Journal* 15:177-185.
Bromley, D.W., 1991. Testing for Common versus Private
    Property: Comment. *Journal of Environmental Economics and
    Management* 21:92-96.

B. Common Pools
Neher, pp. 256-266

C. Fisheries--Static
Neher, pp. 11-26
C.G. Ploude, 1970. A Simple Model of Replenishable Natural
    Resource Exploitation. *American Economic Review* 60:518-522.

D. Fisheries--Dynamic
Neher, pp. 40-44, 177-180 and 195-199
Brown, G.M., 1974. An Optimal Program for Managing, Common
    Property Resources with Congestion Externalities. *Journal
    of Political Economy* 82:163-173.
Clark, C.W. and G.R. Munro, 1975. The Economics of Fishing
    and Modern Capital Theory: A Simplified Approach. *Journal
    of Environmental Economics and Management*
    2:92-106.

E. Extinction
Neher, pp. 35-40
Clark, C.W., 1973. Profit Maximization and the Extinction
    of Animal Species. *Journal of Political Economy* 81:950-961.

F. Dynamic Behavior
Neher, pp. 30-35, 180-188 and 204-217
Tu, P.N.V. and E.A. Wilman, 1992. A Generalized Predator-
    Prey Model: Uncertainty and Management. *Journal of
    Environmental Economics and Management* 23:123-138
Clarke, F.H. and G.R. Munro, 1987. Costal States, Distant
    Water Fishing Nations and Extended Jurisdiction: A
    Principal-Agent Analysis," *Natural Resource Modeling* 2:81-
    107.

V.FORESTS (April 11-April 20)
Neher, pp. 59-80.
Samuelson, P.A., 1976. Economics of Forestry in an Evolving
    Society. *Economic Inquiry* 16:466-492.
Chang, S.J., 1983. Rotation Age, Management Intensity, and
    the Economic Factors of Timber Production: Do Changes in
    Stumpage Price, Interest Rate, Regeneration Cost, and Forest
    Taxation Matter? *Forest Science* 29:267-277.
Hartman, R., 1976. The Harvesting Decision When a Standing
    Forest Has Value. *Economic Inquiry* 14:52-58.
Binkley, C.S., 1987. When is the Optimal Economic Rotation

Longer than the Rotation of the Maximum Sustained Yield. *Journal of Environmental Economics and Management* 14:152-158.

COURSE SCHEDULE

Jan. 12
Jan. 17   Due: Verbal Report #1-Solow
Jan. 19   Due: Verbal Report #2-One of Scott, Lofgren or Young
Jan. 24   Due: Verbal Report #3-Hotelling
Jan. 26   Due: Verbal Report #4-Dorfman
Jan. 31   Due: Mathematical Report #1-Dorfman, pp. 818-828
Feb. 2
Feb. 7
Feb. 9
Feb. 14   Due: Verbal Report #5-Slade
Feb. 16   Due: Verbal Report #6-Stiglitz
       Mathematical Report #2-Stiglitz
Feb. 21   Due: Problem Set #1
Feb. 23   Due: Verbal Report #7-Farzin
       Verbal Report #8-Porter
Feb. 28   Due: Verbal Report #9-Arrow and Fisher
       Mathematical Report #3-Arrow and Fisher
Mar. 2   Due: Verbal Report #10-Olson
       Verbal Report #11-Bishop
Mar. 7   Due: Literature Review #1
       Student Presentations
Mar. 9   Student Presentations
SPRING BREAK
Mar. 21   Due: Problem Set #2
       Verbal Report #12-Ciriacy-Wantrup and Bishop
      or Bromley
       Verbal Report #13-Ploude
Mar. 23   Due: Verbal Report #14-Clark and Munro
       Mathematical Report #4-Clark and Munro (pp. 92-102)
Mar. 28   Due: Initial Draft Literature Review #2
Mar. 30   Due: Peer Comments on Literature Review #2
       Verbal Report #15-Clark
       Verbal Report #16-Clarke and Munro
Apr. 4   Due: Final Draft Literature Review #2
       Student Presentations
Apr. 6   Due: Student Presentations
Apr. 11   Due: Problem Set #3
Apr. 13   Due: Verbal Report #17-Samuelson
       Verbal Report #18-Chang
       Mathematical Report #5-Chang (pp. 267-273)
Apr. 18   Due: First Draft Modelling Assignment
Apr. 20   Due: Peer Comments on Modelling Assignment
       Verbal Report #19-Hartman
       Verbal Report #20-Binkley
Apr. 25   Due: Final Draft Modelling Assignment
       Student Presentations
Apr. 27   Student Presentations
       Final Exam Distributed
May 2   Due: Problem Set #4

6

32

May 10   Due: (by 4:30 pm)   Final Exam

SAMPLE VERBAL REPORT FORM

Identification: (Citation)
General Problem Area: (Topics by Key Words)
Economic Question(s):
Significance of Economic Question(s):
Key Assumption(s):
Modelling Approach:
Key Results:
Significance of Key Results:
Possible Further Research:

Remember that each verbal report should be a **maximum** of 1 single-spaced page.   (For clarity, please double-space between sections.)

SIMON FRASER UNIVERSITY
DEPARTMENT OF ECONOMICS   G

COURSE: ECON 864-4   **SEMESTER:**   Fall 1992

TITLE: Studies in Economic Fisheries Management   **INSTRUCTOR:** P. Copes

PREREQUISITES: ECON 863 or equivalent, or permission of the instructor.

Content:

The course will include:

I.   A review and extension of economic fisheries management analysis as dealt with in ECON 863. Emphasis will be on practical applications, taking account of:

    (a)   the achievement of socioeconomic objectives,
    (b)   social and political constraints,
    (c)   stock assessment and management,
    (d)   the practicalities of enforcement and administration.

II.   Examination of several cases of economic fisheries management, illustrating different objectives, techniques and constraints.

III.   A critical assessment of current practices and policy proposals regarding fisheries management and regulation.

Format:

There will be approximately 48 hours of lecture/seminar work during the semester, at times agreed upon by instructor and course participants. Each student will be assigned an ongoing study project on which the student must deliver one or more reports in the seminar.

Readings:

Students will be required to become thoroughly familiar with the final report of the Pearse Commission on Pacific Fisheries and the two Copes reports on South Australian prawn fisheries. Selected readings from other reports and articles will also be required.

Grading:

The course grade will be based on the results of:

      Examination   50%
      Project Report   40%
      Seminar Participation   10%

SIMON FRASER UNIVERSITY

Department of Economics

Economics 864   EXAM   Fall 1992

Studies in Economic Fisheries Management   Three hours

Answer the number of sub-questions required for each of Questions 1, 2, 3 and 4. Each Question is worth one-quarter of the total exam grade.

---

1. Answer **two** of the following sub-questions:

(a) What is "the critical size" in cohort analysis? Explain its significance in designing an optimal fisheries management strategy.
(b) Explain the advantages and disadvantages of transferability of individual fishing rights.
(c) Explain the reasons for introducing area management regulations.

2. Answer **two** of the following sub-questions:

(a) Compare the usefulness of traps and weirs, as against nets and gaffs, in a river fishery on mixed salmon stocks.
(b) Explain the effect that Pearse's proposed auctioning of salmon licenses would have on the amount of producer's surplus generated in the B.C. salmon fishery.
(c) Discuss the main reasons why an individual quota regime would not be effective in the B.C. salmon fishery.

3. Answer **two** of the following sub-questions:

(a) Explain why it is appropriate to set different size criteria in fishing concentrations of prawns in different parts of Gulf St. Vincent.
(b) Explain the advantages of a larger mesh size for trawl nets in the Gulf St. Vincent prawn fishery and describe the circumstances that have made improvement in gear selectivitiy particularly important in that fishery.
(c) Discuss the logic of biovalue calculations for the Gulf St. Vincent prawn fishery and explain shortcomings in the calculations actually used.

4. Answer **two** of the following sub-questions:

(a) Discuss the pros and cons of maintaining traditional fishing rights in Papua New Guinea.
(b) Describe the initial position of the U.S. with regard to the Law of the Sea in respect of tuna stocks. How did it differ from international consensus?
(c) Discuss the prospects of an international tuna fishing regime run by the Nauru Group.

SIMON FRASER UNIVERSITY

DEPARTMENT OF ECONOMICS   G

COURSE: ECON 863-4   **SEMESTER:**   Fall 1994

TITLE: Fisheries Economics   **INSTRUCTOR:**   P. Copes

Content:

The course will cover four main subject areas:

I.   Bioeconomic Theory of Fisheries
Population dynamics, yield-effort relationships, catch per unit of effort, gear selectivity, fisheries externalities, common property and open access characteristics, effort and output limitation; economic, social and biological aspects of optimum exploitation rates; rights-based fishing.

II.   Fisheries Development and Management
Management systems, their objectives and their effects; protection, conservation, effort and output regulation, gear conflict regulation, seasonal management, catch beneficiation, stock enhancement, interaction with aquaculture, rationalization, rent generation and allocation.

III.   International Aspects of Fisheries
Law of the Sea developments, international fisheries conventions, bilateral and multilateral management agreements, comparative advantage in fisheries exploitation, joint ventures, transboundary stock migration.

IV.   Socioeconomic and Political Aspects of Fisheries
Access and property rights in fisheries, historical development pattern, objectives and management, fisheries rationalization and distributional equity, regional development concerns, settlement patterns, political implications, employment/income trade-offs, education and extension work in fisheries, recreational fishing.

Format:

There will be 48 hours of instruction, at times mutually agreed upon by instructor and students. Each student will be required to complete an essay or project and to present a seminar report thereon.

Grading:

Formal Examination	65%
Essay/Project Work	30%
Seminar Participation	5%

Reference Work:

Stephen Cunningham, Michael R. Dunn and David Whitmarsh, **Fisheries Economics: An Introduction**, New York, St. Martin's Press, 1985.

Extensive readings from the professional literature will be assigned.

SIMON FRASER UNIVERSITY

Department of Economics

Economics 863   EXAM   Fall 1994
Fisheries Economics   Three hours

Answer the number of sub-questions required for each of Questions 1, 2,
3 and 4. Each Question is worth one-quarter of the total exam grade.

1.   Explain and discuss briefly **five** of the following terms (one good
     paragraph each):

     (a) quota busting   (e) MSY
     (b) the slope (of the continental margin)   (f) ITQ
     (c) eumetric yield curve   (g) CPUE
     (d) a race of salmon   (h) recruitment

2.   Explain the equilibrium position that will be achieved in fisheries
     exploitation in **one** of the following cases. Use a diagram and
     indicate areas representing net benefits ('social surpluses').
     Which surpluses (or combinations of surpluses) are maximized and
     which are incidental? The cases to choose from are:

     (a) The fishery is controlled by a management agency acting
          in the general public interest.
     (b) The fishery is controlled by a producers' cooperative.
     (c) The fishery is controlled by a private sole owner.

3.   Answer **two** of the following sub-questions:

     (a) Explain fully the advantages of an ITQ system when there are
     no complicating problems.
     (b) Explain what is a "transitional gains trap" in the context of
     fisheries rationalization. Discuss how this "trap" affects
     government policy objectives and explain the relationship to
     transferability of licenses.
     (c) Explain the nature and impact of high-grading and data fouling
     in ITQ fisheries.

4.   Answer **two** of the following sub-questions:

     (a) Explain what advantages for salmon management would result
     from shifting a significant part of the Skeena River salmon harvest
     from a tidewater to an in-river fishery.
     (b) Explain how social and political constraints have made it
     difficult to improve the economic performance of the Canadian east
     coast fisheries.
     (c) Explain the principal rights and obligations of the coastal
     state, with respect to fisheries, under the Law of the Sea
     Convention.
     (d) Explain why fishing incomes are often low.

University of California Santa Barbara

Natural Resource Economics
Econ. 122

G

Robert Deacon

Winter 1995

Class: TTh. 2:00-3:15 PHELP 3519
Office hours: W 1:00-3:00, or by appointment (893-3679), 3040 North Hall.
Exams: Midterm: Tuesday, February 14 (40%)
            Final: Saturday, March 18, 4:00-7:00 (cumulative, 60%)

Course Description:
This course examines the role of natural resource industries in the U.S. and world
economies, including minerals and fossil fuels, forest resources, fish and game, water
resources, and natural environments. The social issues involved in natural resource use are
broader than this statement would suggest, however. Some resources are
nonreplenishable, and hence are used up in the process of economic activity, and
consequently it is relevant to ask whether or not an economic system based on their
exploitation can continue indefinitely. Natural resources often are characterized by a clear
tradeoff between present and future use, which raises complicated equity questions
regarding future generations. Finally, ownership rights to natural resources often are not
clearly defined. In such cases the interests of some potential resource users will not be
reflected in market outcomes, and the scramble to acquire these unowned assets may be
destructive. These broad themes appear repeatedly throughout the course.

Pre-requisites:
Intermediate microeconomics (Econ. 100A and B or Econ. 104A and B) is required.
Exceptions will be made on an individual basis for Environmental Studies students who
wish to take this course as part of an Economics emphasis. Students in this category
should see me during office hours during the first two weeks of the quarter. Two sets of
concepts will be used during the quarter: welfare economics (concepts of Pareto efficiency,
externalities, and property rights) and intertemporal choice (interest rates, discounting,
saving and investment, capital theory). These concepts will be reviewed briefly in class
and in Section II of the readings, but the time spent will be minimal. Students who
completed their intermediate microeconomics courses some time ago should review as
needed.

Text and Supplementary Readings:
Tom Tietenberg, *Environmental and Natural Resource Economics*, 3rd edition, Harper
    Collins Publishers, 1992.
This text does not cover all of the natural resource topics I intend to examine in the course,
however, so I have placed copies of additional readings in the Reserve Book Room of the
Library. These items are listed below in the outline of topics.

Exams, Term Papers, and Grading:
        Exam dates and weights used in grading were listed above. Both exams will
consist primarily of short essay/problem questions. Old exams, with sample answers,
have been placed in the library as study aids. No make-up exams will be given. Students
who miss the midterm may substitute a term paper in its place. Students also may submit a
term paper in the course for extra credit. I have a 'no fault' policy on extra credit term
papers. That is, such a paper will have no effect on the course grade unless it earns a grade
that exceeds the grade earned in exams. If that condition is met, it will count for 25% of
the course grade.

TOPIC OUTLINE

I. Basic Facts and Concepts
Tietenberg, Chapter 1.
Charles W. Howe, *Natural Resource Economics*, Chapters 1, 3. Reprints are titled "Chapter 1: Overview of the Natural Resources Field", and "Chapter 3. Natural Resources Concern is Not New".
J. Krutilla, "Conservation Reconsidered", *American Economic Review*, Sept. 1967.
A.V. Kneese, *et al.*, "Economics of the Environment: A Materials Balance Approach", in A.C. Enthoven and A.M. Freeman, *Pollution, Resources, and the Environment*, Norton Press, 1973.

II. Welfare Economics, Benefit Cost Analysis and Intertemporal Choice
T. Tietenberg, Chapters 2, 3, 4.
D.W. Pearse and R.K. Turner, "5. The Market Achievement of Optimal Pollution" from *Economics of Natural Resources and the Environment*, Johns Hopkins University Press, 1990, pp. 74-78.
Note: This provides a rather brief review of welfare economics and intertemporal choice. For further depth, review relevant sections of your intermediate microeconomics text, or study the following items on reserve in the library:
R. Pindyck and D.L. Rubinfeld, *Microeconomics*, Macmillan and Co., 1989, Chapter15, Chapter 16, Chapter 18, pp. 617-636.

III. Biodiversity and Species Extinction
R. Sedjo, "Property Rights, Genetic Resources, and Biotechnological Change", *Journal of Law and Economics,* April 1992.
R. T. Deacon and Paul Murphy, "Swapping Debts for Nature: Direct International Trade in Environmental Services", in T. L. Anderson, ed. *NAFTA and the Environment*, Pacific Research Institute, 1993.
W. Harrington and A. C. Fisher, "Endangered Species", in P. R. Portney, *Current Issues in Natural Resource Policy*, Resources for the Future, 1982.

IV. Forest Resources
Tietenberg, Chapter 11.
R.T. Deacon, "The Simple Analytics of Forest Economics", in R.T. Deacon and M.B. Johnson, eds., *Forestlands, Public and Private*, Ballinger, 1986.
R. Repetto, "8. Subsidized Timber Sales from National Forest Lands in the United States", in R. Repetto and M. Gillis, eds., *Public Policies and the Misuse of Forest Resources*, Cambridge Univ. Press, 1988.
R. Repetto, "1. Overview", in R. Repetto and M. Gillis, eds., *Public Policies and the Misuse of Forest Resources*, Cambridge Univ. Press, 1988.
D. Pearse. "An Economic Approach to Saving the Tropical Forests", in D. Helm, ed. *Economic Policy Towards the Environment*, Blackwell, 1991.

V. Fisheries
T. Tietenberg Chapter 11.
D.W. Pearse and R.K. Turner, "16. Renewable Resources" and "17. The Extinction of Species" from *Economics of Natural Resources and the Environment*, Johns Hopkins University Press, 1990, pp. 241-270.

VI. Non-renewable Resources
Tietenberg Chapter 6, 7 pp. 153-155, 161-169.
D.W. Pearse and R.K. Turner, "18. Exhaustible Resources", from *Economics of Natural Resources and the Environment*, Johns Hopkins University Press, 1990, pp. 271-287.

VII. Scarcity, Growth, and Development
Tietenberg, Chapter 13.
A.C. Fisher, "Resource Scarcity: Are There Limits to Growth?", from *Resource and Environmental Economics*, Chapter 4, Cambridge Univ. Press, 1981.

VIII. Water Resources
Tietenberg, Chapter 9.

39

University of Toronto
Department of Economics

Professor D.N. Dewees
150 St. George Street
S205   978-4473

ECONOMICS 313F

Environmental Problems and Policies   **U**

Undergraduate

Fall, 1995

		Abbr.
<u>Buy:</u>		

LIB   T. Tietenberg, <u>Environmental and Natural Resource Economics</u> 3rd ed.
(Harper, Collins, 1992).   TT

<u>Supplementary</u>

R. Dorfman and N. Dorfman, eds., <u>Economics of the Environment</u>, 3rd. ed.,
(Norton, 1993).   D&D

A.M. Freeman, <u>The Measurement of Environmental and Resource Values</u>
(Washington: Resources for the Future, 1993).   FREE

<u>Reference</u>:

W.J. Baumol & W.E. Oates, <u>The Theory of Environmental Policy</u>
(Cambridge U. Press, 1988).   B&O

LIB   Bentkover, Judith D., V. T. Covello, J. Mumpower, <u>Benefits Assessment:</u>
<u>The State of the Art</u>. (Reidel, Dordrecht, Boston, 1986)   BCM

H.E. Daly and K.N. Townsend, <u>Valuing the Earth: Economics, Ecology,</u>
<u>Ethics</u> (Cambridge: MIT Press, 1993).   D&T

R.O. Zerbe and D.D. Dively, <u>Benefit-Cost Analysis in Theory and Practice</u>
(New York: HarperCollins College, 1994)   Zerbe

H.M. Peskin & E.P. Seskin, eds., <u>Cost-Benefit Analysis and Water Pollution</u>
<u>Policy</u>, (Washington: The Urban Institute, 1975).   P & S

J.E. Stiglitz, <u>Economics of the Public Sector</u>, 2nd. ed.
(New York: Norton, 1988).   STIG

A.   Introduction

<u>TT</u> Ch. 1, 2.

* <u>B&O</u>, Ch. 2

1. Theory of Externalities

<u>TT</u> Ch. 12, especially 305-316

<u>Pearce</u>, Ch. 1.2, 1.3, 1.6, 1.8, 1.9 (pp. 2-27).

* <u>STIG</u> 119-137, 213-236.
α <u>B & O</u>, Chs. 3, 4.

2. Environmental Law and Economics

<u>TT</u>, Ch. 3.

Dewees, "The Role of Tort Law in Controlling Env. Pollution", pp. 1-20.

Dewees, "Reducing the Burden of Env. Regulation", pp. 25-34, 36-38, 39-41.

Ontario EPA, Sections 1, 6, 14, Regulation 308 §5 and Appendix.

*Coase, R., "The Problem of Social Cost", in <u>D & D</u>.

3. Dispersion Models and Efficiency

<u>TT</u>, Ch. 14, especially pp. 369-382.

<u>P & S</u>, pp. 195-197.

a) Water

<u>P & S</u>, pp. 191-195.

b) Air

Ontario EPA, Regulation 308, Appendix, <u>supra</u>.

4. Water Pollution Problems

Kneese, A.V., "Costs of Water Quality Improvement, Transfer Functions and Public Policy", pp. 175-191 in <u>P & S</u>.

<u>TT</u>, Ch. 18.

Appendices to Kneese, pp. 191-197 in <u>P & S</u>, <u>supra</u>.

* means optional; α means advanced.

5. Air Pollution Problems - Dispersion Models

TT Ch. 15, 16.

Ontario EPA, Regulation 308, Appendix, supra.

NERA, "Emission Trading Program ... in Ontario" 1992, Apx B, pp. 3-8.

6. Cost-Benefit Analysis

Peskin & Seskin, "Introduction and Overview", pp. 1-33;
[or V.K. Smith, "A Conceptual Overview of the Foundations of Benefit-Cost Analysis" in BCM; or STIG "Cost-Benefit Analysis", 256-276.]

TT, Ch. 4.

* Mishan, Cost-Benefit Analysis, 1975, Chs. 7-15, pp. 24-108; Chs. 25-29, pp. 165-195. Zerbe

B.   Analytical Techniques

1. Abatement Cost Estimation

Kneese, A.V., "Cost of Water Quality Improvement..." in P & S pp. 175-191, supra.

Peskin & Seskin, "Introduction and Overview" pp. 16-22, supra.

TT, Ch. 20.

R.A. Luken, Efficiency in Environmental Reg'n (Boston: Kluwer, 1990), pp. 28-35.

NERA, "Emission Trading in ... Ontario" pp. 37-42, 48-55, Apx A, pp 1, 7-10.

* Mishan, Chs. 10-14; pp. 55-97; Zerbe.

2. Benefit Estimation

Cropper and Oates, "Environmental Economics: A Survey", 30 J.E.Lit. 675, 1992, pp. 700-721.
TT pp. 74-84.

* FREE, Ch. 1-3.
* Mishan, Chs. 7-9; pp. 24-54; Zerbe.
α See, generally, BCM, and FREE

a) Contingent Valuation

42 Cropper and Oates, 1992, supra, pp. 709-720.

Portney, P., "The Contingent Valuation Debate: Why Economists Should Care", J. Econ. Perspectives 8:4, Fall, 1994, pp. 3-18.

* See W. Hanemann, "Valuing the Environment Through Contingent Valuation" and P. Diamond and J. Hausman, "Contingent Valuation: Is Some Number Better than No Number?" in J. Econ. Persp. 8:4, Fall, 1994, pp. 19-64.
* FREE, Ch. 6

b) **Valuing Longevity**

Cropper and Oates, 1992, supra, pp. 708-709, 713-715.

Lave, L. and E. Seskin, "Air Pollution and Human Health" in D & D.

Dewees, D., "Economic Incentives for Controlling Industrial Disease: The Asbestos Case" J. Legal Stud., 15. 1985, pp. 289-290, 297-301, 302-306, 0-319.

* M.J. Moore and W.K. Viscusi, Compensation Mechanisms for Job Risks, 1990, "Workers' Implicit Value of Life" pp. 69-81.
* FREE, Ch. 10

c) **The Valuation Disparity Puzzle**

Knetsch, J. and J. A. Sinden, "Willingness to Pay and Compensation Demanded: ...." Q.J.E. 99:3, August, 1984, pp. 507-521.

d) **Discounting Future Benefits**

Weitzman, M.L. "On the 'Environmental' Discount Rate" JEEM 26, 1994, pp. 200-209.

* FREE Ch. 7, esp. 207-217.

3. Information Problems - Monitoring Stochastic Variables

Dewees, Everson and Sims, Ch. 5, "Monitoring and Information Cost."

Ontario EPA Regulation 308," Section 5, Schedule 1, supra.

Review your statistics text on sampling, confidence limits, estimating population parameters, hypothesis testing.

"The Z-Test" Analytic method for compliance with indoor asbestos concentrations.

* W. R. Ott. "A Physical Explanation for the Lognormality of Pollutant Concentrations" JAWMA 40:10, 1378-1382, 1990.

4. Macro-Models, Long-Run Forecasting, Growth

Jorgenson, D. W. and P. J. Wilcoxen, "Environmental Regulation and U.S. Economic

* means optional; α means advanced.

Growth", <u>Rand J. Econ.</u> 21:2, 314-321, 325-339 parts, 1990.

<u>TT</u>, Ch. 21, 13.

Selden, T.M. and D. Song, "Environmental Quality and Development: Is There a Kuznets Curve for Air Pollution Emissions"?, <u>JEEM</u> 27, 147-162, (1994).

* H.M. Peskin, P.R. Portney, A.V. Kneese, <u>eds.</u>, <u>Environmental Regulation and the U.S. Economy</u> (Johns Hopkins Press, 1981).

5. Sustainable Development

<u>TT</u> Ch. 22.

Solow, R., "An Almost Practical Step Toward Sustainability", RFF Address, October 8, 1992.

Daly, H. E., "Sustainable Growth: An Impossibility Theorem" in <u>D&T</u>, pp. 267-273.

Georgescu-Roegen, N., "Energy and Economic Myths" in <u>D&T</u>, pp. 89-105.

C.   <u>Analysis of Corrective Policies</u>

<u>TT</u>, Ch. 14; especially pp. 362-369.

1.   Standards, Prices and Markets

<u>TT</u> Ch. 15 pp. 393-414, Ch. 17 pp. 466-472.

Hahn, R.W. and G.L. Hester, "Where Did all the Markets Go?", <u>Yale J. Regn.</u> 6, pp. 114-118, 149-153, 1989.

Seskin, E., R.J. Anderson, & R.O. Reid, "An Empirical Analysis of Economic Strategies for Controlling Air Pollution", <u>JEEM</u> 10 (1983), pp. 112-124.

Dewees, "Reducing the Burden of Regulation", pp. 45-56, <u>supra</u>.

NERA "Emission Trading in ... Ontario", pp. 21-32.

"A Slow Start for Emissions Trading", <u>IEEE Spectrum</u>, July, 1994, 49-52.

* W.E. Oates, P.R. Portney, A.M. McGartland, "The <u>Net</u> Benefits of Incentive-Based Regulation:...", <u>AER</u> 79, 1989, pp. 1233-1241.

α <u>B & O</u>, Chs. 5, 11, 12.

2.   Distributional Effect of Alternate Policies

<u>TT</u>, Ch. 20.

44

Dewees, D.N., "Instrument Choice in Environmental Policy," <u>Economic Inquiry,</u>

Vol. 21, January, 1983, pp. 53-70.

3. Effectiveness of Regulation

Dewees, "The Efficacy of Regulation", 1992, pp. 9-18, 22-26.

* means optional; α means advanced.

Bowdoin College

Economics 218   Fall 1994
Economics of Resources and the Environment   Mr. Freeman

<u>SYLLABUS</u>   U

TEXT AND LIBRARY RESERVE MATERIALS

Students should purchase the textbook, Barry Field, <u>Environmental Economics: an Introduction</u>. All of the other required readings listed in the reading assignments are available at the reserve desk of the Library. (Unless noted otherwise, optional readings are NOT on reserve.)

The following abbreviations are used in the reading assignments below:

BF: Barry Field, <u>Environmental Economics: an Introduction</u>.

DD: Dorfman and Dorfman, <u>Economics of the Environment, Selected Readings</u>, 3rd edition.

FHK: Freeman, Haveman, and Kneese, <u>The Economics of Environmental Policy</u>.

PP: Paul Portney, ed., <u>Public Policies for Environmental Protection</u>.

TT: Tom Tietenberg, <u>Environmental and Natural Resource Economics</u>, 3rd ed.

V&P1:   Donald VanDeVeer and Christine Pierce, <u>People, Penguins, and Plastic Trees</u>.

V&P2:   Donald VanDeVeer and Christine Pierce, <u>The Environmental Ethics and Policy Book</u>.

Copies of all but BF are on reserve in the Library.

BACKGROUND INFORMATION ON ENVIRONMENTAL SCIENCE

I will presume that students have a working knowledge of basic environmental science, that is, an understanding of what the greenhouse effect is, the difference between good and bad ozone, etc. Some of this material is covered in FHK, Chapter 3, for students who wish a review.

OPTIONAL READINGS AND TOPICS

I have listed several optional readings and topics. The optional readings go into certain areas in more detail than the required readings. The optional topics could be explored by students looking for term paper topics.

READING ASSIGNMENTS

I.   THE ENVIRONMENT AND THE ECONOMY: AN OVERVIEW

    BF, Ch. 1.
    BF, Ch. 2.
    FHK, Ch. 2, pp. 21-34.

    Optional: FHK, Ch. 3.

II. PRINCIPLES OF ENVIRONMENTAL ECONOMICS

    A.   Introduction

        BF, Ch. 3.

    B.   Markets, Market Failure, and Efficiency

        BF, Ch. 4.
        FHK, Ch. 4.
        Hardin, "The Tragedy of the Commons," in DD, pp. 5-19,
            and in V&P2, pp. 422-430
        BF, Ch. 5.

    C.   Principles of Benefit-Cost Analysis:

        BF, Ch. 6.
        Freeman, "Economics, Incentives, and Environmental
            Regulation," pp. 189-195.
        Freeman, "Equity, Efficiency, and Discounting"
            (Handout).

    D.   Measuring Benefits and Costs

        BF, Ch. 7.
        Freeman, "Nonmarket Valuation by Revealed Preferences."
        BF, Ch. 8.

        Optional:

        A. Kneese, Measuring the Benefits of Clean Air and
            Water, Chs. 2-4.
        DD, Dorfman, "An Introduction to Benefit-Cost
            Analysis," pp. 307-318.
        DD, Knetsch and Davis, "Comparisons of Methods for
            Recreation Evaluation."
        DD, Randall, et al., "Bidding Games for Valuation of
            Aesthetic Environmental Improvements."

E.   Benefit-Cost Analysis: Pro and Con

      S. Kelman, "Cost-Benefit Analysis, Environmental
            Safety, and Health Regulation: Ethical and
            Philosophical Considerations," in V&P1,
            pp. 242-249 and in V&P2, pp. 329-335.
      Freeman, "The Ethical Basis of the Economic View of the
            Environment," in V&P1, pp. 218-227 and in V&P2,
            pp. 307-315.
      Leonard and Zeckhauser, "Cost-Benefit Analysis
            Defended," in V&P1, pp. 249-253 and in V&P2,
            pp. 335-339.
      R. Mitchell and R. Carson, "Property Rights,
            Protection, and the Siting of Hazardous Waste
            Facilities," American Economic Review, May, 1986.

III. ENVIRONMENTAL POLICY ANALYSIS

     A.   Instruments of Policy

          BF, Ch. 9.
          Freeman, "Economics, Incentives, and Environmental
                Regulation," pp. 195 to the end.
          Project 88, Round II, Ch. 1; OR Stavins amd Grumbly,
                "The Greening of the Market: Making the Polluter
                Pay."
          BF, Ch. 10-13.
          DD, Ruff, "The Economic Common Sense of Pollution."

          Optional:

          DD, Coase, "The Problem of Social Cost."

     B.   Water Pollution

          BF, Ch. 14.
          PP, Ch. 4.
          A. Kneese, Measuring the Benefits of Clean Air and
                Water, Ch. 10.
          C. Paulsen, "Cost-Effective Control of Water Pollution
                in Central and Eastern Europe," Resources, Fall
                1993.

     C.   Stationary Source Air Pollution

          BF, Ch. 15. to p. 310.
          PP, Ch. 3.
          A. Kneese, Measuring the Benefits of Clean Air and
                Water, read any two of the following chapters --
                5, 6, 7, and 9.

D.   The Automobile: A Special Set of Problems

      BF, Ch. 15, to the end.
      DD, Krupnick and Portney, "Controlling Urban Air
          Pollution: A Benefit-Cost Assessment."
      Harrington, Walls, and McConnell, "Shifting Gears: New
          Directions for Cars and Clean Air," Resources for
          the Future Discussion Paper, 94-26.
      Repetto, et al, Green Fees: How a Tax Shift Can Work
          for the Environment and the Economy, pp. 35-52.

      Optional:

      J. MacKenzie, et al., The Going Rate: What it Really
          Costs to Drive.
      K. Small, et al., Road Work: A New Highway Pricing and
          Investment Strategy.

E.   PODS AND OZONE HOLES

      BF, Ch. 20, pp. 420-429.
      Project 88, Harnessing Market Forces, pp. 32-41.

      Optional:

      T. Barthold, "Issues in the Design of Environmental
          Excise Taxes," Journal of Economic Perspectives,"
          Winter, 1994.

F. GREENHOUSE GASSES AND GLOBAL CLIMATE CHANGE

      BF, Ch. 20, pp. 429-442.
      DD, Schelling, "Some Economics of Global Warming."
      J. Darmstadter, "Estimating the Cost of Carbon Dioxide
          Abatement," Resources, Spring, 1991.
      National Academy of Sciences, Policy Implications of
          Greenhouse Warming.
      W. Nordhaus, "Reflections on the Economics of Climate
          Change," Journal of Economic Perspectives, Fall,
          1993.
      Repetto, et al, Green Fees: How a Tax Shift Can Work
          for the Environment and the Economy, pp. 53-70.

G. THE ENERGY/ENVIRONMENT CONNECTION

      Kozloff and Dower, A New Power Base: Renewable Energy
          Policies for the 1990's and Beyond, Ch. 3 and 4.
      "Conservation Power", Business Week, September 16, 1991
      Project 88, Harnessing Market Forces, Ch. 4, pp. 70-80.
      Project 88, Round II, Ch. 2, pp. 30-38.

Optional:

Pace University, <u>Environmental Costs of Electricity</u>,
pp. 13-48, (on reserve).

<u>Optional Topic:Toxic Substances, Hazardous Waste, Solid Waste</u>

BF, Ch. 16, Ch. 17, pp. 354-364.
PP, Chapters by Dower, Shapiro.
DD, Passell, "Weighing Alternatives for Toxic Waste
Cleanup."
DD, Russell, "Economic Incentives in the Management of
Hazardous Wastes."
Macauley, Bowes, and Palmer, <u>Using Economic Incentives
to Regulate Toxic Substances</u>.
Repetto, et al, <u>Green Fees: How a Tax Shift Can Work
for the Environment and the Economy</u>, pp. 1-34.

IV. ECONOMICS OF NATURAL RESOURCES

   A. <u>NonRenewable Resources</u>

       TT, Ch. 6.

       Optional:

       DD, Dorfman, "The Economics of Resources or the
       Resources of Economics."

   B. <u>A Renewable Resource with Competing Uses: Water</u>

       TT, Ch. 9.
       Lee and Kneese, "Fish and Hydropower Vie for Columbia
       River Water," <u>Resources</u>, Winter 1989.
       <u>Project 88, Round II</u>, pp. 69-77.

   C. <u>A Renewable Resource with Competing Uses: Forests</u>

       TT, Ch. 11.
       <u>Project 88, Round II</u>, pp. 77-86.

   D. <u>The Fishery</u>

       TT, Ch. 12.
       Schlager and Ostrom, "Property-Rights Regimes and
       Natural Resources: A Conceptual Analysis," <u>Land
       Economics</u>, August, 1992.

   E. <u>Biodiversity</u>

       Randall, "What Mainstream Economists Have to Say About
       the Value of Biodiversity," in V&P2, pp. 501-505.

V. SOME ECONOMICS OF SUSTAINABILITY

    BF, Ch. 18, pp. 393-396.
    DD, Solow, "Sustainability: An Economist's Perspective."
    Solow, "An Almost Practical Step Toward Sustainability."
50 M. Toman, "Economics and Sustainability: Balancing Tradeoff
    and Imperatives."

ESSAY #1

You are the chief advisor on environmental economics to Newt-Kemp Cuomo, the leading candidate for her party's nomination to run for president. You have received the following memo from her:

I understand that many parts of the US are presently not in attainment of the Primary National Ambient Air Quality Standard for ozone and that it will be very difficult to achieve attainment in the most severely polluted of these cities. I also understand that this "non=attainment" problem could be made worse if the PNAAQS were revised downward as many environmentalists and health scientists are urging.

I have been scheduled to give a speech before a combined meeting of the Detroit chapter of the Sierra Club and the Automotive Manufacturers of America. Please write me a memo on:

-the nature of this problem, especially its economics dimensions;

-what policy options are being considered in the public debate;

-from the broadest possible perspective, what options should I be considering as I formulate my position on this issue;

-what do you recommend.

This memo should be no more than six pages long. I will not have time to read more than that. Also, I want your objective analytical perspective; do not consider questions of political feasibility. I will worry about that.

SECOND ASSIGNED ESSAY

This course has emphasized an economic approach to analyzing environmental pollution and resource management problems. Write a 5-6 page essay in which you:

explain what you think an "economic approach" means; and

identify the most important insights that this approach has provided you about the causes of, consequences of, and methods of dealing with environmental and resource problems.

Problem Set #2

1. Suppose that an individual's preferences over environmental
    quality (Q) and (M) to purchase market goods can be
    represented by the utility function:

    $$U = U(M, Q)$$

    $$= 5M^{.7} \cdot Q^{.2}$$

    At an income of $500, what is this individual's willingness
    to pay for an increase in Q from Q = 10 to Q·12?

2. Suppose that a travel cost model has been used to estimate
    the demand function for visits to a beach. The result is

    $$V = 40,000 - 1250P + 2000 Q$$

    where   V = visits per year

               P = price

               Q = a measure of annual average water quality.

    a. For P = $1 and Q = 5, what is the predicted number of
        visits? What is the economic value of the beach to
        those who visit it? What is the "Choke" price, that
        is, the price at which V = 0?

    b. How many visits will occur per year if Q is increased
        to 6 and nothing else changes?

    c. Assuming that the conditions for weak complementarity
        are satisfied, what is the economic benefit of an
        increase in Q to 6?

3. Suppose that a hedonic wage equation has been estimated and
    the result is

    $$W = 30,000 + 1000R + 250,000R^2$$

    where W is the annual wage and R is the probability of being
    killed in an accident on the job.

    a. What is the wage premium for a job with a probability
        of .01 of accidental death? a probability of .02 of
        accidental death?

52

Economics 218   Fall 1994
Economics of Resources and the Environment   Mr. Freeman

(Note: These probabilities are much higher than the
probabilities in typical American manufacturing jobs.)

b.   What is the value of statistical life implied by the
      hedonic wage function for a policy that reduces the
      risk of death from .02 to .01?

c.   Assuming that people's preferences for avoiding
      environmental health risks are similar to their
      preferences regarding job risks and that all people are
      alike, calculate the economic benefit of a pollution
      control policy that reduces the probability of dying
      from .02 to .01 for an exposed population of 10,000
      people.

4.   Suppose that the demand and supply functions for market good
     X are:

              Demand: $X_D = 500 - 4P$

              Supply: $X_S = -120 + 4P + 4Q$

     What is the economic benefit of an increase in Q from 5 to
     15? How much is this benefit accrues to consumers? to
     producers?

DUE: Wednesday, Obctober 5, 1994

FIRST HOUR EXAM

I.   (33%) For each of the following two cases:

   (1) What do you think is the most persuasive reason (or
        reasons; there could be more than one) to use benefit-
        cost analysis to decide whether to undertake the
        policy?

   (2) What do you think is the most persuasive reason (or
        reasons; there could be more than one) NOT to use
        benefit-cost analysis to decide whether to undertake
        the policy?

   (3) What is your position on whether or not to use benefit-
        cost analysis to decide whether to undertake the
        policy?

Case A: On a separate island community, all of the citizens are
involved in the production of widgets. Given current practices,
widget production involves emissions of a chemical that increases
the probability of contracting fatal cancer by 0.001 for each of
the equally exposed citizens. There is a proposal to build a
device to control emissions, the costs of which would be borne in
equal shares by all of the citizens.

Case B: Currently logging in old growth forests threatens the
extinction of the northern spotted owl, an endangered species.
The owls can be protected only by prohibiting logging in these
forests. The prohibition would impose long term costs on people
who buy houses and use other lumber products and short term
transition costs on people engaged in logging and lumber
processing.

II. (66%) Choose and TWO (2) of the following terms and for
each write an essay in which you:

   A. Define and explain the term; and

   B. Describe its role and its importance in the economic
analysis of environmental and resource problems and policies.

   Liability as an incentive for controlling pollution.

   Cost effectiveness

   External cost

   Implicit price

54

Second Hour Exam

I. Choose any TWO (2) at 25% each.

A. Describe and evaluate from an economic perspective the key
features of the sulfur allowance trading program that was
introduced as part of the Clean Air Act Amendments of 1990.
Specifically address the following points:

  - What is the objective of this program and on what basis
  was this objective chosen?

  - What mechanism was chosen to achieve this objective?

  - From an economic perspective, what are the major pros and
  cons of this program?

B. Suppose that Congress has established an ambient
environmental quality standard (Q*) for a pollutant.

  - What would the pollution control agency need to know in
  order to set a tax or charge on pollution so as to achieve
  Q*? Describe how this information would be used to set the
  tax.

  - What would the agency need to know to determine the
  correct number of tradable emissions permits to issue?
  Describe how this information would be used.

You should consider both the cases of a well mixed or global
pollutant and a local pollutant such as PM10.

C. Pick either the Federal Water Pollution Control Act of 1972
or the Clean Air Act of 1970 and answer the following questions:

  - What are the principal objectives of the Act?

  - What are the principal means or instruments established in
  the Act to meet these objectives.

  - Evaluate the objectives and the instruments from an
  economic perspective.

II. Choose any THREE (3) at 13% each.

A. Describe the economic principles that should be used to
determine the appropriate penalty under a "command and control"
system for controlling pollution.

55

B.   Describe how a pollution tax or a tradable emission permit
system creates incentives for research and development and
innovation.   Do these incentives apply only to end-of-pipe
treatment technologies?   Discuss.

C.   Describe and contrast the macro or top down vs. the micro or
bottom up approaches estimating the costs of reducing carbon
dioxide emissions.

D.   What are the arguments for and against having the government
auction off tradable emissions permits vs. giving them to
polluters?

E.   Explain the term "old source bias."   Give a couple of
examples in which old source bias is created by features of
federal environmental policies.

FINAL EXAM

SUMMARY:

			Recommended time
I. Overview		30%	1 hr
II. Resources	Choose 1	25%	3/4 hr
III. Pollution	Choose 1	25%	3/4 hr
IV. Teasers	Choose 2	20%	1/2 hr
		100%	3 hr

Be sure that you do the right number of questions.

I.   (30%)   POLICY OVERVIEW

        Assume that a new cabinet level department has been created in
the federal government. It is the Department of Environment and
Natural Resources. It consolidates responsibilities that are
presently scattered in several Departments and agencies, including
the Environmental Protection Agency and the Departments of
Agriculture (national forests),Interior (national parks and other
public lands), Energy, and Commerce (marine fisheries). The new
department has responsibility for all environmental and resource
management policy issues for the federal government. You are the
head of the Office of Economic Planning and Policy Analysis. You
have just received the following memo from the newly appointed
secretary of this department.

        I will be making a major public speech on future directions
        for this Department next week. I need your advice. Please
        prepare for me a briefing paper answering the following
        questions:

        --   From an economic perspective, what are the two or three
              most important environmental and/or resource policy
              problems I should be working on during my first year or
              two in this office? Describe the nature of the problems
              and their causes and consequences. Why do you think
              these are the most important, that is, why should I give
              them priority?

        ___   What is your criterion for defining "important"?

        --   For each of these problems, what are the policy options?
              Which of these policies or options would you recommend
              that I work for? Why?

        Your answer to this question will be evaluated in part on the
basis of the knowledge of the policy issues discussed in class and
in the readings that you demonstrate, and in part on how well you
use economic reasoning and analysis to justify your choice of
problems and policy options.

57

II.   (25%)   RESOURCE MANAGEMENT

Choose ONE (1) of the following questions:

A.   Pick an example of a multiple product resource system, that
is, a natural resource system that produces two or more
environmental and/or resource service flows.

     -- Describe the various service flows from the example you
     have picked. Describe and explain the tradeoffs among service
     flows.

     -- Explain how an economic framework can be developed to
     identify and analyze the management options.

     -- Explain how to determine the optimum or most efficient set
     of service flows.

     -- Under what conditions will the optimum set of service flows
     be obtained without any governmental intervention?

B.   Choose either the selection of a time path of extraction of a
depletable resource or the selection of a level of effort and rate
of harvest from a commercial fishery stock.

     --Derive and explain the conditions from an optimal or
     efficient solution to the resource management problem;

     -- What kinds of market failures might prevent the achievement
     of an efficient solution?

III. (25%)   PRINCIPLES OF POLLUTION POLICY

Choose ONE (1) of the following questions:

A.   Assume that the Agency knows both the marginal damage of
emissions curve and the marginal abatement cost curve for
emissions.

     -- Explain how the Agency would use this information to
     determine the optimal or efficient rate of tax or charge on
     emissions. What is the optimal charge? Identify and explain
     the changes in net economic welfare (NEW) that result from
     imposing this charge.

     -- Explain how polluters would respond to this charge.

     -- Discuss the possible uses of the revenues that the
     government would collect from the charge.

B. Explain what is meant by a "revealed preference" method of estimating the value of an environmental change, for example, the benefit of controlling pollution.

-- For one of the following beneficial effects of an environmental improvement:

reduction in cases of respiratory disease
reduction in risk of death due to air pollution
increased recreation opportunities due to improved water quality

select one of the revealed preference methods that were discussed in the course and describe how it would be used to estimate the benefit of this change. You should explain what the term "benefit" means, what data would be required, and how the data would be used.

IV. (20%)   MISCELLANEOUS TEASERS

Choose TWO (2) of the following questions.

A. In a review of a recent book by Donella Meadows and Dennis Meadows (Beyond the Limits), Robert Stavins writes:

The authors recommend minimizing the use of nonrenewable resources. This recommendation does not, as a general rule, make sense. The authors urge society to 'recycle whenever possible,' which also would be flawed public policy.

Who is right? Are these recommendations flawed public policy? Explain.

B. Several years ago, an environmental organization released the following statement:

POLLUTION CONTROL IS GOOD FOR THE ECONOMY

A recent government study shows that industry compliance with new clean air and clean water requirements will result in the creation of half a million new jobs.

Is this really good news? Explain.

C. Suppose that authorities in southern California are considering a requirement that ALL people commuting to work in cars between 7 AM and 10 AM must be part of a car pool. Supporters of the proposal argue that there will be benefits because of reduced auto emissions and highway congestion and the costs will be negative (!) because of reduced auto operating expenses for car owners. Is this really a negative cost policy? Explain.

Bowdoin College

Economics 318
Environmental and Resource Economics

Fall 1993
Mr. Freeman

READING ASSIGNMENTS

Notes: I have placed copies of thee books of readings on reserve.
Some of the articles listed below are reprinted in one or more of
these collections. In the assignments below, each collection will be
referred to by its editor's name:

Dorfman = Robert Dorfman and Nancy Dorfman, Economics of the
Environment, 3rd ed.

Markandya = Anil Markandya, Environmental Economics.

Oates = Wallace Oates, The Economics of the Environment.

TOPIC 1: A REVIEW OF OPTIMIZATION AND MATHEMATICAL TECHNIQUES

Readings:
"Mathematics for Microeconomics" Handout.

Freeman, Intermediate Microeconomic Analysis, Mathematical
Appendices to Chs. 2, 7, 9, 11.

Optional Readings:
Baumol, Economic Theory and Operations Analysis, 4th ed., Ch. 4
(an elementary treatment of calculus as marginal analysis).

Henderson and Quandt, Microeconomic Theory, 3rd ed., Chs. 1, pp.
5-18, 32-34, Ch. 4, pp. 64-80, 98-101, (A more rigorous
treatment of the application of calculus to economic
analysis.)

Key Points: The first and second order conditions for a maximum and
their economic interpretation; constrained optimization and the
Lagrangian multiplier.

TOPIC 2: ECONOMIC EFFICIENCY, APPLIED WELFARE ECONOMICS, AND BENEFIT-
COST ANALYSIS

Readings:
Freeman, Intermediate Microeconomic Analysis, Chs. 5, 14, 17, and
18.

Freeman, "The Methodology of Benefit-Cost Analysis," pp. 1-18.

Key Points: Pareto optimality; the conditions for an efficient
allocation; the Pareto improvement criterion (Hicks and Kaldor);
the definitions of benefits and cost; how all of these relate to
benefit-cost analysis.

TOPIC 3: THE PRINCIPLES OF BENEFIT-COST ANALYSIS

Readings:
> Freeman, "The Methodology of Benefit-Cost Analysis," pp. 18-41,
>   skip pp. 30-32.
>
> RTI, Benefit-Cost Assessment Handbook, Chap. 1, Chap. 2

Key Points: With vs without scenarios; when indirect effects should be
counted as benefits and costs; how to deal with what you don't
know for sure.

TOPIC 4: TIME, DISCOUNTING, AND THE INTEREST RATE

Readings:
> Freeman, Intermediate Microeconomic Analysis, Chap. 13, esp.
>   pp. 355-373.
>
> Henderson and Quandt, Microeconomics Theory, 3rd ed., Ch. 12,
>   pp. 322-326, pp. 341-342.
>
> Chaing, "Handout."
>
> Lind, "The Conceptual Basis for Discounting."

Key Points: Discounted present value in both the discrete time and
continuous time cases; using present values for investment and
project evaluation decisions; the choice of discount rate; the
shadow price of capital.

TOPIC 5: THE THEORY OF EXTERNALITIES

Readings:
> Coase, "The Problem of Social Cost," Jour. of Law and Economics,
>   vol 3, 1960; also available in Dorfman, and in Oates. This
>   is a "classic." It is also difficult because of the Because
>   of the nonrigorous style of argumentation. We will discuss
>   this article after you have read the other items in this
>   topic; but you should read it first to get a sense of the
>   evolution of economic thinking on this topic.
>
> Pearce and Turner, Economics of Natural Resources and the
>   Environment, Chaps. 4 & 5.
>
> Varian, "Production Externalities," pp. 548-553. To be handed
>   out.
>
> Freeman, "Measuring Values and Benefits," pp. 19-23.
>
> William Baumol and Wallace Oates, The Theory of Environmental
>   Policy, 2nd ed., Chap. 3 to p. 25 and Chap. 4 to p. 47.

61

Key Points: What is the "Coase" theorem? Under what conditions does
    it hold? Define an externality. What is the economic
    consequence of a negative externality for Pareto optimality?

TOPIC 6:   THE THEORY OF CONTROLLING EXTERNALITIES

Readings:
    Pearce and Turner, Economics of Natural Resources and the
        Environment, Chaps. 6-8.

    Bohm and Russell, Ch. 10 of Kneese and Sweeney, Handbook of
        Natural Resource and Energy Economics, vol. 1, to p. 415.

Key Points: How taxes and marketable permits work to correct
    externality type market failures. Can direct regulation of the
    externality alone achieve an efficient allocation of resources?

TOPIC 7:   APPLICATIONS OF THE THEORY: COST EFFECTIVENESS

Readings:
    Herzog, "Economic Efficiency and Equity in Water Pollution
        Control," Journal of Environmental Economics and Management,
        1976, pp. 170-174.

    O'Neil,,et. al., "Transferable Charge Permits and Economic
        Efficiency," Journal of Environmental Economics and
        Management, December 1983, also available in Oates.

    Seskin, Anderson, and Reid, "An Empirical Analysis of Economic
        Strategies for Controlling Air Pollution," Journal of
        Environmental Economics and Management, 1983, pp. 112-124,
        also available in Oates.

Key Points: Concept of cost effectiveness; how the environment is
    modelled (Q as a function of emissions); economic implications of
    alternative policies; why are some policies less costly then
    others?

TOPIC 8:   APPLICATIONS OF THE THEORY: EMISSION TRADING

Readings:
    Tietenberg, "Transferable Discharge Permits and the Control of
        Stationary Source Air pollution," Land Economics, 1980,
        pp. 391-416, also available in Oates and in Dorfman.

    Bohm and Russell, Ch. 10 of Kneese and Sweeney, Handbook of
        Natural Resource and Energy Economics, vol. 1, pp. 419-428.

    Hahn and Noll, "Designing a Market for Tradable Emissions
        Permits."

Atkinson and Tietenberg, "The Empirical Properties of Two Classes
of Designs for Transferable Discharge Permit Markets,"
Journal of Environmental Economics and Management, 1982, pp.
101-121.

Tietenberg, "Economic Instruments for Environmental Regulation,"
in Markandya.

Key Points: Difference between trading emissions and trading ambient
permits. Problems of market power.

TOPIC 9: THE THEORY OF WELFARE MEASUREMENT

Readings:
Freeman, "Defining and Measuring Welfare Changes: Basic Theory,"
pp. 39-56, 60-66.

Freeman, "Models for Indirect Benefit Estimation: Basic Theory,'
pp. 93-103, 104-108, 115-118, 124-131.

Markandya, "The Value of the Environment: A State of the Art
Survey," in Markandya.

Key Points: How to derive the indirect utility function and
expenditure function; their use in defining welfare measures; how
models of individual choice and behavior can be used to draw
inferences about the values of things not purchased in markets.

TOPIC 10: SOME EXAMPLES OF WELFARE MEASUREMENT

Readings:
Harrington, Krupnick, and Spofford, "The Economic Losses of a
Waterborne Disease Outbreak," Journal of Urban Economics,
1989, pp. 116-137, also available in Oates.

Fisher, Violette, and Chestnut, "The Value of Reducing Risks of
Death: A Note on New Evidence," Journal of Policy Analysis
and Measurement, 1989, pp. 88-100.

Gerking, De Haan, and Schulze, "The Marginal Value of Job Safety:
A Contingent Valuation Study," Journal of Risk and
Uncertainty, 1988, pp. 185-200.

Bishop and Heberlein, "Measuring the Values of Extramarket Goods:
Are Indirect Measures Biased? American Journal of
Agricultural Economics, 1979, pp. 926-930, also available in
Markandya.

63

Ridker and Henning, "The Determinants of Residential Property
   Values with Special Reference to Air Pollution," Review of
   Economics and Statistics, 1967, pp. 246-257, also available
   in Oates. See if you can spot the error that they make in
   interpreting their empirical results.

Brookshire, Thayer, Schulze, and D'Arge, "Valuing Public Goods: A
   Comparison of Survey and Hedonoic Approaches," American
   Economic Review, 1982, pp. 165-177, also available in Oates.

Hazilla and Kopp, "Social Cost of Environmental Quality
   Regulations: A General Equilibrium Analysis," Journal of
   Political Economy, 1990, pp. 853-873, also available in
   Oates.

TOPIC 11: AGRICULTURAL BENEFITS OF CONTROLLING OZONE POLLUTION

Readings:
   ES&T, Outlook: "Crop Losses from Air Pollutants."

Kopp, et al., "Implications of Environmental Policy for U.S.
   Agriculture: The Case of Ambient Ozone Standards," Journal
   of Environmental Management, 1985, pp. 321-331.

McGartland, "The Implications of Ambient Ozone Standards for U.S.
   Agriculture: A Comment and Some Further Evidence," Journal
   of Environmental Management, 1987, pp. 139-146.

Bruce Madariaga, "Ambient Air Quality Standards for U.S.
   Agriculture: The Correct Welfare Measure Revisited,"
   Journal of Environmental Management, 1988.

Kopp and Krupnick, "Agricultural Policy and the Benefits of Ozone
   Control," American Journal of Agricultural Economics,
   December 1987, pp. 956-962.

TOPIC 12: OPTIMAL FORESTRY

Readings:
   Freeman, Intermediate Microeconomic Analysis, pp. 375-377.

Howe, "The Economics of forest Management," pp. 221-231; HANDOUT.

Hartman, "The Harvesting Decision When a Standing Forest Has
   Value," Economic Inquiry, March 1976.

Bowes and Krutilla, Multiple-Use Management: The Economics of
   Public Forestlands, Chs. 1-3.

Optional Readings:

   Bowes and Krutilla, Ch. 12 in Kneese and Sweeney, Handbook of
      Natural Resource and Energy Economics, Vol. 2 (A more
      rigorous treatment of the multiple use problem.)

TOPIC 13: THE MANAGEMENT OF COMMON PROPERTY RESOURCES: THE FISHERIES

Readings:
   Freeman, Intermediate Microeconomic Analysis, PP. 340-343.

   Fisher, Resource and Environmental Economics, Ch. 3.

   Shone, "The Blue Whale."

   Lee Anderson, "Property Rights in Fisheries: Lessons from the
      New Zealand Experience."

TOPIC 14: THE ECONOMIC VALUE OF WETLANDS

Readings:
   Gosselink, Odom, and Pope, "The Value of the Tidal Marsh."

   Shabman and Batie, "Economic Value of Natural Coastal Wetlands, a
      Critique.

   Ellis and Fisher, "Valuing the Environment as an Input."

   Freeman, "Valuing Environmental Resources under Alternative
      Management Regimes," Ecological Economics, 1991, pp. 247-
      256.

TOPIC 15: NONRENEWABLE RESOURCES

Readings:
   Fisher, Resource and Environmental Economics, Ch. 1, p. 10-44.

   Herfindahl and Kneese, Economic Theory of Natural Resources, Ch.
      4, pp. 114-125.

   Mishan, Introduction to Normative Economics, Ch. 61-66, pp.
      477-497.

   Freeman, "Severance Taxes and Depletable Resources," Handout.

   Stiglitz, "A Neoclassical Analysis of the Economics of Natural
      Resources," in V. K. Smith, ed., Scarcity and Growth
      Reconsidered.

Problem Set #1

1. (20%) Why is discounting benefits and costs necessary to assure an
efficient intertemporal allocation of resources? Conceptually, what
is the appropriate basis for selecting a discount rate for discounting
future benefits and costs accruing to individuals?

2. (70%) Assume the following facts about the lighting system in your
company's office:

-it presently uses 10,000 kWh of electricity per year.

-it will last exactly 30 more years

-the price of electricity is now $.11/kWh and is expected to
be constant at this level for the next 30 years.

Show all of the calculations that you base your answers on. If you
use a spread sheet or computer program, provide adequate documentation
so that I can see how you got your answers.

A. You are told that there is now available a new high
efficiency lighting system that will use only 3,000 kWh per year. It
will also last exactly 30 years. It would cost the company $10,000
now to rip out and dispose of the present system in an environmentally
safe manner and to purchase and install the new system. The
opportunity cost of funds for your company is 8%.

-is purchasing the new lighting system a good investment for
your firm? Explain

-is it a good investment from society's point of view?
In other words, is it economically efficient? Explain.
(For this question, assume that 8% is the correct social
discount rate.)

B. Assume the same facts as in #2.A except that the opportunity
cost of funds is 5%.

-is purchasing the new lighting system a good investment for
your firm? Explain

-is it a good investment from society's point of view?
In other words, is it economically efficient? Explain.

- What do you conclude about the role of the interest rate in
influencing investments in conservation?

C. Assume the same facts as in #2.A (including the 8% cost of
funds) except that the price of electricity is $.13/kWh.

-is purchasing the new lighting system a good investment for
your firm? Explain

66

-is it a good investment from society's point of view?
In other words, is it economically efficient? Explain.

- What do you conclude about the role of the price of
electricity in influencing investments in conservation?

D. Assume the same facts as in #2.A (including the 8% cost of
funds and $.11/kWh electricity). Suppose that emissions of sulfur
dioxide associated with generating electricity cause damages to others
that are valued at $.02/kWh.

-is purchasing the new lighting system a good investment for
your firm? Explain

-is it a good investment from society's point of view?
In other words, is it economically efficient? Explain.

- Discuss policy options which could be used to create
incentives for private agents such as your company to
make the economically efficient or socially desirable
decisions in this case.

3. (5%) Suppose that it has been established that the world
population of mosquitoes was 3.12 million on January 1, 1993 and that
this population is growing continuously at the rate of 0.1% per day.
What will the population be on January 3, 1994?

4. (5%) Consider the sum of $1000 due in exactly 20 years. Calculate
its present value using a discount rate of 8% per year:

a. Assuming compounding annually;

b. Assuming continuous compounding.

DUE: In class, Wednesday, September 22.

67

Problem Set No. 2
DUE DATE: Class on Wednesday, October 13

You are given the following information about a river basin.

A.   There are two factories (No. 1 and 2) discharging wastes (D_1, D_2)
     at the locations shown in the Figure. The quantities of wastes
     are measured in tons of B.O.D. per day.

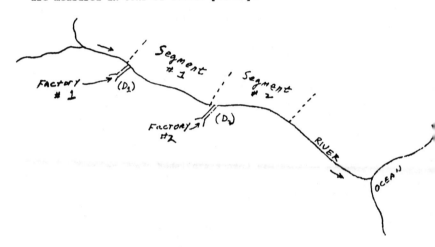

B.   The production processes at the two factories result in the
     generation of waste products, X_1 and X_2.

     $X_1 = 50$ tons/day, $X_2 = 100$ tons/day

C.   Wastes can be removed by treatment. R = tons of wastes
     removed. Therefore:

     $D_1 = X_1 - R_1$,

     $D_2 = X_2 - R_2$

D.   The quality of the water in each segment of the river is
     measured in Dissolved Oxygen and indicated by Q_1 and Q_2.
     Quality depends on the discharges from the two factories in
     the following way:

     $Q_1 = 15 - a_{11}D_1 - a_{12}D_2$

     $Q_2 = 16 - a_{21}D_1 - a_{22}D_2$

68

E. There are legally established water quality standards
    ($\hat{Q}_1$, $\hat{Q}_2$) for each segment of the river. The ambient water
    quality standards are:

    $\hat{Q}_1 \geq 5$

    $\hat{Q}_2 \geq 6$.

F. Treatment costs are linear functions of the wastes removed
    (T).

    $C_1 = c_1 R_1$;

    $C_2 = c_2 R_2$

G. The parameters of the system are:

    $a_{11} = .4$ $a_{12} = 0$

    $a_{21} = .20$ $a_{22} = .25$

    $c_1 = 30$ $c_2 = 50$

As Chief of the Water Quality Division of the Pollution Control
Agency, your task is to decide how much treatment (R) each
factory should undertake. Formally, your problem is to determine
values for the decision variables, R_1 and R_2, so as to achieve the
ambient water quality standards at least total cost.

Show your work either in the space provided or on a separate
sheet.

1. a. State your objective function in algebraic form.

    b. State the constraints in algebraic form as functions of
        R_1 and R_2.

    c. Using graph paper, plot the constraints and clearly
        mark the feasible set, i.e., those combinations of R_1
        and R_2 that will meet the water quality targets.

    d. Draw in at least one iso-cost line (from the objective
        function)

2. The solution requires the following levels of treatment:

    R_1 = _____

    R_2 = _____

    cost is C = _____

69

3. If these levels of treatment are undertaken, the resulting
    water quality is:

       Q_1 = _____

       Q_2 = _____

    why is $Q_1 > \hat{Q}_1$?

4. How could you use a system of taxes on pollution discharges
    to achieve the least-cost solution? At what levels would
    you set the taxes? Why are they different for the two
    factories?

5. Given your solution in Question 2, what is the marginal cost
    of raising the water quality standard in segment #1 to 10,
    i.e., $\hat{Q}_1 \geq 10$? Should such a step be taken? Discuss.

6. Given your solution in Question 2, what is the marginal cost
    of raising the water quality standard in segment #2 to 7;
    i.e., $\hat{Q}_2 \geq 7$? Should such a step be taken? Discuss.

7. Assume a strategy of uniform percentage removal/treatment
    for all dischargers. Specifically assume a 70% removal
    requirement: R_i = .7X_i for i = 1, 2.

       R_1 = _____ R_2 = _____

       Cost C = _____

       Q_1 = _____ Q_2 = _____

70 Compare these with your answers to 2 and 3. Is uniform
    treatment more equitable than the least-cost plan?

Problem Set #3

1. Assume that an individual's preferences for two market goods (X and Y) and environmental quality (Q) can be represented by:

    $$U = aX^b \bullet Y^c \bullet Q^d$$

   Assume that the individual maximizes utility subject to:

    $$M = P_X \bullet X + P_Y \bullet Y$$

   taking Q as given.

   a. Derive the first order condition for a maximum of U. What is the economic interpretation of the Lagrangian multiplier?

   b. Derive the demand functions for X and Y.

   c. Derive the indirect utility function and expenditure function.

2. Assume the following parameter values:

$a = 1$	$c = .3$
$b = .4$	$d = .2$
$M = 100$	$P_Y = 2$
$P_X = 3$	$Q = 5$

   a. Solve for the optimum choices of X and Y.

   b. Compute the CV and EV measures for a decrease in the price of X from 3 to 2. Why are they different?

   c. Compute the marginal value or marginal willingness to pay for a small change in Q, given $Q = 5$.

   d. Compute the CS and ES measures for an increase in Q to 6.

Economics 318   Fall 1993
Environmental and Resource Economics   Mr. Freeman

                            HOUR EXAM

Answer any TWO (2) of the following questions. Plan to spend about 20
minutes on each of the questions you choose.

1. Consider a proposal to require all the widget factories in the US to
install special air filters to prevent the emission of widget dust into
the atmosphere.   Your task is to write about what is involved in
designing and carrying out a benefit-cost analysis of the proposed
requirement. Your answer should cover the following points:

- how to define the benefits and costs;
- what you would need to find out in order to measure the benefits and
    costs;
- how you would go about constructing the relevant scenarios; and
- what it means to say that the proposal is good if its B > C or is
    bad if C > B, in other words, explain the benefit-cost criterion
    and its rationale.

2. Many public policies such as investments in resource development or
regulations on polluters result in streams of benefits and costs that
occur over substantial periods of time.   What is the proper way to
aggregate these sums of economic values (both plus and minus) that
accrue over time, and what is the role of the discount rate in this
aggregation process? Your answer should cover the following points:

- present and explain the mathematical formula for performing this
    aggregation;
- explain why discounting is necessary from an economic perspective;
- explain what discount rate you would use in the case of a perfectly
    competitive economy with no taxes, and why;
- explain what the effect of using a higher (or lower) discount rate
    would be on the decision as to whether to undertake a project
    whose costs occurred in the near future and whose benefits
    occurred mostly in the more distant future.

3.   A tax or charge on pollution can be used either to achieve an
optimal (efficient) level of pollution or to achieve some predetermined
level of "acceptable" pollution (an ambient environmental quality
standard) at minimum cost. Explain:

A. How and why taxes on pollution affect the behavior of polluters; and

B. How to determine the correct tax to charge and the information
required in each of the following cases:

    - achieving the optimal level of a "well mixed" pollutant;
    - achieving the optimal level of pollution when location matters;
    - achieving an ambient standard at minimum cost for a "well
        mixed" pollutant; and
    - achieving an ambient standard at minimum cost when location
        matters.

72

Economics 318   Fall 1993
Environmental and Resource Economics   Mr. Freeman

FINAL EXAM

I. GENERAL ESSAY (35%)

    You should take about one hour to plan and write this essay.

In this course, we have examined a variety of environmental and
resource issues such as:

    - waterborne disease
    - effluent standards at public sewage treatment plants
    - wetlands
    - forests
    - fish

What unifying economic themes or theoretical concepts (one or
several?) do you see that tie together these various issues and give
coherence to our treatment of them in this course?

In your answer you should identify these themes, explain them and show
why they are important, and show how they apply to some or all of the
issues listed above.

II. Answer any TWO (2) of the following questions (25% each)

A.   Consider an environmental improvement that increases the yield of
an agricultural crop or the sustainable harvest in a fishery. Some
people would calculate the benefits of this improvement by multiplying
the increased harvest by the price. Explain what is wrong with this
method. Use an economic model to explain the correct method for
calculating the benefit. Be explicit about what assumptions are
required concerning the role of the government as regulator, manager,
or intervenor in the market for the output.

B.   Define the term "externality." Develop an economic model (with
either algebra or graphs) of a negative externality generated by firms
in a competitive industry and affecting a set of individuals. Be
explicit about the production or cost functions and utility functions
that represent this externality.

    -What conditions characterize the efficient or optimal level of
the externality?

    -Explain how to calculate the correct tax on the externality to
achieve the optimum.

    -Should the tax revenues be used to compensate the individuals
affected by the externality? Explain.

C.   What is meant by the term "user cost?" Explain the role of user
cost in determining the optimal or efficient utilization of renewable
and nonrenewable resources. What economic factors affect the size of
user cost?

D.   Explain the concept of a sustainable economy. What must each
generation do to achieve sustainability? Two important questions are:

-Is the present level of economic welfare sustainable?

-Is ANY level of economic welfare sustainable in the long run?

Discuss the factors that help to determine the answers to these
questions and why firm answers are very difficult to obtain.

III. Pick THREE (3) of the following terms; define or explain them
and indicate what role they play in environmental and resource
economics:

expenditure function	cost-effectiveness
the Coase Theorem	potential Pareto improvement
averting behavior	value of statistical life

Bowdoin College

Environmental Studies 394   Spring 1995
Regulating Chemicals in the Environment   Professor Freeman

<u>COURSE SYLLABUS AND READING ASSIGNMENTS</u> U

I. <u>REQUIRED PURCHASE</u>:

The basic texts and reference sources for this course are:

(1) Cohrssen and Covello, <u>Risk Analysis: A Guide to Principles and Methods for Analyzing Health and Environmental Risks</u>. In the reading assignments below, this book will be referred to as:

  CC, <u>RA</u>.

(2) Joseph Rodricks, <u>Calculating Risks</u>. This book will be referred to as:

  JR, <u>CR</u>

You should purchase both books.

II. <u>RESERVE READINGS AND OPTIONAL READINGS</u>:

Copies of all of the other required readings will be on reserve at the Library. Optional readings provide more in depth coverage of certain topics. They might be sources for research for some term paper topics. The syllabus indicates which optional readings are on reserve.

Articles in journals that the Library holds are marked with an "*". As an alternative to using the Reserve Desk, you can go to the stacks for these items.

Several of the assigned and optional readings are in Glickman and Gough, eds., <u>Readings in Risk</u>. One copy of this book is on reserve. This book will be referred to as:

  GG, <u>Readings</u>

III. <u>PREPARING FOR CLASSES</u>:

At the end of each class, I will tell you which readings will be the basis of the next class meeting. You should read these assignments prior to the next class.

READING ASSIGNMENTS

I. INTRODUCTION:

      CC, RA, Chaps. 1, 2. Also look at Appendix D (pp. 129-132)
          and the Glossary (pp. 355-375); these might come in
          handy during the course.
      JR, CR, Prologue.
      GG, Readings, Wilson, pp. 55-60.
      Probability and Risk Handout.

II. OVERVIEW

      To be read while I am away (January 30 - February 1):

      Misch, "Assessing Environmental Health Risks, in Lester
          Brown, ed., State of the World - 1994.
      Center for Risk Analysis, A Historical Perspective on Risk
          Assessment in the Federal Government.

III. BASICS OF TOXICOLOGY:

      JR, CR, Chaps 1-5.
      Keenan, Finley, and Price, "Exposure Assessment, " Risk
          Analysis, June 1994.

IV. IDENTIFYING CHRONIC TOXIC SUBSTANCES, ESPECIALLY
      CARCINOGENS:

A. Basic Principles

      JR, CR, Chap 6
      Beals, "Testing Hypotheses," Statistics for Economists.
      *Page, On False Positives and False Negatives, taken from
          his article in Ecology Law Quarterly, 1978, pp. 228-
          239.

B. Cancer

      JR, CR, Chap 7 to p. 120
      "Cancer Rates Packet," includes *Gough, "Estimating Cancer
          Mortality," Environmental Science and Technology,
          August 1989, "Experts Clash over Cancer Data, "
          Science, November 16, 1990, and Davis, Dinse, and Hoel,
          "Decreasing Cardiovascular Disease and Increasing
          Cancer ..." Jour. Amer. Medical Assoc., Feb. 9, 1994.

      OPTIONAL: Office of Technology Assessment, <u>Technologies for Determining Cancer Risks...</u>, Chaps. 2 and 3.

C.   Epidemiology

      JR, <u>CR</u>, Chap. 7, pp. 120-130.
      CC, <u>RA</u>, Chap. 3 to p. 38.
      National Academy of Sciences, <u>Environmental Epidemiology</u>, Chap. 1 pp. 27 to 42.

      OPTIONAL: CEP Newsletter, "Public Health: Nuclear Emissions Take Their Toll." (on reserve)
      Maine Yankee Leukemia File. (on reserve)

D.   In Vivo, Animal Tests

      JR, <u>CR</u>, Chap. 7, pp. 130 to end.
      CC, <u>RA</u>, Chap. 3 p. 39 to end.

E.   In Vitro, Short Term Tests

      JR, <u>CR</u>, Chap. 8.
      CC, <u>RA</u>, Appendix A.

      OPTIONAL: Ames, <u>Environmental Chemicals Causing Cancer...</u>

F.   Conclusions.

      "Animal Carcinogen Testing Challenged."

      OPTIONAL: Office of Technology Assessment, <u>Technologies for Determining Cancer Risks...</u>, Chapter 4.
      GG, <u>Readings</u>, Ames, et al., including comment and response, pp. 76-100.
      Allen, Crump, and Shipp, "Correlation Between Carcinogenic Potency of Chemicals in Animals and Humans," <u>Risk Analysis</u>. December, 1988, pp. 531-544, and Commentary, pp. 549-561.
      Lave and Omenn, "Cost-effectiveness of Short-term Tests for Carcinogenicity." <u>Nature</u>, 6 November 1986.
      Lave, et al., "Information Value of the Rodent Bioassay," <u>Nature</u>, 15 December 1988.

V.   <u>RISK ASSESSMENT</u>:

A.   Overview

      CC, <u>RA</u>, Chap 4.
      JR, <u>CR</u>, Chap. 10.

B. Dose-Response and Extrapolation

    JR, CR, Chap. 9.
    Environ, Elements of Toxicology..., pp 38-41 and Table 9..

    OPTIONAL: Office of Technology Assessment, Technologies for
        Determining Cancer Risks..., Chapter 5
    Anderson, "Quantitative Approaches in Use to Assess Cancer
        Risk," Risk Analysis, December 1983, (skim the
        Appendix).

C. Federal Policy and Guidelines:

    CC, RA, pp. 190-196, 278-289.

    OPTIONAL: CC, RA, all of Appendices G and H.

D. Modelling Uncertainty and the Conservatism Issue.

    Nichols and Zeckhauser, "The Perils of Prudence: How
        Conservative Risk Assessments Distort Regulation,"
        Regulatory Toxicology and Pharmacology, pp. 61-75,
        1988.
    Burmaster and Harris, "The Magnitude of Compounding
        Conservatisms in Superfund Risk Assessments," Risk
        Analysis, April, 1993.
    *Finkel, "Has Risk Assessment Become Too 'Conservative'?,"
        Resources, Summer, 1989.
    Finkel, "Stepping out of your own Shadow," Risk Analysis,
        October 1994.

F. Is Cancer All That Matters?

    Travis and Morris, "The Emergence of Ecological Risk
        Assessment," Risk Analysis, June 1992, and attached
        materials.

VI. RISK MANAGEMENT:

A. Introduction

    JR, CR, Chaps. 11 and 12.
    GG, Readings, Morgan, pp. 17-29.
    *Travis and Hattemer-Frey, "Determining an Acceptable Level
        of Risk," Environmental Science and Technology, August
        1988.

B. Economics

    Freeman, Benefit-Cost Analysis and Environmental Policy,

Freeman and Portney, "The Rational Management of Risk,"
    1989.
Viscusi, "The Dangers of Unbounded Risk Regulation
    Commitments," presented at American Enterprise
    Institute Conference, Oct. 27, 1994.
GG, Readings, Kelman, and reply, pp. 129-138.

C.   Risk vs. Risk, Do Regulations on Chemicals Kill People?

    Keeney, "Mortality Risks Induced by Economic Expenditures,"
        Risk Analysis, March, 1990.
    Regulation Costs Lives Handout

D.   Federal Policy: In Principle and in Practice

    Portney, Public Policies for Environmental Protection, Chaps
        5, 6.
    Gough, "How Much Cancer Can EPA Regulate Away?," Risk
        Analysis, March 1990.
    *Travis, et al, "Cancer Risk Management," Environmental
        Science and Technology, May, 1987.
    Travis, et al, "Cost-Effectiveness as a Factor in Cancer
        Risk Management," Environment International, pp. 469-
        474, 1987.
    Van Houtven and Cropper, "When is a Life too Costly to
        Save?: The Evidence from Environmental Regulations."

E.   The Courts: Private Law Suits as a Remedy?

    *Menell, "The Limitations of Legal Institutions for
        Addressing Environmental Risks," Journal of Economic
        Perspectives, Summer, 1991.

VII. CASE STUDIES:

We will not do all, or even most, of these cases. View this as a
menu of possibilities. You should feel free to pursue any of
these as possible research paper topics.

A.   Dioxin:

    Dioxin Handout.
    Gough, "Science Policy Choices and the Estimation of
        Cancer Risk Associated with Exposure to TCDD," Risk
        Analysis, September 1988.
    Finkel, "Dioxin: Are We Safer Now Than Before?" Risk
        Analysis, June 1988.

B.   Proposition 65 in California:

PROP 65 Packet
Pease et al, "Risk Assessment for Carcinogens Under
    California's Proposition 65," Risk Analysis, June 1990.

C.   The Delaney Clause - Food Additives:

Cooper, "Stretching Delaney Till It Breaks," Regulation,
    November-December 1985.
GG, Readings, Rodricks and Taylor, pp. 143-155.

D.   The Delany Clause - Pesticides in Food:

National Academy of Sciences, Regulating Chemicals in Food,
    Executive Summary.
*Archibald, "Review," Land Economics, February, 1989.
Archibald and Winter, "Pesticides in Food: Assessing the
    Risks," in Winter, et al, eds., Chemicals in the Human
    Food Chain, 1990.

E.   Pesticides:

Pesticide Packet.
*Zilberman, et al., "The Economics of Pesticide Use and
    Regulation," Science, 1991.

F.   Lead:

Whitfield and Wallsten, "A Risk Assessment for Selected
    Lead-Induced Health Effects: An Example of a General
    Methodology," Risk Analysis, June 1989.
Silbergeld, "Lead in the Environment," Risk Analysis, June
    1989.
Benefit-cost analysis of removing lead from gasoline.

G.   Perchloroethylene

Chapter 6 in John Graham, Harnessing Science for
    Environmental Regulation.

H.   Formaldehyde

Chapter 7 in John Graham, Harnessing Science for
    Environmental Regulation.

I.   Benzene

GG, Readings, White et. al. including comment and response,
    pp. 165-178.

J.   Air Toxics

Gray and Graham, "Risk Assessment and Clean Air Policy," and
Finkel, "Edifying Presentation of Risk Estimates: Not
as Easy as it Seems," <u>Jour. of Policy Analysis and
Management</u>, Spring, 1991, pp. 286-303.

ENVIRONMENTAL AND NATURAL RESOURCE ECONOMICS   U

University of Texas, Fall 1994
Department of Economics, Ec 350K
Professor Don Fullerton

I. Introduction	V. Exams
II. Office Hours	VI. Calendar
III. Is this Course Theoretical?	VII. Readings
IV. Assignments	

I. Introduction

This semester-long course will study the economics of public policy toward natural resources and the environment. It is designed primarily for undergraduates in economics. Microeconomics is a prerequisite.

We will start with the concepts of externalities, public goods, property rights, market failure, and social cost-benefit analysis. Within this framework, we will consider a few additional problems such as information, uncertainty, and risk analysis. The first set of applications of these tools will involve natural resources. Other applications include air pollution, water pollution, solid waste management, and hazardous substances. In addressing each of these problems, we will compare public policy responses such as administrative regulation, marketable permits, tax incentives, and direct subsidies.

In the case of nonrenewable resources, such as fossil fuels, we will consider the "efficient" rate of extraction, the private market rate of extraction, and possible public interventions that might achieve the efficient rate. In the case of renewable resources, such as forests and fisheries, we will consider the common property problem and public policies to correct it. We will also look at the disposal of wastes through landfills and incineration, policies to encourage alternatives such as recycling, and policies to discourage other alternatives such as illegal dumping or burning.

Goals: You will learn some of the tools useful in evaluating environmental policy and proposals with respect to the sometimes conflicting criteria of administrative and economic efficiency, horizontal and vertical equity, simplicity, certainty, and flexibility. Alternative explanations will make frequent use of algebra and occasional use of calculus for those who understand it, but the latter is not a prerequisite.

Requirements: There will be short papers due every second week, jointly determining fifty points or 25% of your total grade. The midterm exam will make up 50 points or 25% of the total, and the final will account for the remaining hundred points or 50%. Scores out of the two hundred possible points will be ranked on a relative scale, but grades will be assigned on an absolute scale. In other words, the curve might be concentrated at the high end, or the low end, depending on performance. See "Exams" and "Calendar" for more detail.

Reading Material: The text is <u>Environmental and Natural Resource Economics</u> by Tom Tietenberg. Further readings are required from <u>Public Policies for Environmental Protection</u>, edited by Paul Portney. We will read all of both books. Third, you will need a packet with copies of additional articles. See Section VII "Readings" below.

Social Contract: The first requirement of this course is that you read this entire syllabus. Though lengthy, it contains rules, regulations, procedures, and due-dates that are essential for participation in the course. Because they are listed here, you will be responsible for all requirements or assignments whether or not you hear the announcements in class. There will be no extensions. If you remain in this course, I will presume that you agree to these conditions. You give up some flexibility, but the advantage is that you know well in advance exactly what is expected.

II. Office Hours

Office: ECB 3.144	Monday 1:30 - 3:00pm at ECB
Phone: 471-3211 ext.173	Wednesday 1:30 - 3:00pm at the Law School
Home Phone: 329-9881	Friday 9:30 - 11:00am at ECB

You are welcome to drop in at other times. If I am engaged or under deadline when you drop in, however, then we will arrange an appointment for later. If things get particularly busy, I might extend my hours with a sign-up sheet on my door. Sign up for one 20 minute slot if you have a short question, or two consecutive slots for a longer one. During extended hours, I may be gone if the sheet is blank.

III. Is This Course Theoretical?

You might find this course to be "theoretical", but I think of it as "conceptual". We could give a course with a lot of hard facts about externalities, regulations, and public policy. For example, we could tell you which government agencies spend how much money to provide what environmental services. I suspect that you would not find such a course to be useful, however, because the few facts or numbers that you remember will soon be out-of-date. Rather, we will try to teach techniques for evaluating public policy. You will learn concepts and methodology which should prove useful in doing policy analysis yourself. Hopefully you will learn to think like an economist.

Thus, we might use equations with Greek letters in place of numbers, without ever giving the input numbers or the current numerical answers. Once you get an idea of how to obtain the right input numbers, you will always be able to use these techniques and derive your own current answers. No need to memorize old numbers. Some of you may not become economists, but all of you will want to read and understand what economists write.

IV. Assignments

One of the most constructive features of courses like this in the past has been the biweekly papers. They reinforce your knowledge of the course by putting it to immediate use, they help keep everybody up with the readings, they give you examples of the kinds of questions I am likely to ask on exams, and they give me useful feedback from students. Your answers will be strictly limited to three typed double-spaced pages in order to encourage succinct and incisive reasoning. By shifting a relatively small typing burden onto each of you, the grader can save a very large cumulative burden of time and effort. Because I do not want to judge the quality of excuses or the quality of handwriting, no untyped papers will be accepted.

There are six assignments which will count for fifty points or 25% of your final grade. Each assignment will be scored from a possible ten points, and I will select your highest five grades for the possible fifty points. You might recognize that this means you can drop one assignment, but I highly recommend doing all six: it can only help your grade as well as your understanding of the material. Also, a word on joint efforts: much can be learned from your peers, and I encourage discussion of the assignments. The most effective method seems to be maximum individual effort with occasional hints from your friends. There is nothing to be gained from wallowing about, if you don't have a clue on what to do next. But avoid doing entire sections of homework together, because you will only learn how to approach these problems if you get some practice at doing it alone. (More concretely, do not copy on the homeworks).

The calendar provides relevant dates for these assignments. If you miss a class when homework is distributed, be sure to get a copy from a friend or from me. Homeworks are due no later than the beginning of the class indicated.

"Sample Answers" to the homeworks will be distributed in the week after each is due. Because

- you know about due-dates well in advance
- you have a week for each homework,
- it should only take a couple of hours, if you're up on the readings,
- everybody has other assignments
- and I don't want to judge the quality of excuses,

there will be a one point penalty on every late paper. After distribution of the sample answers, I am willing to correct a late homework for you, but I cannot count the score. (This apparently picky approach helps avoid the more picky business of deciding what excuses qualify.)

V. Exams

Do not ask me if you can move an exam. I will follow only university procedures for rescheduling examinations.

The Midterm will be held in class on Wednesday November 2. It will probably include a few short warm-up questions such as definitions or identification of key concepts. The longer question(s) will be similar in nature to the previous assignments. There will be no choice on the midterm. Fifty points on the midterm will make up 25% of your total grade. A review session will be held two days beforehand.

The Final Exam will be held on schedule. Again, it will include some short questions and some longer questions, but there will be some choice on the final. This will enable you to concentrate on those issues which you find the most interesting. One hundred points on the final will make up half of the total grade. A review session will be held two days beforehand.

VI. Calendar

A separate sheet shows the whole semester at a glance, so you might want to mark your other assignments and exams on it.

VII Readings

Required purchases: Tom Tietenberg, Environmental and Natural Resource Economics, Third Edition (1991) by Harper Collins, and Paul R. Portney, editor, Public Policies for Environmental Protection (1990) by Resources for the Future, Washington DC. The attached list also includes other required readings, available in a xerox packet.

To ensure a fairly uniform starting place, students should already be familiar with concepts like the Edgeworth box diagram, marginal conditions for Pareto Optimality, social welfare functions, economic efficiency, and the theory of the second best. These concepts are discussed in all intermediate microeconomics textbooks, such as Mansfield's Microeconomics: Theory and Applications. Please re-read corresponding sections from your text.

Separate topics are not shown on the calendar because we will be flowing from one to another. Though I do not wish to be constrained on the timing of any particular topic, you will notice that there are 14 topics and 28 lectures. Thus, though the average topic will take two lectures, some may take only one. You should keep up on readings accordingly, and always be prepared to start the next topic.

1. **Introduction: The Role of Government**

    Tietenberg, Chapters 1 and 2.

    Rosen, Harvey S., Public Finance, Irwin, 1988, pp. 39-53 and 58-59.

    Ruff, Larry E., "The Economic Common Sense of Pollution", The Public Interest, Spring 1970, pp. 69-85.

2. **Public Goods**

    Rosen, Harvey S., Public Finance, Irwin, 1988, pp. 62-72.

    Ruckelshaus, William D., "Toward a Sustainable World", Scientific American, September 1989, pp. 166-74.

3. **Externalities**

    Tietenberg, Chapter 3.

    Rosen,Harvey S., Public Finance, Irwin, 1988, pp. 124-146.

4. **Cost-Benefit Analysis**

    Tietenberg, Chapters 4 and 5.

    Portney, Chapters 1 and 2.

    Maloney, Michael T. and Robert E. McCormick, "A Positive Theory of Environmental Quality Regulation", Journal of Law & Economics, Vol. 25, April 1982, pp. 99-123.

5. **Comparing Alternative Policies**

    Hahn, Robert W., "Economic Prescriptions for Environmental Problems: How the Patient Followed the Doctor's Orders", Journal of Economic Perspectives, Vol. 3, No. 2, Spring 1989, pp. 95-114.

4

Barthold, Thomas A., "Issues in the Design of Environmental Excise Taxes", Journal of Economic Perspectives, Vol. 8, No. 1, Winter 1994, pp. 133-51.

6. Depletable Resources

Tietenberg, Chapters 6 - 8.

7. Water Resources

Tietenberg, Chapter 9 (and 18).

Portney, Chapter 4.

Desvousges, William H., V. Kerry Smith and Ann Fisher, "Option Price Estimates for Water Quality Improvements: A Contingent Valuation Study for the Monongahela River", Journal of Environmental Economics and Management 14, September 1987, pp. 248-267.

8. Food and Forests

Tietenberg, Chapters 10 and 11.

9. The Common Property Problem

Tietenberg, Chapters 12 and 13.

Haveman, Robert H., "Common Property, Congestion, and Environmental Pollution", Quarterly Journal of Economics, May, 1973, pp. 278-87.

10. Air Pollution

Tietenberg, Chapters 14 - 17 (and 18).

Portney, Chapter 3.

11. The Greenhouse Effect

Schmalensee, Richard, "Symposium on Global Climate Change," Journal of Economic Perspectives, Vol. 7, No. 4, Fall 1993, pp. 3-10.

Nordhaus, William D., "Reflections on the Economics of Climate Change," Journal of Economic Perspectives, Vol. 7, No. 4, Fall 1993, pp. 11-25.

12. Garbage and Recycling

(Tietenberg, Chapter 8)

Portney, Chapter 5

O'Leary, Philip R., Patrick W. Walsh and Robert K. Ham, "Managing Solid Waste",

5

Scientific American, Vol. 259, No. 6, December 1988, pp. 36-42.

13. Toxic Substances

Tietenberg, Chapter 19.

Portney, Chapter 6.

Kunreuther, Howard, Paul Kleindorfer, Peter Knez, and Rudy Yaksick, "A Compensation Mechanism for Sitting Noxious Facilities: Theory and Experimental Design", Journal of Environmental Economics and Management, 14, December 1987, pp. 371-383.

14. Overview

Tietenberg, Chapters 20 - 23.

Portney, Chapters 7 and 8.

Environmental Economics, Econ 350k
University of Texas, Department of Economics

Fall 1994   Professor Don Fullerton

First Assignment

Use the terminology and tools that you have learned so far in this course to discuss the choice described below of whether or not to allow development of a natural lake. As stated in the syllabus, your answer is limited to three double-spaced pages, must be typed, and must be submitted by the beginning of class next Wednesday.

The following warning should be obvious, but let me state it just once: you may have valuable experiences that can be helpful on environmental problems, but these homeworks are intended to develop your facility with certain economics tools. In other words, even though your first reaction may be quite valid, based on your existing training and experience, it may not be the answer I am looking for. The homework is an opportunity to practice using concepts from THIS course, so think about which of the particular circumstances described below relate to concepts such as rivalness, excludability, Pareto optimality, consumer surplus, externalities, marginal benefits, marginal costs, MRS, PPF, MRT, UPF, SWF, etc, etc. Do not waste space on definitions, but choose which terms are applicable, and then apply them correctly.

Most lakes in this country are man-made, either by dredging a swamp or by building a dam. Surprisingly few are natural. Puedam Lake is natural, lies away from any main road, and is owned privately. Some birds and animals use it, but they are not endangered and can go elsewhere. The RE Development, Inc., has made a sizable offer for the property and plans to build: a road to the lake, some houses and condos around it, a swimming beach, and boat access. The beach and boat-ramp will be open to the public for a fee. As a real estate community, it will be maintained and secure from improper entry and from improper use that might damage the lake and surrounding development. They view it as a responsible plan that will allow many more people to enjoy the natural environment of the lake than do currently.

Local residents protest that the lake should be kept pristine for the good of all current and future citizens. Once developed, the lake can never again be truly natural, and an important environmental asset will be lost. Their most preferred solution is for the state government to buy the property and maintain its integrity. They recognize that the state would likely use such a purchase to make a state park with an entry road and some public facilities, but they envisage strict controls that would maintain the pristine nature of the lake. They argue that the lake is not the only commodity here to be bought and sold, but encompasses many aspects providing value that cannot each be provided by the private market.

How should the state analyze this decision? In particular, let me remind you of the framework suggested by the fundamental theorem of welfare economics: private markets will achieve an optimal allocation of resources on their own, with no government interference, if no "market failure" such as public goods, externalities, taxes, monopoly, increasing returns to scale, or information problems. Government intervention MIGHT be justified, however, if you can make a case that private markets fail in one or more of these respects.

Second Assignment

Advertising billboards along the highway are visual pollution to those who value the scenery. Others value the benefits to their businesses from the additional advertising. In three double spaced pages, plus at most one page for any figure(s), use this example to find and describe each of the eight conceptual solutions presented in class.

Specifically, suppose Farmer One has land along the highway and can put up a maximum of 30 square meters of billboard space. He is paid according to a particular schedule, and he might make adjustments for his own aesthetic costs, but his net marginal benefit starts at $60 and falls at a rate of two dollars per square meter (the equation is $MB1 = 60 - 2x$, where x is the number of square meters of billboard). Farmer Two lives just across the road and dislikes the whole idea. If Farmer One had 30 square meters of billboard, then Farmer Two would value reductions starting at $30 per square meter and falling by $1 per additional square meter reduced ($MB2 = 30 - y$, where y is the number of the 30 possible square meters not put into billboards).

Start with just two individuals and the Coase solution. Analyze case a) where One has the property rights, and then b) where Two has property rights. What wording in the law would assign property rights in each case? Describe how much one person might offer to pay the other. How and why do they arrive at a particular point? How much does each gain or lose?

Then suppose a thousand different individuals just like One and a thousand just like Two. In other words, 30,000 square meters are possible. Each of type One has the MB1 schedule above, and these are added horizontally (why?). All of the type Two together have $\mathcal{E}MB2 = 30 - y$ where y is counted per thousand square meters reduced, added vertically (why?). What would be required for the Coase solution to work? How likely is that? Now assume it does not work, and describe each of the other six solutions. How would the law have to be worded: who must pay what amount to whom for what? In each case, give the dollar value to each agent.

In this assignment, the math should be easy. The point is to apply the concepts appropriately, interpret the results, and trace the dollar flows.

Third Assignment

The cost-benefit literature devotes considerable attention to the issue of discounting future benefits and costs. Discussion involves risk, imperfect capital markets, and the choice for social rate of discount. But the procedure of discounting effectively puts lower weight on future dollar values received by future generations. Why should those individuals count as any less important than today's individuals? The issue appears to involve "intergenerational equity" within a social welfare function that somehow adds together utility levels for a lot of different individuals, and it might seem that the "fair" procedure would weight all individuals equally. If so, dollars to future generations should be weighted the same as dollars to current generations, and thus the social rate of discount should be zero. Right?

Environmental and Natural Resource Economics, Econ 350k
University of Texas, Department of Economics

Fourth Assignment

Wait a minute here: fish, forests, minerals and oil are all natural resources that can be depleted (used up) and therefore need to be conserved. Why do we need to distinguish among them? In order to save <u>any</u> of these resources for future use, while relying on private markets, the owners of these resources must earn at least the market rate of interest for continuing to hold the resource (or else they would sell it now and put the money in an interest-bearing bank account). So why did we introduce three different models in class? Are there really any essential differences among these resources?

To a certain extent, this question asks you to distill the essential elements from the textbook and lectures, and put them in your own words. It is not a hard "problem" per se, but an opportunity to solidify your grasp of the key issues by writing about them yourselves. For this reason, our grading will put more emphasis on the quality of your writing. Therefore, please think about the key distinctions among these resources, organize the presentation of your first draft, write clearly, and edit the final paper. Your job is to explain the important elements most clearly in just three double-spaced pages.

Fifth Assignment

Read the attached newspaper article (from the June 21, 1989, Wall Street Journal), and try to formalize the problem in an economic model. Start with the simplest possible model, with too many simplifying assumptions, so that you can reach an explicit solution for the social optimum amount of garbage, and, for the market equilibrium amount of garbage. The model should include a single specific reason if these differ: what exactly is the externality or public good, and why? The model might be as simple as a single diagram, or you might want to write down a utility function of several arguments, with a budget constraint, and perform the constrained optimization. In this case, you are welcome to outline such a procedure, without actually solving it.

Use class notes from about 6 weeks ago to list the necessary simplifying assumptions. Then, discuss what is too simple about that model. What other important considerations are omitted? How might the model be amended to incorporate these other interesting considerations?

Sixth Assignment

Under the topic of "toxic substances," we will talk about the problem of where to put noxious facilities. You may want to read more under that heading before trying to address this question. The problem is called "NIMBY" because everyone says "not in my back-yard."

But why does this have to be such a problem? If analysts can design a policy to achieve the "efficient" allocation of resources, i.e. the "best" location with the "right" amount of toxic waste, then the sum of the social benefits of the proposed site necessarily exceeds the sum of the social costs. The efficient solution is a potential Pareto improvement, so everyone can gain. What is the problem with this idea? Is it just in implementation, or is it something more fundamental?

A bit more specifically, describe the nature of the externality and the Pigouvian tax solution. Does this solution guarantee that everyone is better off? If not, what amendment would make everyone better off? What is the implication for NIMBY? Describe specific ideas.

Environmental and Natural Resource Economics, Econ 350k
University of Texas, Department of Economics

<u>Fall 1994</u>   <u>Professor Don Fullerton</u>

Midterm Exam

Answer all three questions. Each counts equally. Each answer should be fairly short, and to the point, so each should take only 15 minutes. You have plenty of time, so please relax. When you are done, make sure your name is on the cover of the blue-book, and then fold back the cover and place it in a pile on the desk at the front of the room.

What is wrong with each of the following statements? Please describe the main conceptual error, using tools from the course. You may also wish to provide a counter-example, but be specific about how it would work and how it refutes the statement.

1. Chincotegue Island, in the Atlantic just along the coast of Virginia, has had wild ponies in a nature preserve for hundreds of years. One bridge connects the island to the mainland, serving many visitors every year. Therefore, in this case, a private owner of the island could easily charge admission and earn a return. With no "market failure" to justify public intervention, the government should sell the land to a private provider.

2. The world's estimated reserves of oil are about 100 billion barrels, and this year's use is about 1 billion barrels. If consumption were not growing, simple arithmetic suggests that this stock would last 100 years. Because of population and income growth, however, overall consumption grows at 2% per year. Therefore, in this case, all known reserves of oil would be exhausted in 55 years.

3. Instead of requiring a specific pollution control technology, marketable pollution permits provide the right to pollute. Such permits may induce firms to use the cheapest forms of pollution control, but the firms save money, and others still breathe dirty air. Therefore permits cannot be part of a Pareto improving policy.

Midterm Sample Answers

(What is wrong with each of the following statements? Please describe the main conceptual error, using tools from the course. You may also wish to provide a counter-example, but be specific about how it would work and how it refutes the statement.)

A primary general reaction is that many students did not use diagrams that could help explain the important concepts. The question says to use tools from the course. The homeworks and midterm are practice for the final which counts 50% of your grade, so these are the places to try your hand. I'll put diagrams into my sample answers.

(1. Chincotegue Island, in the Atlantic just along the coast of Virginia, has had wild ponies in a nature preserve for hundreds of years. One bridge connects the island to the mainland, serving many visitors every year. Therefore, in this case, a private owner of the island could easily charge admission and earn a return. With no "market failure" to justify public intervention, the government should sell the land to a private provider.)

The key to this question is the separate definitions of nonexcludable and nonrival. The point of using an island is that visits are excludable. The owner can easily charge admission, and it is more difficult to circumvent in this case than for another park on the mainland somewhere else. This is not a source of market failure. However, some individuals who do not even visit the park may receive a "nonuse" value from the existence of the park. This nonuse benefit is not excludable. If the owner cannot charge people in Indiana for the existence of this park in Virginia, then the owner does not see the social marginal benefit curve and may stop short of the socially optimum provision. In addition, the existence value is nonrival. This means that the social valuation of existence is the vertical sum of individual marginal benefits. The Samuelson Solution is where this $\sum$MB is equal to marginal cost of another acre. It tells us the right number of acres:

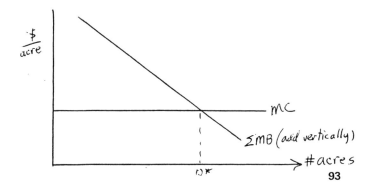

93

Finally, it is very important to distinguish MC of another acre from the MC of another user. If visits to the island are nonrival, the MC of another user is zero. Efficiency requires visits up to where the MB of another visit equals the MC of another visit, maximizing benefits under the demand curve below. Any private owner, whether monopolist or not, would have to charge a positive price to stay in business. Consumers lose surplus (area 1 and 2), the provider earns a return (area 1), for a net loss of area 2.

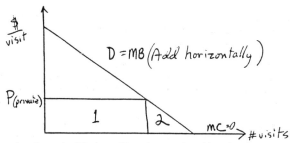

With congestion, the optimal fee is positive, since another visitor does impose costs on others. If it is both excludable and rival, then the private owner might charge just the right price, with no need for government intervention. The owner's price may not exactly match the congestion cost, however, and the owner still ignores existence value.

(2. The world's estimated reserves of oil are about 100 billion barrels, and this year's use is about 1 billion barrels. If consumption were not growing, simple arithmetic suggests that this stock would last 100 years. Because of population and income growth, however, overall consumption grows at 2% per year. Therefore, in this case, all known reserves of oil would be exhausted in 55 years.)

Your responses noted a number of fallacies. First, more oil may be discovered. Second, new technologies may be discovered. Difficult extraction may be made more economically feasible, and/or more energy may be obtainable from a given amount of oil. Third, and most important to state explicitly, the statement seems to assume that every year's use will be the same or growing. Yet we have good reason to believe that the price will be rising. As price continues to rise, the quantity demanded each year will fall. Thus it lasts longer. If the demand approaches the vertical axis asymptotically, as in the left diagram below, the price continues to rise forever. Then the quantity continues to fall, but some oil is always saved for the next generation who value it at higher and higher prices. It never runs out. If demand hits the vertical axis, as in the right diagram, the last drop of oil will be purchased when the price hits Pmax.

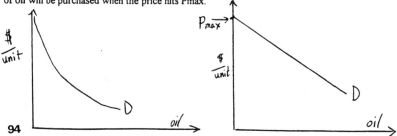

Moreover, we even know the rate at which the price (or royalty) will rise over time. If it were to rise at a rate less than the rate of interest, some companies would sell off more oil and drive down the current price. If price were to rise at a rate more than the rate of interest, some would hold oil off the market and drive up the current price. In equilibrium, the current price (Po) is determined such that the price will rise at the rate of interest. It may rise forever as in the left diagram above, or it may rise only to Pmax as in the right diagram. Equivalently, it may only rise to the price of a backstop technology (Pb):

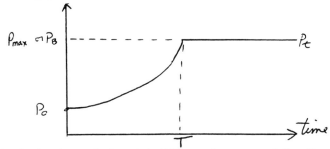

As price rises, the quantity demanded will <u>fall</u>, so a given amount of oil could easily last longer than any calculation which assumes that the quantity demanded will be constant (100 years) or growing (55 years).

(3. Instead of requiring a specific pollution control technology, marketable pollution permits provide the right to pollute. Such permits may induce firms to use the cheapest forms of pollution control, but the firms save money, and others still breathe dirty air. Therefore permits cannot be part of a Pareto improving policy.)

Many of you pointed out that we don't want zero pollution, because then we couldn't drive cars at all or use any fossil-fuel-fired generation of electricity. Our course involves determining the "right" amount. Actually, that "cost-benefit analysis" may be too difficult, because the benefits may be too hard to measure (the value of health improvements, lives saved, improved visibility, etc.). Therefore, if Congress were to guess at the right amount, we could devote our attention to a "cost-effectiveness analysis." Command and control regulation (CAC) <u>could</u> get the least-cost method of pollution abatement, but the regulators would have to be virtually omniscient. The least-cost method can more easily be attained via permits. If a firm must pay $p to emit one more ton of SO2, then it has the incentive to undertake any abatement that can reduce a ton of SO2 for less than $p. The firm undertakes the cheapest method without being told what to do. This cheapest method is found not only within a firm, but across firms. If one firm can undertake more abatement more cheaply than another firm, it just sells more permits to the other firm. The industry might be described by the following diagram, where Q is units of electricity, SMC is the social marginal cost including the pollution externality, Qc is the competitive solution, and Q* is the "optimum."

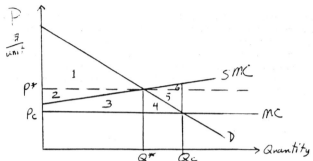

If Q*-worth of permits are given to existing firms, then output will fall to Q* (either by all firms contracting, or by some firms selling off all their permits and going out of business). The price rises from Pc to P*, so consumers lose consumer surplus of areas 2+3+4. The firms make profits of area 2+3. Victims of pollution gain from the reduction of pollution, area 4+5+6. The net gain is area 5+6. However, this is not a Pareto Improvement, as requested in the question, because consumers lose.

As one alternative, the government could sell Q* at auction rather than give them out to existing firms. Then 2+3 is not profits to the firm but revenue to the government. Victims still gain 4+5+6, but consumers still lose 2+3+4. How can we rearrange things such that everybody shares in the net gain? Imaginative policy-making can help. In this case the government would have to take back some of the gains to the victims, in some kind of lump sum tax of at least area 4. Then the government would have an amount of money 2+3+4 that it could pay out in lump-sum amounts to the consumers of this output, to protect them from loss. Payments need to be lump-sum so as to avoid further distortions in behavior. Clearly, this task is too difficult.

We might be able to get close, however. First, net gains might already be shared if we all consume the good, all benefit from what government does with the revenue, and all breathe the air. Second, higher energy taxes are designed to discourage energy use but have the unintended effect of hitting low-income families disproportionately. In this case an earned income tax credit or other aid for low-income families might help offset the higher energy taxes.

Environmental and Natural Resource Economics, Econ 350k
University of Texas, Department of Economics

<u>Fall 1994</u>   <u>Professor Don Fullerton</u>

Final Exam

This exam has three parts, each with several questions. All three parts together include eleven questions, worth ten points each. You must answer ten of these eleven questions, for a total of 100 points. I recommend that you try all eleven questions, and then decide which to cross out. But you must indicate which ten answers you want to count. If you leave answers for all eleven, I will simply count the first ten (not the best ten).

Do not use a calculator. You will not need a calculator. If you think you want a calculator, you are doing it wrong. The math is easy if you have the concepts correct. Each answer should be fairly short, and to the point, so each should take only 10 to 12 minutes. Ten answers times 12 minutes is 120 minutes, or two hours. You have <u>three</u> hours, so please relax. Write carefully. No credit for answers I cannot read. When you are done, make sure your name is on the cover of the blue-book, and then fold back the cover and place it in a pile on the desk at the front of the room.

Part I. (Four questions, ten points each) Your job is policy analyst in the Environmental Protection Division (EPD) of the Industry Performance Section (IPS). Your boss is worried about how to reduce air pollution to an appropriate level while minimizing economic costs and maximizing social welfare. Currently, the industry is not subject to any regulatory restrictions. You describe to her the various conceptual solutions you learned in your undergraduate environmental economics class. She says that sounds great, but let's put some meat on those bones. She asks you to study industry demand and cost functions, diagram them, demonstrate each solution, and explain how it works. Your study of industry demand finds that the output demanded, Q, can be expressed as:

$$Q = A + BP + CY$$

where Q is measured in millions of units (so Q=20 really means 20 million of aggregate demand), P is the price in dollars per unit, and Y is aggregate income (in millions of dollars). When this equation is estimated, you find that the coefficient A is 10 (millions of units), the estimated coefficient B is -1.0, and C is 2.0. Aggregate income for the relevant area is 20 (millions of dollars), and it is not expected to change for any reason.

Current output is 30 (million units), and the current total cost of production is 60 (millions of dollars). Upon further investigation, you decide that production exhibits no fixed costs, with constant returns to scale, and plenty of competition. You use that information to derive private marginal cost (PMC). Finally, you use estimates (from studies of health effects, visibility, etc.) to find that marginal external cost (MEC) is $Q/2$. In other words, the first unit of output (at Q=0) has no environmental cost at all, but at the current output level (Q=30), one more unit of output imposes $15 of external cost (assuming at each level of output that we cannot change the external cost per unit of output). You use all of this information together to draw PMC, MEC, SMC, Demand, current (competitive) output Q^e, and the socially optimum output Q^*.

Questions 1, 2, 3, and 4: Analyze each of the four conceptual solutions to the externality problem, each with version A and B. (If you choose to skip a question here, then fully analyze any three of the solutions, each with version A and B.) For each solution analyzed, indicate: What assumptions are required for this solution to work properly? With those assumptions, how does that policy redirect the economy from the competitive outcome to the optimal outcome? What is the dollar value for five outcomes: the change in consumer surplus, the change in government revenue, the change in industry profits, the change in environmental damages, and the net change in welfare. If you choose to answer all four of these questions (provide all eight solutions 1A through 4B), you can provide these five results for each of eight solutions in the attached matrix with 40 entries. If you answer three questions here, use the first six rows (30 entries). If you use this matrix, please put your social security number on it and staple it into your blue book.

Part II. (Three questions, ten points each) Having sorted out the conceptual issues, in Part I above, we now turn to environmental policy in practice. Describe actual air and water pollution policy in the United States (or elsewhere), using what you learned in this course, either from lectures or from the books:

   5. How do command and control (CAC) policies actually work? What is a technology-based standard, in general and by example? What is a performance-based policy, in general and by example? How are these enforced? What information is required?

   6. Can you describe any real-world example(s) of an "incentive-based policy" (IBP)? How would it be enforced? What information is required?

   7. What is the meaning of "cost-effectiveness analysis"? Can you apply this concept to the choice between CAC and IBP? Which is likely to be more cost-effective, and why?

Part III. (Four questions, ten points each) Various models of natural resources are useful for analyzing changes in the economy, and how those changes affect prices. We used different models for natural resources such as oil, timber, and fish. For each of the scenarios below, use the relevant model to show how each change in the economy is likely to affect the price for each natural resource. Start with the simplest model in each case, but indicate the simplifying assumptions (what effects are omitted).

   8. Suppose we experience a sudden unexpected increase in the market rate of interest. What is the likely effect on the current price, and on the future price path, for oil, for timber, and for fish?

9. Suppose a new environmental regulation in the U.S. requires mining firms to use a more expensive but cleaner technology for mining minerals such as zinc and magnesium. What is the likely effect on the current price and future price path of those minerals? Now suppose further investigation reveals that one of these minerals (say zinc) is primarily produced in the U.S., while the other (say magnesium) is primarily produced overseas and imported. How does that affect your answer?

10. Currently, a barrel of synthetic fuel made from shale can be produced at about three times the current price per barrel of oil. Suppose, however, that a new invention reduces the cost of this synthetic fuel to only two times the current price per barrel of oil. Would this invention have any affect on the current price of oil, or on the price path over time, and if so, how?

11. Much of our analysis of oil and minerals assumed that each landowner owns all of the resource on his or her property and can choose when and how much to sell. However, much oil is found in large underground pools that do not respect legal boundaries. A single pool of oil may extend under many different plots of land. How does this affect the optimal time to extract the oil? How does it affect the optimal time to sell the oil? How does it affect the workings of the private market and the justification for government intervention?

Economics 779B: Environmental Damage Assessment

University of South Carolina

G

Instructor:	Professor Glenn W. Harrison
	Room BA 427, phone 777-4943.
Office Hours:	By appointment.
Class:	Monday, 10-12.30, BA 801H.

Objective

One way to protect the environment is for society to place a monetary value on it, and then sue any firm or individual that damages it. But how can society measure the economic damage caused by environmental injury? The traditional tools of benefit assessment used by economists do not readily apply here, mainly due to the non-market nature of the damaged good. This course reviews the controversies that arise in the assessment of damages for such goods, with particular emphasis on the use of the Contingent Valuation Method (CVM). The course has three themes. One is a general discussion of the policy issues involved in undertaking cost-benefit analysis for non-market goods such as the environment, and how one can bring traditional microeconomic theory to bear on them. The second theme is a detailed case-by-case study of major efforts at environmental damage assessment in recent years, particularly in the context of significant pieces of litigation such as followed the *Exxon Valdez* oil spill. The third theme is an evaluation of implications for corporations operating under current U.S. law and accounting regulations with respect to environmental liabilities. The potential impact on corporations of pending changes in those laws and regulations will also be discussed.

Outline

The purpose of having one long session per week is to be able to plan to cover a specific topic or two in each class. There will also be a series of brownbags and seminars dealing with the CVM and environmental damage assessment, and these will be listed below in the final course outline. They should be considered as regular class times. The references in curly brackets indicate readings appropriate for each class. Virtually all of the remaining articles or excerpts from books will be available on 2-hour reserve at the BA library.

Class 1: General introduction and review of the major issues in environmental damage assessment. This class will briefly review the various components of a CVM study. It will also review current and pending legal and accounting responsibilities of corporations operating under U.S. law {Coller and Harrison [1995]}.

Class 2: What are we measuring? Non-use values: their economic meaning and measurement. How should we allow for altruism and moral judgements in benefits assessment? {Cummings and Harrison [1995]}.

Class 3: How have we been measuring it? Critical review of the older CVM literature {Cummings and Harrison [1994]}.

Class 4: The Exxon *Valdez* oil spill {Carson et al. [1994]}.

Class 5: The *Kakadu* Conservation Zone study {Carson, Wilks and Imber [1994], Carson [1992]}.

Class 6: Statistical interpretation and analysis of responses to CV surveys {Harrison and Kriström [1995]}.

Class 7: Must CV surveys cost so much? {Harrison and Lesley [1995]}.

Class 8: Is the referendum approach the answer? A critical review of the "dichotomous choice" approach to damage assessment {Cummings, Harrison and Rutström [1995], Cummings, Elliot, Harrison and Murphy [1994]}.

Class 9: Exam!

Class 10: The *Nestucca* oil spill {Rowe, Shaw and Schulze [1992]}.

Class 11: Experimental methods for private goods evaluation {Neill, Cummings, Ganderton, Harrison and McGuckin [1994], Rutström [1994]}.

Class 12: Calibrating CVM responses for hypothetical bias. Are the responses to hypothetical surveys informative, but biased, measures of true valuations? {Blackburn, Harrison and Rutström [1994]}.

Class 13: WTA *or* WTP? {Nape, Frykblom, Harrison and Lesley [1994]}.

Class 14: Information and the role of substitutes. How much information should subjects be given, and about what?

Class 15: A critique of the NOAA Panel report {NOAA [1993]}.

Class 16: Valuing life and limb? The valuation of risk. {Gerking, Haan and Schulze [1988], Viscusi [1991; ch.5], Moore and Viscusi [1990; chs. 5, 6]}.

Class 17: Discounting lives and monetary damages? {Cropper, Aydede and Portney [1992], Coller and Williams [1994], Kopp [1994]}.

Class 18: Environmental damage assessment, poor countries, and environmental priorities on a global scale {Whittington, Lauria and Mu [1991]}. Environmental equity and environmental racism {Cutter [1995], Kanninen and Kriström [1993]}.

Assessment

One mid-term exam, and the choice of either a final exam or an essay.

References

Blackburn, McKinley; Harrison, Glenn W., and Rutström, E. Elisabet, "Statistical Bias Functions and Informative Hypothetical Surveys", *American Journal of Agricultural Economics*, 76, December 1994, forthcoming.

Carson, Richard T., "Kakadu Conservation Zone", in K.M. Ward and J.W. Duffield (eds.), *Natural Resource Damages: Law and Economics* (New York: Wiley, 1992).

Carson, Richard T.; Wilks, Leanne; and Imber, David, "Valuing the Preservation of Australia's Kakadu Conservation Zone", *Discussion Paper 94-09*, Department of Economics, University of California at San Diego, June 1994; forthcoming, *Oxford Economic Papers*.

101

Carson, Richard T.; Mitchell, Robert C.; Hanemann, W. Michael; Kopp, Raymond J.; Presser, Stanley; and Ruud, Paul A., *A Contingent Valuation Study of Lost Passive Use Values Resulting From the Exxon Valdez Oil Spill* (Anchorage: Attorney General of the State of Alaska, November 1992).

Carson, Richard T.; Mitchell, Robert C.; Hanemann, W. Michael; Kopp, Raymond J.; Presser, Stanley; and Ruud, Paul A., "Contingent Valuation and Lost Passive Use: Damages from the Exxon Valdez", *Discussion Paper 94-18*, Resources for the Future, Washington, DC, March 1994.

Coller, Maribeth, and Harrison, Glenn W., "On the Use of the Contingent Valuation Method to Estimate Environmental Costs", *Advances in Accounting*, 15, 1995, forthcoming.

Coller, Maribeth, and Williams, Melonie, "Eliciting Individual Discount Rates", *Unpublished Manuscript*, Department of Economics, College of Business Administration, University of South Carolina, 1994.

Cropper, Maureen L.; Aydede, Sema K., and Portney, Paul R., "Public Preferences for Life Saving", *Discussion Paper CRM 92-01*, Center for Risk Management, Resources for the Future, May 1992.

Cummings, Ronald G.; Elliot, Steven; Harrison, Glenn W.; and Murphy, James, "Homegrown Values and Hypothetical Surveys: Are Referenda Incentive Compatible?", *Unpublished Manuscript*, Department of Economics, College of Business Administration, University of South Carolina, 1994.

Cummings, Ronald G., and Harrison, Glenn W., "Was the *Ohio* Court Well Informed in Their Assessment of the Accuracy of the Contingent Valuation Method?", *Natural Resources Journal*, 34(1), Winter 1994, 1-36.

Cummings, Ronald G., and Harrison, Glenn W., "The Measurement and Decomposition of Nonuse Values: A Critical Review", *Environmental and Resource Economics*, 4, 1995, forthcoming.

Cummings, Ronald G.; Harrison, Glenn W., and Rutström, E.E., "Homegrown Values and Hypothetical Surveys: Is the Dichotomous Choice Approach Incentive Compatible?", *American Economic Review*, 85, March 1995, forthcoming.

Cutter, Susan L., "Race, Class and Environmental Justice", *Progress in Human Geography*, 1995, forthcoming.

Gerking, Shelby; Haan, Menno; and Schulze, William, "The Marginal Value of Job Safety: A Contingent Valuation Survey", *Journal of Risk and Uncertainty*, 1, 1988, 185-199.

Harrison, Glenn W., and Kriström, Bengt, "On the Interpretation of Responses to Contingent Valuation Surveys", in P.O. Johansson, B. Kriström and K.G. Mäler (eds.), *Current Issues in Environmental Economics* (Manchester: Manchester University Press, 1995, forthcoming).

Harrison, Glenn W., and Lesley, James C., "Must Contingent Valuation Surveys Cost So Much?", *Journal of Environmental Economics and Management*, 28, 1995, forthcoming.

102

Imber, David; Stevenson, Gay; and Wilks, Leanne, *A Contingent Valuation Survey of the Kakadu Conservation Zone* (Canberra: Australian Government Publishing Service for the Resource Assessment Commission, 1991).

Kanninen, Barbara J., and Kriström, Bengt, "Welfare Benefit Estimation and Income Distribution", *Working Paper #21*, Beijer Institute, Royal Academy of Sciences, Stockholm, 1993.

Kopp, Raymond, "Discounting for Damage Assessment", *Discussion Paper 94-31*, Resources for the Future, Washington, DC, May 1994.

Mitchell, Robert C., and Carson, Richard T., *Using Surveys to Value Public Goods: The Contingent Valuation Method* (Baltimore: Johns Hopkins Press, 1989).

Moore, Michael J., and Viscusi, W. Kip, *Compensation Mechanisms for Job Risks* (Princeton: Princeton University Press, 1990).

Nape, Steven; Frykblom, Peter; Harrison, Glenn W.; and Lesley, James C., "Hypothetical Bias and Willingness to Accept", *Unpublished Manuscript*, Department of Economics, College of Business Administration, University of South Carolina, 1994.

National Oceanic and Atmospheric Administration, "Contingent Valuation Panel, Public Meeting, Wednesday, August 12, 1992," *Certified Official Transcript*, 283 pp., Department of Commerce, Washington, DC., 1992.

National Oceanic and Atmospheric Administration, "Report of the NOAA Panel on Contingent Valuation", *Federal Register*, 58, no.10, January 11, 1993, 4602-4614.

National Oceanic and Atmospheric Administration, "Natural Resource Damage Assessments; Proposed Rules", *Federal Register*, 59, no.5, January 7, 1994 (Part II).

Neill, Helen R.; Cummings, Ronald G.; Ganderton, Philip T.; Harrison, Glenn W., and McGuckin, Thomas, "Hypothetical Surveys and Real Economic Commitments", *Land Economics*, 70(2), May 1994, 145-154.

Rowe, Robert D.; Shaw, W. Douglass; and Schulze, William, "*Nestucca* Oil Spill", in K.M. Ward and J.W. Duffield (eds.), *Natural Resource Damages: Law and Economics* (New York: Wiley, 1992).

Rutström, E.E., "Home-Grown Values and Incentive Compatible Auction Design", *Unpublished Manuscript*, Department of Economics, College of Business Administration, University of South Carolina, 1993.

Viscusi, W. Kip, *Reforming Products Liability* (Cambridge, MA: Harvard University Press, 1991).

Whittington, Dale; Lauria, D.T., and Mu, X., "A Study of Water Vending and Willingness to Pay for Water in Onitsha, Nigeria", *World Development*, 19, 1991, 179-198.19, 1991, 179-198. World Development.

103

University of Colorado

ECONOMICS 8535

Seminar in Natural Resource Economics   **G**
Fall, 1994
Professor Chuck Howe

Famous Quotes:

"In economic terms, the belief seems to be that natural resources
are scarce; that the scarcity increases with time; and that
resource scarcity impairs levels of living and economic growth...
But in our view, these propositions are neither self-evident nor
easy to formulate in meaningful terms." (Barnett & Morse, p. 49).

"For if growth and welfare are inescapably subject to an economic
law of diminishing returns, the necessary social policies and the
moral and human implications are surely different than if they are
not." (Barnett & Morse, p. 3).

Note: This is a Ph.D. level seminar. The purpose of 8000-
level seminars is to investigate current and even frontier topics
in the field. Another major purpose here at C.U. is to provide
an opportunity for the Ph.D. candidate to try a research topic
that could serve as a Ph.D. dissertation. All participants are
urged to look upon their research paper in this way--as a likely
start on their dissertation. Grading in the seminar--especially
on the research paper--will be based on those assumptions.

There will be a comprehensive final exam on the topics
below, counting 40% of the grade. The research paper will count
40% of the grade, and class participation 20%. Class
participation, based on adequate preparation, is important and is
expected. Selection of research topic must be discussed with and
approved by Professor Howe as well as the final presentation.

Text: Pack of materials available in graduate lounge and in
            the Reserve Room at Norlin.

Classics in the field:

Barnett, Harold J. and Chandler Morse. Scarcity and Growth: The
     Economics of Natural Resources Availability, Baltimore:
     Johns Hopkins University Press, 1963.

Ciciacy-Wantrup, S. V., Resource Conservation: Economics and
     Policies, Division of Agricultural Sciences, Agricultural
     Experiment Station, University of California-Berkeley, 3rd
     Edition, 4th printing, 1976.

Hays, Samuel P., Conservation and the Gospel of Efficiency: The
     Progressive Conservation Movement; 1890-1920, Harvard
     University Press, 1959.

1

Scott, Anthony, <u>Natural</u> Resources: <u>The</u> <u>Economics</u> <u>of</u>
<u>Conservation</u>, Ottawa: Carleton University Press (orig. 1955,
now 1983).

Useful **References:**

Clark, Colin W., <u>Mathematical</u> <u>Bioeconomics:</u> <u>The</u> <u>Optimal</u>
<u>Management</u> <u>of</u> <u>Renewable</u> <u>Resources</u>, Wiley-Interscience,
1976.

Conrad, Jon M. and Colin Clark, <u>Natural</u> <u>Resources</u> <u>Economics:</u>
<u>Notes</u> <u>&</u> <u>Problems</u>, Cambridge University Press, 1987.

Dasgupta, P. S. and G. M. Heal, <u>Economic</u> <u>Theory</u> <u>and</u> <u>Exhaustible</u>
<u>Resources</u>, Cambridge University Press, 1979.

Kneese, Allen V. and James L. Sweeney, <u>Handbook</u> <u>of</u> <u>Natural</u>
<u>Resource</u> <u>and</u> <u>Energy</u> <u>Economics</u>, Vols. I-III, Amsterdam-New
York: North-Holland Press, 1985.

Krutilla, John V. and Anthony Fisher, <u>The</u> <u>Economics</u> <u>of</u> <u>Natural</u>
<u>Environments</u>, Johns Hopkins University Press, 1975.

Smith, V. Kerry (ed.), <u>Scarcity</u> <u>and</u> <u>Growth</u> <u>Reconsidered</u>,
Resources for the Future by Johns Hopkins University Press,
1979.

Smith and Krutilla (eds.), <u>Explorations</u> <u>in</u> <u>Natural</u> <u>Resource</u>
<u>Economics</u>, Johns Hopkins University Press, 1982.

Data **Sources:**

Landsberg, Hans H., Leonard Fishman, and Joseph L. Fisher,
<u>Resources</u> <u>in</u> <u>America's</u> <u>Future</u>, <u>1960-2000</u>, Johns Hopkins
University Press, 1963 (statistics).

Manthy, Robert S., <u>Natural</u> <u>Resource</u> <u>Commodities</u> <u>-</u> <u>A</u> <u>Century</u> <u>of</u>
<u>Statistics:</u> <u>Prices,</u> <u>Output,</u> <u>Consumption,</u> <u>Foreign</u> <u>Trade,</u> <u>and</u>
<u>Employment</u> <u>in</u> <u>the</u> <u>United</u> <u>States,</u> <u>1970-1973</u>, Johns Hopkins
University Press, 1978 (an update of <u>Trends</u> <u>in</u> <u>Natural</u>
<u>Resource</u> <u>Commodities</u> by Potter and Christy, 1962).

Major **Journals** **in** **the** **Field:**

Journal of Environmental Economics and Management (JEEM),
Academic Press, USA.

Environmental and Resource Economics, Kluwer, USA and The
Netherlands.

2

Natural Resources Journal, The University of New Mexico School of
Law.

Land Economics, University of Wisconsin.

American Journal of Agricultural Economics

Water Resources Research, American Geophysical Union.

International Journal of Water Resources Development,
Butterworth, USA and UK.

Resources and Energy, North Holland.

Natural Resource Modeling, Rocky Mountain Math Consortium,
Arizona State University.

Ecological Economics, Elsevier Science Publishers, The
Netherlands.

Natural Resources Forum (A United Nations Journal), Butterworth,
USA and UK.

Energy Economics, Butterworth, USA and UK.

Resources Policy, Butterworth, USA and UK.

Beginning and Intermediate Level Texts:

Hartwick, John M. and Nancy D. Olewiler, The Economics of Natural
Resource Use, Harper & Row, 1986.

Tietenberg, Tom, Environmental and Resource Economics, 3rd
edition, Scott, Foresman and Co., 1988.

General Bibliography on Natural Resources and Environment:

The reading packet contains an excellent taxonomy of issues
in the NR/E area with corresponding bibliography. This was
assembled by Porter Hoagland (Woods Hole) and Rob Stavins (The
Kennedy School, Harvard). It is recommended that you copy this
for your professional files.

3

Note: An asterisk (*) indicates suggested but non-required
            reading.

Topic 1:   The History of Natural Resource Concern
            a.   Howe, Chap. 1, 2 Overview and NR production.
            b.   Howe Chap. 3, Natural Resource Concern Is Not New.
            c.   Howe, Chap. 7, Factors Mitigating New Scarcity.
            d.   Rosenberg, Nathan, 1973, "Innovative Responses to
                 Materials Shortages, AER, May.

Topic 2:   Indicators of Natural Resource Scarcity and Non-
           Renewable Resources
            a.   Howe, "Environment and Primary Activities,"
                 Science of the Total Environment, 55 (1986)
                 3-24.
            b.   Howe: Introduction to the Hotelling Model, plus
                 Problems 1 and 2.
            c.   Solow, Robert M., 1974, "The Economics of
                 Resources or the Resources of Economics," AEA
                 Proceedings, May.
            d.   Howe note on control theory.
            e.   Slade, Margaret E., 1982, "Trends in Natural
                 Resource Commodity Prices," Journal of
                 Environmental and Resource Economics, 9(2).
            f.   Norgaard, Richard B., 1990, "Economic Indicators
                 of Resource Scarcity: A Critical Essay,"
                 JEEM 19 (19-25).
            g.   Farrow, Scott and Jeffrey A. Krautkraemer, 1991,
                 "Comment: Economic Indicators of Resource
                 Scarcity," JEEM 21 (190-195).

            h.* Slade, Margaret E. and Henry Thille, 1993,
                 "Hotelling Confronts CAPM: A Test of the
                 Theory of Exhaustible Resources."
            i.* Slade, Margaret E., 1988, "Grade Selection Under
                 Uncertainty: Least-Cost Last and Other
                 Anomalies," JEEM, Vol. 15, 189-205.

Topic 3:   Renewable Resources
            a.   Morey, Edward R., 1980, "Fishery Economics: An
                 Introduction and Review," Natural Resources
                 Journal, 20, October.
            b.   Howe, Chap. 11, Forestry.
            c.   Howe, Chap. 14, Water Resources.

Topic 4:   Sustainability and Intergenerational Equity
            a.   Krutilla, John V., 1967, "Conservation
                 Reconsidered," AER, September.
            b.   Toman, Michael A. John Pezzey and Jeffrey
                 Krautkraemer, 1993, "Neoclassical Economic
                 Growth Theory and 'Sustainability'."

4

c.* Pezzey, John, 1992, "Sustainability: An Interdisciplinary Guide," _Environmental Values_.

d. Hartwick, John M., 1994, "Sustainability and Constant Consumption Paths in Open Economics with Exhaustible Resources."

e. Howe, 1993, "Intergenerational Equity, Sustainability, and Economic Efficiency: New Paradigms and Old Prescriptions," (xerox) University of Colorado, June.

f.* Hyde, William F. and Gregory S. Amacher, 1994, "Sustainability in World Forestry and Forest Land Use: Theory, Empirical Evidence and Policy Implications."

g. Kennedy, Peter W., 1994, "Rethinking Sustainability."

h. Lozada, Gabriel A., 1991, "Why the Entropy Law Is Relevant to the Economics of Natural Resources Scarcity," (xerox), December.

Topic 5: Sustainability and the National Accounts

a. Repetto, Robert, 1992, "Earth in the Balance Sheet: Incorporating Natural Resources in National Income Accounts," _Environment_ 34-7. September.

b. Maler, Karl-Gören, 1991, "Natural Accounts and Environmental Resources," _Environmental and Resource Economics_, 1(1), 1-15.

c.* Prince, Raymond and Patrice Gordon, 1994, "Greening the National Accounts," Congressional Budget Office, March (not in packet).

d.* Survey of Current Business, 1994, "Integrated Economics and Environmental Satellite Accounts," April (not in packet).

Topics Not Covered: there is a vast energy literature, much of the recent material being related to CO_2 and greenhouse warming. See the instructor and the Hoagland-Stavins bibliography. The energy crisis of 1973 led to an interesting controversy over the substitutability of capital for energy. The key articles were:

a. Berndt, Ernst R. and David O. Wood, 1975, "Technology, Prices and the Derived Demand for energy," _Rev. of Ec. and Stat_; August 1975.

b. Griffin, James M. and Paul R. Gregory, 1976, "An Intercountry Translog Model of Energy Substitution Responses," _AER_, December.

c. Berndt, Ernst R. and David O. Wood, 1979, "Engineering and Econometric Interpretations of Energy-Capital Complementarity," _AER_, Vol. 69, No. 3.

5

There also is an interesting property rights and contracting literature, like the following:

a.   Libecap, Gary D., 1985, "The Influence of Private Contractual Failure on Regulation: The Case of Oil Field Unitization," <u>JPE</u>, Vol. 93, No. 4.
b.   Calabresi, Guido and A. Douglas Melamed, 1972, "Property Rules, Liability Rules and Inalienability," <u>Harvard Law Review</u>, Vol. 85, No. 6.

Then there is the vast literature on open access resources (often mistakenly called "common property resources.").

Spring, 1995

Part I: Pollution Control and Environmental Valuation

This portion of the course will examine the application of economic principles to problems of pollution control and the valuation of environmental improvements. After a brief review of the theory of public goods, externalities and property rights, the design of environmental policy will be considered. In this section, we will examine the use of Pigouvian taxes, marketable permits, regulatory standards and subsidies as potential pollution control tools, both in terms of their theoretical properties and practical potential as policy instruments. Additionally, empirical studies examining many of these questions will be considered.

On the second topic, we will examine various methods economists have employed to value improvements of the environment. This section will start with a brief review of the theory of welfare measurement and will be followed by a discussion of methods used to value non-market resources. The methods we will examine include recreation demand models, hedonic models, and contingent valuation studies.

Texts:
W. Baumol and W. Oates, *The Theory of Environmental Policy*, Second edition, Cambridge University Press, Cambridge, 1988.
A. M. Freeman, *The Measurement of Environmental and Resource Values: Theory and Methods*, Resources for the Future, 1993.

An excellent survey article that touches on essentially all aspects of this course is :
M. Cropper and W. Oates. "Environmental Economics: A Survey," *Journal of Economic Literature* (1992): 675-740.

I. Introduction. Market Failure in Natural Resource Markets

A. Externalities: a basic model and implications
*Baumol and Oates, *The Theory of Environmental Policy*, Chapters 2, 3 and 4.
Samuelson, Paul. "The Pure Theory of Public Expenditure," *Review of Economics and Statistics* 36(1954): 387-389.
Cornes, R. and T. Sandler. *The Theory of Externality, Public Goods, and Club Goods*, Cambridge University Press, 1986, Chapters 3 and 4.

B. The Coasian solution and implications
Coase, R. "The Problem of Social Cost," *Journal of Law and Economics*, (1960): 1-44
*Varian, H. "A Solution to the Problem of Externalities when Agents are Well-Informed," *American Economic Review*, 84(1994): 1278-1293.
*Turvey, R. "On Divergence Between Social Cost and Private Cost," *Economic Journal* (1963): 309-313.

C. Nonconvexities
*Baumol and Oates, *The Theory of Environmental Policy* Chapter 8.
*Burrows, P. "Nonconvexity Induced by External Costs on Production: Theoretical Curio or

110

Policy Dilemma?" *Journal of Environmental Economics and Management*, 13(1986): 101-128.Starret, D. "Fundamental Nonconvexities in the Theory of Externalities," *Journal of Economic Theory*, 4(1972): 180-199.

II. The Design of Environmental Policy

A. Taxes vs. Standards
*Baumol and Oates, *The Theory of Environmental Policy*, Chapter 5.
*Adar, Z. and J. Griffin, "Uncertainty and the Choice of Pollution Control Instruments," *Journal of Environmental Economics and Management*, 3(1976): 178-188.
Weitzman, M. "Prices vs. Quantities," *Review of Economic Studies*, (1974): 477-491.
*Helfand, G. "Standards vs. Standards: The Effects of Different Pollution Restrictions," *American Economic Review*, 81(1991): 622-634.

B. Taxes, Subsidies, and Longrun Optimality
*Baumol and Oates, *The Theory of Environmental Policy*, Chapters 11 and 14.
Spulber, D. "Effluent Regulations and Long-Run Optimality," *Journal of Environmental Economics and Management*, 12(1985): 103-116.
Palmquist, R. "Pollution Standards and Multiple Local Optima", *Land Economics*, 66(1990): 394-401
*Lans Bovenberg, A. and R.A. De Mooij. "Environmental Levies and Distortionary Taxation," *American Economic Review*, 84(1994): 1085-1089.
Karp, L. and J. Livernois. "Using Automatic Tax Changes to Control Pollution Emissions," *Journal of Environmental Economics and Management*, 27(1994): 38-48.

C. Marketable Pollution Permits
*Baumol and Oates, *The Theory of Environmental Policy*, Chapter 12.
Montgomery, W.D. "Markets in Licenses and Efficient Pollution Control Programs," *Journal of Economic Theory*, 5(1972): 387-396.
*McGartland, A. and W. Oates. "Marketable Permits for the Prevention of Environmental Deterioration," *Journal of Environmental Economics and Management* 15(1985):207-228.
*Atkinson, A. and T. Tietenberg. "Market Failure in Incentive-Based Regulation: The Case of Emissions Trading," *Journal of Environmental Economics and Management* 21(1991): 17-31.
*Rubin, J. and C. Kling. "An Emission Saved is an Emission Earned: An Empirical Study of Emission Banking for Light-Duty Vehicle Manufacturers," *Journal of Environmental Economics and Management*, 25(1993): 257-275.
*Oates, W., P. Portney, and A. McGartland, "The Net Benefits of Incentive-Based Regulation: A Case Study of Environmental Standard Setting," *American Economic Review*, (1989): 1233-42.

D. The Effect of Market and Firm Structure on Environmental Policy Design
Baumol and Oates, *The Theory of Environmental Policy*, Chapter 6.
*Barnett, A. "The Pigouvian Tax Rule Under Monopoly," *American Economic Review*, 70(1980): 1037-1041.
*Hahn, R. "Market Power and Transferable Property Rights," *Quarterly Journal of Economics*, (1984): 753-765.
*Coggins, J. and V. Smith. "Some Welfare Effects of Emission Allowance Trading in a Twice-Regulated Industry," *Journal of Environmental Economics and Management*, 25(1993): 275-297.

111

E. Controlling Nonpoint Source Pollution

*Griffin, R. and D. Bromley, "Agricultural Runoff as Nonpoint Externality: A Theoretical Development," *American Journal of Agricultural Economics*, 64(1982): 547-552.

*Segerson, K. "Uncertainty and Incentives for Nonpoint Pollution Control," *Journal of Environmental Economics and Management*, 15(1988): 87-98.

*Malik, A., D. Letson, and S. Crutchfield. "Point/Nonpoint Source Trading of Pollution Abatement: Choosing the Right Trading Ratio," *American Journal of Agricultural Economics*, 75(1993): 959-967.

F. Enforcement Issues in Pollution Control

*Malik, A. "Markets for Pollution Control When Firms are Noncompliant," *Journal of Environmental Economics and Management*, 18(1990): 97-106.

*Keeler, A. "Noncompliant Firms in Transferable Discharge Permit Markets: Some Extensions," *Journal of Environmental Economics and Management*, 21(1991): 180-189.

Malik, A. "Enforcement Costs and the Choice of Policy Instruments for Controlling Pollution," *Economic Inquiry*, 30(1992): 387-396.

G. Current Issues and Case Studies

*Hahn, R. "Economic Prescriptions for Economic Problems: How the Patient Followed the Doctor's Orders," *Journal of Economic Perspectives*, 3(1989): 95-114.

Portney, P. "Policy Watch: Economics and the Clean Air Act," *Journal of Economic Perspectives*, (1989): 95-114.

Schelling, T. "Some Economics of Global Warming," *American Economic Review* (1992):1-14.*Mendelsohn, R., W. Nordhaus, and D. Shaw, "The Impact of Global Warming on Agriculture:A Ricardian Analysis," *American Economic Review*, 84(1994):753-771.

Cronshaw, M. and J. Kruse. "An Experimental Analysis of Emission Permits with Banking and the Clean Air Act Amendments of 1990," working paper, 1992.

III. The Valuation of Environmental Amenities: Theory

A. The Measurement of Welfare

*Just, R, Hueth, D. and A. Schmitz. *Applied Welfare Economics and Public Policy*, (1982), Chapters 5 and 6.

Willig, R. "Consumer's Surplus Without Apology," *American Economic Review*, 66(1976): 589-597.

Randall, A. and J. Stoll. "Consumer's Surplus in Commodity Space," *American Economic Review*, 70(1980): 449-455.

Hausman, J. "Exact Consumer's Surplus and Deadweight Loss," *American Economic Review*, (1981): 662-676.

*Freeman, M. *The Measurement of Environmental and Resource Values*, Chapters 1-4.

Bockstael, N. and K. McConnell, "Public Goods as Characteristics of Non-Market Commodities," *Economic Journal*, (1993):

*Hanemann, M. "Willingness to Pay vs Willingness to Sell: How Much Can They Differ?" *American Economic Review*, 81(1991): 635-647.

*Shogren, J., S. Shin, D. Hayes, and J. Kliebenstein. "Resolving Differences in Willingness to Pay and Willingness to Accept," *American Economic Review*, 84(1994): 255-270.

B. Measuring Welfare Change Under Uncertainty

*Freeman, M. *The Measurement of Environmental and Resource Values*, Chapter 8.

Smith, V. "Valuing Environmental Resource under Uncertainty: A Skeptical View of Recent Resolutions," *Journal of Environmental Economics and Management*, (1990): 283-290.

*Larson, D. and P. Flacco. "Measuring Option Prices from Market Behavior," *Journal of Environmental Economics and Management*, 22(1992): 178-198.

IV. The Valuation of Environmental Amenities: Applications

A. Recreation Demand and Discrete Choice Models
*Freeman, M. *The Measurement of Environmental and Resource Values*, Chapter 13.
*Bockstael, N., K. McConnell, and I. Strand. "Recreation," Chapter 8 of Braden and Kolstad, *Measuring the Demand for Environmental Quality*, (1991).
*Kling, C. "The Reliability of Estimates of Environmental Benefits from Recreation Demand Models," *American Journal of Agricultural Economics* 70(1988): 892-901.
Kling, C. "Estimating the Precision of Welfare Measures," *Journal of Environmental Economics and Management*, 21(1991): 244-259.
Burt, O. and D. Brewer. "Estimates of Net Social Benefits for Outdoor Recreation," *Econometrica*, 39(1971): 813-827.

B. Hedonic Models
*Freeman, M. *The Measurement of Environmental and Resource Values*, Chapter 11 and 12.
Rosen, S. "Hedonic Prices and Implicit Markets: Product Differentiation in Pure Competition," *Journal of Political Economy*, 82(1974): 34-55.
*Palmquist, R. "Hedonic Methods," Chapter 4 of Braden and Kolstad, *Measuring the Demand for Environmental Quality*, (1991).
Roback, J. "Wages, Rents, and the Quality of Life," *Journal of Political Economy*, 90(1982): 1257-1278.
Cropper M., L. Deck, J. Kishor, and K. McConnell. "Valuing Product Attributes Using single Market Data: A Comparison of Hedonic and Discrete Choice Approaches," *Review of Economics and Statistics* (1993): 225-232.
Blomquist, G.C, M.C. Berger, and J.P. Hoehn. "New Estimates of Quality of Life in Urban Areas," *American Economic Review* 778(1988): 89-107.

C. Contingent Valuation Methods
*Freeman, M. *The Measurement of Environmental and Resource Values*, Chapter 5 and 6.
*Carson, R. "Constructed Markets," Chapter 5 of Braden and Kolstad, *Measuring the Demand for Environmental Quality*, (1991).
*NOAA Panel on Contingent Valuation (Arrow, Solow, Leamer, Portney, and Radner) "Natural Resource Damage Assessments under the Oil Pollution Act of 1990," *Federal Register*, 58(1993): January 15.
Hanemann, M. "Welfare Evaluations in Contingent Valuation Experiments with Discrete Responses," *American Journal of Agricultural Economics*, (1984): 332-341.
Cameron, T. "A New Paradigm for Valuing Non-market Goods Using Referendum Data: Maximum Likelihood Estimation by Censored Logistic Regression," *Journal of Environmental Economics and Management*, 15(1988): 355-379.
Smith, V. "Arbitrary Values, Good Causes, and Premature Verdicts," *Journal of Environmental Economics and Management*, 22(1992): 71-89.

D. Reliability and Validity of CVM
*Duffield, J. and J. Patterson. "Field Testing Existence Values: An Instream Flow Trust Fund for Montana Rivers," 1992.
*Neill, H., R. Cummings, P. Garderton, G. Harrison, and T. McGuckin. "Hypothetical Surveys and Real Economic Commitments," *Land Economics*, 70(1994): 145-154.

Sagoff, M. "Should Preferences Count," *Land Economics*, 70(1994): 127-144.

Boyle, K., W. Desvousges, F. Johnson, R. Dunford, and S. Hudson. "An Investigation of Part-Whole Biases in Contingent-Valuation Studies," *Journal of Environmental Economics and Managament*, 27(1994): 64-83.

*Portney, P.R. "The Contingent Valuation Debate: Why Economists Should Care," *Journal of Economic Perspectives* 8(1994): 3-17.

*Hanemann, M. "Valuing the Environment through Contingent Valuation," *Journal of Economic Perspectives* 8(1994): 19-43.

*Diamond, P.A. and J.A. Hausman. "Contingent Valuation: Is Some Number Better than No Number?" *Journal of Economic Perspectives* 8(1994): 45-64.

*McFadden, D. "Contingent Valuation and Social Choice," *American Journal of Agricultural Economics* 76(1994): 689-708. E. Comparing Methods for Measuring Nonmarket Values

Bishop, R. and T. Heberlein. "Measuring Values of Extra-Market Goods: Are Indirect Measures Biased?" *American Journal of Agricultural Economics* 61(1979): 926-930.

Smith, V., W. Desvousges, and A. Fisher. "A Comparison of Direct and Indirect Methods for Estimating Environmental Benefits," *American Journal of Agricultural Economics*, 68(1986): 280-290.

*Brookshire, D. and D. Coursey. "Measuring the Value of a Public Good: An Empirical Comparison of Elicitation Procedures," *American Economic Review*, 77(1987): 554-566.

F. Combining Methods

*Cameron, T. "Combining Contingent Valuation and Travel Cost Data for the Valuation of Nonmarket Goods," *Land Economics*, 68(1992): 302-317.*Adamowicz, W., J. Louviere, and M. Williams. "Combining Revealed and Stated Preference Methods for Valuing Environmental Amenities," *Journal of Environmental Economics and Management*, 26(1994): 271-292.

*Cameron, T. "Nonuser Resource Values," *American Journal of Agricultural Economics*, 75(1992): 1133-1138.

114

UNIVERSITY OF ILLINOIS   G

Economics/ Ag Economics/Environmental Studies 464

ENVIRONMENTAL ECONOMICS: THEORY AND APPLICATIONS

Prof. Charles D. Kolstad
Office: 485 Commerce West   Fall 1992
Office Hours: Tues, 1-3pm or by appt   Mon, Wed 3-4:15
Phone: 333-9897   115 David Kinley Hall

[Prof. Kolstad is now at the University of California in Santa Barbara]

Course Requirements:

There are five basic requirements for the course. Each is approximately equal in weight in the final grade. The basic requirements of the course are:

1.   Term paper
            A major aspect of this course is researching and writing a paper on a topic of your choice in environmental economics. While you have some latitude in choosing your paper topic, you must commit to a topic relatively early. You may also write the paper with others in the class, as a joint effort; in this case correspondingly higher standards will be applied in grading the paper.
            The paper should be an original and interesting contribution although it need not be earthshaking enough to publish in a journal (however, that should be the goal if at all possible). The paper can be theoretical, extending a theoretical finding in the literature; empirical, applying existing methods to a new problem (this would most likely be an study measuring the demand for an environmental good); institutional, such as a critical economic review of environmental regulations/reform in a country of your choice, where such a review is not commonly available. There are other possibilities. A list of possible topics will be distributed early in the course.
            To facilitate timely preparation of a good paper, the following deadlines apply:

1.	one-page proposal (with name(s) of contributors)	Oct 26
2.	1-2 page detailed outline	Nov 9
3.	Draft of paper	Nov 30
4.	Final version of paper	Dec 9

2.   Midterm exam--October 21

3.   Final exam--1:30-4:30, Tuesday, Dec. 15

4.   Homework. Occasional assignments which must be handed in on time.

5.   Class participation. You should attend the class, read the assigned articles before the class meeting and contribute to the discussion of these articles. You should also actively participate in class rather than simply passively absorbing information.

115

Prerequisites: Economics 300 or 400 (intermediate microeconomics); Economics 402 is strongly recommended.

Texts:

1.   The following are required:

William J. Baumol and Wallace E. Oates, The Theory of Environmental Policy, 2nd edition (Cambridge University Press, 1988) [Referred to as B&O].

Paul R. Portney (ed), Public Policies for Environmental Protection (Resources for the Future, Washington, DC, 1990) [Referred to as Portney].

2.   The following are recommended for the course and are on reserve in the Commerce Library:

J. Braden and C. Kolstad (eds), Measuring the Demand for Environmental Quality (North-Holland, 1991) [Referred to as B&K].

World Resources Institute, World Resources 1992-3 (Oxford University Press, 1992).

NB: The texts may be listed at the bookstore under EnvSt 464.

Outline and Reading List:

You are not expected to read all of the readings on this list. The readings with a * should be read. Due to recent changes in interpretation of the copyright laws, a set of readings will only be available on reserve at the Commerce Library. Books are also on reserve in the Commerce Library. Journals are abbreviated:

AER--American Economic Review
CJE--Canadian J of Economics
EJ--Economic Journal
ERE--Envir & Resource Economics
JEEM--J of Environ Econ & Mgmt
JEI--J of Economic Issues
JEL--J of Economic Literature
JEP--J of Econ Perspectives
JET--J of Economic Theory
JLE--J of Law and Economics
JPE--J of Political Economy
JPuE--J of Public Economics

JUE--J of Urban Economics
LE--Land Economics
NRJ--Natural Resources Journal
QJE--Quarterly J of Economics
REStat--Review of Econ & Stat
REStud--Review of Econ Studies
RJE--Rand (formerly Bell) J of Economics
SEJ--Southern Economic Journal
SJE--Scandinavian (formerly
      Swedish) J of Economics
YJR--Yale Journal on Regulation

I.   The Environment and Economics [1 week]

   A.   Scope of the Problem

*Portney, chapters 1 & 2.
*World Development Report 1992, The World Bank, Washington, DC, overview (pp 1-24).
Council on Environmental Quality, Where We Stand, 21st Annual Report (US Govt Printing Office, Washington, DC, 1991), chapter 1.
OECD, The State of the Environment (OECD, Paris, 1991).
World Resources Institute, World Resources (Oxford University Press, 1990), chapters 2 & 3.
"A Survey of the Global Environment," Economist (May 30, 1992).

   B.   Environmental Regulation in Practice

      1.   USA

*Portney, ch. 3-6.
*Paul R. Portney, "Economics and the Clean Air Act," JEP, 4:173-81 (1990).
*Robert W. Hahn, "Economic Prescriptions for Environmental Problems: How the Patient Followed the Doctor's Orders," JEP, 3: 95-114 (1989).
Robert W. Hahn and Gordon L. Hester, "Where Did All the Markets Go? An Analysis of EPA's Emissions Trading Program," Yale Journal on Regulation, 6:109-53 (1989).
Helen Ingram, "The Political Rationality of Innovation: The Clean Air Act Amendments of 1970," in A Friedlaender (ed), Approaches to Controlling Air Pollution (MIT Press, Cambridge, Mass, 1978).

      2.   International

*Raymond J. Kopp, Paul R. Portney and Diane E. DeWitt, "International Comparisons of Environmental Regulation," Resources for the Future Discussion Paper QE90-22-REV (Washington, DC).
Frederic N. Bolotin, International Public Policy Sourcebook, Vol 2 (Greenwood Press, New York, 1989).

   C.   The Environment in the Economics Paradigm

*Kneese, Allen V. and William D. Schulze, "Ethics and Environmental Economics," chapter 5 in A.V. Kneese and J. L. Sweeney (eds), Handbook of Natural Resource and Energy Economics, vol I (North-Holland, Amsterdam, 1985).
*d'Arge, Ralph C., William D. Schulze and David S. Brookshire, "Carbon Dioxide and Intergenerational Choice," AER, 72(2):251-6 (May 1982).
Cropper, Maureen L and Wallace E. Oates, "Environmental Economics: A Survey," JEL, 30:675-740 (1992).
Robert V. Bartlett, "Ecological Rationality: Reason and Environmental Policy," Environmental Ethics, 8:221-39 (1986).
Terry L. Anderson and Donald R. Leal, "Free Market Environmentalism," particularly chapter 2 (Pacific Research Institute, San Francisco, 1991).
Steven Kelman, "Cost-Benefit Analysis: An Ethical Critique," Regulation, 5:33-40 (1981) [reprinted in Glickman and Gough (eds), Readings in Risk, Resources for the Future, Washington, DC, 1990]

II.   Theory of Externalities and Public Bads [3 weeks]

   A.   Nature of Public Bads and Externalities

*B&O, Chapters 2 and 3.
*Walter P. Heller and David A. Starrett, "On the Nature of Externalities," in Steven A.Y. Lin (ed.), Theory and Measurement of Economic Externalities (Academic Press, New York, 1976).
*A. Myrick Freeman III, "Depletable Externalities and Pigouvian Taxation," JEEM, 11, 173-179 (1984).

Meade, James E., The Theory of Externalities (AW Sijthoff, Leiden, 1973), chapter 2.
Alan Randall, "The Problem of Market Failure," NRJ, 23, 131-148 (1983).
James M. Buchanan and William Craig Stubblebine, "Externality," Economica, 29, 371-384 (1962).
David Starrett, Foundations of Public Economics (Cambridge, 1988), Chapter 4: "Theory of Collective Goods."
E.J. Mishan, "The Postwar Literature on Externalities: An Interpretive Essay," JEL, 9(1)1-28 (1971).
Henry M. Peskin, "One More Externality Article," JEEM, 15:380-1 (1988).
Charles R. Plott, "Externalities and Corrective Policies in Experimental Markets," EJ, 93, 106-127 (1983).
A.C. Pigou, The Economics of Welfare, Fourth Ed. (MacMillan, London, 1962), chapter 9.

B. Corrective Policies and Market Structure

*B&O, Chapter 6, 14.
*A. Mitchell Polinsky, "Notes on the Symmetry of Taxes and Subsidies in Pollution Control," CJE, 12(1)75-83 (1979).
Barnett, A.H., "The Pigouvian Tax Rule under Monopoly," AER, 70:1037-41 (1980).
Daniel F. Spulber, "Effluent Regulation and Long-Run Optimality", JEEM, 12(2)103-116 (1985).
Dennis W. Carlton and Glenn C. Loury, "The Limitations of Pigouvian Taxes as a Long-Run Remedy for Externalities," QJE, 95, 559-566 (1980).
R.E. Martin, "Externality Regulation and the Monopoly Firm," JPuE, 29: 347-62 (1986).
Donald Whittman, "Pigouvian Taxes Which Work in The Small Numbers Case," JEEM, 12(2)144-154 (1985).
James M. Buchanan, "External Diseconomies, Corrective Taxes, and Market Structure," AER, 59(1)174-177 (1969).

C. Problems with Nonconvexities

*B&O, Chapters 4,8.
*David Starrett and Richard Zeckhauser, "Treating External Diseconomies--Markets or Taxes?," in John W. Pratt (ed.), Statistical and Mathematical Aspects of Pollution Problems (Marcel Dekker, New York, 1974).
*Cooter, Robert D., "How the Law Circumvents Starrett's Nonconvexity," JET, 22:499-504 (1980).
Paul Burrows, "Nonconvexity Induced by External Costs on Production: Theoretical Curio or Policy Dilemma," JEEM, 13: 101-28 (1986).
David A. Starrett, "Fundamental Nonconvexities in the Theory of Externalities," JET, 4, 180-199 (1972).

D. Property Rights and Transactions Costs

*R.H. Coase, "The Problem of Social Cost," JLE, 3, 1-44 (1960)
*Carl J. Dahlman, "The Problem of Externality," JLE, 22(1)141-162 (1979).
*Vadouj A. Aivazian and Jeffrey L. Callen, "The Coase Theorem and the Empty Core," JLE, 24(1)175-181 (1981).
Elizabeth Hoffman and Mattew L. Spitzer, "The Coase Theorem: Some Experimental Tests," JLE, 25(1)73-98 (1982).
Donald H. Regan, "The Problem of Social Cost Revisited," JLE, 15, 427-437 (1972).
William Schulze and Ralph C. d'Arge, "The Coase Proposition, Information Constraints and Long-Run Equilibrium," AER, 64(4)763-772 (1974).
Guido Calabresi, "Transaction Costs, Resource Allocation and Liability Rules--A Comment," JLE, 11,67-73 (1968).

III. Regulating the Environment [5 weeks]

A. Basic Issues in Environmental Regulation

*Sappington, DEM and JE Stiglitz, "Information and Regulation," in E. Baily (ed), Public Regulation (MIT Press, Cambridge, Mass, 1987).

*W. David Montgomery, "Markets in Licenses and Efficient Pollution Control Programs," JET, 5, 395-418 (1972).

*Wallace Oates and D. Strassmann, "The Use of Effluent Fees to Regulate Public-Sector Sources of Pollution: An Application of the Niskanen Model," JEEM, 5:283-91 (1978).

W.E. Oates and D.L. Strassman, "Effluent Fees and Market Structure," JPuE, 24: 29-46 (1984).

Thomas Roemer and H Rosenthal, "Modern Political Economy and the Study of Regulation," in E. Bailey (ed), Public Regulation (MIT Press, Cambridge, Mass, 1987).

Thomas H. Tietenberg, "Specific Taxes and the Control of Pollution: A General Equilibrium Analysis," QJE, 87(4)503-522 (1973).

B. Command-and-Control vs. Economic Incentives

1. Theoretical issues

*B&O, chapters 11,12

*C.D. Kolstad, "Uniformity vs. Differentiation in Regulating Externalities," JEEM 14: 386-99 (1987).

*Thomas H. Tietenberg, "Transferable Discharge Permits and the Control of Stationary Source Air Pollution: A Survey and Synthesis," LE, 56(4)391-416 (1980).

*Robert W. Hahn, "Market Power and Transferable Property Rights," QJE, 99: 753-65 (1984).

Thomas H. Tietenberg, "Uncommon Sense: The Program to Reform Pollution Control Policy," in LW Weiss and MW Klass (eds), Regulatory Reform (Little, Brown, Boston, 1986).

Susan Rose-Ackerman, "Effluent Charges: A Critique," CJE, 6(4)512-528 (1973).

David Besanko, "Performance Versus Design Standards in the Regulation of Pollution," JPuE, 34: 19-44 (1987).

Brian Beavis and Martin Walker, "Random Wastes, Imperfect Monitoring and Environmental Quality Standards," JPuE, 21, 377-387 (1983).

James M. Buchanan and Gordon Tullock, "Polluters Profits and Political Response: Direct Controls Versus Taxes," AER, 65(1)139-147 (1975).

Thomas H. Tietenberg, Emissions Trading, Chapters 1-2.

K. Segerson, "Uncertainty and Incentives for Nonpoint Pollution Control," JEEM, 15: 87-98 (1988).

Robert A. Collinge and Wallace E. Oates, "Efficiency in Pollution Control in the Short and Long Runs: A system of Rental Emission Permits," CJE, 15(2)346-354 (1982).

2. Empirical Analyses of Efficiency

*Scott E. Atkinson and T.H. Tietenberg, "The Empirical Properties of Two Classes of Designs for Transferrable Discharge Permit Markets," JEEM, 9, 101-121 (1982).

Albert M. McGartland and Wallace E. Oates, "Marketable Permits for the Prevention of Environmental Deterioration", JEEM, 12(3)207-228 (1985).

Eugene P. Seskin, Robert J. Anderson, Jr, and Robert O. Reid, "An Empirical Analysis of Economic Strategies for Controlling Air Pollution," JEEM, 10, 112-124 (1983).

Charles D. Kolstad, "Empirical Properties of Economic Incentives vs. Command-and-Control Regulations for Air Pollution Control," LE, 62: 250-268 (1986).

C. Information and Uncertainty

1. Sticky Instruments

*Martin L. Weitzman, "Prices vs. Quantities," REStud, 41(4)477-491 (1974).

*Marc J. Roberts and Michael Spence, "Effluent Charges and Licenses Under Uncertainty," JPuE, 5, 193-208 (1976).

Martin L. Wietzman, "Optimal Rewards for Economic Regulation," AER, 68:683-91 (1978).

Jean Jacques Laffont, "More on Prices vs. Quantities," REStud, 44(1)177-186 (1977).

James M. Malcomson, "Prices vs. Quantities: A Critical Note on the Use of Approximations," REStud,

45(1)203-207 (1978).

Evan F. Koenig, "Indirect Methods for Regulating Externalities Under Uncertainty," QJE, 100: 479-93 (1985).

2.   Asymmetric Information

*Spulber, Daniel F., "Optimal Environmental Regulation under Asymmetric Information," JPuE (1988)

*David P. Baron, "Design of Regulatory Mechanisms and Institutions," in Handbook of Industrial Organization, R. Schmalensee and R. Willig (eds) (North-Holland, Amsterdam, 1989).

*Evan Kwerel, "To Tell the Truth: Imperfect Information and Optimal Pollution Control," REStud, 44,595-601 (1977).

Karl-Goran Maler, "The Acid Rain Game," in H. Folmer and E. van Ierland (eds), Valuation Methods and Policy Making in Environmental Economics (Elsevier, Amsterdam, 1989).

David P. Baron, "Noncooperative Regulation of a Nonlocalized Externality," RJE, 16(4)553-568 (1985).

Dennis Yao, "Strategic Responses to Automobile Emissions Control: A Game-Theoretic Analysis," JEEM, 15: 419-38 (1988).

David P. Baron, "Regulation of Prices and Pollution Under Incomplete Information," JPuE, 28: 211-31 (1985).

J.A. Ordover and R.D. Willig, "The Role of Information in Designing Social Policy Towards Externalities," JPuE, 12, 271-299 (1979).

Partha Dasgupta, Peter Hammond, and Eric Maskin, "On Imperfect Information and Optimal Pollution Control," REStud, 47, 857-860 (1980).

Gerry L. Suchanek, "A Mechanism for Computing an Efficient System of Wastes Emission Quotas," JPuE, 7, 261-269 (1977).

Robert A. Collinge and Martin J. Bailey, "Optimal Quasi-Market Choice in the Presence of Pollution Externalities," JEEM, 10, 221-232 (1983).

D.   Enforcement

*Portney, ch. 7.

*Malik, Arun S., "Markets for Pollution Control when firms are Noncompliant," JEEM, 18:97-106 (1990).

*Russell, CS, W. Harrington and W.J. Vaughn, Enforcing Pollution Control Laws, chapter 4: "Economic Models of Monitoring and Enforcement" (Resources for the Future, Washington, DC, 1986).

Russell, Clifford S., "Monitoring and Enforcement of Pollution Control Laws in Europe and the United States," unpublished and undated manuscript.

Harford, John D, "Firm Behavior Under Imperfectly Enforceable Pollution Standards and Taxes," JEEM, 5:26-43 (1978).

Viscusi, WK and R. Zeckhauser, "Optimal Standards with Incomplete Enforcement," Public Policy, 27:437-56 (1979).

Harrington, Winston, "Enforcement Leverage when Penalties are Restricted," JPuE, 37:29-53 (1988).

Polinsky, A. Mitchell and Steven Shavell, "The Optimal Tradeoff between the Probability and Magnitude of Fines," AER, 69:880-91 (1979).

Downing, PB and WD Watson, "The Economics of Enforcing Air Pollution Controls," JEEM, 1:219-36 (1974).

E.   Risk, Torts and Insurance

*Martin Katzman, "Pollution Liability Insurance and Catastrophic Environmental Risk," Journal of Risk and Uncertainty, 55:75-100 (1988).

*C.D. Kolstad, T. Ulen and G. Johnson, "Ex Ante Regulation vs. Ex Post Liability for Harm: Substitutes or Complements?," AER (Sept. 1990).

*Daniel A. Graham, "Cost-Benefit Analysis Under Uncertainty," AER, 71: 715-725 (1981).

*V.K. Smith and W.H. Desvousges, "The Valuation of Environmental Risks and Hazardous Waste Policy," LE, 64: 211-219 (1988).

T.H. Tietenberg, "Indivisible Toxic Torts: The Economics of Joint and Several Liability," LE, 65: 305-

319 (1989).

E. Lichtenberg and D. Zilberman, "Efficient Regulation of Environmental Health Risks," QJE, 103: 167-78 (1988).

Kathleen Segerson, "Risk and Incentives in the Financing of Hazardous Waste Cleanup," JEEM, 16: 1-8 (1989).

W.K. Viscusi, W.A. Magat, and J. Huber, "An Investigation of the Rationality of Consumer Valuations of Multiple Health Risks," RJE, 18: 465-79 (1987).

R.L. Raucher, "The Benefits and Costs of Policies Related to Groundwater Contamination," LE, 62: 33-45 (1986).

V.K. Smith and W.H. Desvousges, "An Empirical Analysis of the Economic Value of Risk Changes," JPE, 95: 89-114 (1987).

Phillip J. Cook and Daniel A. Graham, "The Demand for Insurance and Protection: The Case of Irreplaceable Commodities," QJE, 91: 143-56 (1977).

Mark A. Cohen, "Optimal Enforcement Strategy to Prevent Oil Spills: An Application of a Principal-Agent Model with Moral Hazard," JLE, 30: 23-51 (1987).

Steven Shavell, "A Model of the Optimal Use of Liability and Safety Regulation," RJE, 15:271:80 (1984).

IV. Trade and Development [1 week]

A. Trade

*B&O, ch 16, 17.

*Oates, Wallace E., "Global Envrionemntal Management: Towards an Open Economy Environmental Economics," University of Maryland Working Paper No. 91-17, College Park, MD.

*Tobey, James A., "The Effects of Domestic Environmental Policies on Patterns of World Trade: An Empirical Test," Kyklos, 43:191-209 (1990).

WE Oates and RM Schwab, "Economic Competition among Jurisdictions: Efficiency Enhancing or Distortion Inducing?," JPuE, 35:333-54 (1988)

B. Development

*Pezzey, John, "Economic Analysis of Sustainable Growth and Sustainable Development," Environmental Department Working Paper No. 15, The World Bank, Washinton, DC (March 1989). [particularly Part I]

Partha Dasgupta and Karl-Goran Maler, "The Environment and Emerging Development Issues," Proc., World Bank Annual Conference on Development Economics, 1990, pp101-131.

V. The Demand for Environmental Goods and Services [3 weeks]

A. Basic Theory

*B&K, chapter 2.

*WM Hanneman, "Willingness to Pay and Willingness to Accept: How much can they differ?," AER, 81:635-47 (1991).

B. Revealed Preference

1. Hedonic Methods

*Sherwin Rosen, "Hedonic Prices and Implicit Markets: Product Differentiation in Perfect Competition," JPE, 82, 34-55 (1974).

*David Harrison Jr. and Daniel L. Rubinfeld, "Hedonic Housing Prices and the Demand for Clean Air," JEEM, 5(1)81-102 (1978).

*A. Mitchell Polinsky and Steven Shavell, "Amenities and Property Values in a Model of an Urban

Area," JPuE, 5:119-29 (1976).

*Jennifer Roback, "Wages, Rents and the Quality of Life," JPE, 90:1257-78 (1982).

T.J. Bartik, "The Estimation of Demand Parameters in Hedonic Price Models," JPE, 95: 81-8 (1987).

B&K, chapter 4.

S. Scotchmer, "The Short-run and Long-run Benefits of Environmental Improvement, JPuE, 30: 61-81 (1986).

J.R. Neill, "Another Theorem on Using Market Demands to Determine Willingness to Pay for Non-traded Goods," JEEM, 15: 225-32 (1988).

A. Myrick Freeman III, "Hedonic Prices, Property Values and Measuring Environmental Benefits: A Survey of the Issues," SJE, 81, 154-173 (1979).

Mark Bayless, "Measuring the Benefits of Air Quality Improvements: A Hedonic Salary Approach," JEEM, 9, 81-99 (1982).

2.   Household Production

*B&K, chapter 3.

*Paul N. Courant and Richard Porter, "Averting Expenditure and the Cost of Pollution," JEEM, 8, 321-329 (1981).

*S. Gerking and L.R. Stanley, "An Economic Analysis of Air Pollution and Health: The Case of St. Louis," REStat, 68: 115-21 (1986).

T.J. Bartik, "Evaluating the Benefits of Non-marginal Reductions in Pollution Using Information on Defensive Expenditures," JEEM, 15: 111-22 (1988).

W. Harrington and P.R. Portney, "Valuing the Benefits of Health and Safety Regulation," JUE, 22: 101-12 (1987).

Mark Dickie and Shelby Gerking, "Willingness to Pay for Ozone Control: Inferences from the Demand for Medical Care," JEEM, 21:1-16 (1991).

C.   Constructed Markets/Direct Revelation

*B&K, chapter 5.

*Daniel Kahneman and Jack L. Knetsch, "Valuing Public Goods: The Purchase of Moral Satisfaction," JEEM, 22:57-70 (1992).

*Richard C. Bishop, Thomas A. Heberlein and Mary Jo Kealy, "Contingent Valuation of Environmental Assets: Comparisons with a Simulated Market," NRJ, 23,619-633 (1983).

*TC Bergstrom, DL Rubinfeld and P Shapiro, "Micro-based Estimates of Demand Functions for Local School Expenditures," ECTA, 50:1183-1206 (1982).

Peter A. Diamond, J. A. Hausman, G.K. Leonard, M.A. Denning, "Does Contingent Valuation Measure Preferences?: Experimental Evidence," in Contingent Valuation: A Critical Assessment, proc. conference on Exxon Valdez oil spill, sponsored by Exxon Corp., Washington, DC (April 2-3, 1992).

D.S. Brookshire, W.D.Schulze, M.A.Thayer and R.C. d'Arge, "Valuing Public Goods: A comparison of Survey and Hedonic Approaches," AER, 72(1)165-177 (1982).

T.A. Cameron, "A New Paradigm for Valuing Non-Market Goods Using Referendum Data: Maximum Liklihood Estimation by Censored Logistic Regression," JEEM, 15: 355-79 (1988).

A. Randall, B. Ives and C. Eastman, "Bidding Games for Valuation of Aesthetic Environmental Improvements," JEEM, 1(2)132-149 (1974).

R.D. Rowe, R.C. d'Arge and D.S. Brookshire, "An Experiment on the Economic Value of Visibility," JEEM, 7(1)1-19 (1980).

Peter Bohm, "Estimating Demand for Public Goods: An Experiment," EER, 3:111-30 (1972).

JM Bowker and JR Stoll, "Use of Dichotomous Choice Nonmarket Methods to Value the Whooping Crane Resource," AJAE, 70:372-81 (1988).

William D. Schulze et al., "The Economic Benefits of Preserving Visibility in the National Parklands of the Southwest," NRJ, 23:149-73 (1983).

V.   Dynamics and Irreversibility [1 week]

9

A. Economic Growth

*CG Plourde, "A Model of Waste Accumulation and Disposal," CJE, 9:91-101 (1976).
*Kolstad, Charles D., "The Optimal Control of Stock Externalities with Learning," University of Illinois working paper (1992).
Karl-Goran Maler, "National Accounts and Environmental Resources," ERE, 1:1-15 (1991).
D.L. Brito, M.D. Intrilligator, "Stock Externalities, Pigovian Taxation and Dynamic Stability," JPuE, 33: 59-72 (1987).
Charles Plourde and David Young, "A Model of Industrial Pollution in a Stochastic Environment," JEEM, 16:97-105 (1989).
Emmett Keeler, Michael Spence and Richard Zeckhauser, "The Optimal Control of Pollution," JET, 4:19-34 (1971).
RC d'Arge and KC Kogiku, "Economic Growth and the Environment," REStud, 40:61-77 (1973).
Jeffrey A. Krautkraemer, "Optimal Growth, Resource Amenities and the Preservation of Natural Environments," REStud, 52:153-70 (1985).
Vernon L. Smith, "Dynamics of Waste Accumulation: Disposal Versus Recycling," QJE, 86:600-16 (1972).
Bruce Forster, "Optimal Consumption Planning in a Polluted Environment," Economic Record, 49:534-45 (1973).

B. Preservation and Irreversibilities

*Kenneth J. Arrow and Anthony C. Fisher, "Environmental Preservation, Uncertainty, and Irreversibility," QJE, 88, 312-319 (1974).
*Gardner Brown Jr., and Jon H. Goldstein, "A Model for Valuing Endangered Species," JEEM, 11:303-9 (1984).
*Martin Weitzman, "On Diversity," Harvard University Working Paper (Sept. 12, 1991).
Lars J. Olson, "Environmental Preservation with Production," JEEM, 18: 88-96 (1990).
Maureen Cropper, "Regulating Activities with Catastrophic Environmental Effects," JEEM, 3:1-15 (1976).
W.K. Viscusi and R. Zeckhauser, "Environmental Policy Choice Under Uncertainty," JEEM, 3,:97-112 (1976).
Jose M. Usategui, "Uncertain Irreversibility, Information and Transformation Costs," JEEM, 19: 73-85 (1990).
Richard C. Bishop, "Option Value: An Exposition and Extension," LE, 58(1)1-15 (1982).
A.C. Fisher and W.M. Hanemann, "Quasi-Option Value: Some Misconceptions Dispelled," JEEM, 14: 183-90 (1987).
Jon M. Conrad, "Quasi-Option Value and the Expected Value of Information," QJE, 94, 813-820 (1980).
W.K. Viscusi, "Environmental Policy Choice with an Uncertain Change of Irreversibility," JEEM, 12: 28-44 (1985).
John V. Krutilla, "Conservation Reconsidered," AER, 57:777-86 (1967).

[read464.92/8 March 1995]

DUKE UNIVERSITY
School of the Environment
ENV 270 ECO 270
PPS 272
Fall 1994
Randall Kramer

UG

Resource and Environmental Economics
Course Syllabus

Nature of Course: This course will examine economic perspectives on the allocation of natural resources and the management of environmental quality. Emphasis will be placed on the economic impacts of public policies. The objective of the course is to develop students' skills in using economic theory to critically analyze natural resource and environmental pollution problems.

Course instructor: Randall Kramer, School of the Environment
A120 Levine Science Research Center
Phone: 613-8072   E-mail: kramer@env.duke.edu
Fax: 684-8741
Office hours: Tuesday 1:30-2:30, Thursday 1:30-3:00 and by appointment.

Teaching assistants: Joe Aldy   **Graders:** David Bynum
John Hall   Sumie Utsunomiya
Erin Sills
Subhrendu Pattanayak
Office hours: to be announced

Readings: The main textbook for the course is Tom Tietenberg, Environmental and Natural Resource Economics, 3rd ed., 1992. A number of other chapters and journal articles will be assigned. Most of these will be available in a course-pack at the bookstore. There is a substantial amount of reading for the course.

Course format: The lecture periods will be used to present main themes and conceptual material. Active student discussion is encouraged. In addition there will be weekly discussion periods which are an integral part of the course. These periods will be used to review basic economic concepts, to develop benefit-cost analysis techniques, and to discuss and debate course readings. Your class participation grade will depend on your participation in the discussions and presentations during these weekly sessions.

Prerequisites: At least one course in microeconomic theory. It is assumed that students are familiar with basic concepts such as demand, supply, production functions, opportunity cost, marginal analysis and time discounting. In addition, a basic knowledge of calculus is required.

Grading: The final grade will be determined as follows:

Problem sets:	15%
Midterm exam:	25%
Final exam:	35%
Class Participation	15%
Review Article:	10%

Problem sets: There will be 3 major and one shorter problem sets. The problem sets are due one week after being handed out. Late problem sets will be penalized. No problem set grades will be dropped.

Examinations: The midterm will be given on October 13. Please note there will be no makeup midterm exams. The date of the final examination will be announced later.

Journal Article Review: Each student will review one journal article published in the past 5 years pertaining to resource and environmental economics. The purpose of the review is to encourage familiarity with current literature in the field and to demonstrate ability to apply "the economic way of thinking." More detailed instructions will be distributed later in the term.

2

READING LIST

Week			Topic

Aug. 30 I. **Introduction**
    A. Scope of course and field
        Tietenberg, chapter 1
    B. Markets and efficiency
        Tietenberg, chapter 2

Sep. 6   C. Sustainability and macroeconomics
        Solow, R.M., "Sustainability: An Economist's Perspective" in R. Dorfman and N. Dorfman (eds) Economics of the Environment, 1993, pp. 179 - 187.
        Daly, H., "Towards an Environmental Macroeconomics," Land Economics, V. 67, May 1991, pp. 255-259.
        Peskin, H.M. and E. Lutz, "A Survey of Resource and Environmental Accounting Approaches in Industrialized Countries" in E. Lutz (ed) Toward Improved Accounting for the Environment, World Bank, 1993.

Sep. 13 D. Resource Scarcity and Population Growth
        Tietenberg, chapter 13, 5
        Ridker, R.G., "Population Issues," Resources, Winter 1992: 11-14.
    E. Property Rights, Externalities and Public Goods
        Tietenberg, chapter 3
        Schalgler, E., and E. Ostrom, "Property Rights Regimes and Natural Resources: A Conceptual Analysis," Land Economics 1992, V. 68 (3): 249-262.

Sep. 20 F. Benefit-Cost Analysis
        Tietenberg, chapter 4.
        Anderson, D., "Cost Benefit Analysis: Empirical Background," Chapter 4 in The Economics of Afforestation, World Bank, 1987.

Sep. 27 II. **Allocation of Nonrenewable Resources**
    A. Energy
        Tietenberg, chapters 6 and 7
        Darmstadter, J. "Energy Transitions," Resources, Winter 1992: 29-32.
        Anderson, D., and K. Ahmed, "Where We Stand with Renewable Energy," Finance and Development, June 1993: 40-43.
    B. Minerals
        Tietenberg, chapter 8

Oct. 4 III. **Allocation of Renewable Resources**
    A. Land Use and Food
        Tietenberg, chapter 10
        Carlson, G., and D. Zilberman, "Emerging Resource Issues in World Agriculture," Chapter 11 in Agricultural and Environmental Resource Economics, G.A. Carlson, D. Zilberman, and J.A. Miranowski (eds), 1993: 491-517.

Oct. 11 B. Water
        Tietenberg, chapter 9
        Frederick, K.D., "Managing Water for Economic, Environmental, and Human Health," Resources, Winter 1992: 22-25.

Oct. 18   C. Forests
          Tietenberg, chapter 11
          Sandler, T., "Tropical Deforestation and Market
              Failures," Land Economics, 1993, V. 69 (3):
              225-233.
          Vincent, J., and C. Binkley, "Efficient Multiple-
              Use Forestry May Require Land-Use
              Specialization," Land Economics, 1993, V. 69
              (4): 370-376.
Oct. 25   D. Fisheries
          Tietenberg, chapter 12
          Huffaker,R., et al., "Institutional Feasibility of
              Contingent Water Marketing to Increase
              Migratory flows of Salmon on the Upper Snake
              River," Natural Resources Journal, 1993, V.
              33: 671-697.
          E. Biodiversity
          Randall, A, "The Value of Biodiversity,"Ambio, V.
              20, April 1991: 64-68.
          Conrad,J., and G. Salas, "Economic Strategies for
              Co-evolution: Timber and Butterflies" Land
              Economics, 1993, 69 (4): 404-415.
Nov. 1   IV. **Environmental Valuation**
          Smith, V.K., "Can We Measure the Economic Value of
              Environmental Amenities?" Southern Economic
              Journal, 1990, V. 56: 865-878.
          OECD, "Direct Valuation Techniques" and "Indirect
              Valuation Procedures," Chapters 4 and 5 in
              Environmental Policy Benefits: Monetary
              Valuation, Paris, 1989.
          Carson, R., N.F. Meade, and V.K. Smith, "Contingent
              Valuation and Passive Use Values: Introducing
              the Issues," Choices, Second Quarter, 1993: 4-
              8.
          Randall, A., "Passive-Use Values and Contingent
              Valuation - Valid for Damage Assessment,"
              Choices, Second Quarter, 1993: 12-15
          Walsh, R.G., F.A. Ward, and J.P. Olienyk,
              "Recreational Demand for Trees in National
              Forests," Journal of Environmental Management,
              1989. Vol 28: 255 - 268.
Nov. 8   V. **Economics of Pollution Control**
          A. Alternative environmental policy instruments
          Tietenberg, chapter 14
          Stavins, R.N., and B.W. Whitehead, "Dealing with
              Pollution," Environment, V. 34, 1992: 7-11,
              29-42.
Nov. 15   B. Control of air pollution
          Tietenberg, chapters 15, 16, 17
          Schelling, T.C., "Some Economics of Global
              Warming," American Economic Review, V. 82,
              1992, 1-14.
          Harrington, W. and M. Walls, "Shifting Gears: New
              Directions for Cars and Clean Air," Resources,
              Fall 1993: 28-31.
          C. Control of water pollution
          Tietenberg, chapter 18
          Paulsen, C.M., "Cost Effective Control of Water
              Pollution in Central and Eastern Europe,"
              Resources, Spring 1994: 2-6.
Nov. 22   D. Control of toxics

            Tietenberg, chapter 19
            Macauley, M.K. and K.L. Palmer, "Incentive-Based
                Approaches to Regulating Toxic Substances,"
                Resources, Summer 1992: 5-9.
Nov. 29   E. Management of solid waste
            Reschovsky,   J.D.,   and   S.E.   Stone,   "Market
                Incentives   to   Encourage   Household   Waste
                Recycling: Paying for What You Throw Away,"
                Journal of Policy Analysis and Management,
                Winter 1994: 120-139.
        VI. A Look to the Future
            Tietenberg, chapters 22 and 23

Randall A. Kramer

Spring 1994

ENV 373 Advanced Environmental Economics
Course Syllabus

G

<u>Nature of the Course</u>: This course will focus on the two main areas of environmental economics: (1) economic rationale for and evaluation of public policies for managing environmental quality, and (2) economic valuation of environmental quality.

<u>Instructor</u>:

Randall Kramer

School of the Environment

office: 107D Biological Sciences Building

phone: 613-8072 e-mail: kramer@env.duke.edu

office hours: Mon. 2:00-3:00, Fri. 3:30-4:30, and by appointment

<u>Prerequisites</u>:

microeconomic theory, calculus, econometrics

<u>Readings</u>:

Three textbooks are available at the bookstore. The required texts are: (1) A. Myrick Freeman III, <u>The Measurement of Environmental and Resource Values,</u> Resources for the Future, 1993, and (2) William J. Baumol and Wallace Oates, <u>Theory of Environmental Policy</u>, second edition, Prentice Hall, 1988. Those who have not taken a previous course in environmental economics are encouraged to do background reading in David W. Pearse and R. Kerry Turner, <u>Economics of Natural Resources and the Environment</u>, Johns Hopkins Press, 1990, especially chapters 1, 4-10. These primary texts will be supplemented by journal articles and other readings.

<u>Course Requirements</u>:

Midterm examination	25%
Term paper	25%
Written assignments	10%
Classroom participation	15%
Final examination	25%

<u>Course Format</u>:

The course will be run as a seminar with active student participation. The instructor will present basic material on each topic and then readings will be discussed by the class with designated discussion leaders. In addition, students will participate in several debates on controversial issues in the field. There will be several guest lectures.

<u>Term Paper Instructions</u>:

Each student is required to prepare a paper on a research topic relevant to the course material. The paper may be empirical or conceptual. The paper should be creative. Literature reviews are acceptable if they are interpretive. The paper should be no longer than 20 pages (exclusive of figures, tables, and references). The paper should include a clear problem and objectives statement, review of relevant literature, and analysis of the problem. All information or arguments drawn from the literature should be carefully cited. Time will be allotted near the end of the semester for each student to make a short presentation summarizing his or her paper. To encourage early progress, the following deadlines should be observed:

February 23	Selection of paper topic, brief problem statement and preliminary list of references
March 23	Tentative detailed outline and revised list of references
April 20	Completed typed paper

<u>Course Outline and Tentative Reading List</u>

I. Introduction

  A. History and Overview of Environmental Economics

  Allen V. Kneese, "The Economics of Natural Resources," <u>Population and Development Review</u> 14(1989): 281-309.

  B. Critiques of the Standard Orthodoxy

  James A. Swaney, "Elements of a Neoinstitutional Environmental Economics," <u>J. of Econ. Issues</u> 21(1987): 1739-1775.

  Richard B. Norgaard, "The Case for Methodological Pluralism," <u>Ecological Economics</u> 1(1989): 37-57.

  Mark Sagoff, "Some Problems with Environmental Economics," <u>Environmental Ethics</u> 10(1988):

55-74.
II. Externalities and Property Rights
    Alan Randall, "Sources of Inefficiency," Resource Economics, 2nd ed. John Wiley and Sons, 1988, ch. 9.
    Baumol and Oates, chapters 2-4
    James T. Hamilton, "Politics and Social Costs: Estimating the Impact of Collective Action on Hazardous Waste Facilities," RAND J. of Econ. 24(1993): 101-125.
III. The Design of Environmental Policy
  A. Subsidies, Charges and Standards
    Baumol and Oates, ch. 10, 11, 14, 15
    Lawrence J. White, "U.S. Automotive Emissions Controls: How Well Are They Working?" AER 72(1982): 332-335.
    Peter Bohm, "Incomplete Cooperation to Reduce CO_2 Emissions: Alternative Policies," JEEM 23(1993): 258-271.
    Seonghoon Hong et al., "An Economic Analysis of Household Recycling of Solid Waste: The Case of Portland Oregon," JEEM 25(1993): 136-146.
  B. Marketable Permits
    Baumol and Oates, ch. 12
    Eugene P. Seskin and Robert J. Anderson, Jr. "An Empirical Analysis of Economic Strategies for Controlling Air Pollution," JEEM 10(1983): 112-124.
    Scott E. Atkinson and T.H. Tietenberg, "Market Failure in Incentive-Based Regulation: The Case of Emissions Trading," JEEM 21(1991):17-31.
    N. Kete, "The U.S. Acid Rain Control Allowance Trading System," in Climate Change: Designing a Tradeable Permit System, OECD, Paris, 1992.
IV. Valuation of Environmental Quality
  A. Theory and Overview
    Freeman, Chapters 1-3.
    V. Kerry Smith, "Nonmarket Valuation of Environmental Resources: An Interpretive Appraisal, Land Econ. 69(1993): 1-26.
  B. Contingent Valuation
    Freeman, chapters 5 and 6.
    Richard T. Carson, "Constructed Markets," chapter 5 in Jon B. Braden and Charles D. Kolstad, Measuring the Demand for Environmental Quality. New York: North-Holland, 1991.
    Robert C. Mitchell, and R. T. Carson. 1989. Using Surveys to Value Public Goods: The Contingent Valuation Method. Resources for the Future, chapter 5-7.
    Don A. Dillman, "Mail and Other Self-Administered Questionnaires." In P. H. Rossi et al., eds. Handbook of Survey Research,. Academic Press, 1993.
    Dale Whittington, et al. 1990. "Estimating the Willingness to Pay for Water Services in Developing Countries: A Case Study of the Use of Contingent Valuation Surveys in Southern Haiti." Economic Development and Cultural Change 38(2): 293-311.
    Daniel Kahenman and Jack Knetsch, "Valuing Public Goods: The Purchase of Moral Satisfaction," JEEM 22(1992): 57-70 (see also comments by Kerry Smith and response from authors).
    Thomas Holmes and Randall A. Kramer, "Yea-Saying and Contingent Valuation," unpublished paper, 1993.
    Kevin J. Boyle et al., "The Role of Question Order and Respondent Experiences in COntingent-Valuation Studies," JEEM 25(1993): 580-599.
    NOAA Panel Report on Contingent Valuation, 58 Fed. Reg. 4601-4614 (Jan. 15, 1993).
    V. Kerry Smith, "Lightning Rods, Dart Boards, and Contingent Valuation," NRJ (forthcoming).
  C. Recreation Demand Models
    Freeman, chapter 13.
    Jeffrey Englin and Robert Mendelsohn, "A Hedonic Travel Cost Analysis for Valuation of Multiple Components of Site Quality: The Recreation Value of Forest Management, JEEM 21(1991): 275-290.
    Edward R. Morey, et al., "A Discrete-Choice Model of Recreation Participation, Site Choice, and Activity Valuation When Complete Trip Data Are Not Available," JEEM 20(1991): 181-201.

D. Hedonic Methods

Freeman, chapters 11 and 12.

Raymond B. Palmquist, "Hedonic Methods," chapter 4 in Braden and Kolstad.

B.A. Payne, S. Jay Olshansky, and T.E. Segal, "The Effects on Property Values of Proximity to a Site Contaminated with Radioactive Waste", <u>Natural Resources Journal</u> 27(1987):579-590.

E. Other Methods

Freeman, chapter 9 and 10.

W. Kip Viscusi and Michael J. Moore, "Rates of Time Preference and Valuation of the Duration of Life," <u>J. of Public Economics</u> 38(1989): 297-317.

Mark Dickie and Shelby Gerking, "Valuing Reduced Morbidity: A Household Production Approach," <u>SEJ</u> 57(1991): 690-702.

F. Other issues

David S. Brookshire, et al. "Valuing Public Goods: A Comparison of Survey and Hedonic Approaches," <u>AER</u> 72(1982): 165-177.

V. Kerry Smith and Yoshiaki Kaoru, "What Have We Learned Since Hotelling's Letter? A Meta Analysis," <u>Economic Letters</u> 32(1990): 267-272.

Journal Abbreviations:

AJAE	American Journal of Agricultural Economics
JEEM	Journal of Environmental Economics and Management
AER	American Economic Review
QJE	Quarterly Journal of Economics
SEJ	Southern Economic Journal
NRJ	Natural Resources Journal

Syllabus and Course Outline Economics 435
Economics of Resource Scarcity
Fall, 1994
Thompson Hall, Room 105; Tuesday, Thursday 12:45 - 2:00

Texas A & M University

Professor J.R. Moroney
Office: 402B Harrington
Phone: 845-1363
Office Hours: Tuesday, Thursday, 2:00-3:30

Texts: Energy Economics and Policy, (2nd Edition), by James M. Griffin and Henry B. Steele (Academic Press, 1986).
Also a packet of required readings (marked with *) can be purchased at the TAMU Copy Center in the Reed McDonald Building behind the Bus Stop Snack Shop.

This course is an introduction to natural resource economics. The main approach will be analytical. I will assume that all students have a thorough understanding of microeconomic analysis (Economics 322 or 323), a working knowledge of plane geometry and differential calculus, and a basic understanding of statistical inference.

Your grade depends on two criteria. First, 40% is based on the midterm examination. Second, 60% is attributable to either the final examination or a term paper. All graduating seniors must write a term paper, which should consist of original research dealing with some aspect of resource use, resource supply, measures of resource scarcity, international or interregional trade, etc. The paper should be 20 to 30 pages of typescript, with thorough documentation and a listing of all data used in the analysis. Term papers are due on 17 November 1994. A suitable topic should be chosen no later than 13 October. Students who are not graduating seniors may elect either to write a research paper or to sit for the final examination. You must make a choice by 13 October.

I.   What Are Natural Resources?

Physical viewpoint: Elements and compounds occurring in nature

Economic viewpoint: Are they economically exploitable?

A worldwide view:

*Harold Barnett and Chandler Morse, Scarcity and Growth (Baltimore: Johns Hopkins University Press, 1963), Ch. 1

*H. E. Goeller and Alvin Weinberg, "The Age of Substitutability," Science, (20 February, 1976).

*H. E. Goeller and A. Zucker, "Infinite Resources: The Ultimate Strategy," Science (3 February, 1984).

II.   Renewable and Nonrenewable (Exhaustible) Resources

Exhaustible nonfuel minerals
Exhaustible fuels: coal, gas, oil, uranium
Renewable resources

*J. R. Moroney, "Must Growth Be Limited?" in Roland H. Ebel and F. F. Hrubecky, Perspectives on the Energy Crisis, pp. 63 - 83.

*Herman E. Daly, "The Economics of the Steady State," American Economic Review, May, 1974, pp. 15 - 21.

III.   Energy Production and Consumption: Facts

Text, Ch. 1

Robert S. Manthy, Natural Resource Commodities -- A Century of Statistics (covers the period 1870 - 1973 and includes production, consumption, and prices of various energy resources, as well as important nonfuel minerals and renewable resources).

More recent information on resource production, consumption, and prices is found in annual editions of Commodities Yearbook, available in the Evans Library.

*J. R. Moroney, "Output and Energy: An International Analysis," The Energy Journal, Volume 10, Number 3 (1989), pp. 1 - 18.

*J. R. Moroney, "Energy, Capital, and Technological Change in the United States," Resources and Energy, 14 (1992), pp. 363 - 380.

Much information concerning energy production and consumption can be found in:

Monthly Energy Review (Energy Information Administration)
Annual Energy Review (Energy Information Administration)
Basic Petroleum Data Book (American Petroleum Institute)
Oil and Gas Journal

Information concerning recent energy prices is found in Energy Prices and Taxes (Organization for Economic Cooperation and Development).

IV.   Optimal Production and Consumption

Text, Ch. 2 Optimal Allocation with Renewable Resources
Text, Ch. 3 Optimality with Nonrenewable Resources: Hotelling's Model and Modifications
*Robert M. Solow, "The Economics of Resources or the Resources of Economics," American Economic Review, May, 1974, pp. 1 -14.

Midterm Examination, Thursday, 6 October 1994.

V.   OPEC: Economics, Politics, and Fragility of the Cartel

Text, Ch. 4

VI.   Energy and the Environment

Text, Ch. 5

Chapter 2. Industrial Countries (OECD) consumption of Metals and energy)

Chapter 24. Atmosphere and Climate (CO_2 emissions, sulfur and nitrogen emissions)

VII.   Conservation: Demand-Side and Supply-Side

Text, Ch. 7

*J. R. Moroney, "The Economic and Political Consequences of Higher Gasoline Taxes," Center for Energy and Mineral Resources, Texas A&M, January 1994.

VIII.   Federal Policies Toward Energy

Text, Ch. 8

IX.   Energy for the Future

Text, Ch. 9

*Cutler J. Cleveland, R. Costanza, C. Hall, and R. Kaufman, "Energy and the U.S. Economy: A Biophysical Perspective," Science, (31 August, 1984), pp. 225.

*Robert Solow, "An Almost Practical Step Toward Sustainability," Invited Lecture delivered at the 40th Anniversary of Resources for the Future, October 8, 1992.

Reread "The Age of Substitutability: by Goeller and Weinberg.

Term papers due Thursday, 17 November.
Final Examination on Wednesday, 14 December, 1994, 8:00-10:00 a.m.

VANDERBILT UNIVERSITY
Frank Parker and Cliff Russell
UG
ECON 269/CE 278: Technical Basis for Environmental Policy

Spring 1995

Frank Parker
Department of Environmental
& Water Resources Engineering
Phone: 32371

Office Hours:
3-5 W-TH-F
or by appt.

Cliff Russell
Vanderbilt Institute for Public
Policy Studies
1207 18th Avenue, So. (Peabody)
Phone: 28512

Office Hours:
2-4 TH
1:30-3:30 TU
or by appt.

TEXTBOOKS:
Paul R. Portney, Public Policies for Environmental Protection.

All non-textbook readings will be available in the reserve room of the central library. A few public access readings will be reproduced as an informal classpak.

OBJECTIVES:
1. To expose students to the tools of analysis used in environmental engineering and economics--with excursions into risk analysis and ecological modeling--and, most importantly, to point out how these tools fit together to inform policy.
2. To allow students themselves to work as members of interdisciplinary teams on computer modeling problems and on the writing and presentation of a term paper.
3. To demonstrate that important policy problems do not have purely technical solutions and that even at the technical level there can be disagreements about methodology.

Outline of Technical Background
to Environmental Policy

Weeks or Parts	Subject	Class Date
1	Intro: Technical	
	Intro: Policy	17 January
2	Air Pollution: Technical	24 January
3	Air Pollution: Policy	31 January
4	Lab (Air Modeling)	7 February
5	Surface Water Pollution: Technical	14 February
6	Lab (Water Modeling)	21 February
7	Surface Water Pollution: Policy	28 February
8	Ground Water & Hazardous Waste: Technical (Physical)	
	Ground Water & Hazardous Waste: Technical (Risk Ass't)	14 March
9	Ground Water & Hazardous Waste: Policy	21 March
10	Preservation of Species & Ecosystems: Technical	
	Preservation of Species & Ecosystems: Policy	28 March
11	Global Climate Change: Technical	
	Global Climate Change: Policy	4 April
12	Rad Waste: Technical	
	Rad Waste: Policy	11 April

Grading basis for TBEP:

	%
Assignments	20
Paper	30
Final	35
Class Participation	15
	100

Honor Code: The University's Honor Code will be enforced. Collaboration will be encouraged on computer assignments and term papers for which teams will be assembled. Other assignments and the take-home final should be your own work.

READING LIST KEYED TO TOPICS

Introduction

Technical

1.   Jorgensen, Sven Erick, "Ecological Engineering Principles," pp. 21-37 in Ecological Engineering, 1989.
2.   Rich, Linvil, pp. 1-86 in Environmental Systems Engineering, 1973
3.   Haith, Douglas A., "Environmental Systems Analysis," pp. 1-39 in Environmental Systems Optimization, 1982.
4.   Morgan, Granger and Max Henrion, "An Overview of Quantitative Policy Analysis," pp. 916-946 in Uncertainty, 1990.

Policy

5.   Textbook, Chapters 1 & 2, pp. 1-25
6.   Yellin, Joel, "Science, Technology and Administrative Government: Institutional Designs for Environmental Policymaking," pp. 1300-33 in Yale Law Journal, vol. 92, 1983.
7.   Downing, Paul B., "Basic Concepts in Economics and Pollution Control," pp. 21-37, in Environmental Economics and Policy, 1984.
8.   Downing, Paul B., "Measuring the Benefits and Costs ofEnvironmental Improvements," pp. 86-116 in Environmental Economics and Policy, 1984
9.   Hammond, P. Brett and Rob Coppock, eds, "Conclusions," pp. 189-208 in Valuing Health Risks, Costs, and Benefits, National Academy Press, 1990.

Air Pollution

Technical

10.   Elsom, Derk, "The Atmospheric Pollution Problem" and Particulates and Gaseous Pollutants," pp. 3-91 in Atmospheric Pollution: Causes, Effects, and Control Policies, 1987.
11.   Pacyna, Jozef M., "Methods for Pollution Abatement," pp. 93-104 in Atmospheric Pollution, 1993.
12.   Corcoran, Elizabeth, "Cleaning Up Coal," pp. 107-116 in Scientific American, May 1991.

Policy

13.   Textbook, Chapter 3, pp. 27-96
14.   Russell, Clifford S., "Achieving Air Pollution Goals in Three Different Settings," pp. 233-266 in To Breathe Freely: Risk, Consent, and Air, 1985.
15.   Brajer, Victor, Jane V. Hall, and Robert Rowe, "The Value of Cleaner Air: An Integrated Approach," pp. 81-91 in Contemporary Policy Issues, vol. IX, 1991.

Surface Water Pollution
Technical
16. Vesilind, P. Aarne, J. Jeffrey Pierce and Ruth F. Weiner, Chapters 8 & 9, Environmental Engineering, pp. 137-214.
17. Basta, D.J. and B.T. Bower, eds. Chapter 5, Analyzing Effects on Natural Systems and Receptors, pp. 114-169.

Policy
18. Textbook, Chapter 4, pp. 97-150.
19. Letson, David, "Point/Nonpoint Source Pollution Reduction Trading: An Interpretive Survey," pp. 219-232 in Natural Resources Journal, 1992.
20. Davidson, John H. "Little Waters: The Relationship Between Water Pollution and Agricultural Drainage," Environmental Law Reporter, 17ELR10074-10081, March 1987.

Ground Water and Hazardous Waste
Technical (Physical)
21. Anderson, Mary P., John A. Cherry, Robert W. Gillham, and James F. Barker, "Movement of Contaminants in Groundwater," pp. 37-45 in Groundwater Contamination, 1984.
22. "Groundwater Contamination," pp. 1-20 in Groundwater, 1987.
23. "Groundwater Restoration," in Groundwater, Environmental Protection Agency, pp. 35-50.

Technical (Risk Assessment)
24. Morgan, M. Granger, "Risk Analysis and Management," pp. 32-41 in Scientific American, July 1993.
25. Freudenburg, William R., "Perceived Risks, Real Risks: Social Science and the Art of Probabilistic Risk," pp. 44-49 in Science, vol. 242, 1988.
26. Gold, Lois Swirsky, Thomas H. Slone, Bonnie R. Stern, and Neela B. Manley, "Rodent Carcinogens: Setting Priorities," pp. 261-265 in Science, 1992.

Policy
27. Text, Chapters 5 & 6, pp. 151-242.
28. Abelson, Philip H., "Toxic Terror; Phantom Risks," p. 407 in Science, 1993.
29. Russell, Milton, E. William Colglazier, and Mary R. English, "Hazardous Waster Remediation: The Task Ahead," pp. 1-8 from the University of Tennessee, December 1991.
30. Walsh, William J., "Making Science, Policy, and Public Perception Compatible," pp. 206-249 in Ground Water and Soil Contamination Remediation: Toward Compatible Science , 1990.
31. Kopp, Raymond J. and V. Kerry Smith, "Benefit Estimation Goes to Court: The Case of Natural Resource Damage Assessments," pp. 593-612 in Journal of Policy Analysis and Management, 1989.
32. Mitchell, Robert Cameron and Richard T. Carson, "Property Rights, Protests, and the Siting of Hazardous Waste Facilities," pp. 285-290 in American Economic Review, 1986.
33. Amato, Ivan, "The Crusade Against Chlorine," pp. 152-154 in Science, vol. 261, 1993.

Preservation of Species and Ecosystems
Technical
34. Suter, Glenn W., II. "A Critique of Ecosystem Health Concepts and Indexes," pp. 1-

7 in <u>Environmental Toxicology and Chemistry</u>, vol. 12, 1993.
35.   Russell, Clifford S., "Old Lessons and New Contexts in Economic-Ecological Modeling," forthcoming in a conference volume.
36.   Hall, Charles A.S. and John W. Day Jr., Chapter 1, pp. 6-36 in <u>Ecosystem Modeling in Theory and Practice</u>, 1977.

Policy
37.   Bishop, Richard C. "Endangered Species and Uncertainty: The Economics of a Safe Minimum Standard," pp. 10-18, <u>American Journal of Agricultural Economics</u>, vol. 60, 1978.
38.   Ready, Richard C. and Richard C. Bishop, "Endangered Species and the Safe Minimum Standard," pp. 309-12 in <u>American Journal of Agricultural Economics</u>, 1991.
39.   Balick, Michael J. Robert Mendelsohn, "Assessing the Economic Value of Traditional Medicines from Tropical Rain Forests" pp. 128-130 in <u>Conservation Biology</u>, vol. 6, 1991.
40.   Mendelsohn, Robert and Michael Balick, "The Value of Undiscovered Pharmaceuticals in Tropical Forests," unpublished, 1994.
41.   Tobias, Dave and Robert Mendelsohn, "Valuing Ecotourism in a Tropical Rain-Forest Reserve," pp. 91-93 in <u>Ambio</u>, vol. 20, 1991.

Global Climate Change
Technical
42.   Lyman, Francesca, "Is Earth Really Getting Warmer?" and "Climate's Evolution and the Industrial Revolution" (Chapters 1 & 2), pp. 1-49 in <u>The Greenhouse Trap</u>, 1991.
43.   Schneider, Stephen H., "The Greenhouse Effect: Science and Policy," pp. 771-781 <u>Science</u>, February 1989.

Policy
44.   Taubes, Gary, "The Ozone Backlash," pp. 1580-1583 in <u>Science</u>, vol. 260, 1993.
45.   Lave, Lester B., "Formulating Greenhouse Policies in a Sea of Uncertainty," pp. 9-21 in <u>The Energy Journal</u>, vol. 12, no. 1, 1992.

Radioactive Waste Management
Technical
46.   Parker, Frank L., "Radioactive Waste Management," pp. 107-129 in <u>Status and Perspectives of Nuclear Energy: Fission and Fusion</u>, 1992.

Policy
47.   "Interim Storage of Low-Level Radioactive Waste," U.S. Nuclear Regulatory Commission.
47.   "Rethinking High-Level Radioactive Waste Disposal," Report from a committee chaired by Frank Parker, pp. 1-12.
48.   Taubes, Gary, "Plutonium Disposal: No Easy Way to Shackle the Nuclear Demon," pp. 629-631 in <u>Science</u>, vol. 263, 1994

Sustainability and the Long Run
49.   Solow, Robert, "An Almost Practical Step Toward Sustainability," pp. 1-22, 1992.
50.   Toman, Michael A. "Economics and 'Sustainability': Balancing Tradeoffs and Imperatives," Working Paper RFFENR91-05 Rev., Resources for the Future.

Environmental Economics

U

Department of Agricultural Economics and Marketing
Cook College
Rutgers, The State University of New Jersey
(11:373:363, 3 credits)

Professor:

Peter J. Parks
212 Cook Office Building
Department of Agricultural Economics and Marketing
(908) 932-9161, (908) 932-8887 FAX
parks@aesop.rutgers.edu

Office Hours: Mondays and Thursdays 11:30 to 12:30 (sign-up sheet posted outside 212 Cook Office Building). Hours can easily be arranged by appointment.

Lectures:

When: 9:50-11:10 Mondays and Thursdays. *Where:* 101 Food Science Building, Dudley Road, Cook College Campus, New Brunswick, New Jersey. During severe weather conditions, class cancellation information is available on the recorded message system at (908) 932-7799.

Course Goals:

By the end of this course, you should be able to:

1. Plan environmental and natural resource decisions (including conservation, development, preservation, and restoration) to accomplish objectives that can be stated in economic terms; these include objectives of individuals, groups, nations, and groups of nations.

2. Understand the most common economic causes of environmental and resource policy problems.

3. Diagnose potential environmental and resource policy problems and understand the major economic policy instruments used to correct these problems in market economies.

4. Apply economic logic to environmental and resource issues at scales ranging from individual users and development projects to national income accounts, national policies, and international agreements.

5. Extend the concepts we discuss in class to help you understand new environmental and resource contexts, and (if you need to) develop and analyze new policies.

Course Policies:

A. Class Participation

This is a participatory class; while in class, you will frequently be asked during class discussions to *(i)* offer your opinions about the realism of major assumptions and *(ii)* draw on your personal experience to offer insight into the logical steps required to arrive at key conclusions. (These responsibilities are much easier to meet if you have done the reading ahead of time.)

B. Required Readings

Our discussions will draw upon an intermediate knowledge of microeconomics. To help you integrate environmental economics with your prior knowledge of economics as quickly as possible, lectures have been prepared presuming you are familiar with the content of required readings before arriving in class. Each required reading within a subject area will be indicated with an asterisk (*); read this before we begin to discuss the listed topic.

C. Other Related Readings

This syllabus has been prepared to serve not only as a guide to the course, but also to give you some exposure to literature in environmental and resource economics. For this reason, this syllabus includes some examples of recent published research from major publishers and journals. The citations are not intended to be an exhaustive list. They have been included to give you examples of influential or representative approaches and to help you gain more from our class discussions. Lectures will frequently make references to related material, but it will never be presumed that you have read any of the other related readings (in contrast to required readings, above). If you are interested in representative articles on subjects other than those listed in the syllabus, please contact me and I will attempt to provide you with additional citations.

D. Lecture Strategy

The lectures will use the readings as starting points, but will contain references to other readings, empirical results, syntheses of trends in the literature, and discussion of key points from the other relevant readings. Missing a lecture will cost you understanding and perhaps a key inspiration you are seeking. We have roughly thirty hours together:[1] try not to miss even one.

E. Rutgers University Policies

All faculty, staff, and students at our University are bound by University policies. All aspects of this course will be conducted according to these policies. (Please see p10 for additional information.)

---

[1] Environmental Economics (11:373:363) includes twenty-four class meetings. When all class meetings run the full class period (1:10:00 per lecture), total class time equals 30 hours. (This calculation does not include time spent taking examinations on February 20 1995, March 27 1995, and May 9 1994, and completing course evaluations on April 20 1995.)

Texts:

This text has been ordered for our class. Whether you purchase it is up to you; however, it is a widely accepted standard reference for our field, and would be a worthwhile addition to your personal library.

> Tietenberg, T. 1992. Environmental and Natural Resource Economics. Third Edition. New York: McGraw-Hill. This introductory book typically gives a well organized, non mathematical treatment; his discussions are well stocked with examples and graphs.

Other books with which you may want to be acquainted include:

> Baumol, W.J. and W.E. Oates. 1988. The Theory of Environmental Policy. Second Edition. New York: Cambridge University Press. An accessible book on important considerations for policies intended to correct for externalities (e.g. emissions, effluent) should be designed.

> Costanza, R. (ed.) 1991. Ecological Economics: The Science and Management of Sustainability. New York: Columbia University Press. A collection of contributed chapters on what has become a major area of worldwide interest. Includes overviews, methods, and case studies.

> Dixon, J.A. and P.B. Sherman. 1990. Economics of Protected Areas: A New Look at Benefits and Costs. Washington, DC: Island Press. This text combines conceptual chapters with case studies drawn from outside the US. The level of economics is introductory, similar to Tietenberg.

> Dorfman, R. and N.S. Dorfman (eds.) 1993. Economics of the Environment: Selected Readings. New York: W.W. Norton and Company. An excellent collection of classic and modern articles. Includes many of the most influential articles written in environmental and natural resource economics.

> Hartwick, J.M. and N.E. Olewiler. 1986. The Economics of Natural Resource Use. New York: Harper and Row Publishers. A good book that is intermediate between Tietenberg and the Cambridge press group. The focus is primarily on resources; pollution externalities are introduced late in the text.

> Freeman, A.M. III. 1993. The Measurement of Environmental and Resource Values: Theory and Methods. Washington: Resources for the Future. A comprehensive overview of microeconomic foundations and key applications of valuation. Empirical references are contained in footnotes.

> Neher, P.A. 1991. Natural Resource Economics: Conservation and Exploitation. New York: Cambridge University Press. The breadth of coverage in this text is quite good, and includes amenities from natural environments.

Lecture/Discussion Schedule:

Basic Principles of Environmental and Resource Economics
Thursday, January 19
Monday, January 23
Thursday, January 26

*Tietenberg, T. 1992. "Visions of the Future." In Environmental and Natural Resource Economics. Third Edition. New York: HarperCollins.

*Tietenberg, T. 1992. "Economics of the Environment: An Overview." In Environmental and Natural Resource Economics. Third Edition. New York: HarperCollins.

World Commission on Environment and Sustainable Development. 1987. Our Common Future. New York: Oxford University Press.

Property Rights, Externalities and Environmental Problems
Monday, January 30
Thursday, February 2

*Tietenberg, T. 1992. "Property Rights, Externalities, and Environmental Problems." In Environmental and Natural Resource Economics. Third Edition. New York: HarperCollins.

Bromley, D.W. (ed.) 1992. Making the Commons Work: Theory, Practice and Policy. San Francisco: Institute for Contemporary Studies.

Cornes, R. and T. Sandler. 1993. The Theory of Externalities, Public Goods, and Club Goods. New York: Cambridge University Press.

Gordon, H.S. 1954. "The Economic Theory of Common Property." Journal of Political Economy 62(1): 124-142.

Regulating the Market, Information and Uncertainty
Monday, February 6
Thursday, February 9

*Tietenberg, T. 1992. "Regulating the Market, Information and Uncertainty." In Environmental and Natural Resource Economics, Third Edition. New York: HarperCollins.

141

Mishan, E.J. 1976. Cost-Benefit Analysis. Second Edition. New York: Praeger Publishers.

Kelman, S. 1981. "Cost-Benefit Analysis: An Ethical Critique." Regulation (January/February): 33-41.

Economics of Pollution Control: An Overview
Monday, February 13

*Tietenberg, T. 1992. "Economics of Pollution Control: An Overview." In Environmental and Natural Resource Economics, Third Edition. New York: HarperCollins.

Hahn, R.W. 1989. "Economic Prescriptions for Environmental Problems: How the Patient has Followed the Doctor's Orders." Journal of Economic Perspectives 3(Spring): 95-114.

Group Discussions and Presentations I
Thursday, February 16

Midterm Exam I
Monday, February 20

Economics of Pollution Control: An Overview, continued
Thursday, February 23

*Tietenberg, T. 1992. "Economics of Pollution Control: An Overview." In Environmental and Natural Resource Economics, Third Edition. New York: HarperCollins.

Hahn, R.W. 1989. "Economic Prescriptions for Environmental Problems: How the Patient has Followed the Doctor's Orders." Journal of Economic Perspectives 3(Spring): 95-114.

Local, Regional, and Global Air Pollution
Monday, February 27
Thursday, March 2

*Tietenberg, T. 1992. "Stationary Source Local Air Pollution." In <u>Environmental and Natural Resource Economics</u>, Third Edition. New York: HarperCollins.

*Tietenberg, T. 1992. "Regional and Global Air Pollutants: Acid Rain and Atmospheric Modification." In <u>Environmental and Natural Resource Economics</u>, Third Edition. New York: HarperCollins.

Tietenberg, T. 1992. "Mobil-Source Air Pollution." In <u>Environmental and Natural Resource Economics</u>, Third Edition. New York: HarperCollins.

Portney, P. (ed.) 1990. <u>Public Policies for Environmental Protection</u>. Washington: Resources for the Future.

Dornbusch, R. and J.M. Poterba (eds.) 1992. <u>Global Warming: Economic Policy Responses</u>. Cambridge: The MIT Press.

Water Pollution
Monday, March 6
Thursday, March 9

*Tietenberg, T. 1992. "Water Pollution." In <u>Environmental and Natural Resource Economics</u>, Third Edition. New York: HarperCollins.

Portney, P. (ed.) 1990. <u>Public Policies for Environmental Protection</u>. Washington: Resources for the Future.

Russell, C.O. 1981. "Controlled Trading of Pollution Permits." <u>Environmental Science and Technology</u> 15(1):1-5.

Spring Recess
Monday, March 13
Thursday, March 16

Toxic Substances
Monday, March 20

*Tietenberg, T. 1992. "Toxic Substances." In <u>Environmental and Natural Resource Economics</u>, Third Edition. New York: HarperCollins.

Group Discussions and Presentations II
Thursday, March 23

Midterm Exam II
Monday, March 27

Pollution Control Policy: Distributional Effects
Thursday, March 30

*Tietenberg, T. 1992. "Pollution Control Policy: Distributional Effects." In <u>Environmental and Natural Resource Economics</u>, Third Edition. New York: HarperCollins.

Peskin, H. 1978. "Environmental Policy and the Distribution of Benefits and Costs." In <u>Current Issues in U.S. Environmental Policy</u>, P. Portney (ed.) Baltimore: Johns Hopkins University Press for Resources for the Future.

Dorfman, R. 1977. "Incidence of the Benefits and Costs of Environmental Programs." American Economic Review 67(February): 333-340.

Whittington, D. and D. MacRae, Jr. 1986. "The Issue of Standing in Cost-Benefit Analysis." <u>Journal of Policy Analysis and Management</u> 5(1986): 665-682.

The Allocation of Depletable and Renewable Resources: An Overview

Monday, April 3
Thursday, April 6

*Tietenberg, T. 1992. "The Allocation of Depletable and Renewable Resources: An Overview." In <u>Environmental and Natural Resource Economics</u>, Third Edition. New York: HarperCollins.

144

Krutilla, J.V. 1967. "Conservation Reconsidered." American Economic Review 47 (1967):777-786.

McInerney, J. 1976. "The Simple Analytics of Natural Resource Economics." Journal of Agricultural Economics 27(1): 31-52.

Solow, R.M. 1974. "The Economics of Resources or the Resources of Economics." American Economic Review 61(1): 1-14.

Recyclable Resources
Monday, April 10
Thursday, April 13

*Tietenberg, T. 1992. "Recyclable Resources: Minerals, Etc." In Environmental and Natural Resource Economics, Third Edition. New York: HarperCollins.

Spofford, W.O. 1971. "Solid Residual Management: Some Economic Considerations." Natural Resources Journal 11(July):561-589.

The Quest for Sustainable Development
Monday, April 17

*Tietenberg, T. 1992. "The Quest for Sustainable Development." In Environmental and Natural Resource Economics, Third Edition. New York: HarperCollins.

Pezzey, J. 1989. "Economic Analysis of Sustainable Growth and Development." World Bank Environment Department Working Paper No. 15. Washington.

Batie, S. 1989. "Sustainable Development: Challenges to the Agricultural Economics Profession." American Journal of Agricultural Economics 71(1989): 1083-1101.

Group Discussions and Presentations III
Thursday, April 20

Course Evaluations
Monday, April 24

Summary and Conclusions
Monday, May 1

*Tietenberg, T. 1992. "Visions of the Future Revisited." In <u>Environmental and Natural Resource Economics</u>. Third Edition. New York: HarperCollins.

Final Examination
Tuesday, May 9

Grading Policies:

4%	Instructor's Discretion
6%	Group Discussions and Presentations (2% Each)
30%	Exam I
30%	Exam II
30%	Final Examination (Comprehensive)
100%	Total

Group Discussions and Presentations:

On three ocassions during the course, the class will participate in group discussions and presentations. Attendance at each group discussion is mandatory, and will earn the student 2% credit toward the course grade. The class will be divided into smaller groups, and each group will be provided a set of related questions to discuss. The discussion will take place during the normal class period, and will lead to a short presentation made during the same class period. A spokesperson for the group will present the group's perspective on its topic; the spokesperson will automatically obtain two percent extra credit (see below).

Options for Extra Credit:

You have several options to earn extra credit in this course; however, no one is required to pursue any of these options to obtain a grade in this course. These include *(i)* authoring a term paper, which can contribute a maximum of ten percent toward your grade (see below); *(ii)* authoring twenty examination questions, which can contribute a maximum of five percent toward your grade (see below); and *(iii)* serving as group spokesperson (see above), which can contribute a maximum of six percent toward your grade.

146

Writing Exam Questions (Extra Credit):

Up to five (5) percent extra credit may be obtained by submitting twenty examination questions comparable in style and difficulty to the examination questions you encounter on the midterms in this course. Requirements for this extra credit assignment include: *(i)* no more than two questions may be drawn from material in the same chapter; *(ii)* no more than seven exam questions may be of the same type (true/false, multiple choice, graphical interpretation); *(iii)* no exam question may have appeared on an exam previously given in this course; *(iv)* all exam questions must be fair, nontrivial, and require no more than two minutes of effort to answer. (These requirements sound formal, but a general guide would be for you to write exam questions that you would like to be asked or would expect your classmates to know.)

Policy Analysis Paper (Extra Credit):

Up to ten (10) percent extra credit may be obtained by writing a policy analysis paper. This extra credit assignment is designed to provide you with an opportunity to test your own knowledge of environmental economic principles on your own time and at your own pace. By successfully completing this assignment, you will have prepared a high-quality paper, and have obtained first-hand experience with applying economic policy analysis to a problem that is important to you. There are only a few general guidelines to help you succeed more easily.

Students must meet with the instructor to discuss topic and general nature of the paper, and must submit a written one-page statement of the topic and a brief outline by 5:00pm Friday, February 24. No paper will be accepted unless it has been discussed with the instructor before writing begins. The final draft of your paper is due by 5:00pm Friday, April 28. Although earlier submissions are welcome, there will be no exceptions to this final deadline.

Drawing on published literature and your experience as an economist and analyst, write a paper that analyzes a resource or environmental issue that *(i)* is the subject of existing policy or *(ii)* should be the subject of new policy. You are free to choose whatever topic is of interest to you. The only restriction is that there is an obvious link between your topic and resources or the environment.

1. (2 Points). At a minimum, comment on the presence or absence of economic efficiency and equity in the context of your topic; both within and between generations. This will require you to state your definition of an efficient condition and an equitable distribution of benefits and costs. These two concepts are to be the heart of your paper, and must be in your own words and applied directly to your topic. (Realize that these efficiency and equity issues may include equity between countries effected by the policy.)

2. (2 Points). In addition, your paper should discuss at least one of the following concepts as it relates to your topic: *(i)* property rights (including excludability and subtractibility attributes); *(ii)* externalities; *(iii)* proposed policies; or *(iv)* existing policies.

3. (2 Points). Your paper must demonstrate original thinking by you that convinces your reader that you have a thorough understanding of your topic. This paper is an important opportunity for you to use your analytical skills and to sharpen your ability to communicate.

4. (4 Points). Your writing should be clear, concise, and directed toward an audience of your peers. Maximum length is ten double-spaced pages, not including figures or references. For general help with economic writing style, see McCloskey, D.N. 1987. The Writing of Economics. New York: MacMillan Publishing Company. For an excellent short discussion of communicating effectively and meeting readers' expectations, see Gopen, G.D. and J.A. Swan. 1990. "The Science of Scientific Writing." American Scientist 78(2):125-134.

Good places to obtain current ideas in our field include journals such as the Journal of Environmental Economics and Management, American Journal of Agricultural Economics, Land Economics and others. The Journal of Economic Literature December issue contains an index to titles in these and many other journals.

Letter Grade Assignments:

At any time you may calculate your grade in this course. There is a total of 100 points possible (see above). Final grades will be assigned using the scale given below. To calculate your expected final grade, simply add the grades from your completed exams with the grades you plan to get on forthcoming exams and refer to the table below.

90+	A
85+	B+
80+	B
75+	C+
70+	C
60+	D
60-	F

Rutgers University Policies:

The reference for Rutgers University policies that will be used in the conduct of this course is pp461-473 in

Rutgers, The State University of New Jersey, Campus at New Brunswick. 1992. New Brunswick Undergraduate Catalog, 1993-1995. New Brunswick.

All sections of this discussion on policy are of vital importance to you as a Rutgers University student; however for the purposes of this course, please pay particular attention to sections on Registration, Attendance, Nondiscrimination, Policy Against Insult, Defamation, and Harassment, Sexual Harassment, Administrative Policy for Responding to Disruptions, Academic Integrity, and the University Student Disciplinary Hearing Procedure.

Should you have any questions about Rutgers University policies, please contact the personnel listed in the Undergraduate Catalog.

Keywords:

After successfully completing this course, you should be able to use (at least) the following terms in your future work relating to environmental economics.

absorptive capacity
allocation
amenity
benefit-cost analysis
benefit-cost ratio
benefits transfer
biodiversity
carrying capacity
cartel
charge
Coase's theorem
command and control
common property
comparative statics
compounding
concession
conjectural variation
constraint
consumer surplus
contingent valuation
cost-effective
current annual
increment
depletable
development
discount rate
discounting
dynamic
ecological economics
efficient
emissions trading
enforceable
entry
equity
excludable
exhaustible
exponential
extraction
fixed cost
flow
fund pollutant
game theory
growth
Hamiltonian
hedonic price
hedonic wage
impact analysis

impulse control
incidence
incentive
income distribution
individual
transferable quota
inflation
intergenerational
internal rate of return
intragenerational
Lagrange multiplier
Lagrangean
market imperfection
market structure
maximum sustainable
yield
mean annual
increment
missing market
monopoly
multiple use
natural resource
damage assessment
net benefits
nonmarket
nonpoint source
nonstationary source
nonuniformly mixed
objective function
off-site
on-site
open access
opportunity cost
optimization
Pareto improvement
perfect market
perfect property rights
permit
point source
present value
preservation
producer surplus
public good
quota
reciprocal externality
recyclable
regulatory control

renewable
rent
rent capture
risk
rival (nonrival)
consumption
royalty
safe minimum
standard
scarcity
static
stationary source
steady state
economics,
stock
stock pollutant
strategic bias
subsidy
sustainable
tax
technology
transaction cost
transferable
transferable permit
transitive externality
travel cost
uncertainty
uniformly mixed
universal
variable cost
willingness-to-accept
willingness-to-pay

Environmental and Resource Economics

G

Department of Agricultural Economics and Marketing
Cook College
Rutgers, The State University of New Jersey
(16:030:509, 3 credits)

Professor:

Peter J. Parks
212 Cook Office Building
Department of Agricultural Economics and Marketing
(908) 932-9161 Extension 46, (908) 932-8887 FAX
parks@aesop.rutgers.edu

Office Hours: Mondays and Thursdays 11:30 to 12:30 (sign-up sheet posted outside 212 Cook Office Building). Hours can easily be arranged by appointment.

Lectures:

When: 8:10 to 9:30 Mondays and Thursdays. *Where:* 226 Cook Office Building, Dudley Road, Cook College Campus, New Brunswick, New Jersey. During severe weather conditions, class cancellation information is available on the recorded message system at (908) 932-7799.

Course Goals:

By the end of this course, you should be able to:

1. Plan environmental and natural resource decisions (including conservation, development, preservation, and restoration) to accomplish objectives that can be stated in economic terms; these include objectives of individuals, groups, nations, and groups of nations.

2. Understand the most common economic causes of environmental and resource policy problems.

3. Diagnose potential environmental and resource policy problems and understand the major economic policy instruments used to correct these problems in market economies.

4. Apply economic logic to environmental and resource issues at scales ranging from individual users and development projects to national income accounts, national policies, and international agreements.

5. Extend the concepts we discuss in class to help you understand new environmental and resource contexts, and (if you need to) develop and analyze new policies.

Course Policies:

A. Class Participation

This is a participatory class; while in class, you will frequently be asked during class discussions to *(i)* offer your opinions about the realism of major assumptions and *(ii)* draw on your personal experience to offer insight into the logical steps required to arrive at key conclusions. (These responsibilities are much easier to meet if you have done the reading ahead of time.)

B. Required Readings

Our discussions will draw upon an intermediate knowledge of microeconomics and calculus. To help you integrate environmental and resource economics with your prior knowledge of economics as quickly as possible, lectures have been prepared presuming you are familiar with the content of required readings before arriving in class. Each required reading within a subject area will be indicated with an asterisk (*); read this before we begin to discuss the listed topic.

C. Other Related Readings

This syllabus has been prepared to serve not only as a guide to the course, but also to give you some exposure to literature in environmental and resource economics. For this reason, this syllabus includes some examples of recent research from major publishers and journals. The citations are not intended to be an exhaustive list. They have been included to give you examples of influential or representative approaches and to help you gain more from our class discussions. Lectures will frequently make references to related material, but it will never be presumed that you have read any of the other related readings (in contrast to required readings, above). If you are interested in representative articles on subjects other than those listed in the syllabus, please contact me and I will attempt to provide you with additional citations.

D. Lecture Strategy

The lectures will use the readings as starting points, but will contain references to other readings, empirical results, syntheses of trends in the literature, and discussion of key points from the other relevant readings. Missing a lecture will cost you understanding and perhaps a key inspiration you are seeking. We have roughly thirty hours together:[1] try not to miss even one.

E. Rutgers University Policies

All faculty, staff, and students at our University are bound by University policies. All aspects of this course will be conducted according to these policies. (Please see p12 for additional information.)

---

[1] Environmental and Resource Economics (16:030:509) includes twenty-four class meetings. When all class meetings run the full class period (1:20:00 per lecture), total class time equals 32 hours. (This calculation does not include time spent taking examinations on February 20 1995 and March 27 1995 and completing course evaluations on April 20, 1995.)

151

Texts:

These texts have been ordered for our class. Whether you purchase them is up to you; however, these are widely accepted references for our field, and would be worthwhile additions to your personal library.

Baumol, W.J. and W.E. Oates. 1988. The Theory of Environmental Policy. Second Edition. New York: Cambridge University Press. An accessible book on important considerations for policies intended to correct for externalities (e.g. emissions, effluents).

Freeman, A.M. III. 1993. The Measurement of Environmental and Resource Values: Theory and Methods. Washington: Resources for the Future. A comprehensive overview of microeconomic foundations and key applications of valuation. Empirical references are contained in footnotes.

Neher, P.A. 1991. Natural Resource Economics: Conservation and Exploitation. New York: Cambridge University Press. The style of this text is similar to Fisher's (below). The breadth of coverage is quite good, and includes amenities from natural environments.

Other books with which you may want to be acquainted include:

Costanza, R. (ed.) 1991. Ecological Economics: The Science and Management of Sustainability. New York: Columbia University Press. A collection of contributed chapters on what has become a major area of worldwide interest. Includes overviews, methods, and case studies.

Dorfman, R. and N.S. Dorfman (eds.) 1993. Economics of the Environment: Selected Readings. New York: W.W. Norton and Company. An excellent collection of classic and modern articles. Includes many of the most influential articles written in environmental and natural resource economics.

Fisher, A.C. 1990. Resource and Environmental Economics. Cambridge University Press, New York. This text emphasizes exhaustible and renewable resources and contains an excellent reference section for empirical and analytical articles published prior to 1980.

Hartwick, J.M. and N.E. Olewiler. 1986. The Economics of Natural Resource Use. New York: Harper and Row Publishers. A good book that is intermediate between Tietenberg and most Cambridge Press books. The focus is primarily on resources; pollution externalities are introduced late in the text.

Tietenberg, T. 1992. Environmental and Natural Resource Economics. Third Edition. New York: McGraw-Hill. This widely-used introductory book typically gives a well organized, non mathematical treatment; discussions are well stocked with examples and graphs.

152

Lecture/Discussion Schedule:

Contexts for Environmental and Resource Economics
Thursday, January 19

Dixon, J.A. and P.B. Sherman. (eds.) 1990. Economics of Protected Areas: A New Look at Benefits and Costs. Washington: Island Press.

*Freeman, A.M. III. 1993. "Resource Evaluation and Public Policy." In The Measurement of Environmental and Resource Values: Theory and Methods. Washington: Resources for the Future.

Krutilla, J.V. and A.C. Fisher. 1985. The Economics of Natural Environments: Studies in the Valuation of Commodity and Amenity Resources. Baltimore: Johns Hopkins University Press for Resources for the Future.

Tietenberg, T. 1992. "Economics of the Environment: An Overview." In Environmental and Natural Resource Economics. Third Edition. New York: HarperCollins.

World Commission on Environment and Sustainable Development. 1987. Our Common Future. New York: Oxford University Press.

Analyzing Benefits and Costs from Environmental Decisions and Policies
Monday, January 23
Thursday, January 26

Dixon, J.A. and M.M. Hufschmidt. 1986. Economic Valuation Techniques for the Environment: A Case Study Workbook. Baltimore: Johns Hopkins University Press.

*Freeman, A.M. III. 1993. "Measuring Values and Benefits: An Overview." In The Measurement of Environmental and Resource Values: Theory and Methods. Washington: Resources for the Future.

Kelman, S. 1981. "Cost-Benefit Analysis: An Ethical Critique." Regulation (January/February): 33-41.

Mishan, E.J. 1976. Cost-Benefit Analysis. Second Edition. New York: Praeger Publishers.

Tietenberg, T. 1992. "Regulating the Market, Information and Uncertainty." In Environmental and Natural Resource Economics, Third Edition. New York: HarperCollins.

Microeconomic Foundations for Changes in Welfare
Monday, January 30
Thursday, February 2

*Freeman, A.M. III. 1993. "Defining and Measuring Welfare Changes: Basic Theory." In The Measurement of Environmental and Resource Values: Theory and Methods. Washington: Resources for the Future.

Johansson, P.O. 1987. The Economic Theory and Measurement of Environmental Benefits. New York: Cambridge University Press.

Just, R.E., D.L. Hueth, and A. Schmitz. 1982. Applied Welfare Economics and Public Policy. Englewood Cliffs: Prentice-Hall, Inc.

Externalities and Property Rights
Monday, February 6
Thursday, February 9

*Baumol, W.J. and W.E. Oates. 1988. "Externalities: Definition, Significant Types, and Optimal Pricing Conditions." In The Theory of Environmental Policy. Second Edition. New York: Cambridge University Press.

*Baumol, W.J. and W.E. Oates. 1988. "Externalities: Formal Analysis." In The Theory of Environmental Policy. Second Edition. New York: Cambridge University Press.

Coase, R. 1960. "The Problem of Social Cost." Journal of Law and Economics 3(October): 1-44.

Tietenberg, T. 1992. "Property Rights, Externalities, and Environmental Problems." In Environmental and Natural Resource Economics. Third Edition. New York: HarperCollins.

Policies and Policy Tools: Introduction
Monday, February 13
Thursday, February 16

*Baumol, W.J. and W.E. Oates. 1988. "Uncertainty and the Choice of Policy Instruments: Price or Quantity Controls?" In The Theory of Environmental Policy. Second Edition. New York: Cambridge University Press.

Portney, P.R. (ed.) 1990. Public Policies for Environmental Protection. Washington: Resources for the Future.

Midterm Exam I
Monday, February 20

Charges, Standards, and Tradeable Permits
Thursday, February 23
Monday, February 27

*Baumol, W.J. and W.E. Oates. 1988. "Efficiency without Optimality: The Charges and Standards Approach." In The Theory of Environmental Policy. Second Edition. New York: Cambridge University Press.

*Baumol, W.J. and W.E. Oates. 1988. "Marketable Emissions Permits for the Protection of the Environment." In The Theory of Environmental Policy. Second Edition. New York: Cambridge University Press.

Hahn, R.W. 1989. "Economic Prescriptions for Environmental Problems: How the Patient has Followed the Doctor's Orders." Journal of Economic Perspectives 3(Spring): 95-114.

Tietenberg, T. 1992. "Economics of Pollution Control: An Overview." In Environmental and Natural Resource Economics, Third Edition. New York: HarperCollins.

Distribution of Benefits and Costs from Environmental Policies
Thursday, March 2

*Baumol, W.J. and W.E. Oates. 1988. "Environmental Protection and Income Distribution." In The Theory of Environmental Policy. Second Edition. New York: Cambridge University Press.

Dorfman, R. 1977. "Incidence of the Benefits and Costs of Environmental Programs." American Economic Review 67(February): 333-340.

Peskin, H. 1978. "Environmental Policy and the Distribution of Benefits and Costs." In Current Issues in U.S. Environmental Policy, P. Portney (ed.) Baltimore: Johns Hopkins University Press for Resources for the Future.

Tietenberg, T. 1992. "Pollution Control Policy: Distributional Effects." In Environmental and Natural Resource Economics, Third Edition. New York: HarperCollins.

Introduction to Exhaustible Resources
Monday, March 6
Thursday, March 9

*Baumol, W.J. and W.E. Oates. 1988. "On the Optimal Pricing of Exhaustible Resources." In The Theory of Environmental Policy. Second Edition. New York: Cambridge University Press.

*Fisher, A.C. 1981. "Exhaustible Resources: The Theory of Optimal Depletion." In Resource and Environmental Economics. New York: Cambridge University Press.

Hotelling, H. 1931. "The Economics of Exhaustible Resources." Journal of Political Economy 30(2): 137-175.

Krutilla, J.V. 1967. "Conservation Reconsidered." American Economic Review 47(1967):777-786.

*Neher, P.A. 1990. "The Mine." In Natural Resource Economics: Conservation and Exploitation. New York: Cambridge University Press.

Solow, R.M. 1974. "The Economics of Resources or the Resources of Economics." American Economic Review 61(1):1-14.

Spring Recess
Monday, March 13
Thursday, March 16

Fisheries and Common Pool Renewable Resources
Monday, March 20
Thursday, March 23

*Fisher, A.C. 1981. "Renewable Resources: The Theory of Optimal Use." In Resource and Environmental Economics. New York: Cambridge University Press.

Gordon, H.S. 1954. "The Economic Theory of Common Property." Journal of Political Economy 62(1): 124-142.

*Neher, P.A. 1990. "The Fishery." In Natural Resource Economics: Conservation and Exploitation. New York: Cambridge University Press.

Neher, P.A. 1990. "Aquifers and Other Common Pools." In Natural Resource Economics: Conservation and Exploitation. New York: Cambridge University Press.

Midterm Exam II
Monday, March 27

Forests and Natural Environments
Thursday, March 30

Hartman, R. 1976. "The Harvesting Decision When a Standing Forest Has Value." Economic Inquiry 14(1976): 52-58.

Krutilla, J.V. and A.C. Fisher. 1985. The Economics of Natural Environments: Studies in the Valuation of Commodites and Amenity Resources. Baltimore: Johns Hopkins University Press for Resources for the Future.

Johansson, P.O. 1987. "Money Measures of the Total Value of Environmental Resources." In The Economic Theory and Measurement of Environmental Benefits. New York: Cambridge University Press.

Loomis, J.B. 1993. Integrated Public Lands Management: Principles and Applications to National Forests, Parks, Wildlife Refuges and BLM Lands. New York: Columbia University Press.

157

*Neher, P.A. 1990. "Amenity Values." In <u>Natural Resource Economics: Conservation and Exploitation</u>. New York: Cambridge University Press.

*Neher, P.A. 1990. "The Environment." In <u>Natural Resource Economics: Conservation and Exploitation</u>. New York: Cambridge University Press.

*Neher, P.A. 1990. "The Forest." In <u>Natural Resource Economics: Conservation and Exploitation</u>. New York: Cambridge University Press.

Samuelson, P.A. 1976. "Economics of Forestry in an Evolving Society." <u>Economic Inquiry</u> 14(1976): 466-492.

Indirect Benefit Estimation and Nonuse Values
Monday, April 3
Thursday, April 6

*Freeman, A.M. III. 1993. "Models for Indirect Benefit Estimation: Basic Theory." In <u>The Measurement of Environmental and Resource Values: Theory and Methods</u>. Washington: Resources for the Future.

*Freeman, A.M. III. 1993. "Nonuse Values." In <u>The Measurement of Environmental and Resource Values: Theory and Methods</u>. Washington: Resources for the Future.

Smith, V.K., W.H. Desvouges, and A. Fisher. 1986. "A Comparison of Direct and Indirect Methods for Estimating Environmental Benefits." <u>American Journal of Agricultural Economics</u> 68(2): 280-290.

Hypothetical Methods for Valuation
Monday, April 10
Thursday, April 13

*Freeman, A.M. III. 1993. "Hypothetical Methods for Direct and Indirect Valuation." In <u>The Measurement of Environmental and Resource Values: Theory and Methods</u>. Washington: Resources for the Future.

Mitchell, R.C. and R.T. Carson. 1989. <u>Using Surveys to Value Public Goods: The Contingent Valuation Method</u>. Washington: Resources for the Future.

Environmental Quality as a Factor Input
Monday, April 17

Ellis, G.M. and A.C. Fisher. 1987. "Valuing the Environment as an Input." Journal of Environmental Management 25(2): 149-156.

*Freeman, A.M. III. 1993. "Environmental Quality as a Factor Input." In The Measurement of Environmental and Resource Values: Theory and Methods. Washington: Resources for the Future.

Course Evaluations
Thursday, April 20

Property Values and Recreation Benefits
Monday, April 24
Thursday, April 27

*Freeman, A.M. III. 1993. "Property Value Models." In The Measurement of Environmental and Resource Values: Theory and Methods. Washington: Resources for the Future.

*Freeman, A.M. III. 1993. "Recreational Uses of Natural Systems." In The Measurement of Environmental and Resource Values: Theory and Methods. Washington: Resources for the Future.

Classes End
Monday, May 1

Policy Paper Presentations
Week of Monday, May 1

Final Examination
Time To Be Announced

Grading Policies:

5%	Professor's Discretion
20%	Exam I
20%	Exam II
25%	Policy Analysis Paper (See Below)
30%	Final Examination (Comprehensive)
100%	Total

Letter Grade Assignments:

At any time you may calculate your grade in this course. There is a total of 100 points possible (see above). Final grades will be assigned using the scale given below. To calculate your expected final grade, simply add the grades from your completed exams with the grades you plan to get on forthcoming exams and refer to the table below.

90+	A
85+	B+
80+	B
75+	C+
70+	C
60+	D
60-	F

Policy Analysis Paper:

This assignment is designed to provide you with an opportunity to test your own knowledge of environmental and resource economic principles on your own time and at your own pace. By successfully completing this assignment, you will have prepared a high-quality paper, and have obtained first-hand experience with applying economic policy analysis to a problem that is important to you. There are only a few general guidelines to help you succeed more easily.

Fifteen percent of the grade will be on your written paper. The remaining ten percent of your grade will be based on a twenty minute presentation (fifteen minutes talk plus five for discussion) made by you in the evening towards the end of the course. We will discuss the timing of presentations as a group during class.

Students must meet with the instructor to discuss topic and general nature of the paper, and must submit a written one-page statement of the topic and a brief outline by 5:00pm Friday, February 24. No paper will be accepted unless it has been discussed with the instructor before writing begins. The final draft of your paper is due by 5:00pm Friday, May 5. Although earlier submissions are welcome, there will be no exceptions to this final deadline.

Drawing on published literature and your experience as an economist and analyst, write a paper that analyzes a resource or environmental issue that *(i)* is the subject of existing policy or *(ii)* should be the subject of new policy. You are free to choose whatever topic is of interest to you. The only restriction is that there is an obvious link between your topic and resources or the environment.

1. (2.5 Points). At a minimum, comment on the presence or absence of economic efficiency and equity in the context of your topic; both within and between generations. This will require you to state your definition of an efficient condition and an equitable distribution of benefits and costs. These two concepts are to be the heart of your paper, and must be in your own words and applied directly to your topic. (Realize that these efficiency and equity issues may include equity between countries effected by the policy.)

2. (2.5 Points). In addition, your paper should discuss at least one of the following concepts as it relates to your topic: *(i)* property rights (including excludability and subtractibility attributes); *(ii)* externalities; *(iii)* proposed policies; or *(iv)* existing policies.

3. (2.5 Points). Your paper must demonstrate original thinking by you that convinces your reader that you have a thorough understanding of your topic. While writing the paper may require some summarizing of existing work as a point of departure, a review of literature is not acceptable by itself. This paper is an important opportunity for you to use your analytical skills and to sharpen your ability to communicate.

4. (7.5 Points). Your writing should be clear, concise, and directed toward an audience of your peers. Maximum length is twelve double-spaced pages, not including tables, figures or references. For general help with economic writing style, see McCloskey, D.N. 1987. The Writing of Economics. New York: MacMillan Publishing Company. For an excellent short discussion of communicating effectively and meeting readers' expectations, see Gopen, G.D. and J.A. Swan. 1990. "The Science of Scientific Writing." American Scientist 78(2):125-134.

Good places to obtain current ideas and examine writing styles include the Journal of Environmental Economics and Management, American Journal of Agricultural Economics, and Land Economics. The Journal of Economic Literature December issue contains an index to titles in these and many other journals.

Rutgers University Policies:

The reference for Rutgers University policies that will be used in the conduct of this course is pp461-473 in

Rutgers, The State University of New Jersey, Campus at New Brunswick. 1992. New Brunswick Undergraduate Catalog, 1993-1995. New Brunswick.

All sections of this discussion on policy are of vital importance to you as a Rutgers University student; however for the purposes of this course, please pay particular attention to sections on Registration, Attendance, Nondiscrimination, Policy Against Insult, Defamation, and Harassment, Sexual Harassment, Administrative Policy for Responding to Disruptions, Academic Integrity, and the University Student Disciplinary Hearing Procedure.

Should you have any questions about Rutgers University policies, please contact the personnel listed in the Undergraduate Catalog.

Environmental and Resource Economics
(16:030:509, Spring 1995)

Midterm Exam I
(Closed Book)

This exam is worth twenty percent of your course grade. There are two problems to this exam, each worth ten points. Answer all questions to obtain full credit. Partial credit will be given, so it is to your advantage to show all your work. Read the entire exam carefully before you begin your work, so that you can allocate your time wisely.

Consider an economic system with j goods ($j=1, ..., m$). Let

$$x_{ji} \quad = \quad \text{the amount of good } j \text{ consumed by individual } i \ (i=1, ..., n),$$
$$y_{jk} \quad = \quad \text{the amount of good } j \text{ produced by firm } k \ (k=1, ..., h),$$
$$s_j \quad = \quad \text{the endowment of good (resource) } j \text{ available to the economy.}$$

For each of the goods, production and consumption must balance via

$$s_j + \Sigma_k y_{jk} - \Sigma_i x_{ji} = 0, \ (j=1, ..., m).$$

Public goods, r, are limited to no more than r^*. A pollutant, d, is perfectly mixed, unavoidable, and undepletable, so that the amount of pollutant experienced by each consumer is equal to aggregate emissions, i.e.,

$$d = \Sigma_k d_k$$

Individual i's utility is $u^i = u^i(x_{ji}, r, d)$ where $\partial u^i/\partial x_{ji} > 0$, $\partial u^i/\partial r > 0$, and $\partial u^i/\partial d < 0$. You may assume whatever you require for concavity and convexity.

Firm k's production is $f^k(y_{jk}, r, d_k)$ where $\partial f^k/\partial y_{jk} > 0$ and $\partial f^k/\partial d_k < 0$. Recognize that *(i)* more output is associated with more pollution, and *(ii)* the firm is immune to pollution under these conditions. You may assume whatever you require about the influence of public goods, r, on the production process.

(1) (10 points) For this economy, the Minister of the Environment and Economic Development is considering using the social welfare function L^I (below) to determine Pareto efficient policies. You may assume an interior solution for all variables.

$$\max L^I = u^I(\,\cdot\,) + \Sigma_{i=2,n}\, \lambda_i\, [u^{i*} - u^i(\,\cdot\,)] - \Sigma_{k=1,h}\, \mu_k\, f^k(\,\cdot\,)$$

$$+ \Sigma_{j=1,m}\, \rho_j\, (\, s_j + \Sigma_k y_{jk} - \Sigma_i x_{ji}\,) + \gamma\,(r^* - r).$$

(a) (3 points) Show that the marginal value of the public good is comprised of its value to consumers and producers. (This may be a net value, depending on your assumptions about the sign of $\partial f^k/\partial r$.)

(b) (3 points) Show that to maximize societal economic welfare, the Minister must equate *(i)* the marginal value of the production permitted by increasing emissions of firm k with *(ii)* the marginal disutility cost that the added pollution imposes.

(c) (4 points) Assuming that the economy is perfectly competitive, write (but do not derive) an externality tax that will lead a competitive firm to operate in a manner that optimizes the Minister's objective.

(2) (10 points) Consider a firm which emits pollution that is unpleasant for the firm's neighbors. Please complete the following table, given the implicit property rights and policy questions to be answered.

For each policy question, indicate **(a)** (6 points) the identity of gainers and losers, and whether a compensating or equivalent measure is needed to measure welfare changes, **(b)** (2 points) whether that measure is willingness to pay (*WTP*) or willingness to accept compensation (*WAC*), and **(c)** (2 points) the *WTP* and *WAC* conditions in your table that are required for the policy to pass a Kaldor potential compensation test.

Implicit Rights	Policy Question	Gainers	Losers
To the present polluter	Require clean up?		
To the potential polluter	Allow pollution?		
To the neighbors	Require clean up?		
To the neighbors	Allow pollution?		

The Ohio State University

Agricultural Economics 831
Resource Economics
Winter, 1995

Schedule: Agricultural Engineering 104
Tuesday and Thursday, 11:00 a.m. - 12:30 p.m.

Instructor: Alan Randall, 333 Agricultural Administration
292-6423

Secretary: Shelley Wehinger
331 Agricultural Administration
292-6971

Books:

1. Textbook:
    Randall, Alan, 1987. *Resource Economics*, Wiley. Second Edition

    Optional:
    Howe, Charles W., 1979. *Natural Resource Economics*, Wiley.

2. Edited reference books:

    D.W. Bromley (ed.) 1995. *The Handbook of Environmental Economics*,
    Blackwell.

    Dorfman, R. and N. Dorfman (eds.) 1992. *Economics of the Environment* (3rd ed.)
    Norton.

    Oates, W. E. (ed.) 1992. *The Economics of the Environment*. Edward Elgar.

    Kneese, A.V. and J.L. Sweeney (eds.) *Handbook of Natural Resource and Energy
    Economics*, North-Holland. Vols. 1 and 2, 1985; Vol. 3, 1993.

3. Theory and applications of welfare change measurement, fundamental to policy
    evaluation and benefit cost analysis, are covered in:

    Boadway, R.W., and N. Bruce, 1984. *Welfare Economics*, Blackwell.

1

Just, R.E., D.L. Hueth and A. Schmitz, 1982. *Applied Welfare Economics and Public Policy*, Prentice-Hall.

4.   Empirical methods of estimating environmental benefits are covered in:

Braden, J.B. and CD Kolstad (eds.), 1991, *Measuring the Demand for Environmental Improvements*, North-Holland.

Freeman, A.M. III, 1993. *The Measurement of Environmental and Resource Values: Theory and Methods*, Resources for the Future.

5.   Dynamic optimization methods, useful in intertemporal resource allocation are introduced in:

Conrad, J.M. and C.W. Clark, 1987. *Natural Resource Economics: Notes and Problems*, Cambridge U. Press.

GRADING:

Midterm exam	30%
Final exam	40%
Term paper	30%
	100%

Make-up examinations will be provided only in the most unusual circumstances and only by prior arrangement with the instructor or upon presentation of evidence of medical incapacitation. In grading examinations and assignments the following criteria will be used.

1.   Logical rigor of the argument.
2.   Correct use of economic concepts in analysis of the topic at hand.
3.   Demonstrated understanding of the social institutional and legal framework within which resource-related conflicts are resolved.
4.   Presentation (i.e., correct use of language, adequate labeling of diagrams and definition of symbols, etc.).

The term paper is due at the last scheduled class period. The paper must address a topic relevant to natural resource and environmental policy, and must demonstrate the use of economic concepts. Topic should be chosen in consultation with the instructor, no later than the end of the third week of class.

2

Topical Outline and Reading List

Reading assignments are identified as followed:

*required
supplementary readings for students seeking advanced material
+classics.

1. **Efficiency and Economic Well Being**

   *Randall, Ch. 5,7.
   +Bator, F.M., "The Simple Analytics of Welfare Maximization," *Am. Econ. Rev.*,
   March 1957 also in *AEA Readings in Welfare Economics*.
   Silberberg. E., 1978. *The Structure of Economics*, Ch. 15.
   Boadway & Bruce, Ch. 2,3,5.
   *Arrow, K., 1967. Chapter 1, S. Hook (ed.) *Human Values and Economic Policy*,
   NYU Press.
   +Arrow, K., 1951. *Social Choice and Individual Values*, Wiley.
   +Bergson, A., 1938. "A Reformulation of Certain Aspects of Welfare Economics,"
   Quarterly Journal of Economics.
   +Lipsey, R. and K. Lancaster, 1957. "The General Theory of Second Best,"
   Rev. Econ. Stud.
   *Davis, O. and A. Whinston, 1965. "Welfare Economics and the Theory of Second
   Best," *Rev. Econ. Stud.*
   Maler, K-G, "Welfare Economics and the Environment," Ch. 1, in Kneese and
   Sweeney.
   Rawls, J. 1971. *A Theory of Justice*. Harvard U. Press. Ch. 3.

2. **Market Failure: Nonrivalry, Nonexclusiveness, Externality**

   *Randall, Ch. 8,9.
   +Samuelson, P., "The Pure Theory of Public Expenditure," *Rev. Econ. and Stat.*,
   1954, 387-89, also in *AEA Readings in Welfare Economics* (and "A
   Diagrammatic Exposition..." RES 1955 p. 53).
   *Davis and Whinston, "On the Distinction between Private and Public Goods," *Amer.
   Econ. Rev.* 57:360-373, 1967.
   *Ciriacy - Wantrup S. and R. Bishop, "Common Property as a Concept in Natural
   Resources," *Nat. Resources J.*, 15:713-728, 1975.
   Smith, V.L., "Experiments with Decentralized Mechanisms for Public Goods
   Decisions,"
   Am. Econ. Rev., 70: 584-599, 1980.
   *Axelrod, R., "The Emergence of Cooperation Among Egoists," *Am. Poli. Sci. Rev.*,
   75: 306-318, 1982.

3

*Randall, "The Problem of Market Failure," *Natural Resources Journal*, 23: 131-148, 1983.

*Randall, "Market Failure and the Efficiency of Irrigated Agriculture," reprint.

*Farrell, J., "Information and the Coase Theorem," *J. Econ. Perspectives*, 1:113-130, 1987.

+Coase, R., "The Problem of Social Cost," *J. Law and Econ.* 3, 1960, 1-44.

+Cheung, S., "The Structure of a Contract and the Theory of a NonExclusive Resource," *J. Law and Econ.*, 15, 1970, p. 49.

+Randall, "Market Solutions to Externality Problems: Theory and Practice," *Am. J. Agr. Econ.*, 54, May 1972, 175-183.

+Buchanan, J. and W.C. Stubblebine, "Externality," Economics 1962, 371-384, also in *AEA Readings in Welfare Economics*.

+Ayres and Kneese, "Production, Consumption, and Externalities," *Am. Econ. Rev.*, 59, 1969, p. 282.

*Fisher, A. and F. Peterson, "The Economics of Environment: A. Survey," *J. Econ. Lit.*, 14: 1-33, 1976.

Maler, K.G., *Environmental Economics* (John Hopkins RFF, 1974).

Baumol and Oates, *The Theory of Environmental Policy*, (2nd ed.) Cambridge University Press, 1988.

*Bromley: Chapters 13, Segerson; 15, Tietenberg.

3.   **Investment Theory, Asset Markets and Intertemporal Allocation of Resources**

*Randall, Ch. 6,15,17,18.

*Howe, Ch. 2, 4-7,10,11,13.

Conrad and Clark, Ch. 2,3.

Randall and E.N. Castle, 1985. "Land Resources and Land Markets," Ch. 13 in Kneese and Sweeney.

+Solow, R., 1974. "Intergenerational Equity and Exhaustible Resources," *Rev. Econ. Stud: Symposium.*

*McInerney, J., 1976. "The Simple Analytics of Natural Resource Economics," *J. Agri. Econ.*, 27:31-52.

*McInerney, J., 1978. "On the Optimal Policy for Exploiting Renewable Resource Stocks," *J. Agri. Econ.*, 29:183-188.

+Dasgupta, P. and G. Heal, 1974. "The Optimal Depletion of Exhaustible Resources," *Rev. Econ. Stud: Symposium.*

Dasgupta, P. and G. Heal, 1979. *Economic Theory of Exhaustible Resources*, Cambridge University Press.

Heal, G., 1986. "Optimal Resource Depletion Policies," Ch. 18 in Kneese and Sweeney.

*Solow, R. 1988 "Growth Theory and After," *Amer. Econ. Rev.* 78:307-317

*Howarth, R.B. and R.B. Norgaard, 1990. "Intergenerational Resource Rights," *Land Econ.* 66: 1-11.

*Bromley: Chapter 7, Toman et al.

4

4. Policy Evaluation

*Randall, Ch. 13,14.
Just et al:
  * Ch. 4-6.
   Ch. 7-9, Appendices A-D.
*Boadway and Bruce, Ch. 7-8.

*Bergland, O. and Randall, 1984. "Operational Methods for Calculating Exact
    Hicksian Consumer Surpluses from Observable Data."
+Hicks, J.R., 1943. "The Four Consumer Surpluses," *Rev. Econ. Stud.*, 11: 31-41.
+Hicks, J.R., 1939. "The Foundations of Welfare Economics," *Econ. J.*,
    49:696-712.
+Kaldor, N., 1939. "Welfare Propositions in Economics," *Econ. J.*, 49: 549-552.
 Peterson, G. and Randall, 1984. *Valuation of Wildland Resource Benefits*, Westview,
    Ch. 1-4.
*Freeman, A.M., 1985. "Methods for Assessing the Benefits of Environmental
    Programs," Ch. 6 in Kneese and Sweeney.
 McConnell, K., 1985. "The Economics of Outdoor Recreation," Ch. 15 in Kneese
    and Sweeney.
+Krutilla, J., "Conservation Reconsidered," *Am. Econ. Rev.*, 57, 1967, 77-86.
*Graham, D., "Benefit Cost Analysis Under Uncertainty," *Amer. Econ. Rev.*, 71,
    113-23, 1981.
 Randall and J. Stoll, 1983. "Existence Value in a Total Valuation Framework," in
    Rowe, R. and L. Chestnut (eds.) *Managing Air Quality and Scenic Resources
    at National Parks and Wilderness Areas*, Westview.
*Meier, C.E., and A. Randall, 1991. "Use Value Under Uncertainty." *Land Econ.*
    67:379-389
*Braden and Kolstad: Chapters 4, Palmquist; 5, Carson; 8, Bockstael, et al; 10,
    Randall,
*Randall, A. 1994 "Biodiversity and a Safe Minimum Standard of Conservation",
    University of Wisconsin, Madison.
*Bromley: Chapters 2, Randall and Farmer; 24. Bishop and Woodward; 25, Ready;
    27, Freeman; 28, Bishop et al.; 29, Bockstael; 30, Freeman.

5

The Ohio State University

AE 831
Resource Economics

Final Examination   Winter, 1995
Time Allowed: 2 hours   March 14, 1995

Answer questions 1, 2, and 3 in the space provided.

---

1. (*60 points*). Answer **FOUR** (4) of the **FIVE** (5) parts. Provide a concise
    explanation, derivation, and/or supporting argument.

    a.   "A farmer approaching retirement is likely to underinvest in soil
         conservation."

         Do you agree or disagree?

    b.   Under baseline conditions, mineral exploration sites are nonexclusive. Show
         how a new policy of auctioning exploration leases would affect:
         •   the price of mineral raw materials.
         •   the quantity of newly extracted minerals.
         •   the asset value of mineral reserves.

    c.   Compared to command-and-control standards, develop the arguments in favor
         of marketable air pollution emissions permits.

    d.   What is the theoretical justification for techniques, such as the travel cost
         method, that use market observations to estimate the value of nonmarketed
         goods?

    e.   Economist Lawrence Summers has recently argued that opportunities exist for
         welfare-enhancing international trade in pollution. Specifically, pollution-
         intensive industries might relocate from high-income countries to low-income
         countries, with beneficial effects on both.

         What do you think?

2. (*20 points*). What role, if any, should benefit cost analysis play in the public decision
    process concerning preservation of natural habitats? Explain.

3. (*20 points*) Answer all parts. Are the statements **TRUE (T), FALSE (F)**, or **UNCERTAIN (U)**? Please circle the correct response. Do not explain your answers.

T   F   U   a.   In a test for potential Pareto-improvements, an increment in q from $q°$ to q' is valued at $e(p°, s°, q', u') - e(p°, s°, q°, u')$.

T   F   U   b.   In a Pareto-efficient economy, there is no unimplemented proposal with a benefit cost ratio greater than one.

T   F   U   c.   A biological resource cannot achieve a sustainable bounded equilibrium unless at some stages of the growth curve $g > r$ and at other stages $g < r$, where g is the growth rate and r is the rate of interest.

T   F   U   d.   With $r > 0$, the optimal age of trees at harvest is less than the age at which stumpage value is maximized.

T   F   U   e.   Accelerated tax write-offs for mineral exploration would tend to decrease the price paid for aluminum cans at the local recycling center.

T   F   U   f.   Where a project may be built at any of several sizes, the most efficient size is that which maximizes the internal rate of return.

T   F   U   g.   With identical preferences and commuting cost per mile, lower-income households will live closer to the city center.

T   F   U   h.   The expectation of eventual conversion to urban uses increases the price of farm land today.

T   F   U   i.   If $u(z,s,q) = u_{z,q}(z,q) + u_s(s)$, the demand system for z contains information on the value of s but not of q.

T   F   U   j.   It is easy to produce a free-market environmentalist. All one needs to do is buy a parrot and teach it to repeat "Property Rights! Property Rights!"

Note: In the midterm, the analogous statement was: It is easy to produce a resource economist. All one needs to do is buy a parrot and teach it to repeat "Market failure! Market failure!"

2

Vanderbilt University

Revised 26 Dec '94

Russell & Weinhold

ECONOMICS 269 (Sec. 3)
Spring 1995

UG

Trade, Economic Development & Environmental Quality
MWF 1:10-2:00 p.m. • Furman 325

This course will explore the relation between economic development (industrialization, mechanization of agriculture, rising real incomes and consumption standards, improving health, etc.) and environmental quality (air and water, ecosystems, species diversity, etc.). We shall consider as well the complications implied by international trade (the movement of goods, including intrinsically polluting substances such as pesticides; the movement of production facilities; and even the movement of wastes).

After reviews of the key concepts in each of the areas of concern, we shall consider the state of thinking in each area as it relates to the central relationship. Then we shall consider what amount to case study problems such as rivers, forests, and agriculture; and cross cutting issues such as the influence of the local governing system.

To the extent possible we want to avoid a lecture/listen format. Students will be expected to do the readings on time and to participate in class discussions. If things are slow we shall call on individuals by name. At least once during the semester (depending on the final class enrollment) each student will be part of a debate team that will take one side of an assigned issue and argue it in front of the class. (Each team will also prepare a briefing paper of 2 or 3 pages outlining its argument.)

[The first topic, with the debate scheduled for the third class period, will be: Resolved: that the concern about the environmental costs of economic development is just part of a plot by Western (industrialized; Northern) nations to keep the "South" poor.]

There will be one short (5 to 10 double space pages) position paper on a case study or problem area not covered in class and readings.

Grades for the course will be determined as follows:

	%
Debate/Briefing paper	15
Position Paper	20
Class participation	25
Take home final	40
	100

The textbook is <u>Sustainable Development</u> by Pearce, Barbier and Markandya (Edward Elgar, 1990), referred to in the reading list as PBM.

1

10   •   Sustainable Development, David Pearce, Edward Barbier, and Amil Markandya (Edward Elgar) Aldershot, Hants, U.K., 1990, (PBM), Chapters 1-3.   (63)

11   •   "Economics and Sustainability: Balancing Tradeoffs and Imperatives," Toman, ENR 91-05 Rev., RFF 1991.   (19)

12   •   "Economic Theory and 'Sustainability'", Toman, Pezzey and Krautkraemer, ENR 93-14-REV, RFF 1993.   (24)

Weeks
4, 5   **Review and Introduction: Issues in Development Economics**

Introduction to Development Economics

13   •   Meier, Gerald M., 1989. "What Do We Mean by "Economic Development?" Leading Issues in Economics Development. Fifth Edition, Oxford University Press.

Ahluwalia, M.S., and Hollis B. Chenery, 1989. "Measuring Development", in Leading Issues in Economics Development. Fifth Edition, Oxford University Press.

14   •   Erlich, Isaac, 1990. "The Problem of Development: Introduction", Journal of Political Economy. Vol. 98, No. 5, pt 2, S1-S11.

15   •   Summers, Lawrence A., and Thomas Vinod, 1993. "Recent Lessons of Development", World Bank Research Observer, Vol. 8, No. 2, July.

The World Wide Process of Development

16   •   Reynolds, Lloyd G., 1983. The Spread of Economic Growth to the Third World: 1850-1980", Journal of Economic Literature, Vol. XXI, September.

17   •   Ranis, Gustav, 1984. "Typology in Development Theory: Retrospective and Prospects" in L.M. Syrquin and L.E. Westphal (Eds.) Economic Structure and Performance. Academic Press.

Weeks
6, 7   **Trade and Macroeconomic Issues in Development**

Economic Development and International Trade

18   •   Bhagwati, Jagdish, and Anne O. Krueger, 1973. "Exchange Control, Liberalization, and Economic Development", American Economic Review, May.

3

19   •   Krueger, Anne O., 1983. "The Effects of Trade Strategy on Growth", <u>Finance and Development</u>. June.

20   •   Grossman, Gene M., and Elhanan Helpman, 1990. "Comparative Advantage and Long-Run Growth", <u>American Economic Review</u>. September.

21   •   Weinhold, D., and Mike Klasen, 1992. "Supplier Networks, Multinationals and Development", Center for U.S.-Mexican Studies Monograph, UCSD.

Empirical Evidence and Discussion

22   •   Easterly, W., M. Kremer, L. Pritchett, and L.H. Summers, 1993. "Good Policy or Good Luck? Country Growth Performance and Temporary Shocks", NBER Working Paper 4474, September.

Weeks 8-13   **Special Topics and Case Studies**

Overview

23   •   "Environment, Income, and Development in Southern Africa," Duane Chapman, EPAT #7, January 1993.   (14)

24   •   "The 'Second India' Revisited: Population, Poverty and Environmental Stress Over Two Decades," Repetto WRI, August 1994.   (4)

Watersheds and Rivers

25   •   PBM Chapter 4 (Java).   (22)

26   •   "The Planning and Management of African River and Lake Basin Development and Conservation," Maher, <u>Natural Resources Forum</u>, February 1989.   (12)

27   •   "Recent Experiences with River Basin Development in the Tropics and Sub-Tropics," Scudder, <u>Natural Resources Forum</u>, May 1994.   (14)

Forests, Forestry, Erosion...

28   •   <u>PBM</u> Chapters 5, 8, 9   (62)

29   •   "Extractive Reserves: Distribution of Wealth and the Social Costs of Frontier Development in the Amazon," Schwartzman 1989.   (17)

Policies and Problems for Governments and Economists

5

Trade

42 • "Trade, Environment and Development: The Issues in Perspective," Ekins, Folkes, and Costanza; Beyer reprint from Ecological Economics, 1994. (12)

43 • "The Greening of Protectionism," Economist, 27 February 1993. (3)

44 • "Environmental Regulation and International Competitiveness: Thinking About the Porter Hypothesis," Oates, Palmer, and Portney, 94-02, RFF, 1994. (24)

45 • Radetzki, Marian, 1992. "Economic Growth and the Environment", in Patrick Low (ed.) International Trade and the Environment. World Bank Discussion Paper 159.

Multilateral Lending

46 • "The Multilateral Development Banks, Environmental Policy and the U.S.," Rich, Ecology Law Quarterly, 1985. (65)

47 • "The Greening of Giving," Economist, January 1994. (3)

48 • Overview Chapter (pp. 2-23) from Making Development Sustainable, The World Bank, 1994. (22)

Country-to-Country Aid

49 • AID Evaluation News, "Focus on the Environment," 1992. (12)

Supporting Nongovernmental Organizations

50 • "Environmentalism South," Durning, Amicus, 1990. (7)

Debt-for-Nature Swaps

51 • "The Structure of an Environmental Transaction: The Debt for Nature Swap," Deacon and Murphy, unpublished, 1994. (27)

52 • GAO, "Developing Country Debt: Debt Swaps for Development and Nature Provide Little Debt Relief," December 1991. (17)

Population

53 • "Population Policy Options in the Developing World," Bongaarts, Science, February 1994, 771-776. (6)

The "Rule of Law"

54 • Deforestation and the Rule of law in a Cross-Section of Countries," Deacon, 1994. (29)

REVISED READING ASSIGNMENTS
ECON 269
Russell/Weinhold
Spring 1995

KEY: [Date / Reading #]

WEEK	MONDAY	WEDNESDAY	FRIDAY
1		11 Jan none	13 Jan 1
2	16 Jan 2	18 Jan none [Debate]	20 Jan 3
3	23 Jan 4	25 Jan 5,6	27 Jan 7,8,9
4	30 Jan 10	1 Feb 11,12	3 Feb 13
5	6 Feb 14	8 Feb 15	10 Feb 16
6	13 Feb 17	15 Feb 18	17 Feb 19
7	20 Feb 20	22 Feb 21	24 Feb none [Debate]
8	27 Feb 22	Mar 1 23,24	3 Mar 25,26,27
		B R E A K	
9	13 Mar 28	15 Mar 29,30	17 Mar 31
10	20 Mar 32	22 Mar 33	24 Mar 34
11	27 Mar none [Debate]	29 Mar 35-38	31 Mar 39-41
12	3 Apr none [Debate]	5 Apr 42,43	7 Apr 44
13	10 Apr 45	12 Apr 46	14 Apr 47,48
14	17 Apr 49,50	19 Apr 51,52	21 Apr 53
15	24 Apr none [Review]		

177

Environmental Economics: Risk, Conflict, and Resolution UG

Econ 579
Spring 95
MWF 9—Heady 162

J Shogren
468 Heady Hall
294-6231
Office Hrs—Mon. afternoon and by appointment

Introduction

This course explores the economics of environmental management. The goal is to introduce students to the theories of environmental risk, conflict and resolution, the empirical tools, and their application to environmental issues such as water pollution control, air quality, biodiversity, and hazardous waste disposal.

Grading

1 Mid-term exam	35%
1 Final exam	35%
1 Paper	30%

Your paper should examine an specific environmental risk or conflict, explaining the economics behind the problem and the economics leading to a potential resolution. The risk or conflict can be local, regional, national or international in scope. You should consider the costs and benefits associated with resolving or ignoring the risk or conflict. Sound economic reasoning is expected.

    —16 page limit on text
    —abstract due by Feb. 10
    —first draft (optional) due by April 14
    —final version due by May 12

Note—early papers are acceptable, late papers are not.

Readings

No assigned text.   A readings packet will be available, and will be on reserve in the Economics Reading Room, 3rd floor of Heady Hall.

Course Outline

- **Introduction**
  - What is the economics of environmental risk, conflict, and resolution
  - What has environmental economics accomplished over the past 25 years
  - What has environmental economics failed to deliver
  - What is the future of environmental economics

- **Environmental Risk**
  - Defining Risk
  - Environmental Risk Analysis
    - Risk Assessment
    - Risk Perception
    - Risk Valuation
    - Risk Management

- **The Theory of Choice under Risk**
  - Expected Utility Theory
  - Endogenous Risk
  - Risk Perception

- **Risk, Markets, and Market Failure**
  - Efficiency, Markets, and Social Welfare
  - Incomplete Markets and Property Rights
  - Externalities
  - Nonexcludable and Nonrival Consumption
  - Nonconvexities
  - Asymmetric Information: Moral Hazard and Adverse Selection

- **Valuing Risks to Life and Limb**
  - Theoretical Framework
    - Economic Measures of Value
    - Value Formation and Preference Learning
    - Risk-Risk Tradeoffs
  - Estimation Methods
    - Indirect Methods: Hedonic Pricing and Averting Behavior
    - Direct Methods: Contingent Valuation and Experimental Auction Markets

- **Regulating Risk**
  - Rules as an Incentive System
    - Quantity Constraints
    - Technological Constraints
  - Prices as an Incentive System
    - Emission Charges
    - Input Charges
    - Output Charges
  - Marketable Permits: Risk-Risk Trading
  - Liability Systems
    - Noncompliance Fees
    - Performance Bonds
    - Deposit-Refund Systems
  - Hazard Warnings

- **The Theory of Environmental Conflict**
  - — Strategy and Definitions
    - Game Theory
    - Normal Form Games
    - Extensive Form Games
  - — Solution Concepts
    - Nash Equilibrium
    - Subgame Perfect Equilibrium
  - — Examples

- **Noncooperative Behavior and Transferable Risk**
  - — Traditional Emission Reduction Game
    - Noncooperative Action
    - Cooperative Action
  - — Transferable Risk
    - Noncooperative Action
    - Cooperative Action

- **Cooperation and Treaties**
  - — Paradox of Environmental Treaties
  - — Siting Hazardous Waste Disposal

- **Bargaining and Negotiation**
  - — Bargaining over Emissions Reduction
  - — Coasian Bargaining
  - — Scope of Environmental Negotiations

- **Monitoring, Enforcement, and Contestable Regulation**
  - — A Model of Monitoring and Enforcement
    - Passive Firm Response
    - Active Firm Response

- **Citizen Suits and the SLAPP**
  - — A Model of Citizen Suits with Asymmetric Reimbursement
    - NIMBYs
    - LULUs
    - LUSTs
  - — Strategic Lawsuits against Public Participation

- **Regulating Risk and Conflict Revisited**
  - — Risk, Conflict, and Technology Choice
  - — Prudence in Risk Assessment and Risk Management
  - — Collective versus Individual Misperception of Risk
  - — Global Risks and Institutional Design
  - — Adverse Selection and Moral Hazard
  - — Public Participation in Enforcement

Reading List

Introduction

1. Zeckhauser, R. and W. K. Viscusi (1991). Risk within Reason. <u>Science</u> 248: 559-564.

2. Morrall, J., III (1986). A Review of the Record. <u>Regulation</u> Nov/Dec: 25-34.

The Theory of Choice under Risk

3. Binger, B. and E. Hoffman (1988). . <u>Microeconomics with Calculus</u>. Chapter 19— Uncertainty: The Basics. Scott, Foresman and Company.

4. Machina, M. (1987). Choice under Uncertainty: Problems Solved and Unsolved. <u>Journal of Economic Perspectives</u> 1: 121-154.

5. Crocker, T. and J. Shogren (1994). Endogenous Risk and Environmental Program Evaluation. <u>Environmental Program Assessment</u>. University of Illinois Press (forthcoming).

Risk, Markets and Market Failure

6. Coase, R. (1960). The Problem of Social Cost. <u>The Journal of Law and Economics</u> 3: 1-40.

7. Cornes, R. and T. Sandler (1986). <u>The Theory of Externalities, Public Goods, and Club Goods</u>. Chapter 3—The Theory of Externalities. Cambridge: Cambridge University Press.

Valuing Risks to Life and Limb

8. Shogren, J. (1994). The Theory of Nonmarket Valuation. Photocopy.

9. Viscusi, W. K. (1992). A Survey of Values of Risks to Life and Health. Chapter 4 in <u>Fatal Tradeoffs</u>. Oxford: Oxford University Press, pp. 51-74.

10. Smith, V., and W. Desvousges (1987). An Empirical Analysis of the Economic Value of Risk Changes. <u>Journal of Political Economy</u> 95: 89-114.

11. Hayes, D. et al. (1995). Valuing Food Safety with Experimental Auction Markets. <u>American Journal of Agricultural Economics</u> (forthcoming).

Regulating Risk

12. Menell, P. (1991). The Limitations of Legal Institutions for Addressing Environmental Risks. <u>Journal of Economic Perspectives</u> 5: 93-114.

13. King, D., P. Crossen, and J. Shogren (1993). Economic Instruments for Environmental Protection in Developing Countries. Paris: OECD Document.

The Theory of Environmental Conflict

14. Binmore, K. (1992). Fun and Games. Chapter 4— Winning Out. Heath Publishers

15. Hargreaves Heap, S., M. Hollis, B. Lyons, R. Sugden, and A. Weale. (1993). The Theory of Choice. Chapter 7—Game Theory. Oxford: Blackwell Press

16. Hirshleifer, J. (1987). The Economic Approach to Conflict. Economic Imperialism. The Economic Method Applied Outside the Field of Economics (G. Radnitzky and P. Bernholz, eds.). New York: Paragon House Publ., pp. 335-364.

Noncooperative Behavior and Transferable Risk

17. Hoel, M. (1991). Global Environmental Problems: The Effects of Unilateral Action Taken by One Country. Journal of Environmental Economics and Management 20: 55-70.

18. Crocker, T. and Shogren, J. (1994). Transferable Risk and the Technology of Environmental Conflict. Society and Natural Resources 7: 181-188.

Cooperation and Treaties

19. Barrett, S. (1991). The Paradox of International Environmental Agreements. Mimeo.

20. Sullivan, A. (1993). Voluntary Auctions for Noxious Facilities: Incentives to Participate and the Efficiency of Siting Decisions. Journal of Environmental Economics and Management 25: S12-S26.

Bargaining and Negotiation

21. Porter, R. (1988). Environmental Negotiation: Its Potential and Economic Efficiency. Journal of Environmental Economics and Management 15: 129-142.

Monitoring, Enforcement, and Contestable Regulation

22. Russell, C. (1990). Monitoring and Enforcement. Public Policies for Environmental Protection (P. Portney, ed.) Washington, D. C.: Resources for the Future, pp. 243-274.

Citizen Suits and the SLAPP

23. Baik, K. and J. Shogren (1993). Citizen Suits and SLAPPs in U.S. Water Disputes. Photocopy.

Candidate Test Questions

1.   As a small business owner you plan on expanding your manufacturing plant. Unfortunately perhaps, the plot of land that you purchased for the expansion was a former gas station.   If the land is found to be contaminated from leaking underground storage tanks, under joint and several liability rules you will be liable for the clean-up.   (a) Discuss how and why this is a market failure for you and society.   The reasons may differ.   (b) Given the probability, p, of the land being contaminated from leaking underground storage tanks and your utility for profits, $U(\pi)$, show and explain your maximum willingness to pay to completely remove the contamination risk associated with the land purchase.   Define the profit function and factors that influence your decision problem.   Illustrate and explain the relative willingness to pay of a more risk averse person.

2.   True. False. Explain.   The decision to invest in self-protection is influenced by the level and misperception of risk.   Discuss the importance of the axioms underlying expected utility theory in your answer.

3.   Prior to 1981, regulations frequently required risk to be reduced to the lowest possible level, often without regard to economic efficiency.   To curb this practice, Executive Order 12291 was issued by President Reagan which requires that new regulations with projected economic impacts of $100 million or more must be justified by its benefits and cost.   Now the Republican's "Contract for America" has proposed reducing this benchmark to $25 million from $100 million, thereby unleashing benefit-cost analysis on even more regulatory decisions.   This will make the explicit economic value of life and limb even more prominent in public policy and industry.   Given that the estimated value of life and limb ranges from $200,000 to $16.2 million, discuss (a) the divergence in these values and why direct and indirect valuation procedures influence these values of life and limb, and (b) how this range of values should be used to guide regulatory policy..

4.   True. False. Explain.   If the social decision is between zero pollution and a level of pollution that exceeds an ecological threshold beyond which there is potentially irreversible damage, a nonconvex damage function dictates zero pollution.

Environmental Economics
Econ 579
J Shogren
2 May 95

Candidate Final Exam Questions

1. True. False. Explain. Noncooperative efforts to reduce pollution will exceed cooperative efforts. Be sure to define your terms in your answer.

2. Define Nash Equilibrium and subgame perfect equilibrium. Explain their role in eliminating incredible threats in a game between two countries who are in conflict over an area of tropical rain forest. Assume the game has two stages such that each player decides (1) when to invest effort, first or second, and (2) how much effort to expand trying to win the conflict. Discuss the role that symmetric and asymmetric ability has on the equilibrium. What practical problems are there in applying these equilibrium concepts to real environmental conflicts? As a budding economist, how would you address theses issues?

3. True. False. Explain. Coase argued that all environmental conflicts can be mediated efficiently through negotiation. Be sure to explain the key assumption underlying your answer.

4. Except for certain aboriginal rights, commercial whaling has been controlled by the International Whaling Commission for some time. Recently, however, Norway and Japan have decided to allow commercial whaling to begin again. Please model their decision to reenter these markets? Under what conditions does it make economic sense and conversely, under what conditions doe it not make sense. You may want to consider the additional element of time.

U.C.L.A   **G**

Economics 204G: Applications of Economic Theory   Professor Hilary Sigman

Environmental Economics   Office: Bunche 9361

Spring Quarter 1995   Phone: 825-2443

This course provides an introduction to current research issues in environmental economics. It aims to familiarize students with the empirical literature on environmental policy and some of the theoretical background for this literature. The course focuses primarily on the design of cost-effective environmental policies and only secondarily on assessment of the benefits of these policies.

Texts. We will draw on:

W.J. Baumol and W.E. Oates, *The Theory of Environmental Policy, second edition* (Cambridge, U.K.: Cambridge University Press, 1988).

A.M. Freeman III, *The Measurement of Environmental and Resource Values: Theory and Methods* (Washington, DC: Resources for the Future, 1993).

Some of the readings listed below are reproduced in:

W.E. Oates, ed. *The Economics of the Environment* (Edward Elgar: Brookfield, Vermont, 1992).

A useful overview of the area may be found in:

M.L. Cropper and W.E. Oates, "Environmental economics: a survey," *Journal of Economic Literature* 30 (1992), 675–740.

Two good sources for general background on environmental policy are:

P.R. Portney, ed. *Public Policies for Environmental Protection* (Baltimore MD: Resources for the Future, 1990) (for the U.S.)

The World Development Report 1992: Development and the Environment (Oxford: Oxford University Press, 1992)

Course outline

I. **Externalities and the role of environmental policy**

Baumol and Oates, chapter 4

R.H. Coase, "The problem of social cost," *Journal of Law and Economics* 3 (1960), 1–44.

E. Keeler, M. Spence, and R. Zeckhauser, "The optimal control of pollution," *Journal of Economic Theory* 4 (1971), 19–34.

J.J. Laffont, *Fundamentals of Public Economics* (Cambridge, MA: M.I.T. Press, 1989), chapter 1.

1

II. Environmental policy instruments

A. Cost effectiveness of conventional policy instruments

W.E. Oates, P.R. Portney, and A.M. McGartland, "The *net* benefits of incentive-based regulation: a case study of environmental standard setting," *American Economic Review* 79 (1989) 1233–1242.

E.P. Seskin, R.J. Anderson, and R.O. Reid, "An empirical analysis of economic strategies for controlling air pollution," *Journal of Environmental Economics and Management* 10 (1983), 112–124.

T. Tietenberg, *Emissions Trading* (Washington, DC: Resources for the Future, 1985), chapters 2–4.

A.L. Nichols, "The importance of exposure in evaluating and designing environmental regulations: a case study," *American Economic Review* 72 (1982), 214–219.

B. Alternative policy approaches: general background

R.W. Hahn, "Economic prescriptions for environmental problems: how the patient followed the doctor's orders," *Journal of Economic Perspectives* 3 (1989) 95–114.

R.W. Hahn and R.N. Stavins, "Incentive-based environmental regulation: a new era from an old idea?" *Ecology Law Journal* 18 (1991), 1–42.

R.N. Stavins and B.W. Whitehead, "Dealing with pollution: market-based incentives for environmental protection," *Environment* 34 (1992), no. 7, pp. 7–11, 29–42.

G.S. Eskeland and E. Jimenez "Policy instruments for pollution control in developing countries," *The World Bank Research Observer* 7 (1992), 145–169.

C. Marketable emissions permits

Baumol and Oates, chapter 12

S.E. Atkinson and T.H.Tietenberg, "The empirical properties of two classes of designs for transferable discharge permits," *Journal of Environmental Economics and Management* 9 (1982), 101-121.

R.W. Hahn and G.W. Hester, "Where did all the permits go? An analysis of EPA's emissions trading program," *Yale Journal of Regulation* 6 (1989), 109–153.

S.C. Kerr "The operation of tradeable rights markets: Empirical evidence from the United States lead phasedown," Harvard University, mimeo, 1994.

Folder of materials on South Coast Air Quality Management District's RECLAIM program.

D. Taxes and subsidies

Baumol and Oates, chapter 14

P. Diamond, "Consumption externalities and imperfect corrective pricing," *Bell Journal of Economics* 4 (1973), 526–538.

J. Green and E. Sheshinski, "Direct versus indirect remedies for externalities," *Journal of Political Economy* 84 (1976), 797–808.

W. Oates and D.L. Strassmann, "Effluent fees and market structure," *Journal of Public Economics* 24 (1984), 29–46.

D. Starrett and R. Zeckhauser, "Treating external economies — markets or taxes?" in J.W. Pratt, ed. *Statistical and Mathematical Aspects of Pollution Control Policies* (New York: Marcel Dekker, 1974), 65–84.

1. Application: carbon taxes

L. H. Goulder, "Effects of carbon taxes in an economy with prior tax distortions: an intertemporal general equilibrium analysis," mimeo, Stanford, 1994.

W.D. Nordhaus, "The cost of slowing climate change: a survey," *Energy Journal* 12 (1991) 37–65.

W.D. Nordhaus, "An optimal transition path for controlling greenhouse gases," *Science* 258 (1992), 1315–1319.

J. Poterba, "Tax policy to combat global warming: on designing a carbon tax," in R. Dornbusch and J.M. Poterba, eds. *Global Warming: Economic Policy Responses* (Cambridge, MA: MIT Press, 1991), 72–98.

A. Shah and B. Larsen, "Global warming, carbon taxes, and developing countries," mimeo, World Bank, 1992.

2. Application: waste management

D. Fullerton and T.C. Kinnaman, "Household demand for garbage and recycling collection with the start of a price per bag," N.B.E.R. working paper, 1993.

D. Fullerton and T. C. Kinnaman, "Garbage, recycling, and illicit burning or dumping," *Journal of Environmental Economics and Management,* forthcoming.

H. Sigman, "A comparison of public policies for lead recycling," *RAND Journal of Economics,* forthcoming.

E. Environmental policy instruments under uncertainty

Baumol and Oates, chapter 5

M.J. Roberts and M. Spence, "Effluent charges and licenses under uncertainty," *Journal of Public Economics* 5 (1976), 193–208.

M. Weitzman, "Prices vs. quantities," *Review of Economic Studies* 41 (1974), 477–491.

F. Environmental liability rules

J.P. Acton and L.S. Dixon, *Superfund and Transactions Costs: The Experiences of Insurers and Very Large Industrial Firms* (Santa Monica, CA: RAND, 1992).

J.J. Opaluch and T.A. Grigalunas, "Controlling stochastic pollution events with liability rules: some evidence from OCS leasing," *RAND Journal of Economics* 15 (1984) 142–51.

S. Shavell, "A model of the optimal use of liability and safety regulation," *RAND Journal of Economics* 15 (1984) 271–80.

III. Enforcement of environmental regulation

D.A. Fuller, "Compliance, avoidance, and evasion: emissions control under imperfect enforcement in steam-electric generation" *RAND Journal of Economics* 18 (1987), 124–37.

J.D. Harford, "Firm behavior under imperfectly enforceable pollution standards and taxes," *Journal of Environmental Economics and Management* 1 (1978), 26–43.

W. Harrington, "Enforcement leverage when penalties are restricted," *Journal of Public Economics* 37 (1988), 29–53.

W.A. Magat and W.K. Viscusi, "Effectiveness of EPA's regulatory enforcement: the case of industrial effluent standards," *Journal of Law and Economics* 32 (1990), 331–360.

C.S. Russell, "Monitoring and enforcement," in P.R. Portney, ed. *Public Policies for Environmental Protection* (Baltimore MD: Resources for the Future, 1990), 243–274.

IV. Environmental regulation, productivity, and growth

A. Effects of regulation on productivity

A.J. Barbara and V.D. McConnell, "The impact of environmental regulations on industry productivity: direct and indirect effects," *Journal of Environmental Economics and Management* 18 (1991), 50–66.

M. Hazilla and R. Kopp "Social cost of environmental quality regulations: a general equilibrium analysis," *Journal of Political Economy,* 98 (4), 853–73.

D.W. Jorgenson and P.J. Wilcoxen, "Environmental regulation and U.S. economic growth," *RAND Journal of Economics* 21 (1990), 314–340.

B. Regulation, innovation, and technology adoption

A.B. Jaffe and R.N. Stavins, "The diffusion of energy conserving windows: the effect of economic incentives and building codes," mimeo, Harvard University, 1993.

A.B. Jaffe and K. Palmer, "Environmental regulation and innovation: a panel data study," Resources for the Future Discussion paper, 1995.

S.R. Millman and R. Prince, "Firm incentives to promote technological change in pollution control," *Journal of Environmental Economics and Management* 17 (1989), 247–65.

V. Policy coordination

A. International environmental policy

Baumol and Oates, chapter 16

K.G. Maler "International environmental problems," *Oxford Review of Economic Policy* 6 (1990), 80–108.

D.M.G. Newbery, "Acid Rain," *Economic Policy* 5 (1990), 297–346.

4

G.M. Grossman and A.B. Krueger, "Environmental impacts of a North American free trade agreement," N.B.E.R. working paper no. 3914, 1991.

A. Steer et al. "Overview," *World Development Report 1992: Development and the Environment* (Oxford: Oxford University Press, 1992), pp. 1–24.

B. Environmental federalism

Baumol and Oates, chapter 17.

A. B. Atkinson and J.E. Stiglitz, *Lectures on Public Economics* (New York: McGraw-Hill, 1980), chapter 17.

A. Levinson, "Environmental regulation and manufacturers' location choices: systematic evidence from the Census of Manufactures" *Journal of Public Economics*, forthcoming.

V.D. McConnell and R.M. Schwab, "The impact of environmental regulation on industry location decisions: the motor vehicle industry," *Land Economics* 66 (1990) 67–81.

W.E. Oates and R.M. Schwab, "Economic competition among jurisdictions: efficiency-enhancing or distortion inducing?"
Journal of Public Economics 35 (1988) 333–354.

M.P. Pashigian, "Environmental regulation: whose self-interests are being protected?" *Economic Inquiry* 22 (1985), 555–84.

VI. Valuing environmental quality

A. Approaches using observed behavior

Freeman, chapters 4, 11 and 12

S. Rosen, "Hedonic prices and implicit markets: product differentiation in pure competition," *Journal of Political Economy* 82 (1974), 34–55.

V.K. Smith and J-C Huang, "Can markets value environmental quality? A meta-analysis of hedonic property value models," *Journal of Political Economy* 103 (1995), 209–227.

B. Contingent valuation

Freeman, chapter 6

D.S. Brookshire, M.A.Thayer, W.D. Schulze, and R. D'Arge, "Valuing public goods: a comparison of survey and hedonic approaches," *American Economic Review* 72 (1982), 165–77.

T.A. Cameron and M.D. James, "Efficient estimation methods for 'closed-ended' contingent valuation surveys," *Review of Economics and Statistics* 69 (1987), 296–76.

P. R. Portney, W.M. Haneman, P.A. Diamond and J.A. Hausman, "Symposium on Contingent Valuation " *Journal of Economic Perspectives* 8 (1994), Fall, 3–64.

C. Health consequences

Freeman, chapter 10

A.J. Krupnick and P.R. Portney, "Controlling urban air pollution: a benefit–cost assessment," *Science* 252 (1991), 522–527.

M.L. Cropper, et al., "The determinants of pesticide regulation: a statistical analysis of EPA decision-making," *Journal of Political Economy* 100 (1992), 175–97.

D. Uncertainty and the value of environmental preservation

K.J. Arrow and A.C. Fisher, "Environmental preservation, uncertainty, and irreversibility," *Quarterly Journal of Economics* 88 (1974), 312–319.

A.C. Fisher and W.M. Hanemann, "Option value and the extinction of species," *Advances in Applied Micro-economics* 4 (1986), 169–190.

A. S. Manne and R.G. Richels, "Decision-making under uncertainty," in *Buying Greenhouse Insurance: The Economic Costs of CO_2 Emission Limits* (Cambridge, MA: M.I.T. Press, 1992).

190

Duke University

EC 163 (NEW TITLE)
Economics of Environmental Resources
Fall 1994

V. Kerry Smith   **U**
Soc. Science: 210
Office Hours: T/TH
          1:00-3:00 p.m.
and by appointment
(613-8052)

Class Location: Soc. Science 213
Time: Tues/Thurs 3:50-5:05 p.m.

I. Background and Course Objectives

The objective of this course is to show you how economic principles can be and are used in private and public policy decisions involving environmental resources. It assumes you have taken at least one economics course that covers aspect of households' and firms' decisions. It does not have to be intermediate microeconomics, though this would be helpful.

The course begins with basic principles. This may be a review for those who had intermediate micro. The focus will be on how these methods are used.

Five case studies will be considered as methods to illustrate the use of economic analysis for current environmental problems. They are:

Case

1. The Monetary Value of Natural Assets: Litigating Oil Spills and Hazardous Waste Dumps

2. Two Years of Auctions for Rights to Pollute: How Do They Work?

3. Is Climate Change Bad?

4. Trade and The Environment

5. Superfund: Is There a Better Way?

II. Requirements

A. Readings (General)

The course deals with very current issues, so there are detailed readings for all of the cases. The text has limited coverage of specifics and is intended for background and development of economic methods.

191

The text is:

B.C. Field, Environmental Economics: An Introduction
(New York: McGraw Hill, 1994)
[available in paperback]

Readings are available on reserve at the library.

B. Readings (Student Prepared Assignments)

The readings for each case assignment will be available on reserve in the library shortly before the assignment is distributed.

C. Grading and Exams

Grades will be based on four sets of information:

(a) random quizzes (given largely at outset of semester to gauge knowledge and to encourage reading of developmental material);

(b) a mid-term exam;

(c) one student prepared case study; and

(d) a final exam. The final exam is comprehensive.

The distribution of weight to each set of information is as follows:

(a) Random quizzes and class participation   10%

(b) Mid-term   [October 13]   30%

(c) Student prepared case study [November 15]   20%

(d) Final Exam   40%

Quizzes **cannot** be made up. The mid-term is optional but encouraged. As a general rule, I rarely give makeup exams for mid-terms. Under unusual circumstances, with advance notice, it is possible to arrange to take the exam prior to the scheduled date. If one selects not to take the mid-term, the weight for that information shifts to the final exam.

It is always in your best interest to take the exams. They provide you and me information. Because I take account of improvement, poor initial performance does not imply your "fate" is sealed. Your goal is to demonstrate to me that you know the material.

D. Student Prepared Cases

I will distribute two case studies. Each student must select one, apply the concepts and methods developed in the class to one selected case study. Some background material will be provided for each case, but library research is also expected.

A case report consists of four, double-spaced, typed pages (standard font size). Supplementary tables, figures or math can be attached provided they are used in the text and cannot exceed three (3) pages.

Do not exceed the length specifications. Reports exceeding the specified length will be returned for editing and considered late. Late reports lose one letter grade.

E. Class Attendance

The grading information rewards class participation. A substantial volume of the material necessary to do problems on the exams and the case studies will be presented in lectures. Nonetheless, attendance is not enforced by taking roll.

III. Course Outline and Readings

A. Background

Frances Cairncross, Costing the Earth
(Harvard Business School Press, 1991)
Chapters 1 and 2

Text, Chapters 1 and 2

B. Economic Concepts

1. Opportunity Cost, Marginal Analysis, Markets and Consumer Surplus

R.H. Frank, Microeconomics and Behavior
(Second Edition 1994)   Chapter 1

Text, Chapter 3

2. Property Rights, Externalities, Open Access Resources, Public Goods

Text, Chapter 4

Frank, Chapters 18, 19

G.M. Brown and V.K. Smith, "Public Goods, Externalities and Congestion"
(Chapter 4 from unpublished manuscript, 1994)

3. Inter-temporal Allocation, Discounting and Uncertainty

Text, Chapter 6

4. Benefit - Cost Analysis

Text, Chapters 7, 8

C. Case 1 - What is a Natural Asset Worth?

Barry J. Breen, "Citizen Suits for Natural Resource Damages: Closing the Gap in Federal Environmental Law," Wake Forest Law Review, Vol. 24, 1989

Jeffrey C. Dobbins, "The Pain and Suffering of Environmental Loss: Using Contingent Valuation to Estimate Non-Use Damages," Duke Law Journal, No. 4, 1984

R.J. Koppand , V.K. Smith, editors, Valuing Natural Assets (Washington, D.C.: Resources for the Future, 1993), Chapters 1 and 7

J. Loomis and P. Anderson, "Idaho vs. Southern Refrigerated Transport," in K.Ward and J. Duffield, editors, Natural Resource Damages: Law and Economics, (John Wiley, 1992), Chapter 16

D. Case 2 - Auctions for Air

Text, Chapter 13

Frank, pp. 240-245

Paul Milgrom, "Auctions and Bidding: A Primer," Journal of Economic Perspectives, Summer 1989

EPA Background Materials 1993, 1994

E. Case 3 - Is Climate Change Bad?

Text, Chapter 20

Richard Lindzen, "Global Warming: The Origin and Nature of the Alleged Scientific Consensus," Regulation, Spring 1992

OTA, Preparing for an Uncertain Climate, Summary, Office of Technology Assessment, Sept. 1993, pp. 1-34

Andrew Jordan, "Paying the Incremental Costs of Global Environmental Protection: The Evolving Role of GEF," Environment, July/August 1994

F. Case 4 - <u>Trade and the Environment</u>

Text, Chapters 18, 21

Roberto Salinas - León. "Green Herrings - NAFTA and the Environment," <u>Regulation</u>, Winter 1993.

Kym Anderson, "The Standard Welfare Economics of Policies Affecting Trade and the Environment," Chapter 2 in <u>The Greening of World Trade Issues</u>, edited by K. Anderson and R. Blockhurst (Ann Arbor: University of Michigan, 1992)

G. Case 5 - <u>Superfund: Is There A Better Way?</u>

Text, Chapter 16 pp. 335-347.

K.N. Probst and P.R. Portney, <u>Assigning Liability for Superfund Cleanups: An Analysis of Policy Options</u>, RFF Report, June 1992

Lloyd Dixon, Deborah S. Drezner and James K. Hammitt, <u>Private Sector Cleanup Expenditures and Transaction Costs at 18 Superfund Sites</u>, Rand Corporation, 1993, Chapters 1, 6

Kent Jeffreys, "Amending Superfund: Reform or Revanche?", <u>Regulation</u>, No. 1, 1994

Duke University

UG

EC 263	Environmental Economics: Theory and Application	Spring 1995

Class Time: Tuesday and Thursday, 9:10-10:25 a.m..
Location: Social Sciences 219

Professor: V. Kerry Smith

Office: Social Sciences 210
LSRC 125A

Office Hours
At SS 210: Tuesday and Thursday   11:00-12:00 a.m.
            Tuesday and Thursday   1:15 - 2:15 p.m.

At LSRC 125A: Tuesday   3:40 - 5:00 p.m.
               and (by appointment,
               contact Ms. Paula Rubio, 613-8084)

A. General Information

The purpose of this course is to provide an overview of the economic theory used to describe how environmental resources get involved in the decisions about resource allocations. This is a large and complex area. As a result, my focus is in three areas.

I. Problems Modeled as Externalities and Public Goods

This section of the course develops the static economic theory associated with externalities problems. It discusses policy instruments that are suggested by economists to deal with these issues and outlines the practice of environmental regulation.

II. Allocation of Environmental Resources

This section describes the theory and practice of benefit-cost analysis, considering how it is used in environmental policy evaluation.

III. Environmental Risk Management

Because the actual implementation of environmental policy is often framed in terms of an effort to reduce or avoid risk, this section discusses the economics model for risk management, compares it with psychologists' views on how people evaluate environmental risk and uses the results to consider the role of information programs for environmental policy.

B.   Requirements

Grades will be based on three aspects of each participant's performance.

(a)   Mid-term exam (March 9)   (35%)

(b)   Short Analysis paper (April 4)   (25%)

(c)   Comprehensive Final Exam   (40%)

The short analysis paper is to be 10 pages typed double spaced, using standard font size. This includes footnotes, tables and references. Longer papers will be returned as unacceptable. The topic must be selected from a set of issues that will be distributed at the outset of the semester. Participants can select the particular economics issue to be addressed within each theme.

Please note that the dates for the mid-term and the short analysis paper are firm. Changes will not be made. Announcement of this policy at this time is regarded as adequate notice for you to plan your schedule to meet the deadlines or to leave the course now. Exceptions later will not be made.

C.   Course Specifics

I.   Texts (both available in paperback):

1.   W.J. Baumol and W.E. Oates, *The Theory of Environmental Policy*, second edition (Cambridge: Cambridge Univ. Press, 1988). [This is a graduate text, but is very readable; the material will be presented in a simplified format using calculus, but it will be presented in graphical and mathematical formats].

2.   D.W. Pearce and R.K. Turner, *Economics of Natural Resources and the Environment* (Baltimore: Johns Hopkins 1990).

II.   Readings

The readings will be on reserve at Perkins Library.

D.   Course Outline

I.   Overview of Environmental Problems

A.   Background on Materials Balance and Economics

B.   Role of Uncertainty

    1.   Baumol and Oates, Chapter 5

C.   Market Structure

    1.   Baumol and Oates, Chapter 6

    2.   A.H. Barnett, "the Pigouvian Tax Rule Under Monopoly", *American Economic Review*, (Dec. 1980): 1037-1041.

D.   Practical Modeling Issues

    1.   W.O. Spofford, C.S. Russell and R.A. Kelly, *Environmental Quality Management: An Application to the Lower Delaware Valley* (Resources for the Future, 1976) pp 3-114.

IV.   Current Air and Hazardous Waste Policies

A.   Background

    1.   P.R. Portney "The Evolution of Federal Regulation" in P.R. Portney (editor) *Public Policies for Environmental Protection* (Washington: Resources for the Future, 1990).

    2.   P.R. Portney "Air Pollution Policy" in P.R. Portney (editor) *Public Policies for Environmental Protection.*

    3.   R. Dower, "Hazardous Wastes" in Portney, *Public Policies for Environmental Protection.*

B.   Experience

    1.   W.E. Oates, P.R. Portney and A.M. McGartland, "The Net Benefits of Incentive-Based Regulation: A Case Study of Environmental Standard Setting" *American Economic Review* Vol. 79 (December, 1989): 1233-42.

    2.   C.S. Russell and V.K. Smith, "Demands for Data and Analysis Induced by Environmental Policy" in E.R. Berndt and J.E. Triplett, editors, *Fifty Years of Economics Measurement* (Chicago: University of Chicago Press, 1990) pp. 299-313 and 327-334.

V.   Using Environmental Economics in Resource Allocation Decisions

    A.   Monetary Measures for Economics Values

        1.   Freeman, "Non-Market Valuation by Revealed Preferences" in Brown and Smith, Chapter 10, *Resource and Environmental Economics.*

        2.   Pearce and Turner, Chapter 9-10

    B.   Benefit-Cost Analysis

        1.   Halvorsen, "Benefit-Cost Analysis" in Brown and Smith Chapter, *Resource and Environmental Economics.*

        2.   President Clinton's Clean Water Initiative: An Analysis of Benefits and Costs (U.S. EPA, March 1994) - Executive Summary pp. 1-22.

VI.   Modeling Environmental Risk

    A.   Conceptual Background and Psychological Issues

        1.   A.M. Freeman, *The Measurement of Environmental and Resource Values: Theory and Methods,* (Washington, D.C.: Resources for the Future, 1993), Chapter 8.

        2.   P. Slovic, "Perception of Risk" *Science*, (April, 1987): 280-285

        3.   K. Halvor Teigin, W. Brun and P. Slovic, "Societal Risks as Seen by a Norwegian Public" *Journal of Behavioral Decision Making (1988): 111-130.*

    B.   Information Policies

        1.   B. Fischhoff, A. Bostrom and M.J. Quadrel, "Risk Perception and Communication" *Annual Review of Public Health*, (1993): 183-203.

        2.   V.K. Smith, W.H. Desvousges, F.R. Johnson and A. Fisher "Can Public Information Programs Affect Risk Perceptions?" *Journal of Policy Analysis and Management*, (1990): 41-59.

        3.   W.H. Desvousges, V.K. Smith and H.H. Rink III, "Communicating Radon Risks Effectively: The Maryland Experience", *Journal of Public Policy and Marketing*, (Fall 1992): 678-78.

VII.   A Good Summary of the Terrain

        1.   M.L. Cropper and W.E. Oates "Environmental Economics: A Survey" *Journal of Economics Literature* (June 1992): 657-740.

Duke University

EB 372* Environmental and Resource Economics   Fall 1995

V. Kerry Smith
Office Hours:

A.   General Information

The purpose of this course is to provide an overview of the theory and empirical practice of economic analysis as it is used in evaluating environmental and natural resource problems. It assumes familiarity with micro-theory, understanding of calculus and constrained optimization, and rudimentary knowledge of applied econometrics (for the applications we shall cover).

In discussing applications involving environmental resources, I will assume you can review, on your own, the institutional background. Some good sources include:

T. Tietenberg, Environmental and Natural Resource Economics, 2nd edition. (Scott Foresman, 1987).

P.R. Portney, Editor, Current Issues in U.S. Environmental Policy (Baltimore: Johns Hopkins University Press, 1978). [See Freeman chapter for overview of early air and water legislation.]

Two general areas will be covered in this course: environmental economics including theory and practice and natural resource economics, including renewable and non-renewable resources. Most of the coverage of these last two topics will be theoretical and empirical, as I have less experience with policy in these areas. The necessary mathematical equipment for the dynamic optimization will be covered as part of the class materials.

B.   Requirements

Grades will be based on four aspects of each student's performance.

(1)   mid-term exam March 2, 1989

(2)   final exam May 2, 1989

(3)   research paper that must be submitted by April 4; no later submissions will be accepted.

(4)   class participation and one oral presentation or referee report.

The weights for each are as follows: (1) 25%

                                                        (2) 30%
                                                        (3) 30%
                                                        (4) 15%

Several criteria are important to how these requirements will be graded. Exams will require analysis of topics covered in class or in the readings. They will require problem solving and modeling, not review and summarization of material. The final exam is not cumulative. It will cover material since the mid-term exam.

Each student will be required to submit a 2-page (typed) outline of his (her) paper by mid February (February 16).

Each student can select either an oral presentation of one topic from a list I will provide or to prepare one referee's report on an unpublished paper I will provide to them. This report must be detailed (3 to 5 typed pages) and demonstrate knowledge of the literature relevant to the topic of the paper (including a list of the relevant references used in evaluating the paper).

The research paper should be 15 to 20 typed pages (no more than 20). It must be either an analytical or empirical paper. No literature reviews will be accepted. The ideal paper will either:

(a)   attempt to modify a specific economic model (from the literature) leading to a positive or normative result and explain its implications; or

(b)   test a specific hypothesis derived from the economic analyses in the readings or in the lectures.

No credit will be given for papers that are late. Plan to start your paper early. It cannot be one used in another class. Discuss the topic with me before you prepare an outline. Schedule an appointment for that discussion.

Item (4) allocates 10% weight to the oral presentation or referee report and 5% to participation in class. If there is limited or no participation in class, the 5% weight will shift to the final exam.

C.   Text and Readings

Two books have been ordered for the class:

Per-Olov Johansson, The Economic Theory and Measurement of Benefits (Cambridge University Press, 1987).

Richard Cornes and Todd Sandler, The Theory of Externalities, Public Goods and Club Goods (Cambridge University Press, 1986).

Both are in paperback editions. It is not essential that you buy either. However, we will read nearly all of both as well as selections from a set of other readings on reserve.

A good supplement that I have not ordered because it is a bit out of date is:

Anthony C. Fisher, Resource and Environmental Economics (Cambridge University, 1981).

It is nonetheless a useful book to read. It has excellent descriptions and insight, and worth acquiring for your personal library if you are interested in resource economics.

Course Outline

I.   Theory of Static Environmental Problems

A.   Pareto Efficiency

1.   Just, Hueth and Schmitz, Applied Welfare Economic and Public Policy (Prentice Hall, 1982) Chapter 2.

2.   Cornes and Sandler, Chapter 2.

3.   Dasgupta and Heal, Economic Theory and Exhaustible Resources (Cambridge University, 1979) Chapter 2.

B.   ·   Externalities and Economic Efficiency

    1.   W.J. Baumol and Oates, Theory of Environmental Policy, second edition (Prentice Hall, 1988) Chapters 2-4, 6, 7, 8.

    2.   Cornes and Sandler, Chapter 3.

    3.   Dasgupta and Heal, Chapter 3.

    4.   Fisher, Resource and Environmental Economics Chapter 6 (overview of literature

C.   Instruments for Environmental Policy

  i. Conventional Cases

    1. Baumol and Oates, Chapters 11, 14.

    2. Cornes and Sandler, Chapter 4.

    3.   P. Bohm and C.S. Russell, "Comparative Analysis of Alternative Policy Instruments" in Handbook of Natural Resource and Energy Economics (North Holland, 1985).

    4.   D.W. Carlton and G.C. Loury, "The Limitations of Pigouvian Taxes as a Long-Run Remedy for Externalities," Quarterly Journal of Economics, November 1980.

    5.   R.E. Kohn, "The Limitation of Pigouvian taxes as a Long-Run Remedy for Externalities: Comment," Quarterly Journal of Economics, August 1986.

    6.   D. W. Carlton and G.C. Loury, "The Limitation of Pigouvian Taxes as a Long-Run Remedy of Externalities: An Extension of Results," Quarterly Journal of Economics, August 1986.

    7.   W. Oates, "The Regulation of Externalities: Efficient Behavior by Sources and Victims," Public Finance, 1983.

    8.   H. Shibata and J.S. Winrick, "Control of Pollution When the Offended Defend Themselves," Economica, 1983.

  ii. Marketable Permits: Theory and Practice

    1.   T. Tietenberg, Emission Trading (Johns Hopkins University Press, 1985) Chapters 1-4, 6.

    2.   Baumol and Oates, Chapter 12.

    3.   A.M. McGartland, W.E. Oates, and P.R. Portney, "The Net Benefits of Least Cost Controls: Setting Environmental Standards in the Real World," University of Maryland unpublished paper, November 1987.

    4.   C. S. Russell and V. K. Smith, "Demands for Data and Analysis Induced by Environmental Policy" in 50th Anniversary Volume Conference on Income and Wealth, NBER (University of Chicago Press, forthcoming).

iii.   Uncertainty

1.   M. Weitzman, "Prices versus Quantities," Review of Economic Studies, 1974.

2.   Z. Adar and J.M. Griffin, "Uncertainty and the Choice of Pollution Control Instruments," JEEM, October 1976.

3.   Baumol and Oates, Chapter 5.

iv.   Relationship between Externalities, Public Goods and Common Property Resources

1.   R. Dorfman, "The Technical Basis for Decision Making," in E.T. Haefele, The Governance of Common Property Resources (Baltimore: Johns Hopkins University Press University, 1974).

2.   Cornes and Sandler, Chapter 5-7.

3.   R.H. Haveman, "Common Property, Congestion and Environmental Pollution," Quarterly Journal of Economics, May 1973.

4.   R. Cornes, C. Mason and T. Sandler, "The Commons and the Optimal Number of Firms," Quarterly Journal of Economics, August 1986.

5.   C. Mason, T. Sandler and R. Cornes, "Expectations, the Commons and Optimal Goup Size," JEEM, March, 1988.

v.   Asymmetric Information and Regulatory Design

1.   E. Kwerel, "To Tell the Truth: Imperfect Information and Optimal Pollution Control," Review of Economic Studies, October 1977.

2.   Charles D. Kolstad, "Uniformity versus Differentiation in Regulating Emissions," JEEM, December, 1987.

3.   Kathleen Segerson, "Uncertainty and Incentives for Nonpoint Pollution Control," JEEM, March, 1988.

D.   Practical Implementation of Static Theory for Policy

i.   Background

1.   V.K. Smith, "A Conceptual Overview of the Foundations of Benefit Cost Analysis," Benefit Assessment: The State of the Art, edited by J.D. Bentkover, V.T. Covello, J. Mumpower (D. Reidel, 1986). (Simplified overview of benefit-cost analysis)

2.   A. Randall, "Valuation in a Policy Context," Natural Resource Economics: Policy Problems and Contemporary Analysis, edited by D.W. Bromley (Kluwer-Nijhoff, 1986) [see also comments by A. Fisher and V.K. Smith].

ii.   Monetary Measures of Welfare Change - Certainty Case

1.   Johansson, The Economic Theory and Measurement of Environmental Benefits, Chapters 1-6.

204

2. Just, Hueth, and Schmitz, Appendix B.

3. A.M. Freeman, "Methods for Assessing the Benefits of Environmental Programs," Handbook of Natural Resource and Energy Economics, Vol I (North Holland, 1985) (an overview of theory and methods).

4. J. Hausman, "Exact Consumer Surplus and Deadweight Loss," American Economic Review, September 1981.

5. Y.O. Varia, "Efficient Methods of Measuring Welfare Charge and Compensated Income in Terms of Market Demand Functions," Econometrica, January 1983.

6. W. Michael Hanemann, "Willingness to Pay and Willingness to Accept: How Much Can They Differ?" American Economic Review, forthcoming.

7. N. E. Bockstael and K. E. McConnell, "Welfare Effects of Changes in Quality: A Synthesis," Unpublished Paper, University of Maryland, 1987.

iii. Monetary Measures of Welfare Change - Uncertainty Case

1. J. V. Krutilla, "Conservation Reconsidered," American Economic Review, September 1967.

2. R. C. Bishop, "Option Value: An Exposition and Extension," Land Economics, February 1982.

3. D.A. Graham, "Cost Benefit Analysis Under Uncertainty," American Economic Review, September 1981.

4. V.K. Smith, "Non-Use Values in Benefit Cost Analysis," Southern Economic Review, July 1987.

5. Johansson, Chapters 10-11.

6. A. M. Freeman, III, "Nonuse Values in Natural Resource Damage Assessment," in Natural Resource Damage Assessment Manuscript, edited by Kopp and Smith, unpublished, 1988.

7. D. C. Cory and B. C. Saliba, "Requiem for Option Value," Land Economics, February, 1987.

8. V. K. Smith and W. H. Desvousges, "The Valuation of Environmental Risks and Hazardous Waste Policy," Land Economics, August, 1988.

iv. Measurement in Practice

1. Johansson, Chapters 7-8. [partial overview of several of the methods].

   a. Hedonic Models

      1. R. B. Palmquist, "Hedonic Methods," unpublished paper.

2.	K. E. McConnell, "Indirect Methods for Assessing Natural Resource Damages Under CERCLA," in Natural Resource Damage Assessment, edited by Kopp and Smith, unpublished, 1988.

3.	T.J. Bartik and V.K. Smith, "Urban Amenities and Public Policy," Handbook on Regional and Urban Economics, (North Holland, 1987).

4.	Y. Kanemoto, "Hedonic Prices and the Benefits of Public Projects," Econometrica, July, 1988.

5.	R. Palmquist, "Welfare Measurement in the Hedonic Model: The Case of Non-parametric Marginal Prices," Journal of Environmental Economics and Management, September, 1988.

b.	Household Production Models

1.	H. Hori, "Revealed Preferences for Public Goods," American Economic Review, December, 1975.

2.	N. E. Bockstael and K. E. McConnell, "Welfare Measurement in the Household Production Framework," American Economic Review, September, 1983.

3.	N. E. Bockstael and C. L. Kling, "Valuing Environmental Quality: Weak Complementarity With Sets of Goods," AJAE, August, 1988.

4.	V. K. Smith, "Household Production Models, Averting Behavior and Valuation: An Overview," Unpublished Paper, 1989.

5.	W. Foster and R. E. Just, "Consumer Valuation of Health Risk: The Case of Heptachlor Contamination of Milk in Hawaii," Unpublished Paper, University of California, Division of Agricultural Sciences, June, 1984.

c.	Travel Cost Recreation Demand Models

1.	K.E. McConnell, "The Economics of Outdoor Recreation," Handbook of Natural Resources and Energy Economics, Vol II (North Holland, 1985).

2.	V. K. Smith, "Travel Cost Recreation Demand Methods: Theory and Implementation," Discussion Paper QE89-03, Quality of the Environment Division, Resources for the Future, Washington, D.C., 1988.

3.   N.E. Bockstael, I.E. Strand and W.M. Hanemann, "Time and Recreational Demand," <u>American Journal of Agricultural Economics</u>, May 1987.

4.   G. Brown and R. Mendelsohn, "The Hedonic Travel Cost Method," <u>Review of Economics and Statistics</u>, August 1984.

5.   Winston Harrington, <u>Measuring Recreation Supply</u> (Resources for the Future, 1987), Chapter 1-4.

6.   K. E. McConnell, "Heterogeneous Preferences for Congestion," <u>JEEM</u>, September, 1988.

d.   <u>Random Utility and Discrete Choice Models</u>

1.   N.E. Bockstael, W.M. Hanemann, C.L. King, "Estimating the Value of Water Quality Improvements in a Recreational Demand Framework," <u>Water Resources Research</u>, May 1987.

2.   W. Michael Hanemann and Richard Carson, Sections of "Southcentral Alaska Sport Fishing Economic Study," prepared for Alaska Department of Fish and Game, November, 1987.

e.   <u>Contingent Valuation and Contingent Behavior Approaches</u>

1.   V.K. Smith and W.H. Desvousges, <u>Measuring Water Quality Benefits</u>, Chapter 4.

2.   R.C. Mitchell and R.T. Carson, <u>Using Surveys to Value Public Goods</u>: <u>The Contingent Valuation Methods</u> (Washington, D.C. Resources for the Future, 1989), Chapters 4, 5, 8.

3.   W.D. Schulze, "The Use of Direct Methods for Valuing Natural Resource Damages," in Kopp and Smith, Ed., <u>Natural Resource Damage Manuscript</u>, Unpublished.

4.   M. Dickie, A. Fisher and S. Gerking, "Market Transactions and Hypothetical Demand Data: A Comparative Study," <u>Journal of the American Statistical Association</u>, March 1987.

5.   W.M. Hanemann, "Welfare Evaluations With Simulated Market Data: Bishop and Heberlein Revisited," <u>American Journal of Agricultural Economics</u>, August 1984.

6. T. A. Cameron, "A New Paradigm for Valuing Nonmarket Goods Using Referendum Data: Maximum Likelihood Estimation by Censored Logistic Regression," <u>JEEM</u>, September, 1988.

7. K. E. McConnell, "Models for Referendum Data," University of Maryland, Unpublished Paper, December, 1987.

v. <u>Putting it Together - Benefit Cost Analysis</u>

1. P. Bohn, <u>Social Efficiency,</u> second edition (Macmillan, 1987) Chapter 4.

2. R. Lind, "A Primer on the Major Issues Relating to the Discount Rate for Evaluating National Energy Options," <u>Discounting for Time and Risk in Energy Policy</u>, edited by R. Lind (Johns Hopkins University Press, 1982).

vi. <u>Emerging Topics - Acidic Deposition and Climate Change</u>

1. W. Harrington, "Acid Deposition: Science and Policy," Discussion Paper QE88-09, Resources for the Future, Washington, D.C., August, 1988.

2. H. Doulatabadi and W. Harrington, "Policies for the Mitigation of Acid Rain: A Critique of Evaluation Techniques," Discussion Paper QE88-08, Resources for the Future, Washington, D.C.

3. I.M. Mintzer, <u>A Matter of Degrees: The Potential for Controlling the Greenhouse Effect</u>, World Resources Institute, 1987.

II. <u>Economic Allocation of Non-Renewable Resources</u>

A. <u>Mathematical Background</u>

1. M.D. Intrillgator, <u>Mathematical Optimization on Economic Theory</u> (Prentice Hall, 1971) Chapters 11-14.

2. Per-Olov Johansson and Karl Gustaf Lo"fgren, <u>The Economics of Forestry and Natural Resources</u> (Basil Blackwell, 1985), Chapter 1.

B. <u>Model of the Firm</u>

1. Dasgupta and Heal, Chapters 6, 11.

2. Fisher, Chapter 2.

3. Johansson and To"fgren, Chapter 2.

4. R. Solow, "The Economics of Resources or Resources of Economics," <u>American Economic Review Proceedings</u>, May 1974 (an overview of firm and economy-wide issues).

C. <u>Tests of Hotelling Framework</u>

1. G. Heal and M. Barrow, "Empirical Investigation of the Long-Term Movement of Resource Prices - A Preliminary Report," <u>Economic Letters</u>, 1981.

2. M.H. Miller and C.W. Upton, "A Test of the Hotelling Valuation Principle," <u>Journal of Political Economy</u>, February 1985.

3. V.K. Smith and J.T. Liu, "A Micro-Evaluation of the Hotelling Valuation Principle," unpublished paper, revised, January 1989.

D. <u>Natural Resources and Economic Well-Being</u>

1. Dasgupta and Heal, Chapter 7.

2. Fisher, Chapter 4.

3. A.C. Fisher, "On Measures of Natural Resource Scarcity," <u>Scarcity and Growth Revisited</u>, edited by V.K. Smith (Johns Hopkins, 1979).

4. V.K. Smith, "The Evaluation of Natural Resource Adequacy: Elusive Quest or Frontier of Economic Analysis," <u>Land Economics</u>, August 1980.

5. M. Slade, "Trends in Natural Resouce Commodity Prices: An Analysis of the Time-Domain," <u>Journal of Environmental Economics and Management</u>, 1982.

III. <u>Economic Allocation of Renewable Resources</u>

A. <u>Model of Firm</u> (Fishery Applications)

1. Fisher, Chapter 3.

2. Dasgupta and Heal, Chapter 5.

3. Johansson and Lo⁺fgren, Chapter 3.

4. L.G. Anderson, <u>The Economics of Fisheries Management</u>, Revised Editions (Johns Hopkins University Press, 1986) Chapters 2-4.

5. P. Dasgupta, <u>The Control of Resources</u> (Harvard University Press, 1982) Chapters 6-7.

6. E.R. Morey, "Fishery Economics: An Introduction and Review," <u>Natural Resources Journal</u>, October 1980.

7. L.G. Anderson, "Marine Fisheries," <u>Current Issues in Natural Resource Policy</u>, edited by P.R. Portney (Johns Hopkins University Press, 1982).

B. <u>Forestry Applications</u>

1. M.D. Bowes and J.V. Krutilla, "Multiple Use Management of Public Forestlands," <u>Handbook of Natural Resources and Energy Economics</u>, Vol II (North Holland, 1985).

2. P. Berck, "The Economics of Timber: A Renewable Resource in the Long Run," <u>Bell Journal of Economics</u>, 1979.

3. R.H. Nelson, "The Public Lands," <u>Current Issues in Natural Resource Policy</u>.

209

4. M. Clawson, "Private Forests," <u>Current Issues in Natural Resource Policy</u>.

Duke University

| EC 363 | Economics of Natural Resource Damage Assessment | Spring 1995 |

Class Time: Tuesday and Thursday, 2:15 - 3:30 p.m.
              Location: 116 Old Chemistry Building

Professor: V. Kerry Smith, Duke
              Dale Whittington, UNC

Office: Social Sciences 210
              LSRC 125A

Office Hours (Smith):

| At SS 210: | Tuesday and Thursday | 11:00-12:00 |
| | Tuesday and Thursday | 1:15 - 2:15 |

At LSRC 125A:	Tuesday	3:40 - 5:00
	and (by appointment,	
	contact Ms. Paula Rubio, 613-8084)	

Office Hours (Whittington):

| Page Building | Tuesday and Thursday | 4:00 - 5:00 |
| (210N. Columbia St.) | | |

A.   General Information

This course will deal with the law, economics and practice involved in natural resource damage assessments. The course assumes a working knowledge at the graduate level of micro theory, applied welfare economics and an introductory (graduate level) knowledge of non-market valuation methods. We will schedule some review sessions for those who want to brush up on the material in these areas. The class format will involve lectures and comments by both of us, with some alternating on who takes the lead. Approximately 45 minutes of lecture; 10 to 15 minutes of reactions and 10 to 15 minutes of student initiated discussion.

The objective is to develop a more detailed knowledge of how environmental economics has been and is being used in the area of natural resource damage measurement.

B.   Requirements

Grades will be based on two aspects of each participant's performance.

(1)   Exams - A mid-term (March 23) and a comprehensive final (60 %).

(2)   Research paper (due April 13; 40%).

C. Books and Readings

Two books have been ordered for the course but there are extensive readings as well. One (Ward and Duffield) is listed as optional because of its high price. Neither book is a "text" in the conventional sense and thus neither is required. The readings use 9 of 14 chapters in Kopp and Smith and 5 of 23 chapters in Ward and Duffield. However the later has a number of other chapters relevant to the area that could help in understanding some of the material on the reading list.

Texts:

R.J. Kopp and V.K. Smith (editors), Valuing Natural Assets: The Economics of Natural Resource Damage Assessment.
(Washington, D.C.: Resources for the Future, 1993).
[available in paperback]

K.M. Ward and J.W. Duffied, Natural Resource Damages: Law and Economics (New York: John Wiley, 1992)

Readings:

The readings are on reserve at Perkins Library. A separate set will be available for students at UNC (and if there is sufficient registration, for NC State students).

D. Research Paper

Each registered student is expected to prepare a research paper on some aspect of one of three recent or pending natural resource damage cases:

(1)   Nestucca Oil Spill

Ward and Duffield, Chapter 20 and R. D. Rowe et. al., Contingent Valuation of Natural Resource Damage Due to The Nestucca Oil Spill, June 15, 1991.

(2)   New Bedford Harbor

R. Mendelsohn, D. Hellerstein, M. Huguenin, R. Unsworth and R. Brazee, "Measuring Hazardous Waste Damages With Panel Models," Journal of Environmental Economics and Management, May 1992.

K. E. McConnell, "The Damages to Recreational Activities From PCBs in New Bedford Harbor," unpublished paper, December 1986.

C. J. Cicchetti, J. A. Dubin and L. L. Wilde, "The Use and Misuse of Surveys in Economic Analysis: Natural Resource Damage Assessment Under CERCLA," unpublished paper 1991.

(3)   Clark Fork River

W. D. Schulze and R. D. Rowe, "Contingent Valuation of Natural Resource Damage Due to Injuries to the Upper Clark Fork River Basin," unpublished, December 1993.

The paper cannot exceed 15 pages typed (double-spaced). This is with normal margins and no smaller than Times Roman - 12-point font. References and tables are extra. The paper can be undertaken independently or collaboratively with no more than two authors.

The paper's deadline is firm. Extensions will not be given. Announcement of this policy at this time is regarded as adequate notice to you to plan your schedule to meet the deadline or leave the course now. Exceptions later will not be made.

E.   Guest Speakers

Because this course deals with real uses of economics, we have arranged to have approximately 6 guest speakers: prominent lawyers from both the public and private sides of the legal community; senior economists who participated (and are continuing to participate in rulemaking for damage assessment); and senior economists serving as experts who presented testimony in the damage assessment hearings we will read about. The schedule for these talks is listed below.

While we believe the use of guest lecturers offers a unique opportunity to hear about the issues in damage assessment directly, it also limits the available class sessions for covering this material. We will cover all the material in the readings. However, a substantial amount of outside effort will be expected of participants. Again, this announcement at this time is regarded as adequate notice for your decision making.

Auditors are invited to the guest lectures, but only registered students can be accommodated in the other class sessions.

F.   Readings

I.   Economic Theory of Liability as a Policy Instrument

1.   S. Shavell, "Liability for Harm versus Regulation of Safety," Journal of Legal Studies, (June 1984): 357-374.

212

2.   S. Shavell, "The Judgment Proof Problem," <u>International Review of Law and Economics</u> 6 (1986): 45-58.

3.   T. H. Tietenberg, "Indivisible Toxic Torts: The Economics of Joint and Several Liability," <u>Land Economics</u>, (Nov. 1989): 305-319.

4.   K. Segerson, "Risk and Incentives in Financing Hazardous Waste Cleanup," <u>Journal of Environmental Economics and Management</u>, (January 1989): 1-8.

II.   <u>Emergence of Natural Resource Damage Liability</u>

1.   B. Breen, "Citizen Suits for Natural Resource Damages: Closing a Gap in Federal Environmental Law," <u>Wake Forest Law Review</u>, Vol. 24, (1989): 851-880.

2.   Kopp and Smith - Chapters 3 and 4.

3.   T. A. Campbell, "Natural Resource Damage Assessments: A Glance Backward and a Look Forward," <u>Baylor Law Review</u>, (Spring 1993): 221-232.

4.   P. Wald, "Judicial Review of Economic Analyses," <u>Yale Journal of Regulator</u>, (1983): 43-62.

III.   <u>Background on Theory and Practice of Non-Market Valuation</u>

A.   <u>Review Materials (assumed knowledge)</u>

1.   A. M. Freeman, <u>The Measurement of Environmental and Resource Values</u>, (Resources for the Future, 1993), Chapters 2,3,4,5,6,11,13.

2.   P. O. Johansson, <u>The Economic Theory and Measurement of Environmental Benefits</u>, (Cambridge Univ. Press, 1987), [alternative source for reviews], Chapters 2,3,4,7.

3.   R. T. Carson, "Constructed Markets" in J. Braden and C. Kolstad, <u>Measuring the Demand for Env. Quality</u>, (North Holland 1991).

4.   Ward and Duffield, Chapters 11,12.

B.   <u>What Do We Know About Methods?</u>

1.   Kopp and Smith, Chapters 8-11.

2. V. K. Smith, "Non-Market Valuation of Environmental Resources: An Interpretive Appraisal", Land Economics, (Feb. 1993): 1-26.

3. R. G. Cummings and G. W. Harrison, "Was the Ohio Court Well Informed in its Assessment of the Accuracy of the Contingent Valuation Method?" Natural Resources Journal, (Winter 1994): 1-36.

4. V. K. Smith, "Lightning Rods, Dart Boards and Contingent Valuation," Natural Resources Journal, (Winter 1994): 121-152.

IV. Regulations Governing Damage Assessment, Ohio Decision NOAA Panel, and Current Status

1. Kopp and Smith, Chapters 5,6.

2. Ward and Duffield, Chapters 7,8.

3. Court of Appeals Decision, Ohio Case, July 14, 1989.

4. Federal Register, DOE Proposal Rules, July 22, 1993, DOI Final Rules, March 25, 1994.

5. NOAA Report, Federal Register, January 15, 1993.

6. Federal Register, OPA Proposal Rules, January 7, 1994.

V. Exxon Critique and One Reaction

1. P. R. Portney, "The Contingent Valuation Debate: Why Economists Should Care," Journal of Economic Perspectives, (Fall, 1994): 1-9.

2. P. Diamond and J. Hausman, "Contingent Valuation: Is Some Number Better Than No Number?" Journal of Economic Perspectives (Fall, 1994): 45-64.

3. K.J. Boyle, et. al., "An Investigation of Part-Whole Biases in Contingent Valuation Studies," Journal of Environmental Economics and Management (July 1994): 64-83

4. D. A. Schkade and J. W. Payne, "How People Respond to Contingent Valuation Questions: A Verbal Protocol Analysis of Willingness to Pay for a Environmental Regulation," Journal of Environmental Economics and Management, (January 1994): 88-109.

214

5. D. McFadden, "Contingent Valuation and Social Choice," <u>American Journal of Agricultural Economics,</u> (Nov. 1994): 689-708.

6. W. M. Hanemann, "Valuing the Environment Through Contingent Valuation," <u>Journal of Economic Perspectives,</u> (Fall, 1994): 19-44.

VI. <u>Alaska Analysis</u>

1. R. T. Carson, R. C. Mitchell, W. M. Hanemann, R. J. Kopp, S. Presser, and P. A. Ruud, "Contingent Valuation and Lost Passive Use: Damages from the Exxon Valley," Resources for the Future QE Discussion Paper, 94-18, March 1994.

2. R. T. Carson, et. al., "Some Answers for the NOAA Panel's Questions: the No-Vote Option," unpublished paper, January 1995.

VII. <u>Conceptual Issues Raised for Valuation</u>

A. <u>Embedding, Scope, and Adding-Up Hypotheses</u>

1. D. Kahneman and J. Knetsch, "Valuing Public Goods: The Purchase of Moral Satisfaction," <u>Journal of Environmental Economics and Management,</u> (January 1992).

2. R. T. Carson and R. C. Mitchell, "Sequencing and Nesting in Contingent Valuation Surveys," <u>Journal of Environmental Economics and Management,</u> forthcoming.

3. P. Diamond, "Testing the Internal Consistency of Contingent Valuation Surveys," <u>Journal of Environmental Economics and Management,</u> forthcoming.

4. V. K. Smith and L. Osborne, "Do Contingent Valuation Estimates Pass a "Scope" Test: A Meta Analysis," Center for Environmental and Resource Economics, Duke University, revised December 1994.

5. R. T. Carson, N. E. Flores and W. M. Hanemann, "On the Creation and Destruction of Public Goods: The Matter of Sequencing," University of California, San Diego, unpublished, April 1994.

B. <u>Non Use Values: Should They Be Included</u>

1. D. H. Rosenthal and R. H. Nelson, "Why Existence Value Should Not Be Used in Cost-Benefit Analysis," <u>Journal of Policy Analysis and</u>

Management, (Winter 1992): 116-122.

2.   R. J. Kopp, "Why Existence Value Should Be Used in Cost-Benefit Analysis," Journal of Policy Analysis and Management, (Winter 1992): 123-130.

3.   R. G. Cummings and G. W. Harrison, "The Measurement and Decomposition of Non Use Values: A Critical Review," Environmental and Resource Economics, forthcoming.

4.   D. M. Larson, "On Measuring Existence Value," Land Economics, (Nov. 1993): 377-388.

VIII. Natural Resource Damage Cases

A.   Eagle River - Comparison of Methods

1.   Kopp and Smith, Chapter 7.

2.   R. Rowe and W. Schulze, "Natural Resource Damages in the Colorado Mountains: The Case of the Eagle Mine," unpublished paper, December 1987.

B.   Idaho vs. Southern Refrigerator Transport - Limits to Benefit Transfers

1.   Ward and Duffield, Chapter 16.

C.   National Gypsum: Habitat Equivalency

1.   Fish and Wildlife Service, Report Regarding National Gypsun Litigation - Operable Unit III (Dietzman Tract) for Great Swamp National Refuge, April 1992.

2.   R. C. Bishop, "The Potential Natural Resource Damages From the Askestos Dump Sites in the Dietzman Tract, Great Swamp National Wildlife Refuge, New Jersey," May 1992.

3.   R. E. Unsworth and R. C. Bishop, "Assessing Natural Resource Damages Using Environmental Annuities," unpublished paper, 1993

4.   R. J. Kopp, "An Analyses of Natural Resource Damages Claimed by the U.S. Government from Dietzman Tract OU-3, Asbestos Dump, Great Swamp National Wildlife Refuge, New Jersey," unpublished paper, May 1992.

IX. Emerging Research Issues

    A. Calibration

        1. T. A. Cameron, "Combining Contingent Valuation and Travel Cost Data for the Valuation of Nonmarket Goods," Land Economics, (Aug. 1992): 302-317.

        2. W. Adamowicz, J. Louviere, and M. Williams, "Combining Revealed Preference and State Preference Methods for Valuing Environmental Amenities," Journal of Environmental Economics and Management, (May 1994): 271-293.

        3. C. Mansfield, "A Consistent Method for Calibrating Contingent Valuation Survey Data." (SOE, Duke University, Dec. 1994)

    B. Cognition and Contingent Valuation

        1. J. A. Krosnick, "Response Strategies for Coping With the Cognitive Demands of Attitude Measures in Surveys," Applied Cognitive Psychology, (1991): 215-236.

        2. N. Schwartz, "Cognition, Communication and Survey Measurement: Some Implications for Contingent Valuation Surveys," unpublished paper, July 1994.

    C. Experiments and Contingent Valuation

        1. H. R. Neill, R. G. Cummings, P. T. Ganderton, G. W. Harison and T. McGucken, "Hypothetical Surveys and Real Economic Commitments," Land Economics, May 1994.

        2. P. A. Champ, R. C. Bishop, T. C. Brown and D. W. McCollum, "Some Evidence Concerning the Validity of Contingent Valuation: Preliminary Results of an Experiment," unpublished paper, 1994.

        3. J. W. Duffield and D. A. Patterson, "Field Testing Existence Values: An Instream Flow Trust Fund for Montana Rivers," unpublished, January 1991.

Duke University

EC 373** Topics in Environmental and Resource Economics · · · · · · · · Fall 1995

Class Time:
Professor: · · · · · · · V. Kerry Smith
Office:
Office Hours:

A. *General Information*

As the title implies, this course will consider current research topics in resource and environmental economics and discuss them in some depth. The purpose is to focus attention on areas for research papers and potential dissertation topics.

Three areas will be covered during the semester.

B. *Requirements*

Grades will be based on three aspects of each participant's performance:

(1) a mid-semester exam on **March 17** and a final oral exam on the research paper and material since the mid-term (50%);

(2) at least two class presentations and associated written summaries (20%);

(3) a research paper that <u>must</u> be submitted by **April 14**. No submissions after this date will be accepted. (30%)

The weights for each component are given in parentheses.

C. *Logistics*

(1) Occasionally I will have to miss a class because of travel commitments. Because of this, I would like to designate a time when we can hold make-up classes. On the attached index card, please fill in your name, year in the program, interests in resource and environmental economics, and feasible times for make-up classes.

(2) All registered participants in class will be expected to prepare a research paper. The topic should be selected in consultation with me before the end of January. Schedule an appointment to discuss ideas. An outline (two typed pages, including a separate, one-page statement of your objectives or hypotheses) is due February 18. Research papers should not exceed 18 typed pages. **All papers must be typed**, including the research summaries described below.

(3) I assume that by registering in this class you have an interest in resource and environmental economics. Because of that interest, I also assume you will want to begin to function like professional economists actively involved in the field. This implies that you are expected to be active participants in the REEP

Workshop, which is usually scheduled on the first and third Tuesday of each month (3:40 - 5:00 p.m., 208 Patterson Hall).

(4)   In each topic covered, I will select issues for in-depth discussion. Participants in the class (either individually or as groups) will be expected to complete at least two in-depth reviews and associated discussion in class. Because this is a requirement, I expect participants to volunteer. In the absence of volunteers, I will be forced to assign tasks. The number of these assignments will depend on the number of class participants.

(5)   There is no text. Each topic will have a set of readings that can be borrowed through Barbara Scott.

AREA I: Contingent Valuation: Framing, Reliability, and Role of Discrete Choice Models

1.   *Background*

R. T. Carson. "Constructed Markets," Chapter V in Measuring the Demand for Environmental Quality, edited by J. Braden and C. Kolstad (North Holland, 1991).

B. Fischhoff and L. Furby. "Measuring Values: A Conceptual Framework for Interpreting Transactions with Special Reference to Contingent Valuation of Visibility. Journal of Risk and Uncertainty, June 1988.

W. D. Schulze. "The Use of Direct Methods for Valuing Natural Resource Damages" in Valuing Natural Assets, edited by R. J. Kopp and V. K. Smith, editors (Washington, DC: Resources for the Future), forthcoming 1992.

o   R. C. Mitchell and R. T. Carson. Using Surveys to Value Public Goods (RFF, 1989), Chapters 1, 4, 5, 6, 7, 9.

2.   *Reliability Issues--Questions*

D. Kahneman and J. L. Knetsch. "Valuing Public Goods: The Purchase of Moral Satisfaction." Journal of Environmental Economics and Management (January, 1992).

V. K. Smith. "Arbitrary Values, Good Causes, and Premature Verdicts." Journal of Environmental Economics and Management (January, 1992).

G. W. Harrison. "Valuing Public Goods with the Contingent Valuation Method: A Critique of Kahneman and Knetsch." Journal of Environmental Economics and Management (forthcoming).

D. Kahneman and J. L. Knetsch. "Contingent Valuation and the Value of Public Goods: A Reply." <u>Journal of Environmental Economics and Management</u> (January, 1992).

* R. Gregory, S. Lichtenstein, and P. Slovic. "Valuing Environmental Resources: A Constructive Approach." Unpublished paper, Decision Research (November 4, 1991).

3. Reliability Issues--Analyses

* J. B. Loomis. "Test-Retest Reliability of the Contingent Valuation Method: A Comparison of General Population and Visitor Response." <u>American Journal of Agricultural Economics</u> (February 1989).

* M. J. Kealy, M. Montgomery, and J. F. Dovidio. "Reliability and Predictive Validity of Contingent Values: Does the Nature of the Good Matter?" <u>Journal of Environmental Economics and Management</u> (November 1990).

* M. Dickie, A. Fisher, and S. Gerking. "Market Transactions and Hypothetical Demand Data: A Comparative Study." <u>Journal of the American Statistical Association</u> (March, 1987).

* W. L. Adamowicz and T. Graham-Tomasi. "Revealed Preference Tests of Nonmarket Goods Valuation Methods." <u>Journal of Environmental Economics and Management</u> (January, 1991).

* W. D. Schulze, G. McClelland, and D. Waldman. "Contingent Valuation Methods and the Valuation of Environmental Resources." Unpublished paper (August, 1991).

o V. K. Smith. "Nonmarket Valuation of Environmental Resources: An Interpretive Appraisal." <u>Land Economics</u> (forthcoming).

4. *Discrete Choice Methods and CVM--The Issues*

W. M. Hanemann. "Welfare Evaluations in Contingent Valuation Experiments with Discrete Responses." <u>American Journal of Agricultural Economics</u> (August 1984).

T. A. Cameron. "A New Paradigm for Valuing Nonmarket Goods Using Referendum Data." <u>Journal of Environmental Economics and Management</u> (September 1988).

K. E. McConnell. "Models for Referendum Data: The Structure of Discrete Choice Models for Contingent Valuation." <u>Journal of Environmental Economics and Management</u> (January 1990).

T. A. Cameron. "Combining Contingent Valuation and Travel Cost Data for the Valuation of Nonmarket Goods." University of California at Los Angeles, unpublished paper (1990).

Y. S. Eom and V. K. Smith. "Linking Revealed and Stated Preference Data in Describing Consumer Responses to Risk." Resource and Environmental Economics Program, N. C. State University, unpublished paper (December, 1991).

5. *Discrete Choice Methods and Experimental Design*

T. A. Cameron. "Sample Design for Estimator Efficiency in Probit-Based Discrete Choice Contingent Valuation Models." University of California at Los Angeles, unpublished paper (1989).

T. A. Cameron and D. D. Huppert. "Referendum Contingent Valuation Estimates: Sensitivity to the Assignment of Offered Values." Journal of the American Statistical Association (December, 1991).

J. W. Duffield and D. A. Patterson. "Inference and Optimal Design for a Welfare Measure in Dichotomous Choice Contingent Valuation." Land Economics (May, 1991).

M. Hanemann, J. Loomis, and B. Kanninen. "Statistical Efficiency of Double-Bounded Dichotomous Choice Contingent Valuation." American Journal of Agricultural Economics (November, 1991).

6. *A Policy Debate: Three "Views" of Valuing Visibility at the Grand Canyon with CVM*

* R. D. Rowe, L. G. Chestnut, M. Skumanech. Controlling Wintertime Visibility Impacts at the Grand Canyon National Park: Social and Economic Benefit Analysis. Prepared for the U. S. Environmental Protection Agency (January, 1990).

* W. E. Bolson, et al. Development and Design of a Contingent Value Survey for Measuring the Public's Value for Visibility Improvements at the Grant Canyon National Park. Decision Focus (1990).

* D. S. Levy, et al. "Comments on Contingent Valuation of Altered Visibility in the Grand Canyon Due to Emissions from the Navajo Generating Station." Rand Corporation (June, 1991).

AREA II: Current Issues in Theory of Nonmarket Valuation

1.   *Nonuse Values: Overview and Emerging Issues*

D. A. Graham. "Cost-Benefit Analysis Under Uncertainty." American Economic Review (September 1981).

D. A. Graham. "Public Expenditure Under Uncertainty: The Net Benefit Criteria." American Economic Review (forthcoming).

A. M. Freeman III. "Nonuse Values in Natural Damage Assessment" in Valuing Natural Assets, edited by R. J. Kopp and V. K. Smith (Washington, DC: Resources for the Future, forthcoming).

o   D. H. Rosenthal and R. H. Nelson. "Why Existence Values Should Not Be Used in Cost-Benefit Analysis." Journal of Policy Analysis and Management (forthcoming, 1992).

R. J. Kopp. "Ethical Motivations and Existence Values." Resources for the Future, unpublished paper (November, 1991).

D. Larson. "Measuring Willingness to Pay for Nonmarket Goods." University of California at Davis, unpublished paper (August, 1990).

A. K. Sen. "Rational Fools: A Critique of the Behavioral Foundations of Economic theory." Philosophy and Public Affairs (Volume 6, 1977).

J. Andreoni. "Impure Altruism and Donations to Public Goods: A Theory of Warm Glow Giving." Economic Journal (June, 1990).

W. Michael Hanemann. "Three Approaches to Defining 'Existence' or 'Nonuse' Values Under Certainty." University of California at Berkeley, unpublished paper (1988).

*   K. J. Boyle and R. C. Bishop. "Valuing Wildlife in Benefit-Cost Analyses: A Case Study Involving Endangered Species." Water Resources Research (May, 1987).

*   J. W. Bennett. "Using Direct Questioning to Value the Existence Benefits of Preserved Natural Areas." Austrian Journal of Agricultural Economics (August/December, 1984).

2.   *Environmental Risk Perception and Behavior*

P. Slovic. "Perceptions of Risk." Science (Volume 36, 1987, pp. 280-285).

W. K. Viscusi. "Prospective Reference Theory: Toward an Explanation of the Paradoxes." Journal of Risk and Uncertainty (September, 1982).

V. K. Smith. "Environmental Risk Perception and Valuation: Conventional versus Prospective Reference Theory" in The Social Response to Risk: Policy Formation in an Age of Uncertainty, edited by D. Bromley and K. Segerson (Kluwer, 1992, in press).

W. N. Evans and W. K. Viscusi. "Estimation of State Dependent Utility Functions Using Survey Data." Review of Economics and Statistics (February, 1991).

3.   General Equilibrium Welfare Measurement

R. E. Just, D. L. Hueth, A. Schmitz. Applied Welfare Economics and Public Policy, Appendix D (Prentice Hall, 1982).

W. N. Thurman and M. K. Wohlgenant. "Consistent Estimation of General Equilibrium Welfare Effects." American Journal of Agricultural Economics (November, 1989).

H. Mohring. "Alternative Welfare Gain and Loss Measures." Western Economic Journal (December, 1971).

L. E. Edlefsen. The Deadweight Loss Triangle as a Measure of General Equilibrium Welfare Loss: Harberger Reconsidered." University of Washington, unpublished paper (December, 1983).

L. E. Edlefsen. "Measurement of General Equilibrium Welfare Loss Using Limited Information." University of Washington, unpublished paper (November, 1983).

W. E. Diewert. "The Measurement of Waste and Welfare in Applied General Equilibrium Models." University of British Columbia, unpublished paper (April, 1985).

*   J. Whalley. "How Reliable is Partial Equilibrium?" Review of Economics and Statistics (August, 1975).

*   M. F. Kokoski and V. K. Smith. "A General Equilibrium Analysis of Partial Equilibrium Welfare Measures: The Case of Climate Change." American Economic Review (June, 1987).

*   M. Hazilla and R. J. Kopp. "Social Cost of Environmental Quality Regulations: A General Equilibrium Analysis." Journal of Political Economy (August, 1990).

*   J. Whalley and R. Wigle. "The International Incidence of Carbon Taxes." University of Western Ontario, unpublished paper (October, 1990).

* D. W. Jorgenson and P. J. Wilcoxen. "Reducing U. S. Carbon Dioxide Emissions: The Cost of Different Goals." Harvard University, Discussion Paper No. 1575 (October, 1991).

* J. Piggott and J. Whalley. "Public Good Provision Rules and Income Distribution: Some General Equilibrium Calculations." Empirical Economics (1991).

4.   Welfare Change Indexes and the Theory of Benefits Transfer

* W. H. Desvousges, M. C. Naughton, and G. R. Parsons. "Benefits Transfer: Conceptual Problems in Estimating Water Quality Benefits Using Existing Studies." Water Resources Research (forthcoming, 1992).

* R. A. Luken, F. R. Johnson, and V. Kibler. "Benefits and Costs of Pulp and Paper Effluent Controls Under the Clean Water Act." Water Resources Research (forthcoming, 1992).

o   V. K. Smith. "On Separating Defensible Benefits Transfers from Smoke and Mirrors." Water Resources Research (forthcoming, 1992).

W. E. Diewert. "Harberger's Welfare Indicator and Revealed Preference Theory." American Economic Review (March, 1976).

M. L. Weitzman. "Consumer Surplus as an Exact Approximation When Prices are Appropriately Deflated." Quarterly Journal of Economics (August, 1988).

W. E. Diewert. "Exact and Superlative Welfare Change Indicators." University of British Columbia, unpublished paper (November, 1989).

AREA III.   Theory and Empirical Issues--Nonrenewable Natural Resources

1.   Background

Per-Olov Johansson and K. G. Löfgren. The Economics of Forestry and Natural Resources (Basil Blackwell, 1985). Chapters 2, 3.

J. M. Hartwick. Nonrenewable Resources, Extraction Programs, and Markets (Harwood Publishers, 1989). Chapters 1, 2, 3, 4, 5.

2.   Application I of Theory: Testing the Hotelling Hypothesis

* S. Farrow. "Testing the Efficiency of Extraction of a Stock Resource." Journal of Political Economy (June 1985).

* R. Halvorsen and T. R. Smith. "A Test of the Theory of Exhaustible Resources." Quarterly Journal of Economics (February, 1991).

* M. H. Miller and C. W. Upton. "A Test of the Hotelling Valuation Principle." Journal of Political Economy (February 1985).

3. *Application II of the Theory: Measuring Natural Resource Scarcity*

* A. F. Fisher. "On Measures of Natural Resource Scarcity" in Scarcity and Growth Reconsidered, V. K. Smith, editor (John Hopkins, 1979).

* R. Halvorsen and T. R. Smith. "On Measuring Natural Resource Scarcity." Journal of Political Economy (October 1984).

---

* Candidate papers for participant presentation

o Optional readings

**Examples of the syllabus that would be used.

John F. Kennedy School of Government
Prof. Robert N. Stavins
ENR-201/Econ 1661

Harvard University
Spring 1995
Handout #1 (11/16/94)

G

ENVIRONMENTAL & RESOURCE ECONOMICS AND POLICY
Monday, Wednesday: 1:00-2:30 PM, Room 140
COURSE SYLLABUS

Nature and Purpose of the Course:

This course provides a survey, from the perspective of economics, of public policy issues regarding the use of natural resources and the management of environmental quality. The course covers both conceptual and methodological topics and recent and current applications. The first part of the course is an introduction to the principles of environmental and resource economics, including private and social benefit-cost models. We develop basic theory and methods, and examine actual practice and politics. In the second part of the course, the focus is on natural resources, both nonrenewable resources (minerals and energy) and renewable resources (water, forests, land, fisheries, and wildlife). In the third part of the course, we examine environmental policy, beginning with air pollution problems, including: local problems (both stationary and mobile sources); regional air pollution (acid rain); and global problems (the greenhouse effect and stratospheric ozone depletion). Next we explore water pollution issues, followed by an investigation of solid and hazardous waste management problems. In the fourth and final part of the course, we focus on political and macroeconomic aspects of environmental policy.

Instructor:	Robert N. Stavins
	Office: Room 265, KSG
	Phone: 495-1820
	Office Hours: Monday, 4-5 pm, and by appointment
	Assistant: Lesly Adkins-Shellie, Room 263, 495-8833
	(leslya@ksg1.harvard.edu)
Course Assistants:	Steve Kafka (Head Teaching Assistant)
	Phone: TBA
	E-Mail: kafka@husc.harvard.edu
	Office Hours: Times to be arranged
	Richard Newell
	Phone: 496-9330
	E-Mail: rgnewell@fas.harvard.edu
	Office Hours: Times to be arranged
	Margaret Madajewicz
	Phone: 628-2484
	E-Mail: madajew@husc3.harvard.edu
	Office Hours: Times to be arranged

Prerequisites: One course in microeconomic theory, or permission of the instructor; an introductory course (such as Social Analysis 10, P-125, API-1-01, or M-221) is adequate preparation. Students should be familiar with basic economic concepts, such as: supply & demand functions, consumers' surplus, opportunity cost, marginal analysis, and time discounting. It may be helpful to review a microeconomics textbook.

1

Reading Material:

There are two required texts for the course:

>   Tietenberg, Tom. *Environmental and Natural Resource Economics*, Third Edition. New York, New York: Harper Collins, Inc., 1992.

>   Portney, Paul R., ed. *Public Policies for Environmental Protection.* Washington, D.C.: Resources for the Future. Distributed by Johns Hopkins University Press, Baltimore, Maryland, 1990.

These books are available at the Harvard Coop, and both are on reserve at the Kennedy School Library, on the ground floor of the Littauer Building. Extensive use will be made of other materials, as indicated on the course reading list (Handout #2). All required readings are available in the Course Materials Distribution Office (Belfer G-6) and are on reserve in the Kennedy School Library; optional readings are only on reserve. If you are unable to find any of the assigned materials, please let the course assistants know as soon as possible. All reading material, with the exception of the starred items, is required. Most of the reading is quite straightforward, but a few of the readings may be more challenging for some students because of the economics and/or mathematics background assumed.

Course Requirements and Grading:

We will meet for a total of 24 class sessions. There will be: three quantitative problem sets (due at the beginning of class on February 22, March 8, and April 5); two problem sets consisting of short essays on policy issues (due at the beginning of class on April 19 and May 3); an in-class midterm exam (March 15); and an "in-class" (closed book) final exam during exam period. Late problem sets will be penalized by a grade adjustment.

Optional review sessions on specific subjects of interest or difficulty will be conducted periodically throughout the semester by the course assistants. These review sessions will be announced in advance and take place on Fridays, from 1:00 PM to 2:30 PM in Room 280, and on Thursdays at a time and place to be announced.

Course grading will be on the following basis:

Problem Sets	25%
Midterm Exam	30%
Final Exam	45%
	100%

There will be no makeup for the midterm exam; instead, the weight assigned to the final exam will be adjusted accordingly. For a detailed picture of the class sessions, see the course reading list (Handout #2). A brief overview of the course is provided on the following page.

2

ENR-201/ECON 1661: COURSE OUTLINE

I.   INTRODUCTION TO ENVIRONMENTAL & RESOURCE ECONOMICS AND POLICY

    A.   Introduction to Environmental & Natural Resource Economics - *Feb 1*

    B.   Principles of Environmental & Natural Resource Policy: Uses and Limits of Conventional Economic Analysis - *Feb 6 & 8*

    C.   Social Benefit-Cost Analysis: Environmental Benefit Evaluation
        1.   Theory and Methods - *Feb 13 & 15*
        2.   Practice and Politics - *Feb 22*   *(Problem Set #1 is Due)*

II.   NATURAL RESOURCE ECONOMICS AND POLICY

    A.   Nonrenewable Resources
        1.   Optimal Extraction & Use of Nonrenewable Natural Resources - *Feb 27*
        2.   Markets, Market Failure, & Nonrenewable Natural Resources - *March 1*
        3.   Energy Economics and Policy - *March 6* (Prof. Adam Jaffe)

    B.   Renewable Resources
        1.   Common-Property Problems, Water Resources - *March 8*   *(Problem Set #2 is Due)*
        2.   Forestry and Forested Wetlands - *March 13*

(Midterm Examination: March 15)

III. ENVIRONMENTAL ECONOMICS AND POLICY

    A.   Overview of the Economics of Pollution Control
        1.   Criteria for Alternative Policies - *March 20*
        2.   Cost-Effective Policies for Pollution Control - *March 22*

    B.   Air Pollution
        1.   Local Air Pollution - *April 3*
        2.   Acid Rain - *April 5*   *(Problem Set #3 is Due)*
        3.   Global Air Pollution: Greenhouse Effect & Stratospheric Ozone Depletion
            a.   Basic Science of Global Change - Monday *April 10* (Prof. William Clark)
            b.   Economics and Policy of Global Change - *April 12 & 17*

    C.   Water Pollution: Overview of Water-Quality Problems and Policy, and Non-point Source Water Pollution & Wetlands - *April 19*   *(Problem Set #4 is Due)*

    D.   Solid and Hazardous Waste Management Problems and Policy - *April 24 & 26*

IV.   THE FUTURE OF NATURAL RESOURCE AND ENVIRONMENTAL POLICY

    A.   Sustainable Development - *May 1*

    B.   Politics and Policy - *May 3*   *(Problem Set #5 is Due)*

3

John F. Kennedy School of Government
Prof. Robert N. Stavins
ENR-201/Econ 1661

Harvard University
Spring 1995
Handout #2 (2/21/95)

ENVIRONMENTAL & RESOURCE ECONOMICS AND POLICY
READING LIST

All readings are required, with the exception of those preceded by an asterisk (*). Readings should be completed prior to class sessions. If possible, selections for each class should be read in the order listed.

FEBRUARY 1 (Wed): INTRODUCTION TO ENVIRONMENTAL & RESOURCE ECONOMICS

Tietenberg, Tom. *Environmental and Natural Resource Economics*. 3rd Edition. New York, New York: Harper Collins, Inc., 1992. Chapter 1 - Visions of the Future, pp. 1-17.

Tietenberg, Chapter 2 - Economics of the Environment: An Overview. pp. 18-43.

Cairncross, Frances. "Costing the Earth: Survey on the Environment." *The Economist*, September 2, 1989, pp. 1-18.

Reilly, William K. "The Greening of EPA." *EPA Journal*, July/August 1989, pp. 8-10.

FEBRUARY 6 (Mon): PRINCIPLES OF ENVIRONMENTAL AND RESOURCE POLICY: USES AND LIMITS OF CONVENTIONAL ECONOMIC ANALYSIS -- PART I

Tietenberg, Chapter 3 - Property Rights, Externalities, and Environmental Problems, pp. 44-71.

Tietenberg, Chapter 4 - Regulating the Market: Information and Uncertainty, pp. 72-74, 83-99.

Passell, Peter. "Life's Risks: Balancing Fear Against Reality of Statistics." *New York Times*, May 8, 1989, pp. 1, D12.

Passell, Peter. "Making a Risky Life Bearable: Better Data, Clearer Choices." *New York Times*, May 9, 1989, pp. 1, C13.

Stavins, Robert N., ed. *Project 88 -- Round II, Incentives for Action: Designing Market-Based Environmental Strategies*. Sponsored by Senator Timothy E. Wirth, Colorado, and Senator John Heinz, Pennsylvania. Washington, D.C., May 1991, Chapter 1, pp. 1-13.

Kelman, Steven. "Cost-Benefit Analysis: An Ethical Critique." *Regulation*, January 1981, pp. 33-40.

DeLong, James V., *et. al.* "Defending Cost-Benefit Analysis: Replies to Steven Kelman." *Regulation*, March/April 1981, pp. 39-43.

FEBRUARY 8 (Wed): PRINCIPLES OF ENVIRONMENTAL AND RESOURCE POLICY: USES AND LIMITS OF CONVENTIONAL ECONOMIC ANALYSIS -- PART II

[See Readings for Monday, February 6]

FEBRUARY 13 (Mon): SOCIAL BENEFIT-COST ANALYSIS: METHODS OF ENVIRONMENTAL BENEFIT EVALUATION I

Tietenberg, Chapter 4 - Regulating the Market: Information and Uncertainty, pp. 74-83.

Pearce, David W. and Anil Markandya. *Environmental Policy Benefits: Monetary Valuation.* Paris: Organization for Economic Co-operation and Development, 1989, pp. 35-47.

Freeman, A. Myrick III. *"Methods for Assessing the Benefits of Environmental Programs."* Handbook of Natural Resource and Energy Economics, Volume I, eds. Allen V. Kneese and James L. Sweeney, pp. 223-224, 250-254, 264-266. Amsterdam: North Holland, 1985.

McConnell, Kenneth E. "The Economics of Outdoor Recreation." *Handbook of Natural Resource and Energy Economics, Volume II,* eds. Allen V. Kneese and James L. Sweeney, pp. 681-706. Amsterdam: North Holland, 1985.

Phillips, Carl V. and Richard J. Zeckhauser. "Contingent Valuation of Damage to Natural Resources: How Accurate? How Appropriate?" *Toxics Law Reporter.* October 4, 1989, pp. 520-530.

FEBRUARY 15 (Wed): SOCIAL BENEFIT-COST ANALYSIS: METHODS OF ENVIRONMENTAL BENEFIT EVALUATION II

Pearce and Markandya 1989, pp. 25-35.

Yang, Edward, Roger C. Dower, and Mark Menefee. *The Use of Economic Analysis in Valuing Natural Resource Damages.* Prepared for National Oceanic and Atmospheric Administration, U.S. Department of Commerce. Washington, D.C.: Environmental Law Institute, 1984, pp. 63-66.

Freeman, A. Myrick III. *"Methods for Assessing the Benefits of Environmental Programs."* Handbook of Natural Resource and Energy Economics, Volume I, eds. Allen V. Kneese and James L. Sweeney, pp. 247-250, 259-261. Amsterdam: North Holland, 1985.

FEBRUARY 22 (Wed): PRACTICE & POLITICS OF SOCIAL BENEFIT-COST ANALYSIS

NOTE: Problem Set #1 is due at beginning of class.

Saving the Tuolumne and *Saving the Tuolumne: Sequel*, case studies C15-86-701.0 and C15-86-701.1. Cambridge: John F. Kennedy School of Government, Harvard University, 1986.

Stavins, Robert. *The Tuolumne River: Preservation or Development? An Economic Assessment.* Berkeley: Environmental Defense Fund, October 1983, pp. 16-18, 25-61.

FEBRUARY 27 (Mon): NATURAL RESOURCE ECONOMICS AND POLICY I: OPTIMAL EXTRACTION & USE OF NONRENEWABLE RESOURCES

Tietenberg, Chapter 6 - Allocation of Depletable and Renewable Resources, pp. 125-152.

MARCH 1 (Wed): NATURAL RESOURCE ECONOMICS AND POLICY II: MARKETS, MARKET FAILURE, AND PUBLIC POLICY

Tietenberg, Chapter 8 - Recyclable Resources: Minerals, pp. 188-200, 210-221.

Tietenberg, Chapter 13 - Generalized Resource Scarcity, pp. 331-359.

Agberyegbe, Terence D. "Interest Rates and Metal Price Movements: Further Evidence." *Journal of Environmental Economics and Management* 16(1989):184-192.

* Slade, Margaret E. "Trends in Natural-Resource Commodity Prices: An Analysis of the Time Domain." *Journal of Environmental Economics and Management* 9(1982):122-137.

MARCH 6 (Mon): ENERGY ECONOMICS AND POLICY (Prof. Adam Jaffe)

Tietenberg, Chapter 7 - Depletable, Nonrecyclable Energy Resources: Oil, Gas, Coal, and Uranium, pp. 153-187.

Cairncross, Frances. Chapter 5, "Energy Efficiency." *Costing the Earth*, pp.111-128. Boston: Harvard Business School Press, 1991.

Jaffe, Adam B. and Robert N. Stavins. "The Energy Efficiency Gap: What Does It Mean?" *Energy Policy* 22(1994):657-665.

* Jaffe, Adam B. and Robert N. Stavins. "The Energy Paradox and the Diffusion of Conservation Technology." *Resource and Energy Economics* 16(1994):91-122.

MARCH 8 (Wed): RENEWABLE RESOURCES I: COMMON-PROPERTY PROBLEMS, WATER USE & ALLOCATION

NOTE: Problem Set #2 is due at beginning of class.

Tietenberg, Chapter 12 - Renewable Common-Property Resources: Fisheries and Other Species, pp. 303-330.

Tietenberg, Chapter 9 - Replenishable But Depletable Resources: Water, pp. 222-247.

Stavins, ed., *Project 88 -- Round II*, "Implementing Water Markets," pp. 69-77.

Stavins, Robert N. *Trading Conservation Investments for Water*. Berkeley: Environmental Defense Fund, March 1983, pp. 137-154.

3

MARCH 13 (Mon): RENEWABLE RESOURCES II: FORESTRY AND FORESTED WETLANDS

Tietenberg, Chapter 11 - Storable, Renewable Resources: Forests, pp. 277-302.

Stavins, ed., *Project 88 -- Round II*, "Eliminating Below Cost Timber Sales on National Forests," pp. 77-86.

Stavins, Robert N. and Adam B. Jaffe. "Unintended Impacts of Public Investments on Private Decisions: The Depletion of Forested Wetlands." *American Economic Review* 80(1990):337-352. [READ AROUND THE MATH]

Stavins, Robert N. "Alternative Renewable Resource Strategies: A Simulation of Optimal Use." *Journal of Environmental Economics and Management* 19(1990):143-159. [READ AROUND THE MATH]

* Hartman, Richard. "The Harvesting Decision When a Standing Forest Has Value." *Economic Inquiry* 14(1976):52-58.

MARCH 15 (Wed): MIDTERM EXAMINATION

MARCH 20 (Mon): ECONOMICS OF POLLUTION CONTROL: OVERVIEW & POLICY CRITERIA

Tietenberg, Chapter 14 - Economics of Pollution Control: An Overview, pp. 360-391.

Portney, Paul R. "The Evolution of Federal Regulation." *Public Policies for Environmental Protection*, ed. Paul R. Portney, pp. 7-25. Washington, D.C.: Resources for the Future, 1990.

Gough, Michael. "Environmental Exposures and Cancer Risks." *Resources*, Winter 1990, pp. 9-12.

U.S. Environmental Protection Agency. *Economic Incentives: Options for Environmental Protection.* Washington, D.C., March 1991, pp. vii-viii, 1-1 to 1-8.

Stavins, Robert N. "Correlated Environmental Uncertainty and Policy Instrument Choice." Discussion paper, John F. Kennedy School of Government, Harvard University, Cambridge, Massachusetts, October 1994.

* Stavins, Robert N. "Transaction Costs and Tradeable Permits." *Journal of Environmental Economics and Management*, forthcoming, Volume 28, No. 4, July 1995.

* Jaffe, Adam B. and Robert N. Stavins. "Dynamic Incentives of Environmental Regulation: The Effects of Alternative Policy Instruments on Technology Diffusion." *Journal of Environmental Economics and Management*, forthcoming, 1995.

MARCH 22 (Wed): COST-EFFECTIVE POLICIES FOR POLLUTION CONTROL

[See Readings for Monday, March 20]

APRIL 3 (Mon): LOCAL AIR POLLUTION - STATIONARY AND MOBILE SOURCES

Tietenberg, Chapter 15 - Stationary-Source Local Air Pollution, pp. 392-421.

Hahn, Robert W. "Economic Prescriptions for Environmental Problems: How the Patient Followed the Doctor's Orders." *Journal of Economic Perspectives* 3(1989):95-114.

Tietenberg, Chapter 17 - Mobile-Source Air Pollution, pp. 450-475.

Portney, Paul. "Economics and the Clean Air Act." *Journal of Economic Perspectives* 4(1990):173-181.

* Portney, Paul. "Air Pollution Policy." *Public Policies for Environmental Protection*, ed. Paul R. Portney, pp. 27-96. Washington, D.C.: Resources for the Future, 1990.

APRIL 5 (Wed): ACID RAIN

NOTE: Problem Set #3 is due at beginning of class.

Tietenberg, Chapter 16 - Regional and Global Air Pollutants: Acid Rain and Atmospheric Modifications, pp. 422-432.

Controlling Acid Rain, 1986. Case Study C15-86-699.0. Cambridge: John F. Kennedy School of Government, Harvard University, 1986.

Stavins, ed., *Project 88*, Chapter 3 - Air Quality Issues, pp. 30-34.

Krupnick, Alan J., Douglas R. Bohi, and Dallas Burtraw. "Emissions Trading in the Electric Utility Industry." *Resources*, Summer 1990, pp. 10-13.

Johnston, James L. "The Trading of Sulfur Dioxide Emission Reductions." *Regulation* 14, no. 4, 1992.

Hahn, Robert W. "Go for the Market -- Warts and All." Letter to the Editor. *Regulation*, Winter 1992.

APRIL 10 (Mon): GLOBAL AIR POLLUTION I: BASIC SCIENCE OF THE GREENHOUSE EFFECT AND STRATOSPHERIC OZONE DEPLETION (Prof. William Clark)

Tietenberg, Chapter 16 - Regional and Global Air Pollutants, pp. 432-449.

Graedel, Thomas E. and Paul J. Crutzen. "The Changing Atmosphere." *Managing Planet Earth*, pp. 13-23. New York: W. H. Freeman and Company, 1990.

Intergovernmental Panel on Climate Change. *Policymakers Summary of the Scientific Assessment of Climate Change*. Report to IPCC from Working Group 1. Bracknell, UK, June 1990.

* Clark, William C. "Managing Planet Earth." *Managing Planet Earth*, pp. 1-11. New York: W. H. Freeman and Company, 1990.

* Schneider, Stephen H. "The Greenhouse Effect: Science and Policy." *Science* 243(1989):771-781.

5

APRIL 12 (Wed): GLOBAL AIR POLLUTION II: ECONOMICS

Brown, Peter G. "Policy Analysis, Welfare Economics, and the Greenhouse Effect." *Journal of Policy Analysis and Management* 7(1988):471-475.

Passell, Peter. "Staggering Cost Is Forseen To Curb Warming of Earth." *New York Times*, November 19, 1989, pp. 1, 18.

Barrett, Scott, Peter Bohm, Brian Fisher, Masihiro Kuroda, J. Mubazi, Anwar Shah, and Robert Stavins. "An Assessment of Greenhouse Policy Instruments." Chapter 10 in the Report of Working Group III, Intergovernmental Panel on Climate Change (IPCC), Geneva, Switzerland, September 30, 1994.

APRIL 17 (Mon): GLOBAL AIR POLLUTION III: POLICY

[See Readings for Wednesday, April 12]

APRIL 19 (Wed): WATER POLLUTION: OVERVIEW OF PROBLEMS & POLICY, AND NON-POINT SOURCES & WETLAND PROTECTION

NOTE: Problem Set #4 is due at beginning of class.

Tietenberg, Chapter 18 - Water Pollution, pp. 476-509.

Portney, Chapter 4 - Water Pollution Policy, pp. 121-145.

Sweedens Swamp Case [to be distributed]

APRIL 24 (Mon): SOLID AND HAZARDOUS WASTE MANAGEMENT PROBLEMS AND POLICY I:

Tietenberg, Chapter 8 - Recyclable Resources: Minerals, Etc, pp. 200-210.

Stavins, ed. *Project 88 -- Round II*, "Solid and Hazardous Waste Management," pp. 40-68.

Porter, Richard. "A Social Benefit-Cost Analysis of Mandatory Deposits on Beverage Containers." *Journal of Environmental Economics and Management* 5(1978):351-375.

Tietenberg, Chapter 19 - Toxic Substances, pp. 510-541.

Portney, Chapter 5 - Hazardous Wastes, pp. 177-189.

APRIL 26 (Wed): SOLID & HAZARDOUS WASTE MANAGEMENT PROBLEMS AND POLICY II:
[See Readings for Monday, April 24]

6

May 1 (Mon): SUSTAINABILITY:

Tietenberg, Chapter 22 - The Quest for Sustainable Development. 3rd Edition, 1992, pp. 599-626.

Solow, Robert M. "Sustainability: An Economist's Perspective." *National Geographic Research & Exploration* 8(1992):10-21.

Pearce, David W. and R. Kerry Turner. *Economics of Natural Resources and the Environment.* Baltimore: The Johns Hopkins University Press, 1990. Chapter 3 - The Sustainable Economy, pp. 43-58.

* Reilly, William K. "The Green Thumb of Capitalism: The Environmental Benefits of Sustainable Growth." *Policy Review*, Fall 1990, pp. 16-21.

May 3 (Wed): THE FUTURE OF NATURAL RESOURCE AND ENVIRONMENTAL POLICY

NOTE: Problem Set #5 is due at beginning of class.

Hahn, Robert W. and Robert N. Stavins. "Incentive-Based Environmental Regulation: A New Era From An Old Idea?" *Ecology Law Quarterly* 18(1991):1-3, 26-42.

Tietenberg, Chapter 20 - Pollution Control Policy: Distributional Effects., pp. 542-565.

Stavins, ed. *Project 88 - Round II,* "Efficiency Equity, and the Politics of Market-Based Environmental Policies," pp. 87-95.

Jaffe, Adam B., Steven R. Peterson, Paul R. Portney, and Robert N. Stavins. "Environmental Regulation and the Competitiveness of U.S. Manufacturing: What Does the Evidence Tells Us?" *Journal of Economic Literature*, forthcoming, June 1995.

Portney, Paul R. "Overall Assessment and Future Directions." *Public Policies for Environmental Protection*, ed. Paul R. Portney, pp. 275-289.

* Tietenberg, Chapter 23 - Visions of the Future Revisited, pp. 627-639.

John F. Kennedy School of Government
Prof. Robert N. Stavins
ENR-201/Econ 1661

Harvard University
Spring 1995
Handout #8

PROBLEM SET #1
[Due: Wednesday, February 22, at beginning of class]

1. There are important trade-offs involved in granting "Wild and Scenic River Status" to portions of a river. The critical issue is how much of this public good, a free-flowing river, should be protected from further development. As an analyst in the Office of Policy Analysis of the U.S. Department of the Interior, you are called upon to make a recommendation, based upon the following information. Each year, one thousand people benefit from the River's various services, exclusively for recreational purposes. A contingent valuation survey carried out by your office has estimated that _each_ beneficiary has the same demand function for river preservation,

$$q = 40 - (0.4)(P)$$

where P is the price-per-mile which persons are willing to pay (per year) for q miles of river preserved. You find that the marginal (opportunity) cost of preservation is $25,000 per mile per year. [Hint: You need to derive the market (aggregate) demand curve for a public good.]

   (a)   How many miles of the river would be preserved in an efficient allocation?

   (b)   What is the magnitude of the total (gross), annual benefits associated with this (efficient allocation) policy?

   (c)   What are the total, annual costs of the policy?

   (d)   What is the magnitude of the total (annual) consumers' surplus?

   (e)   How large are net, annual benefits?

   (f)   If it turns out that the marginal cost of preservation is only $20,000 per mile per year, how many miles of the river would be preserved in an efficient allocation?

   (g)   What if substitute sites were available to beneficiaries, and so it was found that their demands were substantially more elastic, i.e. their individual demand functions for river preservation are

$$q = 40 - (1.2)(P)$$

   In this case, with the original marginal costs of preservation of $25,000 per mile per year, how many miles of the river would be preserved in an efficient allocation?

2. If the total benefits to society of achieving some specific level of pollution control are significantly greater than the total costs to society of doing so, will it necessarily be economically _efficient_ to do so? Explain your answer with words _and_ a graph.

1

236

3.   A survey of all recreational fishermen using Lake Chutzik in the Adirondacks (upstate New York) during the summer of 1990 produced the following information regarding their numbers and their residences (origins):

Origin	Per Capita Visitation Rate	Total "Travel Cost"	Number of Users
#1	0.040	$ 20.00	1,000
#2	0.025	50.00	3,000
#3	0.015	70.00	2,000
TOTAL			6,000

(a)   Plot the participation function on a graph, label the axes and the points representing each origin.

(b)   On a second graph, draw the related demand functions (for each origin) for recreational fishing services from the lake. Label the axes and the demand functions.

(c)   On the second graph, draw the appropriate aggregate (market) demand function.

(d)   Calculate the consumers surplus for all users from each origin, and the total consumers surplus for all users (i.e. from all origins).

(e)   Assuming that the survey data were accurate and exhaustive, does your grand total of consumers' surplus in part (d) provide an unbiased assessment of the economic benefits of the lake for recreational fishing? Explain.

237

John F. Kennedy School of Government
Prof. Robert N. Stavins
ENR-201/Econ 1661

Harvard University
Spring 1995
Handout #10

PROBLEM SET #2

[Due Wednesday, March 8, at beginning of class]

1. Following the reasoning of Harold Hotelling, we might expect the real price of nonrenewable resources to increase continually over time, as resource stocks are depleted. But, empirical evidence (as documented by Margaret Slade) for a number of nonrenewable (mineral) resources indicates that their prices over the past century have not been increasing monotonically; instead, the price paths of a number of nonrenewable resources have been "U-shaped."

    (a) Explain what's going on; i.e. resolve this apparent anomaly between theory and observation. In case you're curious, here are citations to the articles mentioned above:

    Hotelling, Harold. "The Economics of Exhaustible Resources." *Journal of Political Economy* 39(1931):137-175.

    Slade, Margaret E. "Trends in Natural Resource Commodity Prices: An Analysis of the Time Domain." *Journal of Environmental Economics and Management* 9(1982):122-137.

    (b) For a typical nonrenewable resource, would you expect the rate of extraction to increase, be constant, or decrease over time? Why?

2. Under what condition would it be *likely* that the complete *exhaustion* of a nonrenewable natural resource would be socially optimal? Explain.

3. During the consideration in Congress in 1991 of a comprehensive energy act, the debate included many references to "America's excessive dependence on foreign oil." Is there a reasonable need for public policy to address our "dependence on foreign oil," or will the market-generated mix of imports and domestic production provide the appropriate balance in this area? Why, why not?

[PLEASE TURN FOR QUESTION #4]

238

4.	In class, we developed a simple two-period model of dynamically efficient extraction of a nonrenewable resource with a finite stock of 20 units, constant marginal extraction costs of 2.0, and constant demand given by the inverse demand function:

$$p = 8 - 0.4q$$

Everything remains as before (including the 10% interest rate), except for the demand for the resource. We now change the situation in the following manner: we know in period 1 that due to technological change, the demand for the resource will decrease in period 2. Hence, there are now different demand functions for each period. In particular, inverse demand functions for the two periods are:

$$p_1 = 8 - 0.4q_1$$

$$p_2 = 6 - 0.4q_2$$

(a)	What is the socially optimal quantity of resource extraction in the two periods? This part of the question can be satisfactorily approached with a carefully drawn graph. But, in addition, if you're comfortable using some simple algebra, you can get more precise answers by setting up the appropriate equations. It's up to you.

(b)	Compare your optimal extraction in period 1 to the optimal period 1 extraction we derived in class for the case of constant demand. Explain the logic (intuition) behind the similarity or difference.

(c)	What is the optimal real (current) price of the resource in the two periods?

(d)	Compare your optimal price in period 1 to the optimal period 1 price we derived in class for the case of constant demand. Explain the logic (intuition) behind the similarity or difference.

(e)	What is the marginal user cost (or scarcity rent or shadow price) of the resource in the two periods?

(f)	Comment on the applicability of the simple Hotelling Rule developed in class to the context of a nonrenewable resource for which demand is not constant over time. Can you offer any intuition about what's going on?

MIDTERM EXAMINATION

This is a closed-book, closed-notes examination. There are three parts to the exam, with a total of 8 questions. All are required. You have until 2:25 pm to complete your work. The number of points assigned to questions (and the number of minutes you may wish to allot) are indicated at the beginning of each section; there are 70 total points in the exam (and about 70 minutes for you to work).

Please write your answers to the three parts of the exam -- I, II, and III -- in *three* separate blue books, which should be numbered accordingly. Be sure to put your ID number (but *not* your name) on *all* blue books. Also, please be concise with your answers; points will be subtracted if you provide information which, although accurate, does not address the question. Finally, please write neatly; illegible answers will receive zero credit. Good luck!

I. SHORT ANSWERS (30 points; 6 questions; 5 points each)

1.   Under what conditions is it likely that a nonrenewable resource will be exploited more slowly than the dynamically efficient rate?

2.   What justification is there for using an avoided-cost measure of "benefits" in a net present value analysis?

3.   Briefly explain why marginal user cost (scarcity rent) declines over time for a non-renewable natural resource for which extraction costs increase as a function of cumulative extraction.

4.   Briefly describe one potential market failure in energy markets and two alternative public policies for addressing that market failure.

5.   The *Limits to Growth* study, much criticized by economists, predicts "overshoot and collapse." For what kind of natural resource might market behavior result in such a scenario? Be as specific as possible.

6.   What effect is a dramatic increase in South American soybean production likely to have on the rate of forested wetland depletion in the United States? Why?

II. ESSAY (1 question; 20 points -- 5 points for each part)

7.   For each of the following environmental problems, explain which method (or methods) of environmental valuation you would use and why.

   (a)   Exposure of workers to hazardous substances at pesticide factories

   (b)   Emissions from coal-burning power plants causing impairment of visibility at the Grand Canyon

   (c)   New dams and reservoirs on the Columbia River reducing the quality of recreational fishing

   (d)   an oil spill in the open ocean that reduces catches by commercial fishing fleets

(TURN OVER FOR NEXT PROBLEM)

III. PROBLEM (1 question; 20 points -- 4 points for each part)

8. You wish to determine the dynamically efficient rate of extraction of a nonrenewable resource over two time periods, t_1 and t_2. Please assume the simplest case, in which there are no externalities or other complicating factors. The demand function for the resource is known to remain constant over time, and is given by the inverse demand function:

$$p = 150 - 3 \cdot q$$

Marginal extraction costs for the resource are constant at 30 (mec = 30). This question can be addressed with carefully drawn graphs, or you may use a mathematical approach if you prefer. If you use graphs, it is essential that you label the axes and all other elements of your graphs. If you use a mathematical approach, all of your work (equations, etc.) must be shown.

(a) Ignoring scarcity of the resource stock, what would a period-by-period static efficiency criterion suggest as the dynamically efficient rates of extraction in the two periods. Please call these extraction rates q_1 and q_2.

(b) Now, we allow for the reality that the stock of the resource is limited; in fact, the total available stock, S, is 60 units. In the absence of any discounting, what would be the dynamically efficient quantities of resource extraction in the two periods? Again, these extraction rates should be called q_1 and q_2.

(c) Next, we allow for a positive discount rate, i = 0.20 (20%). What are the dynamically efficient quantities of resource extraction in the two periods? Please call these extraction rates Q_1 and Q_2.

(d) What is marginal user cost in each period? Show this on a graph or show your mathematical derivation.

(e) If the total stock of the resource had been 50 units, instead of 60, would the marginal user cost in period 1 have been greater, the same, or less? Use a graph (or math) to demonstrate this, *and* explain in words the logic (intuition) behind your answer.

241

John F. Kennedy School of Government
Prof. Robert N. Stavins
ENR-201/Econ 1661

Harvard University
Spring 1994
Handout #24

PROBLEM SET #3

The purpose of this final problem set, which is really a brief paper, is to provide you with an opportunity to apply some of the concepts learned in the course to a natural resource or environmental policy issue of particular interest to you. Choose only *one* of the following questions.

The paper should be typed, double-spaced, and *no more than 3 pages* in length (*including* any tables, figures, or reference lists you choose to include). Please be sure to tell us the *number* of the question you are answering. Papers are due at the beginning of our final class meeting on Wednesday, May 4th. As always, late papers will be penalized by a grade adjustment. Again, remember to choose only *one* of the following:

1. Following the United Nations Conference on Environment and Development (UNCED), held in Brazil in June of 1992, increasing attention is being given to concerns about worldwide depletion of forests. Prepare a brief memo outlining an international tradeable permit scheme to address this problem.

2. Much attention was given by the news media and the general public to the Exxon Valdez oil spill. How serious was the spill relative to other accidental and chronic releases? How would you compare the threat to other environmental risks? Given predictions made at the time of the Congressional decision to proceed with development of the trans-Alaska pipeline, should the spill be a surprise?

3. What sort of policies would you propose to prevent future oil spills? You may wish to assess some of the actions taken by Congress.

4. Develop some ideas of economic-incentive policies for the control of mobile-source air pollution.

5. Critique the concept and practice of "debt-for-nature swaps" from an environmental perspective, and from the perspective of debtor, developing countries and industrialized (debtee) nations.

6. Analyze peak and seasonal water pricing as potential water policies for Massachusetts.

7. Analyze the wisdom and the practicality of having Federal and state environmental impact statements reflect secondary as well as direct impacts of projects.

8. Develop a policy proposal which would encourage *efficient* levels of recycling in Massachusetts.

9. How could an effective deposit-refund system for containerized hazardous waste be built into a revised RCRA (Resource Conservation and Recovery Act)?

10. How should one go about trying to assess the success of the new tradeable-permit program for acid-rain control?

OVERVIEW OF COURSE TOPICS

In preparing for the final exam, please keep in mind that you are responsible for all required material in the textbook and other sources. In addition, here's a list of major topics covered in our class sessions.

1.   What's a model

2.   What's an economic perspective

3.   Static efficiency

4.   Dynamic efficiency

5.   Relationship between property rights & efficiency

6.   Externalities

7.   Common-property resources

8.   Public "goodedness"

9.   Discount rates - what they represent

10.   Alternative approaches to environmental protection/resource management
      a.   Private negotiation (Coase theorem);
      b.   Court system & liability rules;
      c.   Legislative and administrative regulation;
      d.   Economic-incentive methods

11.   Principles and practice of private (internal) b/c analysis of an environmental issue -- herbicide use in forestry; various technical aspects of b/c analysis and the limits thereof

12.   Theory and methods of social b/c analysis: various methods of valuing externalities
      a.   Preference-revealing survey methods (contingent valuation)
      b.   Inferring WTP from market behavior
            (1)   Hotelling-Clawson-Knetsch method
            (2)   Hedonic equations
                   (a) Property values
                   (b) Wages

13.   Practice and politics of social b/c analysis - Tuolumne River case
      a.   Basics of energy economics, capacity & energy, base & peak
      b.   Basics of hydro projects
      c.   Further lessons of b/c analysis
      d.   Cost-effectiveness analysis
      e.   Option value & existence value
      f.   Uses of econ analysis in env. dispute
      g.   Critique of social b/c, based partly on Kelman
      h.   More general problems of B/C and C/E

1   **243**

14. Basic theory of natural resource economics
    a. Dynamic efficiency and user cost
    b. Stock effects
    c. Hotelling's basic rent-path theory, and modifications for various scenarios
    d. McKelvey diagram

15. Everything that Joe Kalt covered in his lecture

16. Basics of water resources - supply and demand (IID-MWD case)
    a. Importance of marginal costs
    b. Additional opportunity costs of transfers
    c. Evaluating proposal from farmers' points of view
    d. Methods of implementing the proposal (press, etc.)
    e. Environmental concerns of the transfer
    g. Implementation issues as discussed by Tom Graff

17. Fisheries and Wildlife; Endangered Species
    a. Basics of fisheries economics in Tietenberg
    b. How does economic approach to valuation relate to biological species
    c. Causes of species threats and extinctions

18. Forestry and Forested Wetlands
    a. Basics of forestry economics from Tietenberg
    b. Wetland values in situ and through development
    c. How they're protected by law
    * Conversion of forested wetlands to agric. (in MAV)
        (1) How do we believe individuals decide how to use thish land ?
        (2) How can this be tested
        (3) Basic results
        (4) How does this compare with what would be socially optimal?
            (a) How can this be investigated
            (b) Basic results

<-- MIDTERM EXAM -->

19. Overview of Economics of Pollution Control
    a. Efficient allocation (socially optimal level) of pollution control
    b. Market performance
    c. Criteria for good pollution-control policies
    d. Cost-effective policies for uniformly mixed pollutants
        (1) Efficient vs. cost-effective policies
        (2) Identifying cost-effective allocations of pollution-control burden
        (3) Technological standards
        (4) Performance standards (emission standards)
        (5) Emission charges (fees/taxes)
        (6) Transferable emission permits
    e. Cost-effective policies for nonuniformly mixed (surface) pollutants
        (1) Single-receptor case
            (a) Ambient standard
            (b) Ambient charges and ambient tradeable permits
        (2) Multiple-receptor case
    f. Comparison of charges and permit systems
        (1) Responsiveness to change
        (2) Uncertainty regarding costs of control and magnitude of damages

2

244

20. Local Air Pollution -- Stationary Sources
    a.   Criteria Pollutants and the Clean Air Act (CAA)
        (1)   Overview of the Six Criteria Pollutants
        (2)   Basics of Command-and-Control (CAC) Policy in the CAA
        (3)   Assessing the CAC (Command-and-Control) Approach
        (4)   Reform of the Clean Air Act: EPA's Emissions Trading Program
    b.   Hazardous Pollutants under the Clean Air Act
    c.   When are Economic-Incentive and CAC Approaches Appropriate?
    d.   Clean Air Act amendments of 1990

21. Control of Mobile-Source Air Pollution
    a.   Overview
        (1)   What Makes Mobile Sources Special?
        (2)   Are Mobile-Source Emissions Important Quantitatively?
    b.   The Clean Air Act and the Regulation of Mobile-Source Emissions
    c.   Assessing Clean Air Act and Regulation of Mobile-Source Emissions
        (1)   Regulating a Durable Good
        (2)   Problem of overly-strict standards (technology forcing)
        (3)   Regulations
        (4)   Uniform Regulation
        (5)   Deterioration of New Car Emission Rates
    d.   Alternative Approaches to Controlling Mobile-Source Emissions
        (1)   Alternative Regulatory Policies
        (2)   Economic-Incentive Policies

22. Regional and Continental Air Pollution: Acid Rain
    a.   What is acid rain and where does it come from
    b.   The Waxman-Sikorski bill of 1986: pro's and con's
    c.   The costs of acid-rain control
    d.   Alternative methods of acid-rain control
    e.   Benefits of acid-rain control
    f.   Equity considerations and the importance of the compensation issue
    g.   Clean Air amendments of 1990 -- tradeable permit system for acid rain

23. Global Air-Pollution Problems: Stratospheric Ozone Depletion and the Greenhouse Effect
    a.   Basic scientific nature of both problems
    b.   Economic perspective of global climate change
        (1)   Causes
        (2)   Consequences
        (3)   Uncertainty
        (4)   Public attention and policy action
        (5)   new policies
    c.   International trading in greenhouse gas source/sink permits
    d.   Using carbon charges to achieve domestic targets
    e.   Comprehensive least-cost environmental bidding and planning

24. Water Pollution
    a.   Water Quality Problems -- major types of water pollution in the U.S.
    b.   Federal Water Pollution-Control Policy
    c.   Assessing Federal Water-Quality Policy
    d.   Potential Improvements in Federal Water-Quality Policy
        (1)   Point-Nonpoint tradeable permit systems (Dillon Reservoir)
        (2)   Conservation reserve program (USDA)
        (3)   Conventional regulation for ground water sources

3

        (4)   Incentives for environmentally sound farm management practices
        (5)   Tradeable discharge permits for point sources
    e.   Section 404 of the Clean Water Act and Wetland Degradation
        (1)   Basics of 404 regulation
        (2)   The case of Sweedens Swamp
        (3)   The No-Net-Loss Policy

25.   Solid and Hazardous Waste Management
    a.   The problems
        (1)   Municipal solid waste
        (2)   Hazardous waste
    b.   The policy response
    c.   Better price signals for solid waste management
        (1)   Unit charges for collection & disposal
        (2)   Retail disposal charges
        (3)   Virgin material charges
    d.   Using the market to foster recycling: recycling credits
        (1)   Basics of the approach
        (2)   Potential applications
        (3)   Conditions for a successful recycling credit market
    e.   Using market mechanisms to reduce littering and illegal disposal: deposit-refund systems
        (1)   Basics of the approach
        (2)   Potential applications
    f.   Addressing NIMBY: Siting new waste management facilities

26.   Sustainability
    a.   Alternative definitions of the term
    b.   What these definitions imply from an economic perspective
    c.   Making the concept(s) operational

27.   The Politics of Environmental Policy
    a.   Two decades of environmental policy
    b.   How things have changed and how they haven't
        (1)   Administration
        (2)   Congress
        (3)   Federal bureaucracy
        (4)   Environmental organizations
        (5)   Business community
    c.   Why have things changed?
        (1)   Increased understanding?
        (2)   Increased costs of control
        (3)   Changed economic climate
        (4)   New environmental concerns
        (4)   Changed politics
        (5)   New proposals separate out goals and means
        (6)   Coincidences of personnel
    d.   Why things may not change after all
        (1)   Political pressures
        (2)   Distributional issues
        (3)   The problem of constituency
    e.   The next steps

4

John F. Kennedy School of Government
Prof. Robert N. Stavins
ENR-201/Econ 1661

Harvard University
Spring 1994
Handout #29

HANDOUTS DISTRIBUTED

1. Course Syllabus
2. Reading List
3. Periodicals in the Area of Resource & Environmental Economics and Policy
4. National and Regional Environmental Organizations
5. Student Information Questionnaire
6. Net-Benefit and Benefit-Cost Ratio Measures of Welfare
7. Economics and the Environment: Summary
8. Problem Set #1
9. Answer Sheet for Problem Set #1
10. Problem Set #2
11. Natural Resource Economics: Figures to Accompany Lectures
12. *New York Times*: "Greening California"
13. Conversion of Forested Wetlands to Agricultural Uses: Tables & Figures
14. Overview of Course Topics (up to midterm)
15. Answer Sheet for Problem Set #2
16. Midterm Examination
17. Midterm Examination Answer Key
18. Economics of Pollution Control: Tables & Figures
19. *New York Times*: "How Much Is Too Much to Pay To Meet Standards for Smog?"
20. Alternative Solutions to Environmental Externality Problems
21. Mid-Course Commentary
22. Local Air Pollution Economics and Policy: Outline of Topics
23. Clean Air Act Amendments of 1990
24. Problem Set #3
25. *The Economist*: "The Beautiful and the Dammed"
26. Water Pollution -- Outline of Topics
27. Emerson on Nature
28. Overview of Course Topics
29. Handouts Distributed

John F. Kennedy School of Government
Prof. Robert N. Stavins
ENR-201/Econ 1661

Harvard University
Spring 1994
Handout #31

FINAL EXAMINATION

This is a closed-book, closed-notes examination. There are three parts, with a total of 12 questions; all are required. The number of points assigned to questions (and the number of minutes to allot) are indicated at the beginning of each section; there are 142 total points in the exam (and about 180 minutes for you to work). Please write your answers to the three parts of the exam in *three* separate blue books, which should be numbered accordingly. Be sure to put your ID number (but *not* your name) on *all three* blue books. Please be concise with your answers, and write neatly; illegible answers receive zero credit. Good luck!

I.   *SHORT ANSWERS* (70 total points; 7 points each)

1.   Do you agree with the following statement? Why, why not? "A pragmatic alternative to the *efficiency* criterion for environmental policies is a *cost-effectiveness* criterion."

2.   In what situations are tradeable emission permits acceptable substitutes for tradeable ambient permits?

3.   In general, ought we be more concerned as a society about the exhaustion of renewable or non renewable resources? Why?

4.   Evaluate the following statement: "If environmental programs are voluntary, we know that the benefits exceed the costs, and hence that they represent sound public policy."

5.   From an economic perspective, what is the role of "substitutability" in defining the concept of "sustainability?"

6.   Assess the following statement: "All we need in order to develop optimal policy responses to the threat of global climate change is better scientific understanding of the threat."

7.   Is the cost of exploration a useful measure of natural resource scarcity?

8.   Compare performance standards, technology standards, and emission charges in terms of the incentives they provide for *technological change* in pollution control devices.

9.   Given expressed concerns about "environmental justice" (the distribution across income classes of the benefits and costs of environmental protection), comment on the significance of the income elasticity of demand for environmental quality.

10.   Does the equilibrium allocation of permits in a tradeable permit system depend upon the initial allocation? Explain.

(TURN FOR PARTS II AND III)

248

II. *ESSAY* (42 points; 7 points for each part)

11. Consider various types of environmental policy instruments, including: technology standards, performance standards, charges, deposit-refund systems, tradeable permits, liability rules, eliminating government subsidies, and reducing market barriers. For each of the following environmental problems, choose a preferable instrument, and justify your choice, being as specific as possible. (Unless otherwise stated, we will assume that the policy context of your discussion is the United States; *if* this is *not* the case, be sure to *state* the geographic context).

   (a) managing the flow of urban municipal solid waste at minimum cost and subject to appropriate norms of environmental protection;

   (b) reducing emissions of lead particulates at an urban incinerator (note that lead exhibits a non-linear dose-response -- or damage -- function);

   (c) reducing non-point source water pollution from farms;

   (d) reducing U.S. emissions of carbon dioxide in compliance with a fully enforced international agreement;

   (e) preserving particularly valuable ecosystems; and

   (f) achieving efficient use of water by consumers.

III. *PROBLEM* (30 points; 5 points for each part)

You can use graphs or simple algebra to answer the questions; either way, be sure to show all of your work.

12. Two firms can control emissions of a pollutant at the following marginal costs:

$$MC_1 = \$500\,q_1 \qquad\qquad MC_2 = \$300q_2,$$

where q_1 and q_2 are, respectively, the amount of emissions *reduced* by the first and second firms. Total pollution-control cost functions for the two firms are, respectively:

$$TC_1 = \$1000 + \$250\,(q_1)^2 \qquad TC_2 = \$1000 + \$150\,(q_2)^2$$

Assume that with no control at all, each firm would be emitting 40 units of emissions (for aggregate emissions of 80 tons), and assume that there are no significant transaction costs.

   (a) What are the total industry costs of pollution control (for both firms combined) if a *uniform* emission standard is utilized to achieve an aggregate reduction (for both firms combined) of 48 tons of emissions?

   (b) What are the marginal costs of pollution control for firm #1 and for firm #2?

   (c) Compute the *cost-effective* allocation of control responsibility if a total reduction of 48 units of emissions is necessary, i.e. how many units of emissions will each firm *control* under a cost-effective allocation?

   (d) What are the total industry costs of pollution control (for both firms combined) with a cost-effective allocation of control responsibility?

   (e) What equilibrium allocation of the pollution-control responsibility will eventually result with a tradeable permit approach if firm #1 is initially allocated 8 tons of emissions permits and firm #2 is initially allocated 24 tons of permits? What if the initial permit levels for firms #1 and #2 are 20 tons and 12 tons, respectively?

   (f) If the control authority chose to reach its objective of 48 tons of aggregate reduction by the use of an emission charge system, what per-unit charge should be imposed?

249

Economics 231
Colby College
Fall, 1994

Mr. Tietenberg
Office: Miller 234
U   Phone: Ext. 3143
email: thtieten

INTRODUCTION TO ENVIRONMENTAL AND NATURAL RESOURCE ECONOMICS

The following book will be extensively used in the course and is recommended for purchase:

Tom Tietenberg, *Environmental and Natural Resource Economics*, 3rd edition (New York: HarperCollins, 1992) (TT)

Further reading on any topic you wish to pursue further is not difficult to find. A list of supplemental readings is included with each section. Though not required, these works can give you a point of entry for further study of any particular issue.

A number of journals are now devoted either exclusively or mostly to the topics covered in this course. One, *Ecological Economics*, is a new journal dedicated to bringing economists and ecologists closer together in a common search for appropriate solutions for environmental challenges. Interested readers can also find advanced work in the field in *Land Economics, Journal of Environmental Economics and Management, Environmental and Resource Economics, Resource and Energy Economics* and *Natural Resources Journal*, among others.

New resources for student research projects have been made available in response to the growing popularity of the field. Original research on topics related to international environmental and natural resource issues was formerly very difficult because of the paucity of data. A number of good sources now exist including *World Resources: 1993-94* (Washington, DC: Oxford University Press, 1993), which has an extensive data appendix and is published annually, and *OECD Environmental Data* (Paris: Organization for Co-operation and Development, 1989).

The course grade for the three credits will be based on two evening examinations lasting fifty minutes each and a two-hour final examination. These will be weighted 30%, 30%, and 40% respectively. A fourth credit option, involving a 12-15 page research paper, is available for a limited number of participants in the course on a first-come, first-served basis. Choosing this option requires the submission and approval of a topic proposal and research design by October 14.

I. INTRODUCTION

Overview: Many books and articles have suggested recently that mankind is not now living in harmony with the environment and may be incapable of doing so. We shall use this question -- Can our economic and political institutions produce substainable increases in human welfare in the presence of a finite environment? -- as the organizing principle of the course. Following an initial lecture which gives an overview of the course and clarifies some of the administrative details, we begin our inquiry by focusing on the range of specific hypotheses which have been advanced. These hypotheses will then be dissected and the component arguments will be examined in more detail in the rest of the course.

Session 1:   Administrative Details and Overview
September 1
                    TT, "Visions of the Future," Chapter 1

Supplemental Reading:

Hughes, Barry. *World Futures: A Critical Analysis of Alternatives* (Baltimore, MD: The Johns Hopkins University Press, 1985).

Markandya, Anil and Julie Richardson, ed. *The Earthscan Reader in Environmental Economics* (London: Earthscan Publications Ltd., 1992)

Meadows, Donella H., et al., *Beyond the Limits: Confronting Global Collapse, Envisioning a Sustainable Future* (Post Hills , VT: Chelsea Green Publishing Company, 1992).

Oates, Wallace, ed. *The Economics of the Environment* (Cheltenham, UK: Edward Elgar Publishing, 1992).

Pearce, David, Anil Markandya, and Edward B. Barbier. *Blueprint for a Green Economy* (London: Earthscan Publications Ltd,1989).

Simon, Julian L. *The Ultimate Resource* (Princeton, NJ: Princeton University Press, 1981).

World Commission on Environment and Development. *Our Common Future* (Oxford: Oxford University Press, 1987).

United Nations Economic Commission for Latin America and the Caribbean, *Sustainable Development: Changing Production Patterns, Social Equity and the Environment* (Santiago, Chile: United Nations Economic Commission for Latin America and the Caribbean, 1991).

II. PERSPECTIVES

Overview: How anyone views environmental problems and potential solutions to those problems depends on how they organize the various facts, how they interpret them and what kinds of values they bring to bear. Before going into a detailed look at environmental and natural resource problems, it is important to place the ideology of conventional economics in the context of other prevailing ideologies in both the natural and social sciences. In this section we undertake this task.

Sessions 2-3:   Political, Economic and Ecological Paradigms
September 6-8

                        TT, "Economics of the Environment: An Overview,"
                        Chapter 2

                        TT, "Property Rights, Externalities, and Environmental Problems,"
                        Chapter 3

                        TT, "Regulating the Market: Information and Uncertainty,"
                        Chapter 4

Note: The concepts in these chapters are the building blocks for the rest of the course. Make sure you have
        mastered them. Note that the answers to the problems are in the back of the book.

Supplemental Reading:

Anderson, Terry L. and P.J. Hill. "The Evolution of Property Rights: A Study of the American West," *The Journal of Law and Economics,* XVIII (April, 1975): 163-79.

Bromley, Daniel W. "Property Rules, Liability Rules and Environmental Economics," *Journal of Economic Issues,* XII (March, 1978): 43-60.

Cummings, Ronald G., David S. Brookshire, and William D. Schulze. *Valuing Environmental Goods: An Assessment of the Contingent Valuation Method* (Totowa, NJ: Rowman and Littlefield, 1986).

Daly, Herman E. and John B. Cobb, Jr. *For the Common Good: Redirecting the Economy Toward Community, the Environment and a Sustainable Future* (Boston: Beacon Press,1989).

Barde, Jean-Phillipe and David Pearce, ed. *Valuing the Environment: Six Case Studies* (London: Earthscan Publications Ltd., 1991).

Dunford, Richard, "Natural Resource Damages from Oil Spills" in T.H. Tietenberg ed. *Innovation in Environmental Policy* (Cheltenham, UK: Edward Elgar, 1992): 165-193.

Goldfarb, Theodore D., ed. *Taking Sides: Clashing Views on Environmental Issues,* 3rd ed. (Guilford. CT: The Dushkin Publishing Group Inc., 1989).

Hanley, Nick and Clive Spash, *Cost-Benefit Analysis and the Environment* (Cheltenham, UK: Edward Elgar Publishing, 1992).

Kelman, Steven. "Cost-Benefit Analysis--An Ethical Critique," *Regulation* (January/February, 1981), 33-40.

Mitchell, Robert Cameron and Richard T. Carson, *Using Surveys to Value Public Goods: The Contingent Valuation Method* (Washington: Resources for the Future, Inc., 1989).

2

Smith, V. Kerry, ed. *Environmental Policy Under Reagan's Executive Order: The Role of Benefit-Cost Analysis* (Chapel Hill: The University of North Carolina Press, 1984).

Stavins, Robert N., "Harnessing Market Forces to Protect the Environment" *Environment* Vol. 31, No. 1 (1989): 28-35.

III. NATURAL RESOURCE ECONOMICS

Overview: Having examined the major perspectives which shape an understanding of environmental and natural resource problems in general, we turn to an analysis of specific natural resource problems which have arisen and the policy responses to them. A central question is how our economic and political institutions allocate natural resources. Our examination opens with a look at "the population problem" which is a major factor in determining how rapidly problems would be encountered and their severity.

Session 4   Population Growth and Its Control
September 13
                             TT, "The Population Problem," Chapter 5

Supplemental Reading:

Cleaver, Kevin and Gotz, Schreiber, *The Population, Agriculture and Environment Nexus in Sub-Saharan Africa* (Washington: World Bank, 1992).

Cline-Cole, R.A., et. al., "On Fuelwood Consumption, Population Dynamics and Deforestation in Africa" *World Development* Vol. 18, No. 4 (1990): 513-27.

Davis, Kingsley et. al., *Below Replacement Fertility in Industrial Societies: Causes, Consequences, Policies* (New York: Cambridge University Press, 1987).

Johnson, D. Gale and Ronald D. Lee, *Population Growth and Economic Development: Issues and Evidence* (Madison, WI: University of Wisconsin Press, 1987).

Kelly, Allen C., "Economic Consequences of Population Change in the Third World", *Journal of Economic Literature*, Vol. 26 (December, 1988):1685-1728.

Sessions 5-6   Maximizing the Value of Resources
September 15-20
                             TT, "The Allocation of Depletable and Renewable Resources: An
                                 Overview," Chapter 6

Supplemental Reading:

Bohi, Douglas R. and Michael A. Toman. *Analyzing Nonrenewable Resource Supply* (Washington, D.C.: Resources for the Future, Inc., 1984).

Chapman, Duane, "Computation Techniques for Intertemporal Allocation of Natural Resources" *American Journal of Agricultural Economics*, Vol. 69, No. 1 (February, 1987): 134-142.

Toman, Michael A. "'Depletion Effects' and Nonrenewable Resource Supply." *Land Economics*, Vol. 62 (November, 1986): 341-53.

Session 7-8   Energy Choices
September 22-
September 27
                             TT, "Depletable, Nonrecyclable Energy Resources: Oil, Gas, Coal, and Uranium,"
                                 Chapter 7

Supplemental Reading:

Bhatia, R., "Diffusion of Renewable Energy Technologies in Developing Countries: A Case Study of Biogas Engines in India" *World Development* Vol 18, No. 4 (1990): 575-90.

Carpenter, E.H. and S.T. Chester, "Are Federal Energy Tax Credits Effective? A Western United States Survey?" *The Energy Journal* Vol. 5, No. 2 (1984): 134-149.

Clark, William C., "Energy and Environment: Strategic Perspectives on Policy Design" in J.W. Tester, et. al. ed. *Energy and Environment in the 21st Century*, (Cambridge, MA: The MIT Press, 1991): 63-78.

Goldenberg, J., "Solving the Energy Problems in Developing Countries" *Energy Journal* Vol. 11, No. 1 (1990): 19-24.

Griffen, James M., and Henry B. Steele, *Energy, Economics and Policy.* 2nd. ed. (New York:, NY: Academic Press, 1986).

Johansson, Thomas B., et al., *Renewable Energy: Sources for Fuels and Electricity* (Washington, DC: Island Press, 1993).

Ottinger, Richard L. and et. al., *Environmental Costs of Electricity* (New York: Oceana Publications, 1990).

Shea, Cynthia Pollock, "Shifting to Renewable Energy" in Lester R. Brown, et. al. *State of the World: 1988* (New York: W.W. Norton & Co., 1988): 62-82.

Walton, A.L., and E. H. Warrne, Jr., *The Solar Alternative: An Economic Perspective* (Englewood Cliffs, NJ: Prentice-Hall, Inc., 1982).

Session 9	Minerals and Recycling
September 29	

  TT, "Recyclable Resources: Minerals," Chapter 8

Supplemental Reading:

Agarwal, J.C., "Minerals, Energy, and the Environment" in J.W. Tester, et. al. ed. *Energy and Environment in the 21st Century*, (Cambridge, MA: The MIT Press, 1991): 389-395.

Anderson, Anthony B., "Smokestacks in the Rainforest: Industrial Development and Deforestation in the Amazon Basin" *World DEvelopment* Vol. 18 (1990): 26.

Bohm, Peter, *Deposit-Refund System: Theory and Application to Environmental, Conservation, and Consumer Policy* (Baltimore, MD: The Johns Hopkins University Press for Resources for the Future, Inc., 1981).

Clark, Allen L., et. al., "Mineral Development Prospects of the Indochina Area: Potential Exceed Problems" *Natural Resources Forum* Vol. 15, No. 1 (1991): 26.

Curlee, T. Randall, *The Economic Feasibility of Recycling: A Case Study of Plastic Wastes* (New York: Praeger Publishers, 1986)

Roxburgh, Nigel, *Policy Responses to Resource Depletion: The Case of Mercury* (Greenwich, CT: JAI Press, Inc., 1980).

Tilton, John E., ed. *Mineral Wealth and Economic Development* (Washington, DC: Resources for the Future, Inc., 1992).

Session 10:	Water Scarcity
October 4	

  TT, "Replenishable, but Depletable Resources: Water" Chapter 9

Supplemental Reading:

Dinar, Ariel and David Zilberman, ed. *The Economics and Management of Water and Drainage in Agriculture* (Norwell, MA: Kluwer Academic Publishers, 1991).

Easter, K. William, ed. *Watershed Resources Management: Studies from Asia and the Pacific* (Honolulu: East-West Center, 1991).

4

Gibbons, Diana C. *The Economic Value of Water* (Washington: Resources for the Future, Inc.,1986)

Herrington, Paul, *Pricing of Water Services* (Organization for Economic Co-operation and Development, 1987).

Hou, H., "Resolving Problems of Water Shortage in China" *International Journal of Social Economics* Vol. 18, No. 8-9-10 (1991): 167-73.

Lee, T.R., "Managing Water Resources in Latin America" *Natural Resources Journal* Vol 30, No. 3 (1990): 581-607.

Morris, J.R., "Pricing for Water Conservation" *Contemporary Policy Issues* Vol. 8, No. 4 (1990): 79-91.

Morris, J.R., "Water Conservation Progress in Denver" *Contemporary Policy Issues* Vol. 9, No. 3 (1991): 34-45.

Munasinghe, Mohan, "The Pricing of Water Services in Developing Countries" *Natural Resources Forum* Vol. 14, No. 3 (1990): 193.

Saliba, Bonnie Colby and David B. Bush, *Water Markets in Theory and Practice: Market Transfers, Water Values, and Public Policy* (Boulder, CO: Westview Press, 1987).

Torrell, L.A., et. al., "The Market Value of Water in the Ogallala Aquifer" *Land Economics* Vol. 66, No. 2 (1990): 163-75.

Wetzstein, M.E. and T. J. Centner, "Regulating Agricultural Contamination of Groundwater through Strict Liability and Negligence Legislation" *Journal of Environmental Economics and Management* vol. 22, No. 1 (1992): 1-11.

Session 11	Forests
October 6	TT, "Storable, Renewable Resources: Forests" Chapter 11

Supplemental Reading:

Anderson, Anthony D., ed. *Alternatives to Deforestation: Steps Toward the Sustainable Use of the Amazon Rainforest* (New York, NY: Columbia University Press, 1991).

Anderson, Anthony B., et. al., *The Subsidy from Nature: Palm Forests, Peasantry, and Development on Amazon Frontier* (New York, NY: Columbia University Press, 1991).

Barber, Charles, *Cutting Our Losses: Policy Reform to Sustain Tropical Forest Resources* (Washington, DC: World Resources Institute, 1992).

Bautista, G. M., "The Forestry Crisis in the Philippines: Nature, Causes and Issues" *Developing Economies* Vol. 28, No. 1 (1990): 67-94.

Bhat, M.G. and R. G. Huffaker, "Private Property Rights and Forest Preservation in Karnataka Western Ghats, India" *American Journal of Agricultural Economics* Vol. 73, No. 2 (1991): 375-87.

Binswanger, H., "Brazilian Policies that Encourage Deforestation in the Amazon" *World Development* Vol. 19, No. 7 (1991): 821-29

Deacon, R.T., "The Simple Analytics of Forest Economics," *Forestlands: Public and Private*, R.T. Deacon and M.B. Johnson, eds. (San Francisco, CA: Pacific Institute for Public Policy Research, 1985).

Johansson, Per-Olov *Economics of Forestry and Natural Resources* (New York: Basil Blackwell, 1985)

Larson, B.A. and D.W. Bromley, "Natural Resource Prices, Export Policies and Deforestation: The Case of Sudan" *World Development* Vol. 19, No. 10 (October, 1991): 1289-97.

Mcgranahan, G., "Fuelwood, Subsistence Foraging and the Decline of Common Property" *World Development* Vol. 19, No. 10 (1991): 1275-87.

McNeely, Jeffrey A., *Economics and Biological Diversity: Developing and Using Economic Incentives to Conserve Biological Resources* (Gland, Switzerland: IUCN, 1988).

Miller, Kenton and Laura Tangley, *Trees of Life: Protecting Tropical Forests and Their Biological Wealth* (Boston: Beacon Press, 1991).

5

Plotkin, Mark and Lisa Famolare, ed. *Sustainable Harvest and the Marketing of Rain Forest Products* (Washington, DC: Island Press, 1992).

Price, C., "Do High Discount Rates Destroy Tropical Forests?" *Journal of Agricultural Economics* Vol. 42, No. 1 (1991): 77-85.

Program on Social Change, ed. *Social Forestry: Communal and Private Management Strategies Compared* (Washington: Nitze School of Advance International Studies, 1992)

Repetto, Robert *The Forest for the Trees: Government Policies and the Misuse of Forest Resources* (Washington, DC: World Resources Institute, 1988)

Soussan, J. et. al., "Planning for Sustainability: Access to Fuelwood in Dhanusha District, Nepal" *World Development* Vol. 9, No. 10 (1919): 1299-1314.

Southgate, D., et. al., "The Causes of Tropical Deforestation in Ecuador: A Statistical Analysis *"World Development* Vol. 19, No. 9 (1991): 1145-51.

Wibe, Soren and Tom Jones, ed. *Forests: Market and Intervention Failures* (London: Earthscan Publications Ltd., 1992).

Session 12: October 11	Review Session
	This period will be reserved for a review of the preceeding material. The entire session will be devoted to answering your questions.
Session 13 October 11 6:00 pm	******************** FIRST EXAMINATION Location to be announced ********************

Sessions 14-15: Managing the Fisheries
October 20 - 25

TT, "Renewable Common-Property Resources: Fisheries and Other Species," Chapter 12

Supplemental Reading:

Anderson, Lee G., "Enforcement Issues in Selecting Fisheries Management Policy" *Marine Resource Economics*, Vol. 6, No. 3 (1989): 261-77.

Anderson, L. G., "Efficient Policies to Maintain Total Allowable Catches in ITQ Fisheries with At-Sea Processing" *Land Economics* Vol. 67, No. 2 (1991): 141-57.

Barbier, Edward B., et. al., *Elephants, Economics and Ivory* (London: Earthscan, 1990).

Campbell, H. F., "Fishery Buy-Back Programmes and Economic Welfare" *Australian Journal of Agricultural Economics*, Vol. 33, No. 1 (April, 1989): 20-31.

Campbell, H. F. and R.K. Lindner, "The Production of Fishing Effort and the Economic Performance of License Limitation Programs" *Land Economics* Vol. 66, No. 1 (1990): 56-66.

Dupont, D.P., "Rent Dissipation in Restricted Access Fisheries" *Journal of Environmental Economics and Management* Vol. 19, No. 1 (1990): 26-44.

Dupont, D.P. and S.A. Phipps, " Distributional Consequences of Fisheries Regulations" *Canadian Journal of Economics* Vol. 24, No. 1 (1991): 206-20.

Opsomer, J.D. and J.M. Conrad, "An Open-Access Analysis of the Northern Anchovy Fishery" *Journal of Environmental Economics and Management* Vol. 27, No. 1 (1994): 21-37.

Ostrom, Elinor, *Governing the Commons: The Evolutions of Institutions for Collective Action* (Cambridge: Cambridge University Press, 1991).

6

Pearse, Peter H., *Building on Progress: Fisheries Policy Development in New Zealand*, Report (Ministry of Fisheries, July, 1991).

Stevenson, Gelnn. G., *Common Property Economics: A General Theory and Land Use Applications* (New York: Cambridge University Press, 1991).

Townsend, Ralph E., "Entry Restrictions in the Fishery: A Survey of the Evidence" *Land Economics* Vol. 66, No. 4 (1990): 361-378.
Townsend, Ralph, "A Fractional Licensing Program for Fisheries" *Land Economics* vol. 68, No. 2 (1992): 185-190.

Sessions 16   The World Hunger Problem
October 27

              TT, "Reproducible Private-Property Resources: Food,"
              Chapter 10

Supplemental Reading:

Barbier, E. B., "The Farm-Level Economics of Soil Conservation: *Land Economics*   Vol. 66, No. 2 (1990): 199-211.

Batie, Sandra S., "Sustainable Development: Challenges to the Agricultural Economics Profession" *American Journal of Agricultural Economics*, Vol. 71, No. 5 (December, 1989): 1083- 1101.

Gordon, R. Conway and Edward B. Barbier, *After the Green Revolution: Sustainable Agriculture for Development* (London: Earthscan Publishers, Ltd., 1990).

Hall, Darwin C.et. al. "Organic Food and Sustainable Agriculture" *Contemporary Policy Issues* Vol. VII, No. 4 (October, 1989): 47-72.

 Johnson, S. R., et. al., "Coordinating Agricultural and Environmental Policies: A Conceptual Framework" *American Economic review* Vol. 80, No. 2 (1990): 203-07.

Just, R.E. and J. M. Antle, interactions between Agricultural and Environmental Policies: A Conceptual Framework" *American Economic Review* Vol. 80, No. 2 (1990): 197-202.

Lawry, S.W., "Tenure Policy toward Common Property Natural Resources in Sub-Sahara Africa" *Natural Resources Journal* Vol. 30, No. 2 (1990): 403-22.

Lundhal, Mats, *Incentives and Agriculture in East Africa* (London: Routledge, 1990).

Parry, M. L., *Climate Change and World Agriculture* (London: Earthscan Publications, 1990).

Southgate, D., "The Causes of Land Degradation along Expanding Agricultural Frontiers in the Thirld World" *Land Economics* Vol. 66, No. 1 (1990): 93-101.

Young, M.D., *Towards Sustainable Agricultural Development* (London: Bellhaven Press, 1991).

IV. ENVIRONMENTAL ECONOMICS

Overview: Having dealt with the economics of resource extraction and use, we now turn to the other side of the coin--managing the flows of waste back into the environment. In this section we shall begin by identifying the various kinds of pollutants and defining the problems they cause. We then move on to the various possible responses the government could take to adequately protect its citizens from the risks posed, using this framework to evaluate current environmental policy.

Sessions 17-20:   Pollution I - IV
November 1-10

              TT, "Economics of Pollution Control: An Overview," Chapter 14

7

256

TT, "Stationary-Source Local Air Pollution," Chapter 15

TT, "Regional and Global Air Pollutants: Acid Rain and Atmospheric Modification", Chapter 16

TT, "Water Pollution", Chapter 18

TT, "Mobile-Source Air Pollution," Chapter 17

Supplemental Reading:

Barde, J-P. and K. J. Button, *Integrating Transport and Environmental Policy* (London: Earthscan Publishers Ltd., 1990).

Barrett, S., "The Problem of Global Environmental Protection" *Oxford Review of Economic Policy* Vol. 6, No. 1 (1990): 68-79.

Bohm, P. and C. Russell, "Comparative Analysis of Alternative Policy Instruments" in A. V. Kneese and J. L. Sweeney ed. *Handbook of Natural Resource and Energy Economics,* Vol. 1 (Amsterdam: North-Holland, 1985): 395-460.

Bressers, Hans Th. A., "A Comparison of the Effectiveness of Incentives and Directives: The Case of Dutch Water Quality Policy" *Policy Studies Review,* Vol. 7(1988): 500-518.

Brown, G. M. Jr. and R. W. Johnson, "Pollution Control by Effluent Charges: It Works in the Federal Republic of Germany, Why Not in the United States?" *Natural Resources Journal,* Vol. 24(October, 1984): 929-66.

Button, Kenneth and Jean-Philippe Barde, ed. *Transport Policy and the Environment: Six Case Studies* (London: Earthscan Publishers Ltd., 1990).

Churchill, A.A. and R. J. Saunders, "Global Warming and the Developing World" *Finance and Development* Vol. 28, No. 2 (1991): 28-31.

Cline, William R., *The Economics of Global Warming* (Washington, DC: Institue for Internaitonal Economics, 1992).

Dornbush, Rudiger and James M. Poterba, ed. *Global Warming: Economic Policy Responses* (Cambridge, MA: MIT Press, 1919).

Dudek, Daniel J. and John Palmisano, "Emissions Trading: Why is this Throughbred Hobbled?" *Columbia Journal of Environmental Law,* Vol. 13, No. 2 (no month listed, 1988): 217-56.

Eheart, J. Wayland, "Cost-Efficiency of Transferable Discharge Permits for the Control of B.O.D. Discharges" *Water Resources Research,* Vol. 16, No. 6 (December, 1980): 980-986.

Freeman, A. Myrick III, "Water Pollution Policy" in P.R. Portney ed. *Public Policies for Environmental Protection,* (Washington: Resources For the Future, Inc., 1990): 97-149.

French, Hilary F., *Clearing the Air: A Global Agenda,* Report No. 94 (Worldwatch Institute, January, 1990)

Hahn, Robert W. and Gordon L. Hester, "Marketable Permits: Lessons from Theory and Practice" *Ecology Law Quarterly,* Vol. 16(1989): 361-406.

Hahn, Robert W., "Economic Prescriptions for Environmental Problems: How the Patient Followed the Doctor's Orders" *The Journal of Economic Perspectives,* Vol. 3, No. 2 (Spring, 1989): 95-114.

Jorgenson, Dale and Peter Wilcoxen, "The Cost of Controling U.S. Carbon Dioxide Emittions" in D.O. Wood and Y. Kaya ed. *Proceedings of the Workshop on Economic/Energy/Environmental Modeling for Climate Policy Analysis ,* (Cambridge, MA: MIT Center ofr Energy Policy Research, 1991): 234-261.

Luken, Ralph A., *Efficiency in Environmental Regulation: A Benefit-Cost Analysis of Alternative Approaches* (Boston: Kluwer Academic Publishers, 1990).

Mackenzie, James J. and Michael P. Walsh, *Driving Forces: Motor Vehicle Trends and their Implications for Global Warming, Energy Strategies and Transportation Planning* (Washington: World Resources Institute, 1990).

Magat, Wesley A. and W. Kip Viscusi, "Effectiveness of the EPA's Regulatory Enforcement: The Case of Industrial Effluent Standards" *Journal of Law and Economics* Vol. 33, No. 2 (1990): 331-360.

8

Morrison, Steven A., "A Survey of Road Pricing" *Transportation Research*, Vol. 20A, No. 2 (March, 1986): 87-97.

Opschoor, J. B. and Hans B. Vos, *Economic Instruments for Environmental Protection* (Paris: Organization for Economic Co-operation and Development, 1989).

Pearce, David, "The Role of Carbon Taxes in Adjusting to Global Warming" *Economic Journal* vol. 101, No. 407 (1991):   938-48.
Scheraga, J.D., "Combatting Global Warming: *Challenge* vol. 33, No. 4 (1990): 28-32.

Shah, A., "Optimal Pricing of Traffic Externalities: Theory and Measurement" *International Journal of Transport Economics*, Vol. 18, No. 1 (1990).

Tietenberg, T.H., "Economic Instruments for Environmental Regulation" *Oxford Review of Economic Policy*, Vol. 6, No. 1 (March, 1990): 17-33.

Tietenberg, T.H., *Emissions Trading: An Exercise in Reforming Pollution Policy* (Washington, DC: Resources for the Future, Inc, 1985)

United Nations Conference on Trade and Development, *Combatting Global Warming: Study on a Global System of Tradeable Carbon Emission Entitlements* (New York: United Nations, 1992).

Session 21   Review Session
November 15

Session 22:   ********************
November 15   SECOND EXAMINATION
6:00 pm   Location to be announced
                                 ****

Session 23:   Controlling Exposure to Hazardous Substances
November 17
                      TT, "Toxic Substances," Chapter 19

Supplemental Reading:

Dower, Roger C. "Hazardous Waste" in Paul R. Portney, ed., *Public Policies for Environmental Protection* (Washington, DC: Resources for the Future, Inc., 1990):151-194.

Graham, Jon D. Laura C. Green, and Marc J. Roberts, *In Search of Safety: Chemicals and Cancer Risk* (Cambridge, MA: Harvard University Press, 1988).

Katzman, Martin T., "Pollition Liability Insurance and Catastrophic Environmental Risk" *The Journal of Rish and Insurance* Vol. 55, No. 1 (1988): 75-100.

Litan, Robert E. and Clifford Winston, ed. *Liability: Perspectives and Policy* Washington, DC: Brookings Institution, 1988).

Ringleb, A. H. and S. N. Wiggins, "Liability and Large-Scale, Long-Term Hazards" *Journal of Political Economuy* Vol. 98, No. 3 (1990): 574-595.

Shapiro, Michael, "Toxic Substances Policy " *Public Policies for Environmental Protection* (Washington, DC: Resources for the Future, Inc., 1990): 195-242.

Tietenberg, T. H., ed. *Innovation in Environmental Policy: Economic and legal Aspects of Recent Developments in Environmental Enforcement and Liability* (Cheltenham, UK: Edward Elgar Publishing, 1991).

Tietenberg, T.H., "Indivisible Toxic Torts: The Economics of Joint and Several Liability" *Land Economics* Vol. 65 (1989): 305-319.

Viscusi, W. Kip, *Risk By Choice: Regulating Health and Safety in the Workplace* (Cambridge, MA: Harvard University Press, 1983).

Supplemental Reading:

Bullard, Robert D., *Dumping in Dixie: Race, Class, and Environmental Quality* (Boulder, CO: Westview Press, 1990).

Bryant, Bunyan and Paul Mohai, eds., *Race and the Incidence of Environmental Hazards: A Time for Discourse* (Boulder, CO: Westview Press, 1992).

Conrad, Klaus and Catherine Morrison. "The Impact of Pollution Abatement Investment on Productivity Change: An Empirical Comparison of the U. S., Germany, and Canada," *Southern Economic Journal* 55 (January 1989): 684-698.

Bezdek, Roger H., "Environment and Economy: What's the Bottom Line?," *Environment*, 35, 7, (September): 6-11, 25-32.

Bohm, Peter, "Distributional Implications of Allowing International Trade in CO_2 Emission Quotas" *The World Economy* Vol. 15, No. 1 (1992): 107-114.

Bossone, B., "Environmental Protection: How Should We Pay for It?" *International Journal of Social Economics* Vol. 17, No. 1 (1990): 3-15.

Brajer, V. and J. V. Hall, "Recent Evidence on the Distribution of Air Pollution Effects" *Contemporary Policy Issues* Vol. 10, No. 2 (1992): 63-71.

Christiansen, G.B. and T.H. Tietenberg, "Distributional and Macroeconomic Aspects of Environmental Policy" in A. V. K. a. J. L. Sweeney ed. *Handbook of Natural Resource and Energy Economics* (Amsterdam: North-Holland, 1985):.

Pearce, D. W., "Efficiency and Distribution in Corrective Mechanisms for Environmental Externality" in A. Schnaiberg, et. al. ed. *Distributional Conflicts in Environmental Policy*, (Berlin: WZB-Publications, 1985):.

DeMeza, David and J. R. Gould. "Free Access versus Private Property in a Resource: Income Distributions Compared," *Journal of Political Economy* 95 (December 1987): 1317-1325.

Farber, Stephen C. and Robert E. Martin. "Market Structure and Pollution Control under Imperfect Surveillance," *Journal of Industrial Economics* 35 (December 1986): 147-160.

Rose, Adam, Brandt Stevens, and Gregg Davis. *Natural Resource Policy and Income Distribution* (Baltimore: Johns Hopkins University Press, 1988).

Shortle, James S. and Keith D. Willett. "The Incidence of Water Pollution Control Costs: Partial vs. General Equilibrium Computations," *Growth and Change* 17 (April 1986): 32-43.

Stoft, S., "Appliance Standards and Poor Families" *Energy Journal* Vol. 14, No. 4 (1993): 123-28.

V. THE DEVELOPMENT CONNECTION

Overview: You have now been through in some detail the nature of the various limits to growth--the accumulation of waste products, the decline of environmental amenities, and the depreciation of our finite resource base--and the kinds of policies which can be, and have been, taken to circumvent them. We now turn to the second major policy choice which is to control the development process itself. We begin by focusing on how growth occurs in the presence of a finite resource base and continue by considering the desirability of stopping growth vis a vis "reforming" it. Then we speculate on how a zero growth or steady state economy might differ from the one we are used to. Finally we return to an overall assessment of the validity of the competing hypotheses about the future with which we started the course.

10

TT, "The Quest for Sustainable Development" Chapter 22

TT, "Visions of the Future Revisited," Chapter 23

Supplemental Reading:

Adams William M., *Green Development: Environment and Sustainability in the Third World* (New York: Routledge, 1992).

Aniansson, britt and Uno Svedin, *Towards an Ecological Sustainable Economy* (Stockholm: Swedish Council for Planning and Coordination of Research, 1990).

Asian Development Bank, *Economic Policies for Sustainable Development* (Manila, Philippines: Asian Development Bank, 1990)

Brown, Lester R., et. al., "Picturing a Sustainable Society" in *State of the World* (New York: W.W. Norton, 1990): 173-190.

Costanza, Robert, ed. *Ecological Economics: The Science and Management of Sustainability* (New York, NY: Columbia University Press, 1991).

Economic Commission for Latin America and the Caribbean, *Sustainable Development: Changing Production Patterns, Social Equity and the Environment* Santiago: United Nations Economic Commission for Latin America and the Caribbean, 1990).

Hansen, Stein, "Macroeconomic Policies and Sustainable Development in the Third World" *Journal of International Development* Vol. 2, No. 4 (1990): October.

Heaton, George Et. al., *Transorming Techonology: An Agenda for Environmentally Sustainable Growth in the Twenty-First Century* (Washington: World Resources Institute, 1991).

Howarth, R. B. and R. B. Norgaard, "Intergenerational Resource Rights: Efficiency and Intergenerational Optimality" *Land Economics*, Vol. 66, No. 1 (February, 1990): 1-11.

MacNeill, Jim, "Strategies for Sustainable Development," *Scientific American* Vol. 261, No. 3, (September 1, 1989): 154-165.

Panayotou, Theodore, *Green Markets: The Economics of Sustainable Development* (San Francisco: ICS Press, 1993).

Pearce, David, "Economics, Equity and Sustainable Development" *Futures(UK)*, Vol. 20, No. 6 (December, 1988): 598-605.

Tietenberg, T. H., "Managing the Transition: The Potential Role for Economic Policies" in J. Mathews ed. *Preserving the Global Environment: The Challenge of Shared Leadership*, (New York: W. W. Norton & Co., 1991): 187-226.

Victor, P. A., "Indicators of Sustainable Development: Some Lessons from Capital Theory" *Ecological Economics* Vol. 4, No. 3 (1991): 191-213.

World Commission on Environment and Development, *Our Common Future* (New York: Oxford University Press, 1988).

Ec 493
Colby College
Spring, 1994

U

Professor Tietenberg
Miller Lib 234
email: thtieten
Tel: 3143

Advanced Topics in Environmental Economics

This course is designed as a seminar in which all participants are expected to contribute to group learning, not merely to absorb material passively. Three topics which lie on the frontier of environmental economics provide the focus for our inquiry. All three demonstrate the large contributions that economic analysis can make in understanding the nature of the problems and in providing guidance on solutions, but they also raise fundamental questions about the appropriate domain for economic analysis. You will be exposed to both the emerging insights and the controversies and given ample opportunities to develop your own perspective.

Each topic will be examined using both discussion and presentation formats. The early sessions for each topic will follow a discussion format. Having read the background readings, each participant will be expected to contribute to a discussion that extracts the major insights in the readings and assess their validity and import. My role will be to ask leading questions and to probe the responses. The concluding sessions will involve student oral presentations.

The grades in this course will be based upon: (1) class participation (quality and consistency of contributions), 10%, (2) papers (content, analytical depth, organization and style), 40% (20% each), (3) oral presentations (organization, content and delivery), 30% (10% each) and a final exam on the content of the course 20%.

Each student will be expected to have an email address and to check it regularly. I will use email to communicate with participants in the intervals between classes.

Paper and Oral Presentation Assignments:

First Oral Presentation: The first oral presentation (10-12 minutes) will involve a report on the application of the principles of sustainable development and conventional economic analysis to particular environmental problems in particular geographical and cultural settings. Having selected a specific case study (lots of suggestions listed under Session #4 of this syllabus), the author will review this study to identify its objectives, methods and conclusions. The second part of he presentation will assess the success of this application. What were the strengths and weaknesses? What problems in implementing these principles were encountered? What more general lessons might we draw from this experience? This oral report requires original, critical analysis; it is not a simple description of what the authors said. **Presentation Date: March 1.**

Second Oral Presentation (First Paper): The second project will involve choosing one of three topic areas in the area of global warming: (1) an analysis of the two main economic incentive approaches to global warming: transferable permits and emission charges, (2) the economics of energy conservation in the residential, commercial, industrial or transportation sectors or (3) the economics of alternative renewable energy sources including hydrogen, photovoltaics, solar hot water, geothermal, wind, etc. Each student will pick a specific focus within one of the three broad topic areas and summarize what we know about the relevant economic issues in that area. Each seminar participant will write a 12+ page paper and give an oral presentation of 20 minutes each on their selected topic. First paper proposals due at the beginning of class during Session #3. One-page proposals must contain the name of the chosen case study, and some general background on the study. Late or nonresponsive proposals will receive a grade penalty. **Due Date for Papers: April 5. Oral Presentations on March 29 and April 5 as assigned.**

Third Oral Presentation (Second Paper): The third project involves the critical evaluation of a specific economic analysis in the area of trade and the environment. Each seminar participant will pick one (or possibly two, if related) studies in the area and critically evaluate both the analysis itself and the conclusions which were drawn from it. The report (12+ pages) and the oral presentation (20 minutes) will highlight the focus of the study, the approach taken to answer the

261

questions, the strengths and weaknesses of both the author's approach and his/her conclusions and finally what conclusions can be drawn from having looked closely at the study. Second paper proposals due at the beginning of class during Session #8. One-page proposals must contain the name of the chosen case study, and some general background on the study. Late or nonresponsive proposals will result in a grade penalty being imposed on the paper. **Due Date for Papers: May 3. Oral Presentations on May 3.**

I. The Economics of Sustainable Development

Session #1   Overview and Administration
Tuesday, February 8

This session will be devoted to an overview of the material to be covered and the mechanics of coverage. We shall also use this period to record preferences for paper topics and to finalize assignments based upon these revealed preferences.

Session #2   Sustainable Development: An Introduction
Tuesday, February 15

During this session we will investigate the concept of sustainable development and its relationship to traditional economic analysis. What does sustainable development mean? How can it be operationalized?

Required Reading:

"The Meaning of Sustainable Development" in World Resources an al. *Blueprint for a Green Economy* (London: Earthscan Publications, 1989): 28-50.

John Pezzey, *Economic Analysis of Sustainable Growth and Sustainable Development*, World Bank Environment Working Paper No. 15 (March, 1989).

Supplemental Reading:

Barbier, E. B. and A. Markandya, "The Conditions for Achieving Environmentally Sustainable Development" *European Economic Review*, Vol. 34, No. 2-3 (May, 1990): 659-69.

Barbier, Edward, "The Contribution of Environmental and Resource Economics to an Economics of Sustainable Development" *Development and Change*, Vol. 20, No. 3 (July, 1989): 429-.

Batie, Sandra S., "Sustainable Development: Challenges to the Agricultural Economics Profession" *American Journal of Agricultural Economics*, Vol. 71, No. 5 (December, 1989): 1083- 1101.

Common, M. and C. Perrings, "Toward an Ecological Economics of Sustainability" *Ecological Economics* Vol. 6, No. 1 (1992): 7-34.

Costanza, Robert, *Ecological Economics: The Science and Management of Sustainability* (New York, NY: Columbia University Press, 1991).

Lele, S. "Sustainable Development: A Critical Review" *World Development*, Vol. 19, No. 6 (June, 1991): 607-621.

Pearce, David. et. al. "Discounting the Future" and "Economic Appraisal and the Natural Environment" in *Sustainable Development: Economics and Environment in the Third World* (Hants; U.K.: Edward Elgar, 1990): 23-66.

Pezzey, John, "Sustainability: An Interdisciplinary Guide" *Environmental Values*, Vol. 1(1992): 321-62.

Session #3   Implementing Sustainable Development
Tuesday, February 22

Have we already exceeded existing physical limits of sustainability? If so, which ones. If not, why are those who think we have wrong? To the extent that unsustainable activity can be identified what are the social sources of unsustainable behavior? Does it represent a clash between the dictates of efficient exploitation and the moral imperatives of sustainability or is it due to inefficient behavior? Does it make a difference which of those sources is valid? Why or why not? What policies are available to restore sustainability? How can the inertia for unsustainable activity be broken?

Required Reading

Theodore Panayotou, *Green Markets: The Economics of Sustainable Development* (San Francisco: ICS Press, 1993)

Supplemental Reading

Adams, William M., *Green Development: Environment and Sustainability in the Third World* (New York: Routledge, 1992).

Ahmad, Yusuf J., Salah El Serafy, and Ernst Lutz, eds. *Environmental Accounting for Sustainable Development* (Washington, DC: The World Bank,1989)

Asian Development Bank, *Economic Policies for Sustainable Development* (Manila, Philippines: Asian Development Bank, 1990).

Barbier, Edward B., *Economics, Natural-Resource Scarcity and Development: Conventional and Alternative Views* (London: Earthscan, 1989).

Bartelmus, Peter, *Environment and Development* (Cambridge, MA: Unwin Hyman, 1986).

Batie, Sandra S., "Sustainable Development: Challenges to the Agricultural Economics Profession" *American Journal of Agricultural Economics*, Vol. 71, No. 5 (December, 1989): 1083- 1101.

Collard, David, et al., *Economics, Growth and Sustainable Environments* (London: Macmillan, 1988).

Common, M. and C. Perrings, "Toward an Ecological Economic of Sustainability" *Ecological Economics* Vol. 6, No. 1 (1992): 7-34.

Daly, Herman E. and John J. Cobb Jr., *For the Common Good: Redirecting the Economy Toward Community, the Environment, and a Sustainable Future* (Boston: MA: Beacon Press, 1989).

Daly, Herman E. and Kenneth E. Townsend, ed. *Valuing the Earth: Economics, Ecology, Ethics* (Cambridge, MA: MIT Press, 1992).

Dasgupta, Partha and Karl-Goran Maler, "The Environment and Emerging Development Issues" in S. Fischer, et. al. ed. *Proceedings of the World Bank Annual Conference on Development Economics 1990*, (Washington: The World Bank, 1991): 101-132.

Goodland, Robert and G. Ledoc, "Neoclassical Economics and Principles of Sustainable Development" *Ecological Modeling*, Vol. 38(1987).

Holmberg, Johan, ed. *Making Development Sustainable: Redefining Institutions, Policy and Economics* (Washington, DC: Island Press, 1992).

Howarth, R. B. and R. B. Norgaard, "Intergenerational Resource Rights: Efficiency and Social Optimality" *Land Economics*, Vol. 66, No. 1 (February, 1990): 1-11.

Kulik, Omno and Harmen Verbruggen, *In Search of Indicators of Sustainable Development* (Hingam, MA: Kluwer Academic Publishers, 1991).

MacNeill, Jim, et al., *Beyond Interdependence: The Meeting of the World's Economy and the Earth's Ecology* (New York: Oxford University Press, 1991).

MacNeill, Jim, "Strategies for Sustainable Development," *Scientific American* Vol. 261, No. 3, (September 1, 1990): 154-165.

Mikesell, Raymond F., *Economic Development and the Environment* (London, UK: Mansell Publishing Limited, 1992).

Nijkamp, Peter and Frits Soeteman, "Ecologically Sustainable Development: Key Issues for Strategic Environmental Management" *International Journal of Social Economics*, Vol. 15, No. 3-4 (1988): 88-102.

Pearce, D. W. and J. J. Warford, *World Without End: Economics, Environment, and Sustainable Development* (Washington,DC, Oxford University Press for the World Bank, 1993).

Pearce, David and et.al., *Sustainable Development: Economics and Environment in the Third World* (Cheltenham, England: Edward Elgar Publishers Ltd., 1990).

Pearce, David, "Economics, Equity and Sustainable Development" *Futures(UK)*, Vol. 20, No. 6 (December, 1988): 598-605.

Redclift, Michael, *Sustainable Development: Exploring the Contradictions* (London: Methuen, 1987.).

Schramm, Gunter and Jeremy J. Warford, *Environmental Management and Economic Development* (Baltimore, MD: The Johns Hopkins University Press for The World Bank, 1989).

Tisdell, C., "Sustainable Development: Differing Perspectives of Ecologists and Economists, and Relevance to LDCs" *World Development*, Vol. 16, No. 3 (March, 1988): 373-383.

Turner, R. Kerry, *Sustainable Environmental Management: Principles and Practice* (Boulder, CO: Westview Press, 1988).

United Nations Economic Commission for Latin America and the Caribbean, *Sustainable Development: Changing Production Patterns, Social Equity and the Environment* (Santiago, Chile: United Nations Economic Commission for Latin America and the Caribbean, 1991).

Von Weizsacker, Ernst U., *Ecological Tax Reform: A Policy Proposal for Sustainable Development* (London, UK: Zed Books, 1992).

Young, M. D., *Sustainable Investment and Resource Use* (Carnforth, U.K.: The Parthenon Publishing Co., 1992): 49-87.

Session #4 Case Studies
Tuesday, March 1

This period will feature seminar participant presentations on case studies involving the application of economics to examine specific environmental problems from a sustainability perspective. Students are free to pick their own case study but some possibilities are given below. The designations indicate whether they are from the Reserve Desk in the Library (RES) or from my personal collection (TT). You are free, of course, to borrow sources from me.

Anderson, Anthony B., *Alternatives to Deforestation: Steps Toward the Sustainable Use of the Amazon Rainforest* (New York, NY: Columbia University Press, 1990). RES

Anderson, Anthony B., et al., *The Subsidy from Nature: Palm Forests, Peasantry, and Development on an Amazon Frontier* (New York, NY: Columbia University Press, 1991). RES

Berkes, Fikret and A. B. Shaw, "Ecologically Sustainable Development: a Caribbean Fisheries Case Study" *Canadian Journal of Development Studies*, Vol. 7(Summer, 1986): 175-96. RES

Cleaver, Kevin and Götz Schreiber, *The Population, Agriculture and Environment Nexus in Sub-Saharan Africa* (Washington: World Bank, 1992).TT

Cleaver, Kevin. Et. al. Conservation of West and Central African Rainforests (Washington, DC: The World Bank, 1992) TT

Cruz, Wilfredo and Robert Repetto, *Structural Adjustment and Sustainable Development in the Philippines* (Washington: World Resources Institute, 1992). RES

Cruz, Wilfredo, *Accounts Overdue: Natural Resource Depreciation in Costa Rica* (Washington, DC: World Resources Institute, 1991).TT

Faeth, Paul, ed., *Agricultural Policy ans Sustainability: Case Studies from India, chile,the Philippines and the United States* (Washington, DC: World Resources Institute, 1993) RES

McNeely, Jeffrey A., *Economics and Biological Diversity: Developing and Using Economic Incentives to Conserve Biological Resources* (Gland, Switzerland: IUCN, 1988). RES

Repetto, R., *Wasting Assets: Natural Resources in the National Income Accounts* (Washington: World Resources Institute, 1986). TT [Contains an Indonesian Case Study]

Repetto, Robert and Malcolm Gillis, *Public Policies and the Misuse of Forest Resources* (Cambridge,UK: Cambridge University Press,1988). Case studies listed below. RES

> Malcolm Gillis "Indonesia: Public Polices, Resource Management, and the Tropical Forest" pp. 43-113.

> Malcolm Gillis, Malaysia: Public Policies and the Tropical Forest", pp.115-164

> Eufresina L. Boado, "Incentive Policies and Forest Use in the Philippines", pp. 165-203.

> Li Jinchang, Kong Fanwen, He Naihui, and Lester Ross, "Price and Policy: The Keys to Revamping China's Forestry Resources", pp.205-245.

> Malcolm Gillis, " West Africa: Resource Management Policies and the Tropical Forest", pp.299-351.

> Robert Repetto, " Subsidized Timber Sales from National Forest lands in the United States", pp.353-383.

Swanson, Timothy M. and Edward B. Barbier, ed. *Economics for the Wilds: Wildlife, Wildlands, Diversity and Development* (London: Earthscan Publications Ltd., 1992).TT

Tilton, John E., *Mineral Wealth and Economic Development* (Washington, DC: Resources for the Future, Inc., 1992) RES

Turner, Kerry and Tom Jones, ed. *Wetlands: Market and Intervention Failures* (London: Earthscan Publications Ltd., 1991). RES

265

II. The Economics of Global Warming

Session #5
Tuesday, March 8

Global Warming I

Part I: Overview

One of the major environmental problems facing the world today is the threat of global warming. What are the key economic issues that arise in global warming? What differentiates global warming from other pollution problems such as smog, acid rain, or ozone depletion? How secure is the science on which the forecasts depend? What difference should that make to policy makers?

<u>Required Reading</u>:

> William Cline, *The Economics of Global Warming* (Washington, D.C.: Institute for International Economics, 1992): 1-76.

Part II: Benefits

What are the benefits to be derived from a policy to control global warming? How can they be measured? How reliable are the estimates? How large are they?

> William Cline, *The Economics of Global Warming* (Washington, D.C.: Institute for International Economics, 1992): 81-138.

Session #6
Tuesday, March 15

Global Warming II

<u>Required Reading</u>:

Part I: Measuring the Costs

> William Cline, *The Economics of Global Warming* (Washington, D.C.: Institute for International Economics, 1992): 141-194

Part II: Benefit/Cost Analysis

> William Cline, *The Economics of Global Warming* (Washington, D.C.: Institute for International Economics, 1992): 235-320.

Sessions #7 and #8
Tuesday, March 29 and
Tuesday, April 5

Global Warming III and IV

<u>Required Reading</u>:

> William Cline, *The Economics of Global Warming* (Washington, D.C.: Institute for International Economics, 1992): 323-380

Materials for Student Reports:

<u>Emission Charges and Emission Permits</u>

Particpants writing reports in this section will examine the two main economic incentive approaches currently being proposed to deal with the global warming problem-- emission charges and marketable permits. What are the advantages and disadvantages of each system? How are they alike? How are they different? What are the major issues to be confronted before these strategies could be implemented?

OECD, *Climate Change: Designing a Practical Tax System* (Paris: Organization for Economic Cooperation and Development, 1993) RES

OECD, *Climate Change: Designing a Tradeable Permit System* (Paris: Organization for Economic Cooperation and Development, 1992) RES

Rose, Adam and Tom Tietenberg, "An International System of Tradeable CO2 Entitlements: Implications for Economic Development" *Journal of Environment and Development*, Vol. 2, No. 1 (Winter, 1993): 1-36. RES

United Nations Conference on Trade and Development ed. *Combatting Global Warming: Study on a Global System of Tradeable Carbon Emission Entitlements*, (New York: United Nations, 1992). RES

Energy Conservation, Adaptation and "Excessive Consumerism"

In these papers particpants will examine the ecomic issues behind three rather different stategies for dealing with global warming. (1) The Durning book takes on the issue of whether we simply are an excessively consumerist society. How can we tell? What indicators can we use? What do they show? What role should the government play? (2) Other essays deal with adaptation strategies (learning to cope with global warming). Are they an alternative to mitigation? Will normal economic processes produce the optimal amount of adaptation? Why or why not? What role should the government play? (3) The third set of articles deal with the possiblites for using less energy to produce the services we now enjoy in the residential, industrial and transportation sectors.

Durning, Alan, *How Much is Enough: The Consumer Society and the Fututre of the Earth* (New York; W. W. Norton & Co.,1992) TT

MacKenzie, James J., Roger C. Dower, Donald D. T. Chen, *The Going Rate: What It Really Costs To Drive* (Washington, DC: World Resources Institute,1992). TT

OECD, *Cars and Climate Change* (Paris: OECD,1993) RES

OECD, *Market and Government Failures in Environmental Mangement: The Case of Transport* (Paris: OECD,1992) TT

OECD, *Taxing Energy: Why and How?* (Paris:OECD, 1993) RES

Panel on Policy Implications of Greenhouse Warming, National Academy of Sciences, *Policy Implications of Greenhouse Warming: Mitigation, Adaptation, and the Science Base* (Washington, DC: National Academy Press, 1992) TT

"Residential and Commercial Energy Management"
"Industrial Energy Management"
"Transportation Energy Management"
"Adaptation: Findings"

Schipper, Lee and Stephen Meyers, *Energy Eficiency and Human Activity: Past Trends, Future Prospects* (Cambridge, UK: Cambridge University Press,1992). RES

Renewable Energy Sources

In these papers presenters will examine the economics of alternative fuels. Are they economically competitive? Would they become economically competitive if all costs (including environmental costs) were included in the calculations? What is the appropriate role for the government? How effective is technology transfer of renewable energy resources to developing countries? How can that process be improved?

267

Brower, Michael, *Cool Energy: Renewable Solutions to Environmental Problems* Cambridge, MA: The MIT Press, 1993) TT

Jackson, Tim, "Renewable Energy: Summary Paper for the Renewables Series" *Energy Policy Vol. 20*, No. 9 (1992): 861-883. RES

Johansson, Thomas B., Henry Kelly, Amulya K. N. Reddy, and Robert H. Williams, *Renewable Energy: Sources for Fuels and Electricity* (Washington, DC: Island Press, 1993) TT
> "Wind Energy"
> "Photovoltaics"
> "Biomass Fuels"
> "Solar Hydrogen"

III. Trade and the Environment

Session #9 **Trade and the Environment I**
Tuesday, April 12

Recently the conflicts over trade and the environment have intensified. Why? What are the specific issues which have precipitated these conflicts? What is the economic logic that lies behind the presumption that trade is good for the participating countries? What preconditions are necessary for this logic to hold? What has been the basis for the attacks on free trade coming from the environmental community? Is one of these points of view correct? If so, which one and why? If not, where does truth lie?

Required Reading:

Herman Daly, "Problems with Free Trade: Neoclassical and Steady-State Perspectives" in Darwood Zaelke, et al., *Trade and the Environment: Law Economics and Policy* (Washington, DC: Island Press, 1993) RES

Jagdish Bagwadi, "Trade and the Environment; The False Conflict?"in Darwood Zaelke, et al., *Trade and the Environment: Law Economics and Policy* (Washington, DC: Island Press, 1993) RES

Judith Dean, "Trade and the Environment: A Survey of the Literature" in Patrick Low, ed. *International Trade and the Environment* (Washington, DC: World Bank Discussion Papers, 1992)

Patrick Low and Raed Safadi "Trade Policy and Pollution" in Patrick Low, ed. *International Trade and the Environment* (Washington, DC: World Bank Discussion Papers, 1992)

Session #10 **Trade and the Environment II**
Tuesday, April 19

In this session we shall examine the effects of capital mobility on the incentives of governments to set stringent pollution control policies and the effects on the nations receiving the new capital. does capital mobility undermine the desire to protect the environment? Are the developing countries becoming pollution havens? What is the evidence?

Required Reading:

Michael E. Porter, "America's Green Strategy" *Scientific American*, Vol. 264, No. 4(April):168.

Patrick Low "Do 'Dirty Industries' Industries Migrate" in Patrick Low, ed. *International Trade and the Environment* (Washington, DC: World Bank Discussion Papers, 1992)

Robert E. B. Lucas, David Wheeler, and Hemamala Hettige, "Economic Development, Environmental Regulation and the International Migration of Toxic Industrial Pollution:1960-1988" in Patrick Low, ed. *International Trade and the Environment* (Washington, DC: World Bank Discussion Papers, 1992

Nancy Birdsall and David Wheeler, "Trade Policy and Industrial Pollution in Latin America: Where are the Pollution Havens?" in Patrick Low, ed. *International Trade and the Environment* (Washington, DC: World Bank Discussion Papers, 1992)

David Wheeler and Paul Martin, "Prices, Policies and the International Diffusion of Clean Technology: the Case of Wood Pulp Production" in Patrick Low, ed. *International Trade and the Environment* (Washington, DC: World Bank Discussion Papers, 1992)

Sessions #11   **Trade and the Environment III**
Tuesday, April 26

        Lecture by Dr. David Wheeler from the World Bank entitled "Industrial Pollution in the World Economy: The Impact of Trade, Investment and Environmental Regulation Since 1970". Following the lecture the rest of the period will be used for a question and answer session with David.

Sessions #12   **Trade and the Environment IV**
Tuesday, May 3

        Student presentations.

Some Possible Topic Areas for Student Reports (though alternative topic proposals are welcome):

The Tuna-Dolphin Case
Trade in Timber Products and Sustainability
Trade in Agricultural Products and Sustainability
Export of Hazardous Substances
CITES and Trade in Endangered Species
NAFTA and the Environment
The Pollution Havens Hypothesis
The Porter Hypothesis
Multinationals and the Environment

Some Possible Sources:

Anderson, Kym, "Effects on the Environment and Welfare of Liberalizing World Trade: The Cases of Coal and Food" in Kym Anderson and Richard Blackhurst, eds., *The Greening of World Trade Issues* (Ann Arbor: University of Michigan Press, 1993) TT

Anderson, Terry ed. *NAFTA and the Environment* (San Francisco: Pacific Research Instiute for Public Policy, 1993) TT

Barbier, E. B., "Cash Crops, Food Crops, and Sustainability- The Case of Indonesia" *World Development*, 17(1989): 879-895.

Barbier, Edward, et. al. *Elephants, Economics, and Ivory* (London: Earthscan, 1990).

Castleman, Barry I. and Prabir Purkavastha, "The Bhopal Disaster as a Case Study in Double Standards" in J. H. Ives ed. *The Export of Hazard: Transnational Corporations and Environmental Control Issues*, (Boston: Routledge & Kegan Paul, 1985): 213-223.

Castleman, Barry I., "The Double Standard in Industrial Hazard" in J. H. Ives ed. *The Export of Hazard: Transnational Corporations and Environmental Control Issues*, (Boston: Routledge & Kegan Paul, 1985): 60-89.

Charnovitz, Steve, "Exploring the Environmental Exceptions in GATT Article XX" *Journal of World Trade Vol.* 25, No. 5 (1991): 21-35.

Cheru, Fantu, "Structural Adjustment, Primary Resource Trade and Sustainable Development in Sub-Sahara Africa" *World Development*, 20 (April, 1992): 497-512.

Gillis, Malcolm, "Multinational Enterprises and Environmental and Resource Management Issues in the Indonesian Tropical Forest Sector" in C. Pearson ed. *Multinational Corporations, Environment, and the Third World*, (Durham: Duke University Press, 1987): 64-89.

Gladwin, Thomas N., "A Case Study of the Bhopal Tragedy" in C. Pearson ed. *Multinational Corporations, Environment, and the Third World*, (Durham: Duke University Press, 1987): 240-254.

Goldin, Ian, ed. *Open Economies: Structural Adjustment and Agriculture* (Cambridge, UK: Cambridge University Press, 1992).

Goodman, Louis W., "Foreign Toxins: Multinational Corporations and Pesticides in Mexican Agriculture" in C. Pearson ed. *Multinational Corporations, Environment, and the Third World*, (Durham: Duke University Press, 1987): 90-110.

Ives, Jane H., "The Health Effects of the Transfer of Technology to the Developing World: Report and Case Studies" in J. H. Ives ed. *The Export of Hazard: Transnational Corporations and Environmental Control Issues*, (Boston: Routledge & Kegan Paul, 1985): 172-191.

Ives, Jane I., ed. *The Export of Hazard: Transnational Corporations and Environmental Control Issues* (Boston: Routledge & Kegan Paul, 1985).

Larson, B. A. and D. W. Bromley, "Natural Resource Prices, Export Policies and Deforestation: The Case of Sudan" *World Development* 19(1991): 1298-97.

Leonard, H. Jeffrey, *Pollution and the Struggle for the World Product* (Cambridge: Cambridge University Press, 1988).

Lepkowski, Wil, "The Disaster at Bhopal - Chemical Safety in the Third World" in C. Pearson ed. *Multinational Corporations, Environment, and the Third World*, (Durham: Duke University Press, 1987): 223-239.

Levenstein, Charles and Stanley W. Eller, "Exporting Hazardous Industries: 'For Example' is not Proof" in J. H. Ives ed. *The Export of Hazard: Transnational Corporations and Environmental Control Issues*, (Boston: Routledge & Kegan Paul, 1985): 51-59.

OECD Environment Directorate, *Environmental Policies and Industial Competitiveness* (Paris: OECD, 1993) TT

Parthama, Ida-Bagus-P., and Jeffrey R. Vincent, "United States Demand for Indonesian Plywood" *Bulletin of Indonesian Economic Studies* 28(1) (April, 1992): 101-12.

Runge, C. Ford,"Environmental Regulation and Agricultural Trade Competitiveness" in John B. Braden, et al., eds. *Agriculture and Water Quality: International Perspectives* (Boulder, CO: Reinner, 1990): 183-96.

Stonich, Susan C., "The Promotion of Non-Traditional Agricultural Exports in Honduras: Issues of Equity, Environment and Natural Resource Management"*Development and change* 22 (October, 1991): 725-55.

Umana, Alvaro, *Trade and Environment: A Developing Country Perspective* (Washington, DC: World Resources Institute, 1992).

Ural, Engin, "Environmental Protection and Foreign Investment in Turkey" in C. Pearson ed. *Multinational Corporations, Environment, and the Third World*, (Durham: Duke University Press, 1987): 175-197.

Vincent, Jeffrey R., "The Tropical Timber Trade and Sustainable Development," *Science*, 256, (19 June 1992): 1651-1655.

Whalley, John, "The Interface Between Environmental and Trade Policies" *Economic Journal* 101(March, 1991) 180-89.

Young, Michael D., "International Trading Arrangements, the Intensity of Resource Use, and Environmental Qulaity" in John B. Braden, et al., eds. *Agriculture and Water Quality: International Perspectives* (Boulder, CO: Reinner. 1990): 197-215.

COMPREHENSIVE EXAMINATION

Resource and Environmental Economics

Fall 1994   Harberger, Cameron, Sigman

INSTRUCTIONS: There are three parts (and three pages) to this examination.
Each part is worth 80 points for a total of 240 points. Please complete ALL
questions. You have FOUR hours to complete this exam.

PART A. Cost-Benefit Analysis (80 points).

I. (40 points) Write an essay on the conceptual framework underlying
social cost-benefit analysis. In it be sure to cover the following:

a)   What is the common element in all cases where there is a discrepancy
     between social and private benefits or costs?

b)   How is this element reflected in standard measures of social
     opportunity cost of key factors like capital and foreign exchange?

c)   Indicate how, after we have made the full and appropriate use of social
     opportunity costs (say, of foreign exchange and of capital), in a
     typical project evaluation, we would still have to take additional
     discrepancies (between social and private benefits and costs) into
     account. Give one or two examples from standard project evaluation.

d)   In what special ways do discrepancies between social and private
     benefits and costs come into play in environmental economics?

e)   Are there also special ways in which such discrepancies arise in the
     economics of natural resources?

II. (20 points) If a project buys an asset, the cost of that asset should
be accounted for in the period when it is purchased. If a project rents
such an asset, the cost of that asset (to the project) should be accounted
for period-by-period as it is used by the project.

a)   Is the above statement correct, in your opinion?

b)   Is it true that the _social_ costs of a project can (and often will) be
     different if that projects rents an asset rather than buys it? If so,
     explain. If not, why not?

III. (20 points) A common problem in nearly every type of project concerns
when, whether, and how to replace an old asset with a new one. Write an
essay in which you explore carefully the nature of this problem, and the
relevant alternatives open to the typical decision-maker. What key
conclusions do you come to?

271

PART B. Natural Resource Economics (80 points)

(Budget your time carefully, allocating about ten minutes per question.)

I. (20 points) Economics of the Fishery

a) In models that acknowledge that the stock of fish must be treated as a natural asset, how do interest rates and prices affect incentives to conserve or deplete the fishery? Explain.

b) In the basic theory of fishery dynamics, what was the distinction between a "marginal stock effect" and a "stock externality"? How do these two terms enter into the determination of the path to a steady state (in the simple theory)?

II. (20 points) Economics of the Forest

a) Comparative statics for a simplified Faustmann model can be accomplished using a diagram. Employ such a diagram to show how higher interest rates are likely to affect the optimal rotation period for a stand of trees.

b) Suppose a forest also confers amenity value. If amenity values are increasing over time (so that older trees provide more valuable recreational experiences in the forest), how does the optimal rotation period compare to the optimal rotation period in a Faustmann-type model that ignores amenity values? Why?

III. (20 points) Economics of the Mine

a) Consider the simple theory of the mine. Given the interest rate and a known demand curve for the mineral in question, the "reserves constraint" and the "choke price constraint" interact to determine two crucial quantities relevant to the optimal extraction path. What are they? In a carefully labeled four-quadrant diagram, depict how an optimal extraction path can be conceptualized.

b) Stock effects in the Theory of the Mine are usually captured by specifying a cost function $C(x_t, b_t)$ that depends both upon extraction, x_t, and remaining stocks, b_t. In such a model, opportunity costs are different than they would be in a model without stock effects. Explain.

IV. (20 points) Miscellaneous

a) How can exploration activity and discovery of additional reserves be incorporated into the Theory of the Mine? Explain. What additional optimality conditions will the augmented model display?

b) Explain how production externalities might be incorporated into the theory of the firm. Be sure to treat explicitly the natural rate of decay of pollutants in the environment.

272   2

PART C. Environmental Economics

Answer ALL questions: 80 points total.

I. (12 points each; 36 points total) True, false, uncertain and *explain*.

a) "If marginal abatement costs are certain but the marginal benefits of
abatement are uncertain, quantity controls are preferred to price
controls."

b) "There is no option value associated with environmental preservation if
the individuals that experience the costs and benefits of preservation
are risk neutral."

c) "Contingent valuation studies typically find differences between
willingness to pay for improvements in environmental quality (WTP) and
willingness to accept payment for reductions in environmental quality
(WTA). The difference between WTP and WTA is usually of a magnitude that
can be explained by conventional consumer theory."

II. (20 points) Discuss the experience with tradable emissions permits
under the Emissions Reduction Credit program of the U.S. Clean Air Act.
Under what circumstances has trading occurred and why? What lessons should
policy-makers take away from this experience in designing future emissions
permit programs?

III. (24 points) In a hypothetical country, local communities choose the
level of local air quality standards. A federal government agency has asked
you to use the level of the standards chosen by local communities to
evaluate willingness to pay for air quality at a national level. The agency
wants your study to use political decision-making as the basis for the
analysis (i.e., your methodology may not use prices of houses or other
goods, nor can you run a survey).

a) Describe a model of community decision-making that you might use to
undertake this task. What problems would you foresee in applying this
model?

b) What independent variables would you attempt to gather and why? How
would you extrapolate national willingness to pay for air quality
improvements from this model? What additional assumptions are necessary
for this extrapolation?

∅ End of exam ℚ

3   273

University of Colorado

NATURAL RESOURCES/ENVIRONMENT   PhD Comprehensive Examination

January 4, 1995

PART I: **Natural Resources**
Allocate about 1½ hours to Part I. Plan carefully before you start writing.

In the seminar, we covered a range of materials that, hopefully, tie together: empirical evidence on evolving resource scarcity (e.g. Slade, 1982); factors mitigating scarcity (Howe); effects of technological change; the Hotelling model as a normative model (2-period model and original Hotelling article, Howe notes) and as a descriptive model (Solow); sustainability (Pezzey); intergenerational equity (Norgaard); and policy measures towards sustainability and intergenerational equity (e.g. improving the national accounts).

Assuming that human society desires sustainability and intergenerational equity, write a 5 to 10 page essay that includes the following points (but other material may be included):

1.   Are we on the right path?

2.   Is the market dealing appropriately with these issues?

3.   Are discount rates appropriate?

4.   Is R & D sufficient and correctly oriented?

5.   Are existing saving and consumption patterns appropriate?

PART II: Emphasis on Environmental
Allocate approximately one hour and 30 minutes to this part of the exam. Answer all ten questions to the best of your ability in the 90 minutes.

1. (5 minutes) When we discussed intertemporal efficiency conditions we obtained the result that efficiency requires that

$$MRS_{X_1 X_2} = MRT_{X_1 X_2}$$

where X_i is the quantity of the aggregate good in period i. Discuss some conditions that, if they prevailed, would make attainment of this result inconsistent with efficiency.

2. (5 minutes) Does the existence of pollution imply the existence of one or more externalities? Explain.

3. (5 minutes) Is an estimated compensating variation associated with a specific change in prices and/or characteristics a random variable? Explain, and explain why we care.

4. (5 minutes) Should an individual's WTP for an increase in environmental amenities be, or not be, a function of the method of payment. Yes or No and explain.

5. (10 minutes) Argue that some emissions into waterways should not be restricted at their source. Why? What sorts of emissions are you talking about? Would your argument(s) also apply to emissions into the air?

6. (10 minutes) Robert Solow (Science p. 500) states that, "This economizing on information is a second reason for favoring taxes over regulation. The construction of a good schedule of taxes or fees also requires information, but rather less information." Critique this statement.

275

7. (15 minutes) Consider some proposed government policy that can be described as change from (P^o, A^o) to (P^1, A^1) where P is the exogenous price vector and A is the exogenous vector of nonmarket commodities. Now consider the following techniques for evaluating that proposed policy change: a CVM study, a travel-cost study, a hedonic wage study, and a hedonic rent study. Which type of study is most appropriate as a function of the characteristics of the proposal to be evaluated; i.e., consider what characteristics of a proposal make it a good, or bad, candidate for evaluation with each of these four techniques. I want your answer(s) to be expressed in general terms, not in terms of examples. While example free, the types of proposals to be evaluated include, valuing recreational sites, weather, global warming, view, increased or decreased air pollution, earth quake risk, decreased probability of getting cancer in twenty years, etc.

8. (10 minutes) Does CVM valuation of an environmental change require the algebraic specification of a common preference ordering (utility function) for all the individuals in the target population? Yes or No and Explain.

9. (15 pts) Assume two road go to Longmont. The cost (in time) of travelling the wide road is always 60 minutes. Assume that the total amount of time (in minutes) it takes T trucks to travel from Boulder to Longmont on the narrow road is $C(T) = \beta_1 T + \beta_2 T^2$ where $\beta_1 > 0$ and $\beta_2 > 0$. Assume the wide road is a common property resource, but you own the narrow road and 100 trucks, which you do not own, need to get to Longmont everyday. What toll (t - expressed in minutes) will you charge to maximize your profits from the road? Assume the maintenance costs for both roads are independent of the number of trucks that use the roads. How many trucks will pay the toll and take your narrow road? Prove, that the toll will eliminate the gap between MSC(T) and MPC(T), where MSC(T) and MPC(T) are respectively the marginal social cost, and marginal private cost (including the toll), on the narrow road if there are T trucks on the narrow road.

10. (10 minutes) Argue that the market place will not internalize the externalities associated with toxic chemicals in the work environment.

276

University of Colorado

NATURAL RESOURCES/ENVIRONMENT　　　　　　PhD Comprehensive Examination

August, 1994

PART I:　　Spend 1 1/2 hours on this section of the NR/E exam. Answer 1 and 2 and choose one from 3 or 4.

1.　Describe the evidence available to date on the issue of whether or not natural resources (renewable and non-renewable, but not environmental media like water and air) are becoming scarcer. Be sure to cite specific studies. What conclusions do you come to?

2.　The Hotelling model has many variants. Write out a specific optimization model for each of the following cases, showing the first order conditions for a solution. Interpret these conditions.

　　a.　a resource in fixed supply with constant unit recovery costs,

　　b.　the same but with recovery costs dependent on the rate of recovery,

　　c.　the same but with recovery costs dependent on both the rate of recovery and the remaining stock;

　　d.　the same as (c) but with a backstop technology.

3.　Write a carefully structured essay on the meaning(s) of sustainability, how it could be monitored and the economic steps that could be taken to increase the likelihood of achieving it. How does sustainability relate to intergenerational equity?

4.　Choose a specific renewable resource system (e.g. water, forests, fisheries) and describe the main policy issues of current importance in that field. Describe the economic issues and prescriptions available to overcome the problems.

PART II: Spend 1 1/2 hours on this part of the exam. Answer all eight questions.

1. (15 minutes) Discuss when it is, and is not, possible to estimate the CV for a change in the level of an environmental amenities from market data. Why do we care?

2. (10 minutes) Define Maler's "Weak Complimentarity Condition" and explain its relevance to applied welfare economics.

3. (15 minutes) What is the travel-cost method for valuing site-specific recreational activities? Briefly explain what it is and how it can be used to value recreational sites, or changes in the characteristics of the sites.

4. (15 minutes) Consider the designation of a new wilderness area in Colorado. Assume that the economics consulting firm of Snerd, Snerd, and Gomer has accurately determined the CV each hiker and backpacker would associate with designation and that the sum of all these individual CV's is $5 million. Snerd, Snerd, and Gomer included all the aspects of the change in their CV calculation for the hikers and backpackers. However, designation of this Wilderness Area will decrease the availability of water to grow Soy beans on the plains of Colorado. This reduction will cause the price of Tofu to rise by $1 a pound. Assume that before the change, four million pounds of Tofu was produced and sold. This price increase obviously makes Tofu consumers worse off. Note that hikers and backpackers are not in this group; i.e., they never consume Tofu. Convince me whether designating the Wilderness Area is a potential pareto improvement. What if the price increased by $1.50 rather than by $1? Explain your answers.
Your answer could be quite short.

5. (10 minutes) Former Senator Gary Hart was once quoted to the effect that "we don't want to just move pollution around, we want to eliminate it." Discuss.

6. (5 minutes) What is the difference between common property resources and public goods? Your answer should include definitions of both. What are their similarities.

7. (15 minutes) Consider the third party effects associated with toxic substances. The judicial system is often put forward as the appropriate mechanism for internalizing the third party externalities associated with toxic substances. What is this mechanism? Then, discuss the difficulties that the traditional judicial system will have in internalizing these sorts of externalities. How might the system be modified to make internalization through the legal process more likely? Think about the impact of uncertainty, latency, and statistical probabilities on the process.

8. (5 minutes) The compensating variation for a change in the quantity of an environmental amenity is conventionally defined in terms of money. Define, using a direct utility function the compensating variation associated with a change in the quantity of an environmental amenity *in terms of the numeraire good*, where good 1 is defined as the numeraire good.

University of Colorado

NATURAL RESOURCES/WATER

August, 1994

PhD Comprehensive Examination

G

Spend 1 1/2 hours on this section. Answer questions 1 and 2 and choose one (1) from 3 to 5.

1.   Assume we have located a reservoir site at which a dual purpose dam providing irrigation water supply and M & I supply can be built. The objective now is to optimize the design of this dam in terms of its height, H, which determines storage capacity.

    a.   Describe the information you would need to carry out an economic optimization of the dam height.

    b.   Develop a model bringing these elements together so you can optimize H in terms of present value of net benefits.

2.   River basin planning.

    a.   Why is the river basin a natural planning unit for water development?

    b.   Discuss the interdependence of storage projects on a river and how such projects should be evaluated using benefit-cost analysis.

    c.   Why is conjunctive surface water-groundwater management an important component of river basin planning?

    d.   Why is coordinated water supply -- water quality management important?

    e.   What is meant by cost-sharing and why is it important to the attainment of economic efficiency in the political-economy environment of water planning. Give an example or two.

3.   Discuss how you would design an optimal flood control plan for a river valley. Identify the component activities and the roles each would play.

4.   Discuss the weaknesses of the Reclamation Program in the United States since 1902 and what can now be done to make the best of these shortcomings.

5.   Discuss the importance of water markets with examples of some that have been in operation. Discuss the complications that require some degree of social oversight (regulation) of such markets.

NATURAL RESOURCES/ENVIRONMENT

Spend 1 1/2 hours on this section. Answer 1 and 2 and choose one (1) from 3 or 4.

1.   Describe the evidence available to date on the issue of whether or not natural resources (renewable and non-renewable, but not environmental media like water and air) are becoming scarcer. Be sure to cite specific studies. What conclusions do you come to?

2.   The Hotelling model has many variants. Write out a specific optimization model for each of the following cases, showing the first order conditions for a solution. Interpret these conditions.

    a.   a resource in fixed supply with constant unit recovery costs,

    b.   the same but with recovery costs dependent on the rate of recovery,

    c.   the same but with recovery costs dependent on both the rate of recovery and the remaining stock;

    d.   the same as (c) but with a backstop technology.

3.   Write a carefully structured essay on the meaning(s) of sustainability, how it could be monitored and the economic steps that could be taken to increase the likelihood of achieving it. How does sustainability relate to intergenerational equity?

4.   Choose a specific renewable resource system (e.g. water, forests, fisheries) and describe the main policy issues of current importance in that field. Describe the economic issues and prescriptions available to overcome the problems.

University of Colorado

Natural Resources/Environmental   Ph.D. Comprehensive Exam

January, 1994

PART I

NOTE: The examinee is expected to spend about 1.5 hours of the three-hour exam
          period answering all 3 questions.

1.   Take a simple 2 period Hotelling Model (or a more complicated model if you want)
      and do the following:

      a.   derive the basic Hotelling results;

      b.   show how you would modify the model if there is a "backstop technology" in
            the second period;

      c.   add a growth function that applies to the stock that is left after resource use in
            period 1. Derive the optimal results for use in periods 1 and 2.

2.   Write a short essay on current policy issues in <u>one</u> of the following resource areas:

      a.   forest management

      b.   water management

      c.   marine fisheries management

3.   Write a short essay that (a) defines "sustainability;" (b) describes steps that would
      help the industrialized world achieve sustainability; (c) and discusses the relationship
      of sustainability to "intergenerational equity."

PART II - Emphasis on Environmental

NOTE: Allocate approximately one hour and 30 minutes to this part of the exam.

1.   (20 minutes) Argue that one should rank the social desirability of projects by ranking the aggregate CVs for each project where the aggregate CV for each project is obtained by summing each individual's CV for that project. Argue that this method should not be used.

2.   (25 minutes) Discuss when it is, and is not, possible to estimate the CV for a change in the level of an environmental amenities from market data.

3.   (10 minutes) Define the term "pecuniary externality." Explain whether pecuniary externalities cause society's resources to be allocated inefficiently.

4.   (25 minutes) Given the state of technical knowledge, can we hold production, consumption and recycling constant and reduce total emissions? Can we reduce pollution? Explain. What are the implications of your answer for environmental policy?

5.   (10 minutes) Define, and outline the difference between the Pareto Criteria and the Kaldor Criteria. As part of your answer, explain the intended purpose of these two criteria.

University of Colorado

August, 1993

PART A

NOTE: The examinee is expected to spend about 1.5 hours of the three-hour exam period on two questions: Number 1 and either 2 or 3.

I.   Harold Hotelling, among his other brilliant contributions to economics and mathematical statistics, formalized the model of optimal use of an exhaustible resource (1931). Robert Solow, in his famous paper "The Economics of Resources or the Resources of Economics" (1974) elaborated on the Hotelling model, in particular discussing the role of both stock and flow markets.

Another branch of natural resources literature, sometimes related to the Hotelling model (e.g., Scott Farrow) and sometimes not (e.g., Barnett and Morse, Vikerry Smith, Margaret Slade, Hall and Hall) has developed an empirical literature on indicators of resource scarcity. This approach has been criticized on broad conceptual grounds by Richard Norgaard.

Please answer the following questions in as integrated fashion as possible in the time allowed, i.e., try to point out some cross-relationships rather than just finishing one question and going to the next.

1.   Indicate the nature of the basic Hotelling model and state its major conclusion.

2.   Is the model about the firm (micro), the resource sector (macro), or both?

3.   Solow emphasized the interaction of the market for (in situ) resource stocks and for flows of the produced commodity. Discuss briefly how these markets might interact to facilitate the commodity market's adjustment back to the Hotelling path.

4.   Since there is a market for stocks and a market for flows of the produced commodity, there are at least two prices that could be used as indicators of scarcity. In addition, other indicators of scarcity have been used. Discuss briefly what is known about the time paths of these two prices for broad classes of natural resources.

5.   Which indicator (if any) is most appropriate and state reasonable objections to the use of such indicators in general.

II.   It is frequently asserted that the national accounts and related concepts (e.g., GDP, national income, etc.) omit many relevant benefits and costs related to natural resources. Describe some of these shortcomings and suggest ways of making the national accounts more appropriate.

III.   Derive from an apporpriate model the principles that should govern simultaneous extraction from two mines of differing cost characteristics.

The examinee is expected to spend about 1.5 hours of the three-hour exam period on this part of the exam.

1. (15 minutes) Argue that one should rank the social desirability of projects by ranking the aggregate CVs (or EVs) for each project where the aggregate CV (or EV) for each project is obtained by summing each individual's CV (or EV) for that project. Argue that this method should not be used.

2. (15 minutes) Discuss when it is, and is not, possible to estimate the CV for a change in the level of an environmental amenities from market data.

3. (15 minutes) Consider the designation of a new wilderness area in Colorado. Assume that the economics consulting firm of Snerd, Snerd, and Gomer has accurately determined the CV each hiker and backpacker would associate with designation and that the sum of all these individual CV's is $5 million. Snerd, Snerd, and Gomer included all the aspects of the change in their CV calculation for the hikers and backpackers. However, designation of this Wilderness Area will decrease the availability of water to grow Soy beans on the plains of Colorado. This reduction will cause the price of Tofu to rise by $1 a pound. Assume that before the change, four million pounds of Tofu was produced and sold. This price increase obviously makes Tofu consumers worse off. Note that hikers and backpackers are not in this group; i.e., they never consume Tofu. Convince me whether designating the Wilderness Area is a potential pareto improvement. What if the price increased by $1.50 rather than by $1?

    Your answer could be quite short.

4. (15 minutes) When we discussed intertemporal efficiency conditions we obtained the result that efficiency requires that

    $$MRS^i_{x_1 x_2} = MRT_{x_1 x_2} \quad \forall \ i$$

    Discuss some conditions that, if they prevailed, would make attainment of this result inconsistent with efficiency. Why?

5. (15minutes) Pollution from wood bringing stoves is a major problem in many Colorado mountain communities. Why has the problem arisen? Explain why there is a market failure. Suggest a government strategy for internalizing, or reducing, the market failure. Discuss the efficiency, equity and political feasibility of your suggested strategy.

6. (15 minutes) Discuss the relationship between externalities and common property resources. In what sense are they the same? In what sense are they different? As part of your answer define both terms.

University of Colorado

Natural Resources/Environmental PhD

August 17, 1992

PART A

NOTE: The examinees are expected to spend about 1.5 hours of the three-hour exam
period on these two questions, with greatest emphasis on question 1.

I.   Harold Hotelling, among his other brilliant contributions to economics and mathematical
statistics, formalized the model of optimal use of an exhaustible resource (1931). Robert
Solow, in his famous paper "The Economics of Resources or the Resources of Economics"
(1974) elaborated on the Hotelling model, in particular discussing the role of both stock and
flow markets.

Another branch of natural resources literature, sometimes related to the Hotelling model
(e.g., Scott Farrow) and sometimes not (e.g., Barnett and Morse, Vikerry Smith, Margaret
Slade, Hall and Hall) has developed an empirical literature on indicators of resource scarcity.
This approach has been criticized on broad conceptual grounds by Richard Norgaard.

Please answer the following questions in as integrated fashion as possible in the time
allowed, i.e., try to point out some cross-relationships rather than just finishing one question
and going to the next.

1.   Indicate the nature of the basic Hotelling model and state its major conclusion.

2.   Is the model about the firm (micro), the resource sector (macro), or both?

3.   Solow emphasized the interaction of the market for (in situ) resource stocks and for
flows of the produced commodity. Discuss briefly how these markets might interact
to facilitate the commodity market's adjustment back to the Hotelling path.

4.   Since there is a market for stocks and a market for flows of the produced commodity,
there are at least two prices that could be used as indicators of scarcity. In addition,
other indicators of scarcity have been used. Discuss briefly what is known about the
time paths of these two prices for broad classes of natural resources.

5.   Which indicator (if any) is most appropriate and state reasonable objections to the use
of such indicators in general.

II.   It is frequently asserted that the national accounts and related concepts (e.g., GDP, national
income, etc.) omit many relevant benefits and costs related to natural resources. Describe
some of these shortcomings and suggest ways of making the national accounts more
appropriate.

PART B

NOTE: Allocate approximately 1.5 hours to this part of the exam.

Short Answer Question. Each of the four short answer questions should be answered in five
sentences or less.

1.   (Short answer - 5 minutes) What is the difference between a market commodity and a
      nonmarket commodity. As part of your answer define both terms.

2.   (Short answer - 10 minutes) The compensating variation for a change in the quantity of an
      environmental amenity is conventionally defined in terms of money. Define, using a direct
      utility function the compensating variation associated with a change in the quantity of an
      environmental amenity *in terms of the numeraire good*, where good 1 is defined as the
      numeraire good.

3.   (Short answer - 10 minutes) Make a quick argument that it is not worth it to allocate current
      resources to reducing the impact of the Greenhouse Effect.

4.   (Short answer - 10 minutes) Should one expect cross-sectional variations in environmental
      amenities to be reflected in cross-sectional variations in rents and/or wage rates? Why or
      why not?
----
5.   (15 minutes) Define Maler's "Weak Complimentarity Condition" and explain its relevance to
      applied welfare economics.

6.   (15 minutes) Use the expenditure function to explain what determines an individual's
      marginal willingness to pay for an amenity. Explain how one can use the expenditure
      function to determine that marginal willingness to pay. Would you expect that marginal
      valuation to be the same for all individuals? Why or why not? Begin your answer be
      defining both in words, and in functional notation, an expenditure function that includes
      environmental amenities.

7.   (25 minutes) Pollution from wood bringing stoves is a major problem in many Colorado
      mountain communities. Why has the problem arisen? Is there a market failure involved? If
      so, what sort? Should the government do something about it, and if so, what? Discuss taxes
      and regulations from an efficiency, equity and political feasibility perspective.

University of Colorado

Natural Resources/Environment
Ph.D. Comprehensive Examination
August 1990

Part I

Choose 1 of 2 questions. Suggested time: 30 minutes.

1. For a renewable resource, use the Schaeffer-Pearl-Verholst model to derive the long run harvest and population levels that maximize the present value of future income for discount rates of r=0 and 0<r<∞. State underlying assumptions and compare these results to harvest and population levels associated with those for (1) short term profit maximization, and (2) where the objective is to maximize a given social welfare function. Assume perfectly competitive markets for your answer.

2. Discuss the pros and cons of using hedonic methods versus contingent valuation for valuing non-marketed goods.

Choose 1 of 2 questions. Suggested time: 30 minutes.

1. For a non-renewable resource, construct a dynamic (multi-period or continuous time) model that depicts the socially optimum pattern of resource use. Be sure the model contains the dimensions or features you think are important in the real world. Solve for and carefully interpret the first-order conditions.

2. Relate the economic theory of optimum use of renewable and non-renewable resources to the currently popular concept of sustainable economic development. Are the two concepts the same? How are they defined? How do they differ, if at all?

Choose 1 of 2 questions. Suggested time: 15 minutes.

1. Describe the factors that have mitigated resource scarcity in the past. Which of these factors is likely to be most important in the future? Explain.

2. Trace the historical evolution of primary energy sources in the U.S. from 1800 to the present. Discuss reasons why some sources have declined in importance and others have increased in importance.

Choose 1 of 2 questions. Suggested time: 15 minutes.

1. Pick a specific real world resource (forestry, non-fuel minerals, fossil fuels, water, etc.) and discuss the types and causes of deviations between a purely market determined pattern of use over time and a socially optimal pattern.

2. Describe several possible indicators of the scarcity of a resource. Critique each one in terms of its appropriateness.

Part II.

<u>Answer all of the following questions</u> and allocate your time as follows:
Question 1 - 25 minutes, Question 2 - 25 minutes, Question 3 - 20 minutes, and
Question 4 - 10 minutes.

1. Consider the third party effects associated with toxic substances. The
    judicial system is often put forward as the appropriate mechanism for
    internalizing the third party externalities associated with toxic
    substances. Discuss the difficulties that the traditional judicial
    system will have in internalizing these sorts of externalities. How
    might the system be modified to make internalization through the legal
    process more likely? Think about the impact of uncertainty, latency,
    and statistical probabilities on the process.

2. Write a short essay explaining what an expenditure function is and how
    it can be utilized to derive money measures of the changes in welfare
    resulting from changes in nonmarket commodities such as environmental
    amenities and the characteristics of goods. Assume the reader is
    familiar with OCS, CV and EV but has only seen the material presented
    using graphical indifference curve analysis. The reader knows what a
    direct utility function is but not what an expenditure function is.
    Your essay should relate the graphical indifference curve approach and
    the expenditure function approach.

3. Demonstrate that pure competition is incapable of achieving an efficient
    allocation of resources when one of the following conditions prevail:
    a.   one person's utility depends on the amount of good X that another
          person consumes, i.e. $U^A(X^A, Y^A, X^B)$

    b.   one of the resources important to society is a common property
          resource (e.g., $p_k = 0$)

4. What are the differences between common property resources and public
    goods? You should include definitions of both. What are their
    similarities?

288

Duke University

Environmental Economics Field Exam   G
April, 1992

Below is a portion of a memorandum distributed at the EPA
Science Advisory Board Meeting on April 14, 1992. The overall
task of the Committee is to determine the economic impact of the
Clean Air Act. The particular aspect that I would like you to
focus on concerns the benefits associated with the Clean Air Act.
How would you structure a benefits assessment? What are the
principal classes of outcomes that are involved? In particular,
what are the health impacts, what are the non-health impacts,
etc.? What kinds of evidence would you use to value each of
these classes of impacts? Which classes of impacts do you
believe can be valued using the existing studies, and for which
impacts do you believe that EPA should fund new studies? For
the issues where you think our knowledge is soft, how would you
propose to obtain the benefit assessment?

Be thoughtful rather than lengthy.

TOPIC #7:   *Estimating Economic Damages*

Question: What are appropriate techniques for valuing the physical effects estimated in
this assessment?

Discussion:

EPA will review the existing literature on economic valuation to develop valuation
functions for significant physical effects of pollutants regulated under the CAA. Valuation
functions are required for the full range of effects, including mortality, morbidity, welfare and
ecological effects. Valuation functions can take many forms, ranging from unit values for
particular endpoints to more elaborate econometric models (e.g., for agriculture, materials
damages, soiling).

Where appropriate, dollar values or ranges will be assigned to damages. Substantial
economic literature is available on valuation of several key effects (e.g., mortality, visibility, lost
productivity, and others). Other effects have proven more difficult to value satisfactorily in
economic terms. However, to maintain balance between the treatment of costs and benefits, the
potential significance of other key effects will be evaluated using dollar values or range estimates
based on available studies or expert judgment. Where available studies and expert judgments are
insufficient to produce reasonable estimates or ranges, sensitivity analyses will be conducted to

gauge the potential influence of these beneficial effects on the net benefit estimate.

For many effects, it will not be possible to completely value damages. Therefore, it may be useful to categorize damages according to specific attributes as a device for communicating to policymakers the relative importance of different pollutants. Examples include:

> Reversible vs. Non-Reversible Effects
> Fatal vs. Irritant Health Effects
> Hot Spot vs. Regional Effects

Related Questions:

- What is an appropriate methodology for valuing mortality effects?

- Should risk analysis be done in this assessment?

- Are there irreversible effects that should be considered in this assessment? How should they be quantified or characterized?

- What is an appropriate way to report effects when it is not possible to monetize those effects?

Comprehensive Examination   June 15, 1994
Environmental and Natural Resources   9:00-12:00 AM

Instructions: Answer three (3) questions. At least one question
must come from Part A and one from Part B.

Part A

1. Environmental economists have employed a number of "indirect
methods" for estimating the value of environmental goods and
services by which they infer willingness-to-pay from observed
market behavior.

  (a) First, simply enumerate the major "indirect" approaches of
this kind that have been employed by environmental economists.
Define or describe each of them briefly in a couple of sentences.

  (b) Next, select one of these approaches or techniques and
describe it in detail.
    1-Set forth the analytical basis for this technique and
describe the procedures used in its application.
    2-Summarize any findings you are familiar with in the actual
empirical literature from applications of this technique to the
valuation of actual environmental amenities.
    3-Indicate what you see as the major problems and
limitations inherent in this approach.

2. Environmental regulators have employed, among other
incentive-based policy instruments, various systems of tradeable
emissions permits (TDP).

  (a) Explain the basic nature of a TDP system and show how in a
setting of perfect information on both environmental damages and
abatement costs, such a system can be employed to achieve the
optimal level of environmental quality.

  (b) Consider next a setting of uncertainty in which the
information available to the environmental authority has a
stochastic component. Using an appropriate diagram, depict a
case in which the expected welfare gain from the use of a TDP
system exceeds the expected welfare gain from the use of a
Pigouvian tax. Explain the rationale for your result.

  (c) It is claimed that such a TDP system can attain any target
level of environmental quality at the least cost. Provide a
formal proof of this proposition. Be explicit concerning your
assumptions. Then explain how the system must be modified if
these conditions are not satisfied.

(cont.)

(d) Finally, describe one <u>actual</u> TDP system. Indicate its objective and then discuss the (potential) problems that it has encountered in terms of actual design and administration.

3. The hypothesis has been advanced that people place monetary values on environmental goods that are independent of their current use of those goods--socalled "non-use" values.

(a) What sources (or kinds) of non-use values have been suggested in the literature? Discuss briefly the nature of each.

(b) Set forth a conceptual framework for the incorporation of non-use values into basic consumer theory.

(c) Next, discuss that major approach that economists (and others) have employed to measure nonuse values. In your treatment, set out what you see as the major problems inherent in this approach. In particular, point out and discuss the kinds of inconsistencies that have appeared in these studies.

(d) Finally, comment briefly on your sense of the potential of this line of work.

Part D

4. This question concerns depletable resources, economic growth, and sustainability.

(a) Set up the basic Dasgupta-Heal model in extensive variable form and derive necessary conditions for resource depletion to maximize the present value of intergenerational utility. How do these conditions compare to the basic predictions of the theory of the mine? How are they changed if there are amenity values associated with the preservation of undepleted natural resources, as in the Krautkraemer model?

(b) Provide a heuristic discussion of conditions under which constant or increasing consumption over time is (i) feasible and (ii) present-value-maximizing in the Dasgupta-Heal model. Tie these conditions to both the rate of intergenerational time preference and the properties of the economy-wide production function for gross output, and discuss the plausibility of the conditions you are presenting. Discuss also an investment strategy for ensuring a nondecreasing consumption path in this model, and why this investment path is not followed under a discounted utilitarian social welfare function.

(cont.)

2

292

5. This question concerns renewable resources, economic growth, and sustainability.

(a) Set up a simple fishery model in which harvest cost depends only on the harvest rate. For simplicity, assume no open access and an "idealized" population growth law (concave with no minimum viable population). With this model, discuss differences between sustainable and present-value maximizing outcomes. In your discussion, distinguish between sustainability in terms of constant consumption over time and sustainability as asymptotic achievement of some positive fishery stock and rate of consumption.

(b) Embed this model in the Dasgupta-Heal framework in lieu of the depletable resource they assumed. Assume for simplicity that harvest cost is zero. Derive the necessary conditions for present-value maximizing fish harvesting and total consumption/capital accumulation in this modified framework. Discuss the properties of steady state, including conditions for its existence. Compare your findings to those in part (a) of this question.

3

Comprehensive Examination   Monday, June 14, 1993
Environmental & Natural Resources   9:00 a.m. - 12 noon

INSTRUCTIONS: Answer three (3) questions.   At least one must
come from Part A and one from Part B.

Part A

1.   There is a significant debate going on among economists, and
between economists and other experts, regarding the
"sustainability" of economic welfare and environmental quality.
The key issues in this debate appear to be the nature of
technical substitutability and society's intergenerational
preferences. NOTE: Unless otherwise noted, assume below that
population is fixed and represent all variables and functions in
extensive form.

     (a)   Write down a model of growth with exhaustible resources
that addresses these issues. Summarize the basic assumptions of
the model, including those pertaining to the value of
environmental amenities. Using the model, discuss the necessary
conditions for a path of resource depletion to maximize the
present value of utility over time. How does this result relate
to the basic predictions derived from the theory of the mine?

     (b)   Discuss the relationship between the feasibility of
sustained consumption and the nature of the production function.
Address the compatibility or incompatibility of the necessary
conditions on technology with physical laws. How does technical
progress contribute to the feasibility of sustained consumption?
How does growing population make sustained growth more difficult
to attain? What can you say about the prospects for sustaining
environmental amenities?

     (c)   Even if sustained consumption is feasible it may not be
preferred. Assuming society's intertemporal preference ordering
is given by the present value of per-capita utility over time,
discuss conditions under which sustained or growing consumption
per capita is preferred given exhaustible resources.

2.   This question pertains to the economics of fisheries.

     (a)   State the basic assumptions of the efficient fishery
management model. Be sure to distinguish different assumptions
about the relationship between stock size and growth, and between
stock size and harvest technology. Show the basic duality
between models with harvest effort as the decision variable, and
models with catch size as the decision variable.

(b)   What insights does the fisheries literature provide about the time paths of harvest that maximize the present value of net revenues?   (Be sure to answer this for the different types of model considered in part (a), though you do not have to do this for the harvest effort models as well.)   Discuss the similarities (and differences) between the theoretical implications of the fishery models and models from capital theory.   In particular, what can you say about steady-state management and its relationships to capital theory?

(c)   State two different sufficient conditions for extinction of the fishery not to be efficient.   What if the fishery is open-access -- what conditions ensure that extinction does not occur in this case?

Part B

1.   Victims of polluting activities often have recourse to some form of "averting" or "defensive" activities through which to mitigate the effects of the pollution from which they suffer.

(a)   Discuss briefly the nature of such measures and indicate what you see, in practice, to be some of the major forms of averting behavior.

(b)   What difference does the presence or absence of such activities make in the design of economic measures to regulate the polluting emissions of sources?   In your answer, set out a simple model of polluting firms that create disutility among a set of individuals who suffer from the pollution.   Show how the presence of averting behavior is likely to affect the level of a Pigouvian tax on the polluters.   Does averting behavior have any implications for the compensation of victims?

(c)   In their attempts to estimate the value of improved environmental quality, environmental economists have made use of averting activities to construct estimates of the value of pollution reduction.   Explain in conceptual terms just how this can be done.   Next, describe any such studies that you are familiar with in the literature.   What do you see as the strengths and limitations of this approach to measuring the benefits of reducing pollution?

2.   One of the important properties of economic instruments for pollution control is their cost-effectiveness.

(a)   Taking the case of "perfect mixing" where the emissions of all sources are equally damaging, show formally (i.e., prove) that a tax set at the appropriate level per unit of emissions from all sources can achieve any predetermined level of aggregate emissions at the least cost to sources.   What is the relevant efficiency condition that must be satisfied for a cost-minimizing solution?

(b) Taking a dual approach, it must then be true that for any given level of aggregate abatement cost, such a tax can achieve the maximum possible level of emissions reductions. Show this in a diagram in which the axes measure the emissions of two different sources and in which you depict iso-abatement cost functions that indicate aggregate abatement cost. Be explicit about the assumptions you make.

(c) Suppose that an environmental regulator chooses an inefficient set of abatement quotas for the two sources. Depict such a point in another diagram like that you used in part (b). Next show the gains in emissions reductions that would be possible if an efficient policy were followed. How do these gains vary with the various parameters of the problem (e.g., shapes of the abatement cost functions, etc.)?

(d) Finally, discuss briefly the proposed RECLAIM program in Southern California under which some initial tradeable emissions allowances will be distributed to all sources. These allowances (or permits) will then be depreciated at 5 percent per year to reduce air pollution in the Southern California Basin. How does this proposed program relate to your discussion above?

3. How would you respond to the criticism that, because of difficulties in valuing environmental damages, economists should restrict their activities to achieving a given pollution standard at least cost? Organize your answer as follows:

(a) Explain in general terms the rationale for valuing the benefits of pollution abatement. Illustrate your argument with examples of real-world situations where valuing benefits has made (or should have made) a difference in environmental policy.

(b) Of all classes of benefits that economists have attempted to value, which do you think they have been the most successful at valuing? Explain what techniques have been used to value this class of benefits, and why you think economists have been successful.

(c) How would you respond to the criticism that, because it is often difficult to measure the physical consequences of pollution reduction (e.g., number of deaths averted), there is no point in attempting to measure benefits?

UNIVERSITY OF MARYLAND

Comprehensive Examination   Monday, January 11, 1993
Environmental & Natural Resources   9:00 - 12:00 a.m.

INSTRUCTIONS: Answer three (3) questions. At least one must come from
Part A and one from Part B.

PART A

1. Externalities and environmental policy:

(a) Consider a system in which a single polluter imposes costs on a
set of "victims," where these victims have no avenue of escape (i.e., the
level of damages is independent of the choice of location or any other
activity levels on the part of the victims). Set forth a formal model of
such a system and derive the first-order conditions for Pareto efficiency.
Compare these conditions with those that characterize a competitive
equilibrium.

(b) Next, show how an appropriate tax can correct the distortion you
describe in part (a). In particular, indicate the tax base, the tax rate,
and the way in which the tax works to correct the inefficiency. Is
compensation of victims consistent with economic efficiency? Explain why
or why not.

(c) Reconsider the above problem in a setting in which victims can
influence the level of damages that they absorb through various "defensive
activities" (e.g., location decisions or "cleansing" activities). How
would this change your answer (if at all) to both parts (a) and (b)? In
your answer, consider (among other things) how such defensive activities
are likely to influence the level of the tax on the source of the
externality.

(d) In the absence of the above tax, explore the properties of a
system of legal liability under which victims can sue the polluter for any
damages they absorb. Could such a system correct the allocative
distortions? Explain why or why not.

(e) Finally, how would you change your answers to parts (a) and (b) in
a world of costless bargaining among all parties? Explain briefly. What
would be the implication of introducing the tax you describe in part (b)
into a world of costless bargaining? Explain briefly.

2. Write an essay in which you describe two (2) methods that have been
used to estimate the value individuals place on a small change in their
current probability of dying. Be sure to:

(a) Provide theoretical justification for each empirical approach.

(b) Discuss how you would implement each approach empirically.

(c) Discuss problems in implementing the approach and/or theoretical
shortcomings with the approach.

3. Listed below are two categories of pollution damages that economists have attempted to value.

For one (1) category of damages, discuss in detail the theory behind the technique that you think has been most useful in valuing pollution damages. How successful have economists been in applying this technique?

Categories of pollution damages:

Aesthetic damages from urban air pollution
Recreation damages from water pollution

PART B

1. The cornerstone of the fisheries literature is the Gordon-Schaefer model.

(a) What are the assumptions of this model?

(b) How, originally, was this model used to describe optimal fishery management?

(c) How was the model used to describe the consequences of open access fishing?

(d) Do you think that the model has provided any useful insights or policy implications?

(e) Describe how the model has been used as a basis for empirical work in fisheries economics. Evaluate its appropriateness for empirical work.

2. Whether production can be sustained in the presence of exhaustible resources depends on the ease with which capital can be substituted for exhaustible resources in production. Whether continued production is optimal depends not only on the technology but on society's objective function.

(a) Elaborate on the first part of this statement by discussing the relationship between the production function $F(K,R)$, where K is the capital stock and R is the rate of exhaustible resource use, and the feasibility of maintaining constant (growing) output per capita. (Assume zero population growth and no technical progress.)

(b) Elaborate on the second part of the statement by discussing the relationship between the objective functional and the optimal consumption path.

In both cases, be as specific as possible in your answers.

UNIVERSITY OF MARYLAND

Comprehensive Examination   Thursday, August 27, 1992
Environmental & Natural   9:00-12:00 AM
  Resource Economics

INSTRUCTIONS: Answer three (3) questions. At least one
must come from Part A and one from Part B.

PART A

1. Externalities and environmental policy:

(a) Consider a system in which a single polluter imposes
costs on a set of "victims," where these victims have no
avenue of escape (i.e., the level of damages is independent
of the choice of location or any other activity levels on
the part of the victims). Set forth a formal model of such
a system and derive the first-order conditions for Pareto
efficiency. Compare these conditions with those that
characterize a competitive equilibrium.

(b) Next, show how an appropriate tax can correct the
distortion you describe in part (a). In particular,
indicate the tax base, the tax rate, and the way in which
the tax works to correct the inefficiency. Is compensation
of victims consistent with economic efficiency? Explain why
or why not.

(c) Reconsider the above problem in a setting in which
victims can influence the level of damages that they absorb
through various "defensive activities" (e.g., location
decisions or "cleansing" activities). How would this change
your answer (if at all) to both parts (a) and (b)? In your
answer, consider (among other things) how such defensive
activities are likely to influence the level of the tax on
the source of the externality.

(d) In the absence of the above tax, explore the
properties of a system of legal liability under which
victims can sue the polluter for any damages they absorb.
Could such a system correct the allocative distortions?
Explain why or why not.

(e) Finally, how would you change your answers to parts
(a) and (b) in a world of costless bargaining among all
parties? Explain briefly. What would be the implication of
introducing the tax you describe in part (b) into a world of
costless bargaining? Explain briefly.

2. Measuring the benefits of pollution control:

(a) One technique that environmental economists have employed to measure the benefits of improved air quality is the "hedonic approach" as applied to the purchase of houses. Set forth the conceptual basis for this approach and show how it can be used to derive measures of the willingness-to-pay for cleaner air.

(b) Distinguish carefully between the use of the hedonic technique for the measurement of small, marginal changes in air quality and the measurement of larger, non-marginal changes.

(c) This procedure may encounter an "identification problem." Explain the nature of this problem and the methods available for dealing with it.

(d) It has been argued that an upper bound to the value of a nonmarginal environmental improvement can be obtained from the hedonic price function alone. Explain this proposition and its rationale.

(e) Finally, discuss what in practice you see as the major difficulties with using this approach to measuring the value of cleaner air. In your discussion, refer to any relevant studies with which you are familiar.

PART B

1. There is a huge literature on models of growth with exhaustible resources.

(a) What are the main issues that this literature has addressed? [Discuss at least two.]

(b) Set up a model of growth with exhaustible resources. Be explicit about the assumptions you are making regarding each function.

(c) Use this model to illustrate answers to the questions you discussed in (a). State clearly each result, and try to sketch out a proof of the result.

(d) Do you think that the models in this literature have any empirical significance? Discuss.

2. The North American Free Trade Agreement has spurred considerable interest in the issue of environmental regulations and trade.

(a) What do some people in the U.S. fear will be the environmental consequences in the U.S. and in Mexico of the Free Trade Agreement? What do they fear about the effect of U.S. environmental regulations on the migration of jobs to Mexico?

(b) What empirical evidence exists regarding each of these fears?

(c) A related issue concerns the effect of development on the environment. What appear to be the stylized facts regarding development and environmental quality? What could explain these facts?

(d) An official at the World Bank wishes to know whether it is primarily (i) increases in the demand for environmental quality or (ii) changes in technology and in the mix of output that cause environmental quality to improve as a country develops. How would you help him answer this question?

3. The cornerstone of the fisheries literature is the Gordon-Schaefer model.

(a) What are the assumptions of this model?

(b) How, originally, was this model used to describe optimal fishery management?

(c) How was the model used to describe the consequences of open access fishing?

(d) Do you think that the model has provided any useful insights or policy implications?

(e) Describe how the model has been used as a basis for empirical work in fisheries economics. Evaluate its appropriateness for empirical work.

Comprehensive Examination   Monday August 26, 1991
Environmental & Natural Resources   12:30 - 3:30 p.m.

INSTRUCTIONS: Answer three (3) questions. At least one must come from Part A
and one from Part B.

Part A

1. The 1991 Amendments to the Clean Air Act address the problem of acid-rain
deposition by mandating a 10 million-ton (roughly a 50 percent) reduction in
sulfur oxide emissions in the United States over the next decade. This is to
be achieved through the institution of a system of transferable emission
permits under which sources across the country will be able to meet their
allowances either by cutbacks in their emissions or purchases of the requisite
number of permits from other sources.

    (a) The claim is that such a system can achieve the mandated cutback in
aggregate emissions at the minimum aggregate abatement cost. Provide a formal
proof of this proposition and accompany this with an explanation (using, if you
wish, an appropriate diagram). Be explicit concerning any assumptions that are
required for the validity of the argument.

    (b) Assuming (as above) a single nationwide market for emissions permits,
discuss the ability of this system to achieve a given reduction in acid-rain
damage at the minimum cost. The issue here concerns the differential effects
of emissions from differing locations. How might the system be amended to
address this issue?

    (c) Many of the major sources of sulfur emissions are publicly regulated
"utilities"--that is, they are power plants that are subject to various
regulations including, often, a ceiling on the allowable rate of return to
capital. Does this have any implications for your argument in part (a)?
Discuss.

    (d) To set the system in motion, would you recommend that the permits be
allocated through a public auction or distributed without charge to existing
sources? Discuss the efficiency and equity aspects of your proposal.

2. The standard Pigouvian prescription for a polluting firm is a tax on the
firm per unit of emissions equal to marginal social damage. The literature has
considered as an alternative policy instrument a unit subsidy for emissions
reductions.

    (a) Show formally the sense in which these two policy instruments are
equivalent. And accompany your formal presentation with a brief explanation.

    (b) In what ways are taxes and subsidies not equivalent? Explain and
indicate why one is to be preferred to the other.

    (c) Next consider the following "mixed" system. Under this system,
polluters pay a unit tax for emissions above some specified baseline but
receive a unit subsidy (of the same sum as the tax) for any reductions below
the baseline. The right to receive the subsidy payments is limited to existing

firms so that new sources have a baseline of zero. Moreover, this right to subsidy payments can be sold or be exercised even if the firm chooses to leave the industry. Analyze the efficiency properties of this mixed system in the light of your discussion in parts (a) and (b).

(d) Finally, from the perspective of the public revenue system as a whole (which is made up largely of distorting taxes that create deadweight losses), consider the case for taxes against subsidies.

3. Health benefits are both one of the most important classes of benefits from pollution control and one of the most difficult to measure in monetary terms.

(a) Enumerate and discuss briefly the various approaches that environmental economists have used in their attempts to estimate the health benefits from pollution control.

(b) Choose one of these techniques and develop in detail the conceptual framework underlying the approach and describe the actual applications of the approach to the measurement of health benefits.

(c) More generally, discuss and assess the results of studies that have tried to measure health benefits. Indicate what you see as the most promising approaches and the most formidable obstacles to be addressed in this line of research.

Part B

1. One issue brought to the fore in the debate about global warming is the rate at which to discount the utility of future generations.

(a) Present arguments that have been used to justify (i) a zero rate of discount and (ii) a positive one.

(b) What mathematical problems does one encounter in (i) an optimal growth model without exhaustible resources, (ii) an optimal growth model with exhaustible resources, if utility is not discounted?

(c) To avoid the problems you discussed in (b) assume that future utility is discounted at a positive rate. As this rate decreases what, qualitatively, happens to the path of consumption over time? What happens to the rate of return on capital? Justify your answers by setting up a formal model of optimal growth in the presence of exhaustible resources (the no-exhaustible resource case is just a special instance of this). Present the necessary conditions for the model and use them to derive an equation for dC/dt.

2. This question deals with common property exploitation of a renewable resource.

(a) Define what is meant by common property exploitation of a renewable resource. Is this the same thing as open access exploitation of the resource?

(b) There have been several attempts to model common property and/or open access exploitation in the literature. Write a non-technical essay that contrasts and compares these models. Be careful to indicate which features of the problem each model captures and what its main conclusions are. [Be as precise as you can in stating the assumptions of each model. You need not, however, derive each model's results formally.]

(c) What insights do these models offer into the problem of tropical deforestation? In particular, what policies do they suggest with regard to control of this problem?

303

Comprehensive Examination   Monday January 14, 1991
Environmental & Natural Resources   9:00 - 12:00 a.m.

INSTRUCTIONS: Answer three (3) questions. At least one must come from
Part A and one from Part B.

PART A

1. Suppose the government must decide whether or not to allow mineral
production in a wilderness area.

    a. If one views development of a wilderness area as irreversible, the
criteria used to determine whether the area should be developed or not may
be altered, compared to the case in which development is reversible.
Indicate, using a formal model, what the appropriate criteria are for
developing a wilderness area. Contrast these with the criteria when
development is reversible.

    b. Two terms frequently encountered when evaluating the benefits of
preserving a wilderness area are option value and quasi option value.
Define these terms and explain their significance for the problem at hand.

2. Consider the following simple renewable resource model: In the absence
of harvesting, a fish population grows according to

$$dX/dt = aX(t) - bX^2(t) = F(X(t)).$$

The manager of the resource receives utility u(h(t)) from the rate at
which he harvests the resource, h(t). Future utility is discounted at rate
r.

    a. Set up the problem that the manager would solve to maximize the
present discounted value of utility from the resource over an infinite
horizon. Characterize the solution to the problem by drawing a phase
diagram. Interpret the condition that characterizes the steady-state fish
population. Characterize the optimal harvesting path, assuming that
X(0)=a/b.

    b. What parallels can you draw between this problem and optimal
economic growth? Be as specific as you can.

    c. What features of fisheries models are absent from this simple
model? If you were to incorporate them, how, qualitatively, would it alter
the steady-state fish population?

3. Whether production can be sustained in the presence of exhaustible
resources depends on the ease with which capital can be substituted for
exhaustible resources in production. Whether continued production is
optimal depends not only on the technology but on society's objective
function.

a. Elaborate on the first part of this statement by discussing the relationship between the production function $F(K,R)$, where K is the capital stock and R is the rate of exhaustible resource use, and the feasibility of maintaining constant (growing) output per capita. (Assume zero population growth and no technical progress.)

b. Elaborate on the second part of the statement by discussing the relationship between the objective functional and the optimal consumption path.

In both cases, be as specific as possible in your answers.

PART B

1. Economics Incentives for Pollution Control

a. It has been argued that a subsidy per unit of waste reductions is equivalent in its effects on abatement activities to a tax per unit of emissions of the same amount as the subsidy. Using the profit function of a polluting firm, show formally the sense in which this statement is true. Explain the rationale for your answer.

b. Does this equivalence between the tax and subsidy instruments hold in a more general sense? Explain your answer and discuss any special cases where the equivalence does hold.

c. Consider next the problem of choosing between a quantity instrument (i.e., a system of marketable emission permits) and a price instrument (i.e., an effluent charge) in a setting of uncertainty in which the environmental authority knows the marginal benefit function of abatement with certainty but is uncertain concerning the marginal control cost functions of polluters. Draw an appropriate diagram with environmental quality on the horizontal axis in which you give the marginal benefit function a slope of <u>zero</u> and the marginal cost function a positive slope.

1. Indicate in your diagram the expected welfare losses under the use of each policy instrument.
2. In which case is the welfare loss greater? Explain the rationale for your result.

2. Measuring the Value of Environmental Improvements

One approach to valuing environmental improvements takes advantage of the complementarity of environmental quality with private goods that are purchased in the marketplace. This approach has been called the "Weak Complementarity Approach."

a. Set out the basic idea for this approach (using an appropriate diagram if you wish).

b. Next, discuss in more detail the specific conditions that must be satisfied for the validity of this approach. Explain the rationale for each of these conditions.

c. Finally, assess the potential of this approach, in practice, for the valuation of environmental improvements. Be specific concerning what you see as the major problems of implementing this technique. Are there any particular cases where you think this approach might be employed? Discuss.

305

University of Michigan

Preliminary Examination Fall 1994
Natural Resources and Environmental Economics G

Problem 1: Pollution Control with Unknown Technology: I

A regulator wishes to minimize the costs associated with pollution caused by a particular factory. The factory is owned by a company that has private information about the costs of pollution control. The regulator must therefore design an incentive scheme that will lead to the factory undertaking as close to the optimal level of pollution control as possible.

The direct cost to the surrounding community of a level of pollution p is $p^2/2$. If the firm spends nothing on abatement, there will be 5 units of pollution. To reduce pollution by r units costs cr, where c is privately known by the firm. Ex-ante, c takes on the value of 2 with probability $1/2$, and 3 with probability $1/2$. The regulator can observe p, and may tax in order to give proper incentives to the firm.

The regulator wishes to minimize the total costs (direct costs plus abatement costs plus public finance costs) of the pollution. Assume that public finance is costly, or, equivalently, that taxation can be used for public goods, and that every 8 dollars collected in tax is worth one dollar to society. Suppose that the regulator must allow the firm to operate (cannot shut it down). Assume that separate from what it might pay in taxes, the firm is earning 10 dollars in profits from its productive activities; that is, since the firm must be allowed to operate, its taxes plus abatement costs must not exceed 10 dollars.

a. Write out the entire optimization problem to be solved by the regulator, including all constraints.

b. Explain in detail which constraints will and which will not be binding in the optimal solution, and why.

c. (i) Solve for the optimal direct revelation mechanism for the regulator. That is, find the schedule (or mechanism) $(p(c), t(c))$ offered by the regulator, where t represents the tax to be paid by the firm. (Note that because there are only two types of firm, we need only focus on the values of p and t which correspond to the actual levels of cost the firms might have; that is, you only need to define the pair $(p(c), t(c))$ for $c = 2, 3$.

(ii) Verify that your solution is plausible by checking whether the correct constraints bind.

(iii) An alternative approach to offering the menu of contracts described in part (i) is to regulate directly as follows: Present the firm with a tax function $t(p)$ giving tax as a function of realized pollution levels. Give an example of such a tax function that will implement the same outcome as given in part (i). Is this function unique? Would it be unique if there were a continuum of types of firm?

d. Is this solution first-best? That is, does it correspond to an allocation that would arise were there full information? If not, describe in which direction and why distortions occur.

Problem 2: Pollution Control with Unknown Technology: II

Now suppose that public finance is not costly, that is, that taxation is not valuable in itself. Answer parts (a)-(d) of Problem 1 for this new setup. (*Hint:* There are now multiple solutions, whereas in Problem 1, there was a unique solution. Why?)

Problem 3: Least Discounted Cost Disposal of Waste: Formulation

City 1 has an exogenous waste stream w_1 per period and City 2 has an exogenous waste stream w_2 per period. In each period, the two waste streams must be disposed of. Part or all of each city's waste stream can be incinerated locally for the high cost of c per unit of waste; alternatively, it can be transported to either of two landfills. The total distance from City i ($i = 1, 2$) to Landfill j ($j = A, B$) is $c_{i,j}$ miles. Suppose it costs \$1 to ship one unit of waste one mile. Hence, it costs $c_{i,j}$ for each unit of waste shipped from City i to Landfill j. Assume $c_{i,j} < c$ for all i, j. However, these cheaper alternatives have limited capacity and there is no possibility of expanding it. In particular, landfill j can initially accommodate S_j more units of waste. Assume that the discount factor is $\beta \in (0, 1)$.

a. Formulate in discrete time the programming problem of disposing of the waste streams of the two cities over the next T years at *least discounted cost*. Be careful to specify all constraints and nonnegativity conditions.

b. Write down the Kuhn-Tucker conditions which necessarily hold at the optimum. Is every solution to these conditions optimal in this problem?

c. Describe a procedure for solving this Kuhn-Tucker problem.

d. **Reformulate** the problem as a finite-horizon, discrete-time dynamic programming problem where the two state variables are the capacities remaining at the beginning of each period in each landfill. Describe a recursive procedure which could be used to solve this dynamic programming problem.

Problem 4: Least Cost Disposal of Waste: Qualitative Characteristics

The three parts of this question are aimed at developing a characterization of the solution to Problem 3. You may use whichever formulation you like to respond to these three parts. To get credit, you must *justify* your answer by appealing to conditions which necessarily hold at the optimum.

a. True or False. It never minimizes total discounted costs for a city to use a more distant landfill first and then to switch to a closer landfill subsequently.

b. True or False. It never minimizes total discounted costs to switch one city from a closer landfill to a more distant one beyond some date t^* *despite* the fact that the closer one has space remaining and continues to be utilized by the other city.

c. How (qualitatively) would the least discounted-cost solution to Problem 3 change if it was instead known from the outset that landfill A would be available only for the next K periods, where K is shorter than one would have optimally chosen to use landfill A?

Preliminary Exam in Natural Resources—Summer, 1992

Instructions: You have four hours to complete this exam. You may consult notes and books but no individuals.

Question 1: Pollution Regulation Under Uncertainty

Consider two firms which, in the absence of regulation, each discharge 100 units of pollution into a lake. Suppose that the firms can reduce their discharges by using a costly technology but that the output (or outputs) of each firm is fixed and does not depend on how much pollution the firm discharges. Suppose also that it is never socially optimal to shut down either firm. Let q_1 denote the reduction in pollution from 100 units (i.e. the level of cleanup) for firm 1 and similarly let q_2 denote the level of cleanup for firm 2.

The cost to firm i of cleaning up to the level q_i is given by the equation:

$$c_i(q_i) = \gamma_i q_i + (1/2)(q_i)^2 .$$

γ_1 and γ_2 are independent, identically distributed random variables which take one of two possible values. $\gamma_1 = 60$ with probability $1/2$ and $\gamma_1 = 30$ with probability $1/2$.

Let $B(q_1 + q_2)$ denote the social benefit obtained when the pollution of each firm is reduced by the amount indicated.

$$B(q_1 + q_2) = 120(q_1 + q_2) - (1/2)(q_1 + q_2)^2 .$$

Each firm is assumed to know its own cleanup cost function. There is also a risk neutral regulator. It is always assumed that the regulator does not know the realized value of either γ_1 or γ_2. (In question 5, the regulator can learn the value of one of the γ's for a price.) However, the regulator can costlessly observe the cleanup levels of each firm. Except for the realized values of γ_1 and γ_2 all of the above information is assumed to be common knowledge. The regulator wishes to set regulations for the two firms to maximize the expected net benefits from their cleanup, $E(B - c_1 - c_2)$, where E denotes the expectation with respect to γ_1 and γ_2.

When considering the various taxes or subsidies described below, assume that the transfers involved in such payments produce no social benefits or costs. You may also assume that neither firm will shut down as long as the costs imposed by the regulator (both taxes and cleanup costs) are less than 100,000.

Questions.

1. Suppose that the regulator can specify the levels of cleanup for each firm. What are the optimal levels for the regulator to specify? What are the expected net benefits obtained with this type of regulation?

2. Suppose now that the regulator can specify a tax, τ, per unit of pollution. In this case, firm i is assumed to choose the level of cleanup q_i that minimizes the combined cost $\tau(100 - q_i) + c_i(q_i)$. What is the optimal level of τ for the regulator to set?

3. Suppose in this question that the regulator can set a possibly nonlinear pollution tax (or subsidy) that can be different for each firm. Let $T_i(q_1, q_2)$ denote the tax paid by firm i. Note that the payment by (or to) firm i may depend on the cleanup levels of both firms.

Suppose that each firm knows both its own cost function and that of its counterpart (i.e. each firm knows the realized values of *both* γ 's). Suppose also that the two firms simultaneously choose their cleanup levels and that firm i chooses q_i to minimize the cost $T_i(q_1, q_2) + c_i(q_i)$ taking the cleanup level of the other firm as fixed when it makes its own decision. (Negative values for T indicate a subsidy and positive values indicate a tax.) For each pair of realized values for γ_1 and γ_2, a Nash equilibrium pair of cleanup levels can be defined in the usual way.

Specify a pair of tax functions, $T_1(q_1, q_2)$ and $T_2(q_1, q_2)$, such that the Nash equilibrium cleanup levels generated by these functions are the same as those that would be set by a regulator with "full information", that is, a regulator who could observe γ_1 and γ_2 and then set the net-benefit-maximizing levels of cleanup for each firm.

4. Now suppose that each firm knows its own cost function but not that of the other firm. However, the firms can engage in a round of communication with the regulator. Suppose that the regulator asks each firm to report the realized value of its γ. The regulator then specifies for each firm i an output level $q_i(\hat{\gamma}_1, \hat{\gamma}_2)$ and tax (or subsidy) $T_i(\hat{\gamma}_1, \hat{\gamma}_2)$ where $\hat{\gamma}_i$ is the value of γ_i reported by firm i. Each firm wishes to minimize $T_i + c_i(q_i)$.

Specify a set of tax functions $T_i(\hat{\gamma}_1, \hat{\gamma}_2)$ and cleanup functions $q_i(\hat{\gamma}_1, \hat{\gamma}_2)$ so that: 1. It is a dominant strategy for each firm to truthfully report the realized value of its γ and 2. The level of expected net benefits obtained is the same as that which would be obtained by a regulator with "full information."

5. As in question 1, suppose that the regulator cannot impose taxes but can set the level of cleanup for each firm. Suppose also that before setting the cleanup levels the regulator can audit at most one firm to learn (with perfect accuracy) the realized value of γ for that firm. Let the social cost of the audit be A, where A does not depend on which firm is audited.

What is the largest value of A for which it would be optimal for the regulator to conduct an audit?

Question 2: Optimal Harvest Policy for a Fishery.

Denote the biomass of a fish population at the beginning of period t by x_t. The fish population grows according to the equation:

$$x_{t+1} = G(x_t - h_t),$$

where h_t is the harvest during period t and $G(x)$ is a positive, strictly increasing, strictly concave function that describes the growth of the fish population. $0 \le h_t \le x_t$. Suppose that the unharvested fish population has an equilbrium population size of K, that is, $K = G(K)$.

For a feasible harvest policy, h_t, the present value of the profits obtained from the fishery is given by the expression:

$$\sum_0^\infty \frac{1}{(1+\delta)^t} \left[ph_t + c\ln(1 - \frac{h_t}{x_t}) \right],$$

where δ is the one period discount rate, p is the constant price of a unit of harvested fish, and $-c\ln(1-h_t/x_t)$ is the cost of harvesting h_t in period t. (Remember that the logarithm of a fraction is negative.) Let $c \ge 0$. When $c \ne 0$, the cost of harvesting is allowed to depend on the fish population at time t in order to represent the assumption that it is easier to find fish and, therefore, cheaper to harvest fish when there are more of them.

Questions.

1. Let $x_0 = K$. Suppose that the right to harvest the fish population is held by a sole owner who chooses the harvest policy that maximizes the present value of the profits from the fishery subject to the inequality constraints on the harvest $(0 \le h_t \le x_t)$ and the constraint imposed by the population growth equation.

Write down the optimization problem faced by the sole owner. Assume that the population growth function, $G(x)$, is sufficiently well-behaved that the Kuhn-Tucker conditions describe the solution to the optimization and write down the first order conditions that describe this solution.

2. For many reasonable growth functions, the optimal harvest policy for the sole owner reduces the fish population to a particular level, x_{ss}, which depends on the parameters. If $x_t = x_{ss}$, the optimal harvest, h_{ss}, is such that the fish population remains at the "steady-state" level x_{ss} from then on.

Assume that it is optimal for the fish population to approach a steady state and use the first order conditions for an optimum to derive a pair of (implicit) equations which must be satisfied by the steady-state harvest, h_{ss}, and the steady-state fish population size, x_{ss}. These equations should depend only on the parameters p, c, and δ and on $G(x)$.

3. The definition of "steady state" implies that the steady-state harvest and the steady-state fish population size should satisfy the equation $x_{ss} = G(x_{ss} - h_{ss})$. In addition, the following argument suggests that these quantities should also satisfy the equation:

$$1 + \delta = G'(x_{ss} - h_{ss}),$$

where G' denotes the derivative of G. A harvested fish can be deposited as "money in the bank" and return $1 + \delta$ in the next period. A fish left unharvested has value because it increases the size of the fish population in the next period by the factor $G'(x_t - h_t)$ when the fish population size in period t is x_t and the harvest is h_t. When $1 + \delta > G'(x_t - h_t)$, it is optimal to harvest more fish. When $1 + \delta < G'(x_t - h_t)$ it is optimal to harvest fewer fish since leaving the marginal fish in the wild is the better investment. Only when the two returns are equal would a sole owner be indifferent between harvesting or not harvesting the marginal fish.

From the equations for h_{ss} and x_{ss} which you derived in question 2, you should see that the above argument is sometimes but not always correct. In general, the argument in the previous paragraph leaves out an important source of value to fishermen from fish left in the wild. What is this source of value? For what values of the parameters p, c, and δ is the argument correct?

4. Suppose that the population growth function, $G(x)$, has the following form:

$$G(x) = \frac{(1 + r)\tau}{1 + (r/K)x},$$

where r and K are positive parameters.

Suppose also that $c = 0$. For some values of the parameters δ, r, and K, it will be optimal for the fish population to approach a steady state. For other parameter values, the sole owner will find it optimal to drive the fish population extinct (i.e. drive the fish population size to zero).

Describe the set of parameters for which a sole owner would find it optimal to drive the fish population extinct. Provide an economic interpretation for your answer.

Question 3: Monopoly, Competition, and Backstop Technologies for an Exhaustible Resource.

Consider an exhaustible resource with a demand curve for the extracted resource given by the equation:

$$x(t) = x_0 p(t)^{-\epsilon},$$

where $x(t)$ is the quantity of the resource extracted and sold at time t, $p(t)$ is the price of the extracted resource at t, and x_0 and ϵ are positive constants. Recall that ϵ is the price elasticity of demand and assume that $\epsilon > 1$.

Suppose that there is a fixed stock of the resource with an initial level, S_0. Suppose also that there are no extraction costs. Finally assume that the extracted resource is consumed in each period, that is, the resource is not durable.

Questions.

1. Suppose initially that there is no backstop technology for producing a substitute for the resource. Consider the equilibrium price path followed when the resource is owned by a competitive industry (with rational expectations). Consider also the equilibrium price path followed when the entire stock is owned by a monopolist. Explain why, for the constant elasticity demand curve above, the monopoly and competitive equilibrium price paths will be the same (when there is no backstop technology and no extraction costs).

2. Now suppose that a perfect substitute for the extracted resource can be produced at a unit cost, p_B. Suppose that the technology for producing this substitute is owned by a competitive industry that behaves in the following way. When $p(t) < p_B$, the backstop industry produces nothing. When $p(t) > p_B$, it produces an "infinite" amount. When $p(t) = p_B$, the backstop producers observe the extraction of the exhaustible resource and produce whatever is necessary to satisfy the residual demand at the price p_B.

Describe the equilibrium price path followed by a competitive resource industry given the availability of the backstop substitute. Calculate how long the competitive industry will extract while the price is exactly p_B? During this time interval, what is the time path of backstop production?

How would the initial equilibrium price of the resource, $p(0)$, change if the cost of the backstop substitute, p_B, were to increase? Is the initial price lower or higher when the backstop substitute is not available?

3. Continue to suppose that the technology for producing a backstop substitute exists and consider the case where the resource stock is owned by a monopolist. Suppose that, at each time t, the backstop producers allow the monopolist to set the price, $p(t)$, and then behave as described in part 2.

Describe the equilibrium price path followed by a monopolized resource industry when a backstop technology exists. Calculate how long the monopolized industry will extract while the price is exactly p_B? During this interval of time, what is the time path of backstop production?

Compare the initial price charged by the monopolist with the initial price that would be charged by a competitive industry. Compare also the initial prices charged by a monopolist when the backstop substitute is or is not available. Explain your reasoning.

Question 4: Banning Unsafe Pesticides

Your agency is charged with reviewing the safety of new pesticides prior to their introduction to the marketplace. You believe a particular pesticide may be unsafe. You subjectively assess the odds that it is safe as $P(0 < P < 1)$. You have three choices: allow the pesticide on the market, ban the product, or postpone these two decisions until an additional test can be conducted. Alas, the test is not definitive. Safe pesticides pass this test with probability $P_{+|S}$. Unsafe pesticides, unfortunately, pass this test with strictly smaller conditional probability $P_{+|U}$. If you elect additional testing, you can observe whether the product passed or failed the test. But then you must decide whether to ban the pesticide or allow it to be marketed. The cost of the test is passed onto consumers and amounts to T. Consumers receive in gross payoffs (before deducting any cost of testing):

A if you allow production and the pesticide is in fact safe;

C if you allow production and the pesticide is in fact unsafe; and

B if you ban the product (in which case the safety of the pesticide is irrelevant).

Assume $A > B > C$.

Questions. 1. Draw the decision tree for this problem. Distinguish "chance" nodes from "personal" nodes. Indicate the payoffs associated with each outcome (net of testing costs).

2. By Bayes theorem compute the probability that the pesticide is safe (respectively, unsafe) given that it passes (respectively, fails) the test. What is the (unconditional) probability the pesticide will pass the test?

3. State the conditions under which conducting the additional test maximizes the expected net payoff to consumers.

4. Fix $A, B, C, T, P_{+|S}, P_{+|U}$. Determine the interval of subjective assessments (P) which are so high (respectively, so low) that allowing the pesticide on the market (respectively, banning the product without further testing) maximizes the net expected payoff.

UNIVERSITY OF WASHINGTON

NATURAL RESOURCES FIELD EXAMINATION   **G**

Spring 1995

Time: 3 hours
Answer any four of the following five questions.

Committee:
Brown, Chair
Ellis, Halvorsen

1. **Renewable Resources**

    A fishery has a population equation

    $$\dot{X} = f(X) - h = .08 \times - .0002X^2 - h$$

    with X = stock of fish. A polluter earns profit $B(S)$ from discharging waste into the stream,

    $$B(S) = \beta S = 14S$$

    It affects the population dynamics in the following way:

    $$\dot{X} = (1 - S)f(X) - h.$$

    Suppose harvest is costless and sells for $P = 4$ per unit. Discount rate = .04. Suppose the goal is to maximize profit in the polluting and fish harvesting industry.

    (a) What are the optimal steady state values for this problem?

    (b) How can this result be achieved in a decentralized economy?

2. **Non-renewable Resources**

    Consider a non-renewable natural resource in finite supply which is extracted by a perfectly competitive industry. Extraction costs per unit are equal to c, where c is a constant. Derive the effect on the extraction path of each of the following taxes, assuming that they would be imposed on the entire industry.

    (a) A severance tax of w per unit extracted.

    (b) A royalty tax equal to a constant fraction, k, of gross revenues.

    (c) A profits tax equal to a constant fraction, m, of net revenue.

    (d) The addition of a depletion provision to the profits tax in part (c), where the depletion allowance allows a firm to deduct a fixed proportion, b, of its gross revenue in calculating taxable income.

    (e) Under what circumstances, if any, could the tax in part (a) increase economic efficiency?

315

3. **Environmental Policy**

Suppose that the government knows the marginal damage and marginal benefit curves for some type of pollution. Two of the instruments it might use to try to obtain the efficient amount of pollution are a tax per unit of pollution and a subsidy per unit of pollution, each of which would be set equal to the value of marginal damages at the efficient level of pollution. Discuss the relative desirability of these two instruments with respect to each of the following issues:

(a) Attaining the desired level of pollution in the short-run.

(b) Other considerations that might be relevant in the short-run.

(c) Providing incentives for research and development of pollution abatement technologies.

(d) Attaining the desired level of pollution in the long-run.

4. **Enforcement of Environmental Regulations**

(a) Suppose that a significant fraction of firms subject to a particular (uniform) pollution standard is not in compliance with its provisions, so that the level of pollution emitted is inefficiently high. Should the pollution standard necessarily be tightened(i.e., require more pollution abatement) if enforcement expenditures and penalties for noncompliance are held fixed at their current levels? Why or why not?

(b) State-dependent enforcement schemes have received much attention in the environmental economics literature recently (e.g., Harrington, JPubE, 1988, and Harford and Harrington, JPubE, 1991). Why? How do they work, and what is their purported advantage over simpler schemes? Are state-dependent enforcement schemes cost-effective (with regard to aggregate abatement costs), and how does the issue of cost-effectiveness relate to the desirability of the state-dependent approach to enforcement?

5. **Benefit Estimation**

(a) In the context of preserving a natural environment (from immediate development), define the economic concept of quasi-option value. Is risk-aversion a necessary condition for option value to be positive? Is option value related to the value of information? In 1983 the Environmental Protection Agency listed option value as one form of intrinsic benefit that could be included in the benefit-cost analyses of proposed regulations required under the terms of Executive Order 12291. Do you think quasi-option value needs to be calculated when conducting benefit-cost analyses of large-scale development projects? Is so, how might it be measured?

(b) Hedonic analysis of property values has been used in a variety of contexts to measure the value of environmental (dis)amenities. Briefly describe the rationale for the cross-section hedonic property value model. That is, to the extent that the method might provide reliable estimates of amenity values, describe why this is so (in terms of neoclassical microeconomic theory). In practice, many economists advocate the use of a repeat-sales rather than a cross-section approach. Why? If (potential) property owners anticipate future amenity changes, how is the repeat-sales analysis affected?

UNIVERSITY OF WASHINGTON

NATURAL RESOURCES FIELD EXAMINATION

Autumn 1994

Committee:
Ellis, Chair
Brown, Halvorsen

Time: 2.5 hours
Answer any four of the following five questions.

1. **Renewable Resources**

   (a) In a model in which fishing costs do <u>not</u> depend upon the level of the fish stock, describe the rule that characterizes the dynamically efficient sustained yield level of the fish stock. Define each variable and function you write down, and provide intuition for this result. Is this level of the fish stock larger or smaller than the one associated with a management criterion of maximum sustainable yield? If the size of the fish stock <u>did</u> (inversely) affect the cost of fishing, how would your answer to the previous question change?

   (b) Assume that 100 tons of fish per year is the dynamically efficient sustained (steady-state) yield on a particular fishing ground. Assume that the local fisheries council imposes an enforceable total allowable catch (TAC) of 100 tons of fish per year. Once the 100th ton is caught, the fishery is closed for the remainder of the year. Is this an efficient solution to the common property problem? Why or why not? Would your answer be different if the 100 ton quota were divided up into 100 transferable quotas, entitling the holder of each quota to catch one ton of fish? Why or why not?

   (c) The commercial value, V, of a single stand of trees is determined by the volume and the quality of timber the trees can produce. Clearly, V depends on the age, t, of the trees, so that $V = V(t)$. Assume that the value function for a stand of trees is S-shaped: $V'(t) \geq 0$ for $t \geq 0$, $V''(t) > 0$ for $t < t^*$, and $V''(t) < 0$ for $t > t^*$. Let c denote the cost of logging and replanting, so that $V(t) - c$ represents the net value of a stand. Assume that soil productivity and all prices and costs remain constant through time. In an infinite-horizon, multiple-harvest (Faustmann) model of optimal rotation time, derive the condition describing the optimum. How does the optimal rotation time you just characterized compare with the optimal time until harvest in a single-harvest model (i.e., no future use of the land after the first and only stand of trees is felled)?

2. **Benefit Estimation**

   (a) In the context of preserving a natural environment (from immediate development), define the economic concept of option value. When and why should option value be included in benefit-cost analyses of development projects involving pristine natural environments? Is risk-aversion a necessary condition for option value to be positive?

   (b) The travel cost technique has been a popular method for evaluating recreation sites.

   (i) Briefly describe the basic travel cost technique and discuss the issues that arise in applying it.

   (ii) The original travel cost technique provided information on the demand for a site. However, in many cases we are more interested in the demand for the individual characteristics of a site. Discuss how the travel cost technique can be modified to provide information on the demand for characteristics.

3. **Non-renewable Resources**

Consider a non-renewable natural resource in finite supply. The cost of extraction is zero and the elasticity of demand for the extracted resource is constant and greater than unity in absolute magnitude. Suppose that the technology exists to produce a perfect substitute (the "back-stop") at a constant cost per unit of c. Describe the price paths for the resource under each of the following sets of assumptions:

(a)   Both the resource industry and the back-stop industry are perfectly competitive.

(b)   The resource industry is a monopoly and the back-stop industry is perfectly competitive.

(c)   The same monopolist owns the resource and the back-stop industry.

(d)   The resource industry is owned by one monopolist, and the back-stop industry is owned by a different monopolist.

(e)   How, if at all, would your answer to part (b) be affected if the elasticity of demand were less than unity in absolute magnitude?

4. **Environmental Policy**

Suppose that the government of Seattle is concerned about some pollutant that is produced by a large number of firms in the area. Little or no information is available either on the damages caused by the pollutant or the benefits to the polluters. Although it does not know the efficient level of the pollutant, the government has decided that it is desirable to reduce the ambient concentrations in downtown Seattle by half.

(a)   Assuming that the ambient concentration is just equal to the sum of the individual firm's discharges (i.e., it is an aggregate externality), discuss the advantages and disadvantages of each of the following methods of attaining the desired reduction in the ambient concentration of the pollutant.

   (i)   Require all firms to reduce their discharges by half.

   (ii)   Tax all firms the same amount per unit of residuals discharged.

   (iii) Require firms to have permits in order to be allowed to pollute. Create tradable emission permits equal in total to the desired level of pollution and distribute them free to the polluting firms.

(b)   What difference, if any, would it make to your answers in part (a) if the discharges of different firms affected the ambient concentration of the pollutant differently?

5. **Enforcement of Environmental Regulations**

(a)   Suppose that a significant fraction of firms subject to a particular (uniform) pollution standard is not in compliance with its provisions, so that the level of pollution emitted is inefficiently high. Should the pollution standard necessarily be tightened (i.e., require more pollution abatement) if enforcement expenditures and penalties for noncompliance are held fixed at their current levels? Why or why not?

(b)   State-dependent enforcement schemes have received much attention in the environmental economics literature recently (e.g., Harrington, JPubE, 1988, and Harford and Harrington, JPubE, 1991). Why? How do they work, and what is their purported advantage over simpler schemes. Are state-dependent enforcement schemes cost-effective (with regard to aggregate abatement costs), and how does the issue of cost-effectiveness relate to the desirability of the state-dependent approach to enforcement?

UNIVERSITY OF WASHINGTON

NATURAL RESOURCE FIELD EXAMINATION

Spring 1994

Brown, Chair
Ellis
Halvorsen

Time: 3 hours
Answer four of the following five questions.

I. Consider a non-renewable natural resource in finite supply for which there is no backstop technology. Let p be the price of the extracted resource, c be the unit cost of extraction, t be time, r be the rate of discount, S be the stock of the resource, and q be the quantity extracted.

    A. Consider the efficient time path for p in each of the following cases:

        1. $c=0$.

        2. $c=k$, where k is a constant.

        3. $c=c(t)$, with $\dot{c}/c>r$.

        4. $c=c(S)$.

    B. Rank the implied extraction paths in part A from fastest to slowest.

    C. If a monopoly owns the entire stock of the resource, and faces the inverse demand function $p=(q/5)^{.5}$, how will the rate of extraction compare to the efficient rate in each of the following cases?

        1. $c=0$.

        2. $c=k$, where k is a constant.

II. Suppose that the production function for total output is

$$Y_t = G(K_t, R_t, L)$$

where Y is total output, K is capital input, R is a non-renewable natural resource input in finite supply, and L is labor input, which is assumed to be constant over time. Assume that $G(K_t, 0, L) = 0$.

    A. For each of the following cases, briefly describe the conditions under which a constant rate of output *cannot* be maintained forever:

        1. G is a CES production function.

        2. G is a Cobb-Douglas production function.

319

B.   Prove your answer to question A.1 or A.2.

C.   Now suppose that there is capital augmenting technical change. How, if at all, does this change your answer to parts A.1 and A.2?

III.   A company owning two plants which discharge residuals into a lake has been told that the combined discharge must be no greater than Z units per period. With no treatment, the discharge at each plant would be $\overline{R}_1$ at plant one and $\overline{R}_2$ at plant two. Because of age and design differences, the cost of treatment (residual reduction) is different for each plant, but may be approximated by

and
$$C_1 = a_1\left(\overline{R}_1 - R_1\right) + a_2\left(\overline{R}_1 - R_1\right)^2$$
$$C_2 = b_1\left(\overline{R}_2 - R_2\right) + b_2\left(\overline{R}_2 - R_2\right)^2$$

where R_i is the amount of untreated residual discharged from the ith plant and thus $\left(\overline{R}_i - R_i\right)$ is the amount treated.

A.   Derive expressions for the optimal discharges from each plant and determine the conditions for $R_i \geq 0$. That is, in terms of parameter values, initial levels of untreated discharge, and the joint discharge standard, describe the conditions for obtaining interior and corner solutions to the problem of minimizing the joint costs of treatment subject to the combined discharge constraint $Z-R_1-R_2=0$.

B.   If $a_1=10$, $a_2=0.01$, $b_1=5$, $b_2=0.001$, $\overline{R}_1=1{,}000$, $\overline{R}_2=7{,}500$, and $Z=750$, find the optimal values of discharge R_1 and R_2.

C.   Find the optimal values of discharge R_1 and R_2 if $\overline{R}_2$ is initially 5,000 instead.

IV.   Theory of Environmental Regulation

A.   Within the framework of Weitzman's (1974) model, discuss the proposition that under conditions of imperfect information about the benefits and costs of pollution abatement, standards are preferred to effluent taxes "as either the [total] benefit function is more sharply curved or the [total] cost function if closer to being linear." Provide the economic intuition behind Weitzman's conclusion and its relevance for the issue of instrument choice in the "real world."

B.   Suppose that a significant fraction of firms subject to a particular pollution standard is not in compliance with its provisions, so that the level of pollution emitted is inefficiently high. Should the pollution standard necessarily be tightened (i.e., require more pollution abatement) if enforcement expenditures and penalties for noncompliance are held fixed at their current levels? Why or why not?

320

V. Suppose the demand function for harvested fish is

$$P = g(h),$$

the population equation is given by

$$\dot{x} = f(x) - h,$$

and the total harvest cost function is ch and the discount rate is ρ.

A. Provide an economic explanation for the differences and likenesses of two steady state solutions: (i) a monopolist maximizing profit; or (ii) a manager maximizing consumers' surplus.

B. Use your intuition to compare the transition paths for the two regimes. This is only a minor part of the question, so don't spend much time on it.

NATURAL RESOURCE FIELD EXAMINATION

Autumn 1993

Ellis, Chair
Halvorsen

Time: 2.5 hours
Answer four of the following five questions.

1. Consider a non-renewable natural resource in finite supply.

    A. Compare the perfectly competitive and monopolistic extraction paths under each of the following sets of assumptions:

    1. Zero extraction costs, constant elasticity of demand.
    2. Zero extraction costs, non-constant elasticity of demand.
    3. Constant extraction costs, constant elasticity of demand.

    B. How, if at all, would your answer to part A.1 change if there were a perfectly competitive industry that could produce a perfect substitute for the natural resource at a constant per unit cost?

    C. How, if at all, would your answer to part A.2 change if the comparison were between perfectly competitive and duopolistic extraction paths?

2. Suppose that a pulp mill has the right to discharge its wastes into a river. The total damages from the discharges are given by:

(1) $$TD = 4Q + 5Q^2$$

where Q is the quantity of wastes discharged. The total benefits to the pulp mill of discharging its wastes into the river are given by:

(2) $$TB = 60Q - 2Q^2$$

    A. What level of discharges would occur if the pulp mill ignored the damages caused by its wastes?

    B. What is the efficient level of discharges?

    C. Assuming that the pulp mill ignores that damages it causes, the efficient level of discharges could be attained by levying a Pigouvian tax. What is the optimal tax rate (in dollars per unit of discharge)?

322

D. If transactions costs were zero and negotiations occurred between the pulp mill and the people it damaged, what would be the optimal tax rate? What would be the level of pollution that would result from levying the tax you calculated in part C? Why?

E. Returning to the case where the pulp mill ignores the damages caused by its wastes, suppose that the total benefits of discharging wastes are uncertain, with their expected value given by equation (2). Total damages, which are known with certainty, are given by equation (1). Which would be the better type of instrument for the government to use, a pollution tax or a standard? Why?

F. Returning to the certainty case, suppose that, in the absence of any discharges of wastes, the total value of the river would be $540, so that the maximum amount of damages that can occur is also $540. How, if at all, would this limit on the total damages affect the efficient level of discharges? Why?

3. STRATEGIC CONSIDERATIONS IN DESIGNING ENVIRONMENTAL REGULATIONS

a) Consider the problem of issuing environmental regulations in the face of asymmetric information about abatement costs (assume the polluting firm knows its abatement cost function and that the regulator is only imperfectly informed about the costs of abatement). In this context, it may be shown that incentive compatible environmental regulations (those comprised of abatement standard-lump sum subsidy pairs) are not cost-effective if the marginal cost of public funds is positive. Should we conclude that alternative regulatory approaches which are cost-effective are necessarily preferable? Why or why not?

[Hint: Cost-effective schemes are those that equate the marginal cost of abatement across firms; for example, a regulatory scheme relying solely on a per-unit (of abatement) subsidy will be cost-effective.]

b) Suppose that a significant fraction of the firms subject to a particular pollution standard is not in compliance with its provisions. so that the level of pollution currently emitted is inefficiently high. Should the standard necessarily be tightened (i.e., require even more abatement) if enforcement expenditures and penalties are held fixed at their current levels? Why or why not?

4. DYNAMIC EFFICIENCY AND RENEWABLE RESOURCES: THE FISHERY

Derive an equation describing the dynamically efficient steady-state level of a fish stock using the notation that follows. Let $F(X_t)$ be the amount of one-period growth in the fish stock in period t when the level of the fish stock is X_t, let $B(h_t)$ be the gross benefit (total willingness-to-pay) of harvest h_t in period t, let $C(h_t, X_t)$ be the cost of harvesting h_t when the fish stock is X_t, and let r be the discount rate.

(If you prefer to use continuous-time analogues to these one-period functions, you may do so.)

a) Explain the economic intuition behind this condition for dynamic efficiency of a steady-state.

b) Is the common property (open-access) equilibrium level of the fish stock larger or smaller than the dynamically efficient steady-state level?

For parts (c), (d), and (e), consider the special case of the model where costs do not depend on the level of the fish stock (i.e., $C_x(h_t, X_t) = 0$).

c) Is the dynamically efficient steady-state level of the fish stock larger or smaller than the level of the fish stock associated with maximum sustained yield (MSY)?

324

d) Suppose the dynamically efficient steady-state level of the fish stock is 1,000 tons when r=10%. If r falls (unexpectedly) to 5% (and remains at 5% forever), is the dynamically efficient steady-state level of the fish stock larger or smaller than 1,000 tons?

e) Is the dynamically efficient sustained yield larger or smaller after the aforementioned fall in r?

5. REGULATED FISHERY

Assume that a local fishery council imposes an enforceable total allowable catch of 100 tons of fish on a particular fishing ground per year. Assume further that 100 tons per year is the dynamically efficient sustained yield (if the fishery is operating efficiently). The council announces opening day of the fishing season, and once the 100th ton has been caught, the fishery is closed for the remainder of the year.

a) Is this an efficient solution to the common property problem? Why or why not?

b) Would your answer be different if the 100 ton quota were divided up into 100 individual transferable quotas (ITQs), entitling the holder of each ITQ to catch one ton of fish? Why or why not?

UNIVERSITY OF WASHINGTON

NATURAL RESOURCES FIELD EXAMINATION

AUTUMN 1992

Halvorsen, Chair
Brown
Ellis

Answer all four questions, which will receive equal weight. You have two and one-half hours to complete the examination.

1. Non-renewable Resources

Are non-renewable resources extracted according to the Hotelling arbitrage principle? Review the empirical evidence from Slade (1982), Miller and Upton (1985) and Halvorsen and Smith (1991). Discuss the relative methodological merits of the approaches taken by the authors.

2. Benefit Estimation

Snoqualmie Falls is a popular tourist destination not far from Seattle. The rate of water flow over the Falls varies substantially over the year. Puget Power is considering installing new hydro-electric generating units at Snoqualmie Falls that would necessitate reductions in the rate of flow of water over the Falls on some days.

Suppose that you have been assigned the task of estimating the dollar value to tourists of different rates of flow for purposes of calculating the foregone value of the water Puget Power will divert. You have one year in which to collect and analyze data and an "adequate" budget.

Discuss how you would proceed to carry out your assignment in each of the following cases:

a) You are instructed to use a travel cost technique.

b) You are instructed to use a contingent valuation technique.

c) You can use any technique, or combination of techniques, that you think best.

326

3. Renewable Resources

a) Fish:

(i) In a model in which fishing costs do not depend upon the level of the fish stock, describe the rule that characterizes the dynamically efficient sustained yield level of the fish stock. Define each variable and function you write down and provide intuition for this result. Is this level of the fish stock larger or smaller than the one associated with a management criterion of maximum sustainable yield?

(ii) Assume that 100 tons of fish per year is the dynamically efficient sustained yield on a particular fishing ground. Assume that the local fisheries council imposes an enforceable total allowable catch (TAC) of 100 tons of fish per year. Once the 100th ton is caught, the fishery is closed for the remainder of the year.   Is this an efficient solution to the common property problem? Why or why not?   Would your answer be different if the 100 ton quota were divided up into 100 transferable quotas, entitling the holder of each quota to catch one ton of fish? Why or why not?

b) Trees: In William Hyde's infinite-horizon, multiple-harvest model of optimal rotation time, the condition describing the optimum is

$$(p-x)Q_T(T,E^*) = r[(p-x)Q(T,E^*) - wE^*](1 + e^{-rT} + e^{-2rT} + e^{-3rT} + \cdots) .$$

In this expression, $Q(T,E^*)$ is the volume of timber produced on a tract of land during one planting-harvest cycle, where T is the rotation time and E^* is the optimal amount of silvicultural effort. The per unit price of timber (paid at the mill) is p, the constant marginal cost of harvest and transportation to mill is x, the marginal cost of silvicultural effort is w, and the discount rate is r.

Please provide economic intuition for this result.
Is the optimal time until harvest in a single-harvest model (without land rent) longer or shorter than the optimal rotation time described in his infinite-horizon, multiple-harvest model? Why? In the notation employed by Hyde, describe (mathematically) the rule governing the optimal time until harvest in a single-harvest model (without land rent). That is, simplify the above equation so that it describes a single-harvest situation rather than a multiple-harvest one.

4. Environmental Regulation

a) Describe the cost-effective rationale for environmental regulatory schemes that employ effluent taxes or marketable pollution permits (define cost-effectiveness, then explain why effluent taxes and marketable permits may be cost-effective). In practice, are the cost savings from the use of these policy instruments likely to be large (cite evidence from the course readings)? In what sense is the cost-effective criterion of limited value in the formulation of environmental policy?

b) Suppose that a significant fraction of the firms subject to a particular pollution standard is not in compliance with its provisions, so that the level of pollution currently emitted is inefficiently high. Should the standard necessarily be tightened (i.e., require even more abatement) if enforcement expenditures and penalties are held fixed at their current levels? Why or why not?

c) Why might Pigouvian effluent taxes (by themselves) fail to achieve the long run social optimum in a multifirm industry generating pollution, even when the social planner setting the taxes has perfect information about the benefits and costs of pollution abatement?

UNIVERSITY OF WASHINGTON

NATURAL RESOURCE FIELD EXAM   Ellis, Chair
Autumn 1991   Brown
                                                    Halvorsen

Closed Book, 2-1/2 Hours. Answer four questions. including (2). The time limit is designed to encourage choice of what to include.

(1) Characterize the current methods employed in the U.S. to regulate polluters of air and water. As an economist. what specific recommendations for change would you offer policy makers concerning instrument choice and enforcement practices? Why? What gains in efficiency (or some other objective) do you envision following from your policy recommendations?

(2) Suppose you are a fishery manager charged with the task of maximizing the present value of the stream of net benefits generated by a commercial fishery. Let $B(h_t, x_t)$ represent the gross benefit of harvesting h_t units of fish in period t: that is, $B(h_t, x_t)$ is the total willingness to pay for h_t. Assume that $B_h(h_t, x_t) > 0$ and $B_x(h_t, x_t) \geq 0$. Let $C(h_t)$ be the cost of harvesting h_t when the fish stock is of size x_t. $F(x_t)$ is the one-period net growth function. Assume that $F'(x_t) > 0$ for $x_t < x_{msy}, F'(x_t) < 0$ for $x_t > x_{msy}$, and $F'(x_t) = 0$ at $x_t = x_{msy}$, where x_{msy} is the stock of fish consistent with maximum sustainable yield. The rate of discount

a) Derive the equation which describes the dynamically efficient steady–state level of the fish stock. Provide an economic interpretation for the equation.

b) Can you tell whether the dynamically efficient steady–state level of the fish stock is larger or smaller than x_{msy}?

c) For the special case where gross benefits do not depend on the level of the fish stock (i.e., $B_x(h_t, x_t) = 0$), explain why the dynamically efficient steady–state level of the fish stock will be larger or smaller than x_{msy}?

1

d) Would the common property (open–access) equilibrium level of the fish stock be larger or smaller than the dynamically efficient steady–state level? Why?

e) Suppose the dynamically efficient steady–state level of the fish stock is 1.000 tons when $r = 10$ percent. If r falls (unexpectedly) to 5 percent (and remains 5 percent forever), will the dynamically efficient steady–state level of the fish stock be larger or smaller than 1,000 tons? Why?

f) Will the dynamically efficient sustained yield (harvest) be larger or smaller after the aforementioned fall in r? Why?

g) In parts (a) through (f) you implicitly assumed compliance with the optimal harvest quota. h_t, in each period. Now assume that monitoring compliance is costly. Will the dynamically efficient steady–state level of the fish stock be larger or smaller than the level associated with your answer in part (a) (when enforcement costs were zero)? Why?

(3)

a) Within the framework of Weitzman's (1974) model, discuss the proposition that under conditions of imperfect information about the benefits and costs of pollution abatement. standards are preferred to effluent taxes "as either the benefit function is more sharply curved or the cost function is closer to being linear." Provide the economic intuition behind Weitzman's conclusion and explain the root cause (economic) for the non–equivalence of the two policies.

b) Construct a simple numerical example using Weitzman's (1974) framework in which an abatement standard is preferable to an emission tax. Be specific about the benefits and costs of pollution abatement and about the uncertainty (to the risk–neutral regulator) surrounding each. Calculate Weitzman's coefficient of comparative advantage: $\Delta \doteq \frac{\sigma^2 B''}{2C''^2} + \frac{\sigma^2}{2C''}$ where B'' and C'' are the slopes of the marginal benefit and marginal cost functions respectively, and σ^2 is the mean square error in marginal cost.

2

(4) Consider the following two–period model of nonrenewable resource extraction. The inverse demand function for the resource is $p_t = 22 - 2q_t$ for $t = 0, 1$. Total extraction costs in each period are given by $EC_t = 2q_t$, and costs are independent of the resource stock. The rate of discount is $r = 10$ percent, and the total available reserves of the resource are 8.

a) Find the dynamically efficient levels of extraction q_0 and q_1. What are the marginal user costs in each period?

b) A monopolist facing the same level of demand, costs, discount rate, and initial reserves wishes to maximize the present value of profits over the two periods. Find the levels of extraction in each period that maximize the monopolist's present value of profits. Does the monopolist extract the resource more slowly than is dynamically efficient?

c) Would monopolists, in general, extract nonrenewable resources more slowly than is dynamically efficient? What economic factors influence your answer?

(5) Describe, compare and critically evaluate the hedonic technique and the random utility–discrete choice models, alternative ways to estimate non–market values.

UNIVERSITY OF WASHINGTON

NATURAL RESOURCE ECONOMICS FIELD EXAM   Autumn Quarter 1990
Professors Greg Ellis and Gardner Brown

You have **3** hours for the exam. Please answer all three questions. Write neatly
and show your work for partial credit.

Question 1: Environmental Regulation

i.   **Regulation Under Uncertainty**

   a.   Within the framework of Weitzman's (1974) model, discuss the proposition that
        under conditions of imperfect information about the benefits and costs of pollution
        abatement, standards are preferred to effluent taxes "as either the benefit function is
        more sharply curved or the cost function is closer to being linear." Provide the
        economic intuition behind Weitzman's conclusion and explain the important role
        played by the *asymmetry* of information about costs.

   b.   If you, as the social planner, were able to use an additional policy instrument (e.g.,
        a lump sum subsidy (fine)) in conjunction with an abatement standard (or effluent
        tax), how would you design environmental regulations in the face of the
        aforementioned asymmetric information? Why?

ii. **Regulation of Several Firms**

   a.   Why might Pigouvian effluent taxes (by themselves) fail to achieve the long run
        social optimum in a multifirm industry even when the social planner has perfect
        information about the benefits and costs of pollution abatement?

   b.   Marketable pollution permits and effluent taxes have been advocated by some
        economists who claim they are "cost-effective." What do these economists mean
        by the term? How extensively are marketable permits used as regulatory tools in
        the United States?

   c.   How does the optimal uniform abatement standard in the face of costly enforcement
        compare with the optimal uniform standard if full compliance can be assumed (with
        no enforcement costs)? Why?

   d.   Some economists (Russell and Harrington) have recently advocated the use of
        Markov models of enforcement to analyze how firms will respond to a repeated
        game in which current rates of inspection and penalties for detected non-compliance
        depend upon past performance. What lessons should we learn from these models?
        Is there any evidence that regulators behave as described in these formal models?

331

The World Bank's World Development Report (1986) claims that poor performance of agriculture in low-income countries is a result of macroeconomic policies such as agricultural output taxes. As farming grows unprofitable (output prices fall), farmers will deplete their soil.

When is this conclusion true and when is it false? (i) Please give a careful economic *verbal* explanation of your reasoning. (ii) Include in this discussion a specific recommendation for an empirical study to distinguish whether output taxes lead to greater soil depletion.

Model 1: Suppose that soil capital (S_t) changes at a rate, $\dot{S}$, which is increased by natural growth, M, and decreased by cultivation, R_t. Initially, farm output is produced by $F(R_t, S_t)$ and sold at a fixed price, P, per unit. Labor is fixed. The discount rate is ρ.

Model 2: Suppose there is a fertilizer substitute (N_t) for soil depletion which can be purchased at per unit cost W. How does this possibility affect your conclusions?

Question 3:

In the next two years, millions of dollars will be spent in a careful way to improve the quality of contingent valuation (CV) studies. What problems with the CV method do you believe can be solved by this large expenditure and what problems will remain? Justify your classification. In view of the controversy over CV studies, please explain why you would or would not use substitute methods for capturing the values CV is best designed to address.

ECONOMICS READING LISTS, COURSE OUTLINES, EXAMS, PUZZLES & PROBLEMS
Compiled by Edward Tower, *Duke University and The University of Auckland*, September 1995

Volume 1   Microeconomics Reading Lists, 287 pp.
including Experimental, Games, General Equilibrium, Technology, Innovation & Growth
K. Anderson, B. Bennett, M. Berliant, M. Carter, J. Cox, L. De Alessi, P. Diamond, A.K. Dixit, T. Frech,
H. Grabowski, J.K. Hammitt, G.W. Harrison, M. Hviid, M. Kahn, P. Klemperer, G.J. Mailath, I. McLean,
J.P. Neary, A.D. Paltiel, P. Pashigian, J. Pencavel, J. Pischke, L. Putterman, S. Rosen, F.M. Scherer,
R.T. Smith, W.C. Stubblebine, A.G. Wadhawan, M. Waterson, L.E. Westphal, J.A. Weymark, G. Winston,
F.C. Wykoff, D.T. Yang.

Volume 2   Microeconomics Exams, 309 pp.
J.R. Morse, Chicago, Claremont, CO, Duke, Harvard, MD, MI State, MN, NC, Penn, Princeton, UCLA,
VA, WI.

Volume 3   Macro I: Macro, Money, & Financial Economics Reading Lists, 269 pp.
S. Al-Harran, K. Banaian, A. Banerji, C. Bean, O. Blanchard, R. Burdekin, J.Y. Campbell, W.J. Den Haan,
A. Dick, B.M. Friedman, R.E. Hall, K. Hamada, G.C. Harcourt, H.S. Houthakker, K. Kimbrough, M. Kremer,
M. Kuehlwein, M.S. Lawlor, J. Leahy, J.M. Letiche, B. Malkiel, N.G. Mankiw, D. Mann, S. Millán,
F.S. Mishkin, P.F. Peretto, C. Pissarides, S.M. Sheffrin, K. Shell, H.J. Sherman, J. Tobin, E. Tower, H. Uhlig,
C.E. Walsh, R.N. Waud, G. Woglom, F. Wykoff, W.P. Yohe.

Volume 4   Macro II: Macroeconomics Exams, 304 pp.
Chicago, Claremont, CO, Duke, Harvard, MD, MI State, MN, NC, Penn, Princeton, UCLA, VA, WA, WI.

Volume 5   Macro III: Advanced Macro, Monetary & Financial Economics Exams, 303 pp.
Chicago, Duke, MD, MI, MI State, MN, Penn, Princeton, UCLA, VA.

Volume 6   Mathematical Economics, Game Theory,
Computational Economics & Applied General Equilibrium, 252 pp.
S. Achath, D.W. Hands, D. Kendrick, R. Ramanathan, L.E. Westphal, Chicago, CO, MN, Princeton, UCLA.

Volume 7   Econometrics Reading Lists, 246 pp.
M.Y. An, O. Ashenfelter, A.K. Bera, C.F. Christ, J.M. Conrad, H. Dezhbakhsh, R. Gallant, J.J. Heckman,
C. Holsey, J. Horowitz, T.J. Kniesner, G.S. Maddala, R.S. Mariano, B. Meyer, T. Mount, S. Özmucur,
P.C.B. Phillips, R. Piccirillo, R. Ramanathan, P. Schmidt, K.A. Small, W.G. Tomek, F. Wykoff, A. Zellner.

Volume 8   Econometrics Exams, 280 pp.
Chicago, CO, Duke, MD, MI State, MN, NC, Penn, Princeton, UCLA, VA, WA, WI.

Volume 9   Industrial Organization & Regulation Reading Lists, 291 pp.
P. Abrahamse, R.J. Arnould, K. Banaian, K. Basu, S. Borenstein, K.D. Boyer, A. Dick, S. Dowrick,
S. Engerman, M.S. Gaynor, A. Hayri, M. Hviid, J.E. King, R.N. Langlois, J. Likens, R. P. McAfee,
R.A. Miller, D.E. Mills, S. Özmucur, S. Peltzman, J. Poot, R. Porter, C. Ries, N.L. Rose, F.M. Scherer,
G. Shaffer, M. Waterson, A. Zimbalist.

Volume 10   Industrial Organization & Regulation Exams with Transport Economics Reading Lists, 292 pp.
P. McCarthy, T.H. Oum, I. Savage, K.A. Small, K. Stegemann, W.G. Waters II, Chicago, CO, Duke, MD, MI,
MI State, MN, NC, Penn, Princeton, UCLA, VA, WA, WI.

Volume 11   Labor Economics Reading Lists, 289 pp.
S.G. Allen, O. Ashenfelter, J. Betts, S. Davis, J. Dinardo, R.G. Ehrenberg, D. Hamermesh, B. Harrison,
J.J. Heckman, J.E. King, T.J. Kniesner, J. Likens, T.H. Naylor, D. Neumark, J. Pencavel, J. Pischke,
S.W. Polachek, S. Rosenberg, R.T. Ross, J. Schor, D.T. Yang.

Volume 12   Labor Economics Exams With Demography Reading Lists, 247 pp.
C.M. Becker, D. Devoretz, A.C. Kelley, R. Lee, P.A. Yotopoulos, Binghamton, Chicago, CO, Duke, MD, MI,
MI State, MN, NC, Penn, Princeton, UCLA, VA, WA.

Volume 13   International Economics Reading Lists, 293 pp.
J. Adams, K. Anderson, J. Anderson, S.W. Arndt, A. Banerji, P. Bardhan, B. Bentick, S.W. Black, P. Conway,
D. Davis, A. Deardorff, A.K. Dixit, K. Dominguez, D.H. Feldman, A. Field, J. Frankel, Ö. Gökçekus,
B.K. Goodwin, T. Grennes, G.M. Grossman, P. Hallwood, K. Hamada, S. Howson, C. Jing, K. Kimbrough,
A.O. Krueger, J. Levinsohn, K. Maskus, J.P. Neary, D.P. O'Brien, R. Pomfret, M.C. Spechler, K. Stegemann,
D. Weinstein, T.D. Willett, J.G. Williamson, R.J.A. Wilson.

Volume 14   International Economics Exams, 288 pp.
BC, Chicago, Claremont, CO, Duke, MD, MI, MI State, MN, NC, Penn, Princeton, UCLA, VA, WA, WI.

Volume 15   Development I: Reading Lists
including Human Resources, Institutions, Macro Policy, Public Choice, Project Evaluation &
Public Finance in LDCs, 263 pp.
A.H. Amsden, W. Ascher, A. Banerji, P. Bardhan, K. Basu, J.R. Behrman, T. Besley, R. Betancourt,

P. Collier, E. Engel, D.H. Feldman, M. Gersovitz, G.K. Helleiner, G. Jenkins, R. Kelly, T. Kuran, D. Lal,
J. Lodewijks, D. Perkins, R. Pomfret, A.S. Rajkumar, G. Ranis, D. Ray, M. Rosenzweig, T. Sicular,
C.P. Timmer, E. Tower, L.E. Westphal, J. Williamson.

Volume 16 Development II: National Economies, Comparative, Transition & Planning
including Asia, China, Japan, Europe, 219 pp.
K. Anderson, S.W. Black, A. Denzau, T. Frech, K. Hamada, Y. H. Hong, A. Keidel, III, D.D. Li, J.Y. Lin,
J. Lodewijks, T. Lyons, M. Marrese, T. H. Naylor, H. Patrick, K. Polenske, L. Putterman, S. Rosefielde,
T. Sicular, M.C. Spechler, L.E. Westphal, D.T. Yang.

Volume 17 Development III: Exams, 197 pp.
including Ruttan's Reference List on Technology & Development
V.W. Ruttan, Chicago, CO, Duke, MD, MI, MI State, MN, NC, Penn, Princeton, UCLA, VA, WA.

Volume 18 Public Economics I: Taxation & Expenditure Reading Lists, 278 pp.
J. Alm, T. Besley, E.K. Browning, P.N. Courant, D.M. Cutler, C. De Bartolome, D. Donaldson, D. Fullerton,
W. Gentry, J.R. Hines, Jr., H. Hoynes, R. Inman, G. Jenkins, R. Kelly, B. Meyer, J.M. Mintz, E. O. Olson,
A. Randall, H.S. Rosen, G.P. Shukla, W.K. Viscusi, R. Von Haefen, M. Wolkoff.

Volume 19 Public Economics II: Taxation & Expenditure Exams, 272 pp.
Chicago, Claremont, CO, Duke, MD, MI, MI State, MN, NC, Penn, Princeton, UCLA, VA, WA, WI.

Volume 20 Public Economics III: Public Choice, Political Economy, Peace & War, 246 pp.
compiled by Jurgen Brauer, Ronald Friesen & Edward Tower
T. Borcherding, J. Brauer, E.K. Browning, P. Coughlin, L. De Alessi, A. Denzau, A. DiFilippo, P. Dillon,
L.J. Dumas, R.L. Friesen, C. Goodwin, T. Havrilesky, C. Holsey, T. Kuran, A. Markusen, E. Nunn, M. Olson,
F. Raines, S. Rose-Ackerman, S. Rosenberg, W.J. Samuels, A.A. Schmid, H.J. Sherman, S.W. Sommer,
Z. Spindler, K. Stegemann, R.D. Tollison, M. Weidenbaum, MD, MI.

Volume 21 Public Economics IV: Urban, Rural, Regional; Law & Crime; Health, Education, 280 pp.
R.J. Arnould, J. Backhaus, A. Banerji, M. Berliant, C. Clotfelter, P. Cook, P.N. Courant, P. Diamond,
R.G. Ehrenberg, R. Feldman, T. Frech, M.S. Gaynor, H. Grabowski, T. Holdych, D.W. Hughes, K. Jackson,
H.M. Levin, T. Lynch, B.D. Mann, J.P. Newhouse, E.C. Norton, D. O'Flaherty, K.R. Polenske, A.A. Schmid,
F. Sloan, K.A. Small, R.T. Smith, T.H. Tietenberg, P. Vaz, L. Vereeck, W.K. Viscusi, B.A. Weber, Chicago,
Claremont, CO, Duke, NC, WA.

Volume 22 Environmental & Natural Resource Economics, 332 pp.
J.B. Braden, D. Brazee, R.G. Cleetus, P. Copes, R. Deacon, D.N. Dewees, A.M. Freeman III, D. Fullerton,
G.W. Harrison, C. Howe, C. Kling, C.D. Kolstad, R.A. Kramer, J.R. Moroney, F. Parker, P.J. Parks,
A. Randall, C.S. Russell, J. Shogren, H. Sigman, V.K. Smith, R.N. Stavins, T.H. Tietenberg, D.M. Weinhold,
CO, Duke, MD, MI, UCLA, WA.

Volume 23 Agricultural Economics & Agriculture in Economic Development, 214 pp.
A. Featherstone, B.K. Goodwin, A. de Janvry, M.R. Langham, J.Y. Lin, K. Meilke, G. Moschini, M. Nerlove,
J.M. Perloff, S. Rozelle, V.W. Ruttan, E. Sadoulet, C. R. Shumway, L. W. Tauer, C.P. Timmer, T. Tomich,
Chicago, KS State.

Volume 24 Economic History, 286 pp.
J. Anderson, J. Backhaus, H.M. Boot, G.R. Boyer, L.E. Davis, I.M. Drummond, S. Engerman, G. Fleming,
C. Fohlin, D.W. Galenson, C. Goldin, T.W. Guinnane, K. Harley, S. Howson, P. Hoffman, J.A. James,
R.N. Langlois, T. Lyons, P.D. McClelland, I. McLean, G. Meijer, S. Millán, D.E. Moggridge, J.R. Morse,
K.L. Sokoloff, A.M. Taylor, P. van der Eng, A.M. Watson, J.G. Williamson, Chicago, CO, MD, NC,
Princeton, UCLA, VA.

Volume 25 History of Economic Thought, 237 pp.
T. Aspromourgos, R.E. Backhouse, M. Blaug, P. Cain, C.D. Goodwin, P. Groenewegen, L. Haddad,
D.W. Hands, G.C. Harcourt, W. Kaempfer, R.N. Langlois, P. Laumas, M.S. Lawlor, P.E. Mirowski,
D.P. O'Brien, L. Putterman, E. Rothschild, W.J. Samuels, M. Schabas, N.T. Skaggs, J. Skeels, M.C. Spechler,
B. Stein, G. White, MD, MI State, NC, Princeton.

**The price of each volume is $24. The discount price of the complete set of 25 Economics volumes is $395.
A special offer for individuals buying economics volumes: Buy 2 volumes at the regular price, and get
additional volumes for $20 each when ordering directly from Eno River Press. Please add $3/order for
shipping on all orders. Additional postage charges are: US first class and Canadian air @ $3/volume; other
foreign air @ $6/volume. U.S. funds only please.**

BUSINESS ADMINISTRATION READING LISTS AND COURSE OUTLINES

Compiled by Richard Schwindt, *Simon Fraser University*, 1995

Volume 1 ACCOUNTING I: Introductory, Intermediate and Advanced Accounting, Financial Accounting, Auditing, 224 pp.

Volume 2 ACCOUNTING II: Managerial Accounting, International Accounting, Financial Statement Analysis and Tax, 212 pp.

Volume 3 MARKETING I: Marketing Strategy, Management and Research, 237 pp.

Volume 4 MARKETING II: Buyer Behavior, Industrial Marketing, International Marketing, The 4 P's, 292 pp.

Volume 5 FINANCE I: Corporate Finance, 194 pp.

Volume 6 FINANCE II: Investments and Financial Markets, 235 pp.

Volume 7 INTERNATIONAL BUSINESS I: Multinational Management and the International Environment, 274 pp.

Volume 8 INTERNATIONAL BUSINESS II: Comparative Management, Regional Studies (Japan, Russia, Eastern Europe, The Pacific Basin), International Business Law, 197 pp.

Volume 9 INTERNATIONAL FINANCE AND FINANCIAL MARKETS, 166 pp.

Volume 10 INDUSTRIAL RELATIONS AND HUMAN RESOURCES MANAGEMENT, 248 pp.

Volume 11 BUSINESS ETHICS, REGULATION AND LAW, 287 pp.

Volume 12 BUSINESS POLICY AND STRATEGY, 246 pp.

Volume 13 DECISION MAKING UNDER UNCERTAINTY, GAMES AND BARGAINING, 208 pp.

Volume 14 OPERATIONS RESEARCH, 286 pp.

Volume 15 ENTREPRENEURSHIP, 176 pp.

Volume 16 MANAGEMENT COMMUNICATION, 200 pp. *Compiled by Mary Munter*

Volume 17 BUSINESS ECONOMICS, 227 pp.

Volume 18 ORGANIZATIONAL BEHAVIOR I: Organizational Behavior And Theory, 233 pp.

Volume 19 ORGANIZATIONAL BEHAVIOR II: Managerial and Social Psychology, Human Resource Accounting, Leadership, Diversity, Skills, Sensemaking, Organizational Development, 240 pp.

Volume 20 MANAGEMENT INFORMATION SYSTEMS AND BUSINESS STATISTICS, 230 pp.

All volumes are priced at $24 each. The complete set is $350. Please add $3/order for shipping on all orders. Additional postage charges are: U.S. first class and Canadian air @ $3/volume; other foreign air @ $6/volume. Payment accepted in U.S. funds only.

Eno River Press
115 Stoneridge Dr.
Chapel Hill, NC 27514-9737, USA

The Economics Institute Guide to Graduate Study in Economics and Agricultural Economics in the United States and Canada

Ninth Edition
Compiled September 1995 at
The Economics Institute
1030 13th Street, Boulder, CO 80302
Phone: (303) 938-2500
Fax: (303) 492-3006
E-mail: EconInst@Colorado.EDU

The Economics Institute Guide to Graduate Study is an indispensable reference book for prospective graduate students - both domestic and foreign - and their advisors and sponsors.

The ninth edition includes two-page descriptions of 170 programs in economics and agricultural economics. It also contains general information for prospective graduate students and the rankings of economics departments.

The Economics Institute is a nonprofit educational corporation sponsored by the American Economic Association and endorsed by the American Agricultural Economics Association.

ORDER FORM

Mail to: **Eno River Press**
              115 Stoneridge Drive
              Chapel Hill, NC 27514-9737 USA

Value of Books Ordered: ___ copy(ies)@ $24.00 per copy = $ _____
Shipping: $3/order $ 3.00 _____
US first class or Canada air @ $6/volume: $ _____
Other foreign air @ $12/volume: $ _____
Total cost of order: $ _____

Ship to:

Name _____

Address _____

City _____ State _____ Zip Code _____

Country _____

Phone _____ Fax _____

My cheque is enclosed ☐   Charge to: Visa/MasterCard ☐ Expires _____

Card Number _____

Name _____ Signature _____